Michael Waddle
2004

Angola

PALL MALL LIBRARY OF AFRICAN AFFAIRS

The Pall Mall Library of African Affairs is intended to provide clear, authoritative, and objective information about the historical, political, cultural, and economic background of modern Africa. Individual countries and groupings of countries will be dealt with as will general themes affecting the whole continent and its relations with the rest of the world. The library appears under the general editorship of Colin Legum, with Philippe Decraene as consultant editor.

Already Published

T. A. BEETHAM	Christianity and the New Africa
ALFRED G. GERTEINY	Mauritania
RICHARD GREENFIELD	Ethiopia: *A New Political History*
RICHARD HALL	Zambia
ALEX HEPPLE	South Africa: *A Political and Economic History*
JAMES R. HOOKER	Black Revolutionary: *George Padmore's Path from Communism to Pan-Africanism*
RENÉ LEMARCHAND	Rwanda and Burundi
GUY DE LUSIGNAN	French-Speaking Africa Since Independence
HORACE MINER (ed.)	The City in Modern Africa
JOHN G. PIKE	Malawi: *A Political and Economic History*
WALTER SCHWARZ	Nigeria
RICHARD P. STEVENS	Lesotho, Botswana, and Swaziland: *The Former High Commission Territories in Southern Africa*
IMMANUEL WALLERSTEIN	Africa: *The Politics of Unity*
CLAUDE WAUTHIER	The Literature and Thought of Modern Africa: *A Survey*

Angola

DOUGLAS L. WHEELER
and
RENÉ PÉLISSIER

PALL MALL PRESS · LONDON

Pall Mall Press Limited
5 Cromwell Place, London sw7
First published 1971
© 1971 by Pall Mall Press Limited
ISBN 0 269 99330 4
Printed in Great Britain by
The Garden City Press Limited
Letchworth, Hertfordshire

Contents

Maps

Illustrations   *facing pages*

List of Organisations

This list, not intended to be exhaustive, includes most of the many organisations, groups and parties cited in the text. It is felt that the list of abbreviations will be especially helpful to the reader.

Aliança dos Naturais do Zombo	ALIAZO
Alliance du Mayombe	ALLIAMA
Angola Negra	
Associação Africana do Sul de Angola	
Associação das Mulheres de Angola	
Associação de Matabrancos	
Associação dos Bassorongos	
Associação dos Funcionários Públicos	
Associação dos Naturais de Angola	ANA
Associação Regional dos Naturais de Angola	ANANGOLA
Association des Tchokwe du Congo, d'Angola et de Rhodésie	ATCAR
Cartel dos Nacionalistas Angolanos	CNA
Comissão de Defesa dos Indígenas	
Comissão de Luta das Juventudes contra o Imperialismo Colonial em Portugal	
Comité da Unidade Nacional Angolana	CUNA
Comité de Acção da União Nacional de Cabinda	CAUNC
Comité des Bons Offices Angolais	CBOA
Comité Federal Angolano do Partido Comunista Português	
Companhia de Diamantes de Angola	Diamang
Comunidade Cabindense	COMCABI
Conferência das Organisações Nacionalistas das Colónias Portuguesas	CONCP
Conselho de Libertação de Angola	
Conselho do Povo Angolano	CPA
Corpo Voluntário Angolano de Assistência aos Refugiados	CVAAR
Exército de Libertação Nacional de Angola	ELNA
Exército Popular de Libertação de Angola	EPLA
Frente Angolana de Libertação Nacional	FALN
Frente de Libertação do Enclave de Cabinda	FLEC

Angola

Frente Democrática para a Libertação de Angola   FDLA
Frente Nacional de Libertação de Angola   FNLA
Frente Patriótica de Libertação Nacional   FPLN
Frente Patriótica para a Independência do Kongo
   Português   FPIKP
Frente Revolucionária Africana para a Independência
   Nacional das Colónias Portuguesas   FRAIN
Gouvernement Révolutionnaire de l'Angola en Exil   GRAE
Junta Autónoma de Estradas de Angola   JAEA
Junta Revolucionária de Loanda
Juventude do MPLA   JMPLA
Liga Africana
Liga Angolana
Liga Geral dos Trabalhadores de Angola   LGTA
Liga Guineense
Liga Nacional Africana   LNA
Liga Ultramarina
Movimento Anticolonialista   MAC
Movimento de Defesa dos Interesses de Angola   MDIA
Movimento de Independência Nacional de Angola   MINA
Movimento de Libertação de Angola   MLA
Movimento de Libertação do Enclave de Cabinda   MLEC
Movimento de Libertação Nacional   MLN
Movimento de Libertação Nacional de Angola   MLNA
Movimento Nacional Angolano   MNA
Movimento Nacionalista Africano
Movimento para a Independência de Angola   MPIA
Movimento Popular de Libertação de Angola   MPLA
Ngwizako Ngwizani a Kongo   Ngwizako
Nto-Bako
Organisação das Mulheres de Angola   OMA
Organisação Provincial de Voluntários e Defesa Civil   OPVDC
Ovamboland Peoples' Organisation   OPO
Parti de la Solidarité Africaine   PSA
Parti Progressiste Africain   PPA
Partido Africano da Independência da Guiné e Cabo Verde   PAIGC
Partido Comunista de Angola   PCA
Partido Comunista Português   PCP
Partido da Luta Unida dos Africanos Angola   PLUA
Partido Democrático Angolano   PDA
Partido Nacional Africano   PNA
Partido Pro-Angola

Partido Reformista de Angola	
Partido Republicano Colonial	
Polícia Internacional e de Defesa do Estado	PIDE
Rassemblement des Chefs Coutumiers du Kongo Portugais	RCCKP
Serviço de Assistência aos Refugiados de Angola	SARA
South-West African Peoples' Organisation	SWAPO
União das Populações de Angola	UPA
União das Populações do Norte de Angola	UPNA
União dos Defensores de Angola	
União dos Estudantes Angolanos	UEA
União Geral dos Estudantes da Africa Negra sob Dominação Colonial Portuguesa	UGEAN
União Nacional	
União Nacional Angolana	UNA
União Nacional dos Estudantes Angolanos	UNEA
União Nacional dos Trabalhadores de Angola	UNTA
União Nacional para Independência Total de Angola	UNITA
União Progressista Nacional de Angola	UPRONA
União Social dos Maiombes de Luali	
Union Générale des Travailleurs Angolais	UGTA

To the memory of
Richard Blaine McCornack (1919–1959)

⊕

To Elise Pélissier

The authors are indebted to all those who helped them gather the materials for this book. Dr Wheeler is grateful to the University of New Hampshire for a leave of absence, 1966–7, and a CURF grant, which enabled him to complete some of the research in his section; and he would like to thank Dr Norman R. Bennett of Boston University for his reading of chapters 1 to 6 and his offer of valuable criticisms.

Dr Wheeler is grateful to the staff of the Arquivo Histórico Ultramarino of Lisbon who kindly reproduced for him photos 1 to 4.

Photos 6 to 10 were taken by M. Pélissier, and are selected from his collection.

Part One

Douglas L. Wheeler

1. Land, Peoples and Kingdoms

One should attribute the small population of Tropical Africa to
two great scourges: disease and the exploitation of man by man.
High Commissioner Norton de Matos
in *A Provincia de Angola*, 1926.

In 1875, J. J. Monteiro concluded his remarkable book, *Angola and
the River Congo*, with the following eulogy: 'I have now, to the best
of my ability, described the customs and productions of this wonder-
ful and beautiful country, and I shall be glad if the perusal of these
pages should induce others to explore more fully the rich field it presents to the naturalist and geographer.'[1] Nearly a century later, the
visitor to Angola could agree with Monteiro and could add new fields of
knowledge, but could hardly improve upon his enthusiastic description
of the magnificence and beauty of the Angolan landscape. Headline
stories of sensational events and a sombre parade of tragic events
in the past cannot obscure the fact that the land of Angola has a unique
charm. The historian, political scientist, sociologist and anthropologist
who would learn of the environment of Monteiro's favourite African
territory must first study the land itself.

THE LAND

Angola is situated in West Central Africa, south of the equator. It lies
between 5 degrees and 18 degrees south latitude, and between 12
degrees and 24 degrees longitude east of Greenwich. Angola's top-
ography may be divided into three general zones, from west to east
towards the interior. First there is a coastal lowland, at its widest point
little more than one hundred miles, which extends most of the length of
Angola from the extreme north near the Congo river mouth to the
extreme south. Next there is a narrow sub-plateau strip which rises
from 1,000 to 3,500 feet. The eastern-most zone, a true plateau (*planalto*
in Portuguese), rises in a series of tablelands from 4,000 to 7,000 feet.

Angola has a great variety of climate, vegetation and relief. The
territory's size is imposing. It is one of the largest political units in
Africa: over 480,000 square miles in area, equal to the combined areas
of the states of Texas and Arizona, or roughly the combined area of France,
Great Britain and Spain, fourteen times the size of continental Portugal.

Angola

Like its other characteristics, Angola's geographical personality is split. There are at least two major orientations which compete for Angola's attention: to the west, the Atlantic; and, to the north and east, the Congo basin. Moreover, the massive South West African desert extends into south Angola. Several regions—eastern and northern Angola—belong to the great drainage bowl of the Congo, to Central Africa and to the Zambezi-Congo watershed. Coastal and western Angola face the South Atlantic. Angola's major rivers drain towards Brazil, and its major ports of the last century, Luanda and Benguela, have their Brazilian counterparts across the South Atlantic in virtually the same latitudes: Pernambuco (Recife) for Luanda and Bahia (São Salvador) for Benguela. There are further geographical similarities between Brazil and Angola, and, as will be seen, many historical and cultural connections as well. Both countries have extensive highland plateaus behind the low and often unhealthy coastal strips.[2] There is another analogy between them: the subsistence foods of both lands have been the same since the sixteenth century. Manioc, maize and sweet potato are used by the great mass of the population of Angola and all three staple subsistence crops were introduced by the Portuguese from Brazil after the early sixteenth century. Spreading into Central Africa from the Kongo kingdom where they were introduced, these American crops made Angola a botanic outpost for Brazil and provided foods for millions of Angolans and their neighbours. Angola's role in the relationship with Brazil—as a supplier of human labour—had less savoury consequences.

An understanding of the regions of Angola can illuminate the historical developments of the land. An American geographer once suggested that there are six 'geographical provinces' of Angola: Luanda; Congo Border; Benguela; Mossamedes (Moçâmedes); Upper Zambesia; and Kalahari-Desert Border.[3] Although the European administration has divided the territory into a varying series of districts and sub-districts, this geographical division transcends traditional administrative demarcations and incorporates major geographical features of both Angola and Central Africa. The Luanda, Benguela and Mossamedes provinces in this scheme are nuclear provinces or regions stretching inland from the coast. Each with its city on the coast, they were traditional jump-off points for penetration into the *sertão*,* or hinterland; and, under the Portuguese presence, these areas remain not only the termini for long-distance trade routes from Central Africa but also the most developed regions with a high density of population. The three

*The plural of the Portuguese *sertão* (interior, hinterland) is *sertões*, a term commonly used to describe inland Angola and Brazil.

'marginal provinces'—the Congo Border, Upper Zambesia and the Kalahari-Desert Border—have become less marginal over the centuries, but they continue to have a sparse population, little economic activity and climatic problems.

The Luanda region was the first area of European activity in Angola after the first Portuguese contacts with peoples in the Congo Border area south of the Congo river. The Luanda coastal lowland is often desolate and dry and the soil is poor. Any population concentrated at Luanda on the mainland or on Luanda's islands, long sand spits, must look for food to other places: to the north, to the fertile Bengo river valley, for food, fresh water and salt supplies; or to the south, to the nearby Kwanza river valley, where crops could grow. Historically, the tendency to look to the 'north' or up the Kwanza valley for even basic food supplies—not to mention more exotic items—influenced the expansion of the Europeans. The Luanda region has the advantage of containing the Kwanza river, the largest in Angola apart from the Congo. The Kwanza was a corridor of westward migration for African peoples from the east and north. For the white newcomers, the Kwanza acted as a highway for the eastward penetration of commerce and colonisation. This led to a concentration of effort along its banks for centuries, favouring northern Angola to the detriment of the south. In the districts immediately north of the slow-flowing river, the white strangers and African peoples came into very close contact and developed what became the richest agricultural areas in the entire territory. The river is navigable for about 120 miles, being impassable after the Cambambe Falls. The upland region of the Luanda province is reached from the coast by gradual steps, interspersed with some broken country. Yet the Luanda plateau is more accessible from the coast and of a more moderate elevation than are the south-central plateaus of Angola. This very accessibility helped determine the pattern of European penetration and colonisation. The southern plateaus were harder to reach and remained isolated longer than those north of the Kwanza waterway. Within less than a century of the founding of Luanda in 1576, Portuguese settlements reached over 180 miles into the *sertão*, while no comparable settlements reached that far east from the Benguela area for two centuries.

Benguela province has been called the 'core' of Angola, because of its central position, its access to the great Southern African plateaus and its importance as an area of dense population. Its coastal lowland was considered very unhealthy for centuries, yet it was no worse than that of Luanda and its soil is richer than that of Mossamedes, which is nearer the desert. The Benguela sub-plateau, however, is more broken,

3

steeper and less accessible from the coast than the country behind Luanda. Some of the mountains behind Benguela are the highest in Angola and rise to 8,000 feet. On the plateau proper the climate is generally healthy and has had the best reputation of all regional climates. The average annual temperature at Nova Lisboa, the most thickly-settled region, is a dry 60°F. The Benguela plateau has problems of internal transportation since it is crossed and recrossed by many streams and small rivers which were often impassable in the rainy seasons, even in recent years.

Of the three nuclear regions, Mossamedes was the last to be colonised with permanent white settlements. Before the coming of the European, it was apparently sparsely settled. From the dry, desert-like coast, where the sand ends as the town streets begin, the plateau rises sharply to the east, making access to the interior difficult. Though Mossamedes is the healthiest of the regional coasts in Angola, its hinterland is also the driest and its rivers, unlike the Kwanza, are not navigable. To the south of Mossamedes is the barren Kalahari-Desert Border region.

The Congo Border region has long been a scene of African activity and early European and African contact. This area is a part of the periphery of the Congo basin and has generally low relief, heavy forestation and a humid climate. Climate and location as well as vegetation have discouraged the development here of a large European population; until after 1940, the Portuguese population in the Congo district was sparse. The capital of the ancient African kingdom, Mbanza, renamed São Salvador by the Europeans, is located on a low plateau in a relatively isolated position some 100 miles from the nearest point on the Congo river bank, and some 200 miles from the western coast. During the sixteenth century, Luanda, the focus of European interest and development and expansion into the interior, came to rival and then surpass São Salvador.

There is a small piece of Angolan territory north of the Congo river: the Cabinda Enclave, only 2,800 square miles in size. It has no important port and its inhospitable interior has been described as 'miles of steaming, tangled, equatorial rain forest';[4] but its future may well be different as large reserves of petroleum have been discovered offshore in the Atlantic.

The sixth region is Upper Zambesia in the east, bordering on Congo-Kinshasa and Zambia. This region is a part of Central Africa and contains the watershed for the upper Zambezi and the Kasai rivers. Much of it is deserted plateau, descending towards the east into marshy, malarial basins.

The tropical climate of Angola has had a crucial influence on the history of the territory. There are two major seasonal divisions: a rainy season, that begins normally in early October and lasts with variations of rainfall until late April or early May, and a dry season, called *cacimbo* in Angola, that lasts from May to September. Both May and September are transitional months. The *cacimbo* season is named after the typical morning fog of the dry months. The seasons have influenced man's endeavours in war and peace in Angola, as elsewhere, and the *cacimbo* season, by long tradition, has been the time when the Europeans would schedule expeditions to the interior and military campaigns. The rainy season was, and continues to be, a more unhealthy time, when outdoors activities are limited. African military activities, on the contrary, have often been scheduled for the rainy season, when the European would be inconvenienced and at a disadvantage. As recently as 1961, when African insurgents struck during the rainy season, this seasonal fact of life played its role in Angolan affairs.

Until recently, Angola's coastal area and immediate hinterlands in the Kwanza valley were feared as 'white men's graves' where European mortality was high. An anonymous Portuguese poet in the seventeenth century described northern Angola as a sickly place and deadly for the European of his day. His description of 'hot and malignant fever', or malaria, in the early days, could apply to much of Angolan history before the introduction of modern preventives. The climate, to the Portuguese, was 'an enemy'. The peoples of Angola have suffered from many diseases, both endemic and epidemic. The hot and humid climate in the lower altitudes and in the northern part of the country encouraged tropical diseases. Traditional African diseases were malaria, yellow fever, sleeping sickness, hookworm, leprosy and elephantiasis. Until the 1940s malaria was 'hyper-endemic' on the coastal plain from Kongo to the Kwanza and in the northern river valleys, while even in the higher areas heavy rainfall could encourage the prevalence of malarial mosquitoes. Even in the 1960s thousands of Angolans suffer cases of malaria each year. While the battle against malaria began in 1845, the medical campaign against widespread sleeping sickness began only in the first quarter of the twentieth century. In 1928 some 32,723 sleeping sickness cases were reported; the number of reported cases had been reduced to 1,876 in 1957.[5] The European imported several diseases new to the peoples of Angola. Beginning in the late fifteenth century Angolans began to suffer from periodic outbreaks of smallpox, especially serious in epidemics in the eighteenth and nineteenth centuries.[6] Venereal diseases—spread by Portuguese troops[7]—and tuberculosis have also devastated Angolan peoples.

In summarising the nature of the land and its environment, it is

5

important to understand the physical difficulties facing human life in Angola. The great variety in relief, vegetation and climate did not encourage a blending of peoples and cultures. The hot and humid climate and tropical diseases of the coastal areas and sub-plateau discouraged human activity in both native and stranger. Even in the higher altitudes on the healthier plateau, only modern medicines and pesticides could defeat the periodic outbreaks of the same scourges which afflicted the coasts. With the introduction and dissemination of modern medical ideas and practices, sometimes usefully allied with African traditional medicine, both European and African suffered less and could begin to escape from the deadly circle of disease and enervation so common among peoples there in the past. In view of the nature of the land, it is not surprising that modern Angola is a sparsely-settled territory, with an average density of only ten persons per square mile, less than half the average population density of Africa as a whole.

THE AFRICAN PEOPLES AND CULTURES OF ANGOLA

Angola is a plural society, composed of various cultural groups. Before the coming of the Europeans, the Negroid racial group invaded and dominated earlier invaders from the Bushmanoid group. Most of the peoples of Angola are Bantu-speaking, a group which today occupies about one-third of the African continent. In Angola they comprise from ninety to a hundred tribes or sub-groups; this figure is deceptive, however, for many of the groups possess common cultures and values. Despite the ethnic diversity and the variation in physical types of the Bantu-speaking groups of Angola, they are essentially inter-related both culturally and racially. For example, of the twenty-two or more tribes or kingdoms comprising the Ovimbundu peoples of the Benguela plateau, over half were related in a common language and bound by historical ties of tribute and empire. They possessed a strong sense of independence, if not of cultural unity.

The following are the major ethno-linguistic groups among the Angolan peoples: the Bakongo, the Mbundu, the Ovimbundu, the Lunda-Quioco (Chokwe), the Nganguela, the Nyaneka-Humbe, the Herero and the Ambo. The Bakongo, speaking Kikongo, are the northern-most people, located in the Cabinda Enclave and in the north-western areas of Angola. Due to migration and a dearth of reliable census information, it is difficult to know their exact numbers. A constant factor in estimating the Angolan Bakongo population is knowledge of migrations across the frontiers into the two Congo Republics (Brazzaville, formerly French Congo; and Kinshasa, formerly Belgian

6

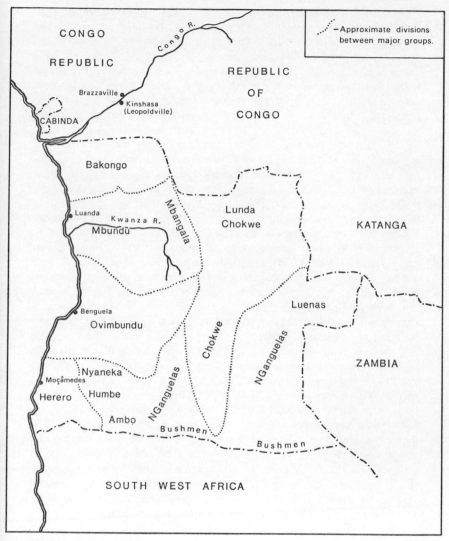

1. Ethnolinguistic map of Angola

Congo). A fair estimate during the 1960s was the figure of 400,000. The Bakongo are oriented to the north and east rather than to the south. Like their neighbours to their immediate south, the Kimbundu-speaking peoples, the Bakongo have had relatively close contact with Europeans since the late fifteenth century. The major ethnic group within the Bakongo are the Kishikongo, including the Muxicongo, many of whom made up the population nucleus of the ancient Kongo kingdom. The Sosso, Pombo, Sorongo and Zombo are other tribes within the Bakongo group.

The Mbundu peoples, speaking Kimbundu, are located mainly in the Luanda area and in the lower Kwanza valley. The Mbundu population totals over 700,000 but can include another 400,000 people whose cultures reflect Mbundu influences. The major tribes in this group are the Mbaka, Ndongo and Mbundu. Like the Bakongo, the Mbundu have been in intimate contact with the Portuguese and their influences for five centuries and, in varying degrees, have become acculturated to European ways. Many have come to live in or near the European urban areas. Included in the Kimbundu-speaking peoples of northern Angola are the Dembo (or Dembos) who rapidly acquired the reputation for being among the staunchest resisters of European intrusion and authority in Angola; this centrifugal tendency in north-west Angola is reinforced, or perhaps in part engendered, by the geographic relief and isolation of Dembos country.

The Ovimbundu, or 'the people of the mist', reside on the plateaus of central Angola. They comprise the most numerous single cultural group of this plural society, more than 1,700,000 people, over one-third of the African population. They live at altitudes of 3–5,000 feet. Migratory rather than sedentary in habit, the Ovimbundu, who speak Umbundu, have participated in a diaspora, spectacular in extent and in historical significance. They have spread from the Benguela coast to the Zambezi watershed and beyond. They have tended to assimilate other cultural sections in Angola rather than being assimilated themselves. Their language, Umbundu, is widely understood in southern-central Angola. Rather than looking northward (as do the Bakongo) or westward (as do the Mbundu), the Ovimbundu have traditionally been self-centred or oriented eastward towards Central-East Africa. Following their trade paths and trails wherever they would lead them, the hardy Ovimbundu tramped across Angola and often lead the European into the interior and back again.

The Lunda-Quioco (Chokwe), with over 500,000 people, live in north-eastern Angola. Living in Katanga in earlier times, the Lunda migrated into eastern Angola from the beginning of the sixteenth

8

century. The Chokwe are more numerous than the Lunda but both peoples are related by historic ties of alliance and intermarriage. Known for their artistic talents, the Chokwe have been moving into Angola from the Congo-Katanga area during the last 150 years, mainly as hunters and traders. Like the Ovimbundu, the Chokwe have been migratory in habit and have ranged over large sections of Central Africa.

The Nganguela peoples (called Ganguela by the Portuguese), estimated to number, in the 1960s, some 350,000, have been caught between the Ovimbundu and Chokwe-Lunda, who have divided up some of the Nganguela homelands. Their name is an example of African ethnocentrism: it is the Umbundu term of the Ovimbundu for 'other peoples'—in effect, 'un-persons'—a term of deprecation applied to the Ovimbundu's eastern and southern neighbours.

The Nyaneka-Humbe people number some 150,000. Unlike many of their neighbours to the north, these people have tended to resist outside influences. They live in the Humpata plateau region in the Huila district and in the Kunene valley. They are chiefly herdsmen, leaving whatever agricultural activities they follow to the women.

The migratory Herero people of south-west Angola number over 20,000 and live in arid lowlands. Cattle are highly prized and are central not only to the Herero economy but also to their cultural value system, for they despise sedentary pursuits. Unlike many of their Angolan neighbours, the Herero have no chiefs. They belong to the cultures of South West Africa as much as to those of south-west Angola.

The Ambo people are a small group, only 60,000 in number, who inhabit the dry plains east of the Kunene. For them, too, cattle constitute an important part of their lives, though they participate in agriculture more than their Herero neighbours. To these people, modern frontiers seem meaningless, and they regularly move in and out of South West Africa. The most famous and strongest of the Ambo people are the Kwanhama, some 50,000 in number, who resisted the Portuguese authority longer than most of their Angolan neighbours. Not until 1915 did they participate in their final battles of resistance, their tribal armageddons fought out in desert Angola.

There are three small non-Bantu groups in Angola, the Khoisan-speaking peoples, which originated from Bushman and Hottentot groups: the Bushman, Cuissi and Cuepe. Numbering only 2,000 to 6,000, they are mainly desert nomads. The last of the ancient hunters and gatherers of old Angola, these small brown men are marginal both in racial and cultural terms. Not exactly within the Negroid racial group, they possess some physical features of the Mongoloid group. They inhabit

9

the remote and arid margins of southern Angola. Not integrated within the modern system which is the product of the last five centuries, they have rejected both Bantu and European influences and they have marched to their own drummers into the inhospitable deserts rather than compete in the better-watered lands of strangers.

The Portuguese

In order to attempt to understand the behaviour of the Portuguese, the dominant minority people in Angola, who began as only a few hundred and today number nearly a third of a million, an introduction to Portuguese culture and history is important. Since the Portuguese Discoveries (1415–1550), events in the colonies have had a profound influence on affairs in Portugal. Conversely, Portuguese affairs influence events in the colonies. This simple but crucial unity of affairs between mother country and colonies can never be forgotten in any analysis of Portugal.

Portugal became an independent kingdom in the middle of the twelfth century, having been a minor portion of the western domains of the King of Leon and Castile. The frontierlands between Portugal and what became the unified kingdom of Spain feature few natural barriers to invasion. Closely related to Spain in culture, kinship and politics, Portugal found that its independence from its much larger and more powerful neighbour was always in doubt for at least six centuries after separation, and, for some Portuguese, even today it may still be hanging in the balance. Portugal's determination to remain independent of Spain, however, became a major feature of its existence. The Portuguese kings rapidly defeated the remaining Moorish forces in Portugal and by 1250 had reconquered the country, nearly two and a half centuries before Castile and Aragon accomplished the same victory over the Moors in their portion of the Peninsula. Nevertheless, Moorish influence remained important in Portuguese culture and economy, and six centuries of intermarriage and miscegenation between the Moors and Portuguese affected Portuguese attitudes towards such relationships with darker peoples. Now having reached its full extent in land area, 34,000 square miles, Atlantic-oriented Portugal was set for expansion overseas. In 1383 a new dynasty of Portuguese kings came to the fore: the Aviz kings, who led the nation to overseas adventures and imperialism. Beginning in 1415 with the capture of the Moroccan town of Ceuta, Portugal entered the brief period when it became a world leader in navigation, exploration, conquest and trade in three continents. Despite a small population of little more than one million people and

poor resources, Portugal enjoyed a glorious age, called in their literature
O Século Maravilhoso ('The Marvellous Century'), lasting from 1415
to about 1515.

Under King Manuel I, 'The Fortunate' (1495–1521), Portugal
reached a precarious apogee of power and prestige. Even at the height
of royal prosperity, however, the Portuguese masses derived little or
nothing from the overseas wealth. Decline came after 1578 when young
King Sebastian was killed and his army slaughtered by Moroccan
forces in a North African campaign. Symbolically, the most celebrated
Portuguese poet, Luís de Camões, died shortly afterwards in 1580 and
is said to have cried on his deathbed that he 'died with the nation'.
Portugal never again achieved world power and entered various phases
of decline, partial regeneration, decline, regeneration, and so on.
Perhaps the greatest of all Portuguese fears—present and past—became
a reality during 1580–1640, when Spain annexed and ruled Portugal. A
national revolution in 1640 freed Portugal again and the country
entered another phase of regeneration. Portugal found a forceful leader
in the Marquis of Pombal (1750–77), who attempted to restore Portugal
to its former greatness by reforming the economy and society. Pombal's
attempt was bold but his results were disappointing and a reaction
followed his fall.

Besides overseas expansion—the major phenomenon of Portuguese
external affairs since 1415—the second major external tradition has
been the Anglo-Portuguese alliance. From the twelfth century, England
protected the independence of Portugal, and later its empire also, in
exchange for certain trade and naval privileges. Strongest during the
seventeenth and eighteenth centuries, the Anglo-Portuguese alliance
has been declining in effectiveness since the early nineteenth century
when the two nations disagreed about affairs in tropical Africa, Asia and
Brazil.

During the first half of the nineteenth century new disasters further
ruined Portugal: the French invasions and the occupation by English
troops (1807–14); the independence of Portugal's largest and most
prosperous colony, Brazil (1822); the disorder and expense resulting
from the political turmoil of a new form of government, constitutional
monarchy (1820–50), and civil wars between constitutionalists and
absolute monarchists. Disorder and debt characterised much of the
nineteenth century. The brief but popular reign of the ill-fated King
Pedro V of Bragança (1853–61) was not enough to speed modernisation
and guarantee stability. The monarchy fell amid political strife in 1910.
A republic took its place but, like the original constitutional monarchy,
had neither the support of the people nor the unity and consistent

judgement of the intellectuals. The democratic republic (1910–26), after half a generation of anarchy, was described by the Portuguese poet, Guerra Junqueira, as 'an heroic march to the sewer'. The republic fell before a 1926 revolt of a cabal of generals, which soon entrenched itself in the government and appointed a civilian leader, Professor of Economics at Coimbra University, Dr António de Oliveira Salazar (1889–1970), to reform the finances. From the Ministry of Finance in 1928, Salazar became, in effect, the political chief of Portugal in 1932 as Prime Minister ('President of the Council of Ministers'). In September 1968, he suffered a paralytic stroke and was replaced as Prime Minister by Dr Marcelo Caetano (born 1906), former Minister of Colonies and Deputy Prime Minister. Salazar died on July 27, 1970. Under Caetano the *Estado Novo* continued many of the same overseas policies while instituting a certain amount of political and economic liberalisation in Portugal.

The foregoing conventional résumé of Portuguese history may be found in general histories by Livermore, Nowell, and Trend.[8] Nevertheless, with the exception of that by Trend, these works tell little about the motivations and psychology of Portuguese behaviour. What have been the major forces in Portuguese history during the period the Portuguese have been active in Angola? Various explanations have been given to explain the decline of Portugal and the persistent but abortive attempts of its leadership to build a modern, fully Westernised society. Trend favours lack of money as an explanation;[9] Livermore, a lack of wisdom, unity and cohesion among the pre-1926 leadership;[10] Salvador de Madariaga believes that Portugal's close alliance with England gave the Portuguese a permanent melancholy and that Portugal should have remained united with Spain;[11] Bragança-Cunha asserts that the ignorance and indifference of the masses and the tyranny of the kings moved Portugal away from the truths and virtues found in Camões's epic, *Os Lusíadas*.[12] Recent works on the post-1926 regime criticise effects thought to derive from the authoritarian *Estado Novo*. Thus Chilcote asserts that the leadership has resisted change;[13] Figueiredo claims that the masses are victimised by a minority, that this oligarchy is disturbed by national inferiority complexes, and that the result is 'an immense moral corruption'.[14]

While there may be some truth in each analysis, all fail to view Portuguese history as a whole and to isolate recurrent behaviour patterns. A fundamental Portuguese problem for centuries has been that Portugal is 'two nations', the rich and the poor, or even 'two races'. The large peasant sector is only partially Westernised and there is a pronounced cleavage—both class and cultural—between the masses and elite. There has been a traditional tendency for the Portuguese common people to be indifferent or even hostile to elite ideas and actions as well as to the outside world. In effect, the masses, or *o povo* in modern parlance, have been opposed or indifferent to the historical developments led by the elite which provide nationalistic inspiration for a modern national revival. The 'other' nation, then, has participated but little in the expansion, colonialism, liberalism, modern government and Westernisation.

Even when there was mass participation in overseas expansion, behaviour could undermine elite reform plans. By acting passively, or by maintaining their tenacious attachment to traditional occupations of petty trading and shopkeeping rather than agriculture or industry, the countrymen, *camponeses* of Minho or Alentejo, have disappointed Lisbon dreamers. In 1915, one close observer noted that the Portuguese were 'not imperially-minded'.[15] Until the mid-twentieth century, the majority of the few who did emigrate to Portuguese Africa (and not Brazil) had no ambition other than to leave Angola, fortune in hand, and retire in Portugal. A respected Portuguese historian recently described the paradoxical character of common Portuguese behaviour in Angola: 'The Portuguese colonist was plastic, humanitarian, and, at the same time, fond of native culture; he was, however, also a devastator of black populations just for the sake of trade.'[16]

The Portuguese masses, however, represent only one fundamental problem. The elite, consisting of the educated Portuguese business class, nobility, clergy and leadership, led the nation through various stages of expansion, decline, regeneration and decline. Without a substantial middle class both as a buffer and as a factor acting to integrate the masses into national society and culture, their reform efforts met little success. Moreover, the Portuguese elite have suffered from various related psychological disabilities which derived partly from their extreme sensitivity to the national plight. Realising the fundamental economic weakness of the country and attempting to remedy this with foreign ideas and aid, the leadership has gone through several moral crises. Manifestations of their psychological problems may be described broadly as variations of inferiority complexes: constant fear of invasions of Portugal by Spain, France or England, fear of the colonies being taken by enemies or lost by rebellion, and fear of Portugal's being the victim of partition, such as that experienced by Poland in the eighteenth century. Such fears of the loss of national independence as recently as 1890 are found in the Angolan diary of the Portuguese settler-trader, António da Silva Porto (1817–90), born of poor peasants.[17] Bursts of hyper-nationalism may well act as a survival

13

mechanism. Psychologists might describe the sum of this complex of Portuguese fears as an extreme case of national paranoia, periodically expressed during time of crises through intense nationalism and patriotism. It has been exacerbated by an acute sense of being heavily outnumbered and the underdog at home and in Africa. Certain melancholy feelings (*saudades**) have been expressed in the popular *fado* (fate) songs.

The Portuguese elite suffered from psychological torments especially during the period from 1600 to 1930. The elite lost confidence and self-respect and the intensely disturbed feelings about the status and future of Portugal were expressed in a high suicide rate, self-deprecation and talk of national suicide. The Jesuit leader, Padre António Vieira, claimed that in the seventeenth century the Portuguese were considered 'the Kaffirs of Europe'.[18] The Portuguese elite, with education and travel outside of Portugal, fully sensed the stagnation and lack of progress at home; they became overly sensitive to the supposed superiority of English, French or German culture, and, when they borrowed ideas from outside, they often failed to blend them with Portuguese traditions. During the nineteenth and early twentieth centuries, the Portuguese elite went through the most trying period of self-criticism and destructive self-flagellation. A former governor of Angola in 1814 wrote of Portugal's contemporary 'degeneration'[19] and suggested that the country needed a strong leader to conquer factionalism and unite the country. The brilliant Portuguese historian Alexandre Herculano wrote in 1851: 'In civilization we are two rungs below Turkey and about the same distance above the Hottentots.'[20] A younger colleague, the economist-writer Oliveira Martins, in 1881 called Portugal 'the sick man of Western Europe', 'this little Turkey of the Occident'.[21] About 1908, a Portuguese friend wrote a revealing letter to the Spanish philosopher Miguel de Unamuno: 'In this cursed country, all that is noble commits suicide; all that is vulgar triumphs. Our illness is a type of moral illness, of moral fatigue. . . . In Portugal, the only belief worthy of respect is the belief in the freedom of death. . . . Europe scorns us; European civilisation ignores us. . . . I do not know where we are going.'[22]

As recently as the 1950s and early 1960s, other writers have observed the torment of certain Portuguese, especially among the elite, despite the fact that the *Estado Novo* has revived a modicum of self-respect and pride during the last generation. Miguel Torga, an Oporto doctor, believes that the Portuguese people have been corrupted by a 'moral

* *Saudade:* nostalgia, sad remembrance of persons and things far away or gone.

14

anemia',[23] that most of Portugal did not willingly follow and sometimes opposed the lead of the Lisbon elite into overseas expansion, and that Lisbon's expansionist activities caused the ruin of Portugal. To Torga, the supreme literary embodiment of the opposition of the Portuguese peasants (as opposed to the city folk of Lisbon) to Portugal's greatest exploits is a character created by Camões in *Os Lusíadas*. *O Velho do Restelo*, the Old Man of Restelo, observing Da Gama's embarkation for India in 1497, warns that Portugal will be ruined by imperialism in Asia and will thus decay at home. In modern colloquial speech, however, *O Velho do Restelo*, does not signify a Cassandra correctly prophesying disaster, but a Doubting Thomas or a spoil-sport. Whatever the validity of Torga's interpretation of the Lisbon-country cleavage, his attributing national decline to overseas expansion is instructive. F. C. C. Egerton, an English observer of Portugal, has analysed what he terms 'the Portuguese soul' by suggesting that Portuguese character contains two conflicting and ambivalent tendencies: *siso*, or sound judgement and wisdom; and *loucura*, or 'heroic madness'.[24] When *loucura* prevails in the national character, he believes, the country is unstable and tormented. Salazar's regime, Egerton asserts, restored the balance between these two traits by means of giving Portugal a new and reconstructed sense of its traditional 'civilising mission' in Africa. Other writers, such as António de Figueiredo in 1961, feel that the modern Portuguese are afflicted with a 'moral corruption' which is blamed on the Salazar dictatorship.[25] Still other writers suggest a less contemporary cause for national decline and point out what some might call a national trait of personal factionalism, carping and bickering. Boxer recently suggested that the trait of Portuguese *murmuração*, 'fault-finding',[26] was observed by Portuguese thinkers as early as 1553. Other literature in Portuguese has described fault-finding or intriguing in terms such as *intrigar* and *maldizer*. At a popular fair in Lisbon in 1962 there were official government regulations forbidding fair employees to 'intrigue' among themselves.

From the above evidence, it seems likely that Portuguese realisation of Portuguese weakness and national disunity both on personal and class levels and sometimes on regional levels had serious consequences for national action at home and in the overseas colonies. An intense feeling of insecurity and a knowledge of the real weaknesses of the nation encouraged certain policies. Leadership policies, and even the awareness of the masses that Portugal had lost a period of glory and might again achieve it in the form of an awaited king or messiah (*Sebastianismo*),[27] usually led in the direction of a national revival to bring back *O Século Maravilhoso*.

How has the leadership attempted to achieve national revival and what are some of the consequences? Since the national decline, Portuguese leaders, whether kings, prime ministers or chancellors, have sought to bring the nation to prosperity by means of three forces, often expressed in policies well entrenched in Portuguese tradition: colonialism, authoritarianism and nationalism. All three have been frequently considered as essential to national independence, and, except for brief periods during the 1820–1926 era, when democratic liberalism was dominant over authoritarianism in Portugal, all three forces have been at work. Clearly, these forces have elements which have led to reform, but they contain also influences and have inspired reactions which have thwarted national revival.

Portuguese thinkers have not been united on the value of colonialism as a means of national revival. While the explorer Serpa Pinto in 1878 could write to the leading colonial activist that colonies were 'the only salvation of Portugal',[28] writers like Ramalho Ortigão, Herculano, Eça de Queiroz and Oliveira Martins asserted that Portugal could not afford colonies and that Portugal, as Oliveira Martins wrote, would be its own best colony.[29] Indeed, it is difficult to find a period in history since 1415 when Portugal did gain from the colonies great profits which were used wisely for internal national development, or when Portugal did not suffer from heavy emigration overseas. Most of the regimes since that date, however, have sought to find in the colonies wealth and prestige not found in Portugal, and colonialism has become since 1928 a major support of the groups in power. Despite post-1945 profits from Portuguese Africa, the ultimate value of colonialism for national revival has not been thoroughly tested.

Besides colonialism—the heritage of the glorious age—the Portuguese elite has continually sought another force for revival: a strong leader, able to end personal and class factionalism. Like Spain, Portugal has found few Iron Surgeons[30] to reform and revive greatness and to save the country from foreign threats and from its own torments and failures. In 1860, Vogel suggested that, since no one class in Portugal had the necessary unity or strength, Portugal could be saved only by a strong monarch or royalty, then embodied in the talented King Pedro v.[31] Since the nation was disorganised and factionalised, authoritarianism was considered by the elite at an early date a virtue of leadership and has been used on several occasions to achieve what the Portuguese call 'unity and order'. Portugal experienced the rule of a number of Iron Surgeons: Marquis of Pombal (1750–77); several nineteenth-century statesmen who allowed civil freedoms but periodically employed force: Mousinho da Silveira (1830s), Sá da Bandeira (various terms in power,

1835–70), Fontes Pereira de Melo (1850s and 1860s), João Franco (1906–08), Sidónio Pais (1917–18), Dr António de Oliveira Salazar (1928–68) and, finally, the present Prime Minister, Dr Marcelo Caetano (since September 1968).

Despite the tradition of authoritarianism and the periodic support found for it among a disillusioned and demoralised elite and an indifferent mass, the feelings of independence and freedom among various regions (especially Oporto and hinterland) and groups (students, urban labour and intellectuals) have opposed centralised leadership. The Portuguese Church, always an ally of the three traditional forces, also experienced the enmity of such elements. It is traditional in modern Portuguese history that when the opposition to an authoritarian regime builds enough strength, the achievements of a strong hand are nullified by the expense and waste of suppressing opponents. The Salazar regime has utilised Portuguese traditions and introduced foreign ideas as well; but, despite its economic successes and its partial revival of national pride and self-respect, it too has suffered from both the consequences of Portuguese national disunity and weakness and from adverse reactions to its policies of authoritarianism, colonialism and nationalism.

Portuguese nationalism has played an important role in the leadership quest for national revival. While it has encouraged unity and an end to factionalism and idleness, it has also encouraged traditional Portuguese tendencies towards xenophobia and paranoic fears of both real and imagined threats from Spain, and more recently threats from Communism, African independent states and various revolutionaries. Using modern techniques of communications, propaganda and security, the *Estado Novo* has emphasised a cult of Portuguese nationalism, cultural revivalism and historical atavism which is directly linked to the other major forces of leadership. Without colonialism, nationalism and authoritarianism, Salazar would not have remained in power for so long. On the other hand, the genuine accomplishments of the regime were possible in part through its use of these three forces, aided as well by post-1945 European recovery, African colonial revenues and assistance from Western allies, including the United States.

This brief survey suggests that, as is the case with the majority of African peoples in Angola, tradition is the most prominent feature of Portuguese culture. Modernisation is slow. The majority of the Portuguese people, with a national illiteracy rate of about 30 per cent and a low per capita income, have not experienced fundamental social revolution. While the elite has begun to taste more than the morsels of Westernisation, it continues to suffer from extreme sensitivity to foreign threats and influences, factionalism and a sense of frustration. The memory of *O Século Maravilhoso*, constantly invoked in scholarship, public speeches, symbols and official pronouncements, is both a spur to national revival and an atavistic burden.

National revival, then, has been the goal of all regimes since the sixteenth-century decline. In this respect the *Estado Novo* has been the most successful of all Portugal's regimes. Because the decline was almost directly the consequence of a rapid overseas expansion without resources adequate to sustain expansion and develop Portugal too, the colonialism policy has played an ambiguous role. Since Portugal's presence in Africa today is pursued as a national policy of revival and the defence of heritage, it would seem that colonialism is as traditional and as perilous as the other forces of revival. If colonialism becomes too costly, of course, national revival is again endangered.

Portuguese behaviour in Angola reflects the strength of tradition, psychological insecurity and a tendency to be intensely nationalistic. In early relations with the peoples of Angola, the Portuguese revealed the highly commercial nature of their expansion and settlement. As 'the most tenacious traders of all the Europeans who have gone to Africa',[32] they tended to demonstrate traits which made modern development difficult at home. The primary source of behavioural explanations lies in Portugal, and only secondarily in Africa. This has become complicated by the increasing African orientation of Portuguese civilisation in Angola and Mozambique and by the rhetoric of national revival used in the last five decades. To the idea of national revival and reform was linked 'the civilising mission' in Africa. Despite the sincere belief in such a mission by certain groups, others did not support it. Moreover, in view of the ambiguous nature of Portuguese commitment to colonialism and colonialism's paradoxical role in national revival, the 'civilising mission' was less altruistic than self-seeking. It was yet another expression of national insecurity. For, if the Portuguese definition of civilising is to create more Portuguese, with more Portuguese national survival is made surer.

In conclusion, much historical evidence suggests that authoritarianism has significant roots in Portugal. The twentieth-century form of authoritarianism, the *Estado Novo*, from Salazar to Caetano, may alter the means of remaining in power, but the goal of national revival remains largely the same. Contrary to a major thesis of the exiled opposition,[33] that the *Estado Novo* is a recent aberration, a peculiar twisting of affairs, evidence suggests that some of the goals and methods are firmly rooted in pre-1926 traditions. It is true that the intellectual and human costs of maintaining such a system are high. It is also true

that the interest groups which support a continuation of authoritarianism do so through self-interest and expediency, motives that have long
undermined the health of democracy in Portugal.

The authoritarian regime, despite its present strength, has a
problematic future. As new generations rise to take over the reins, the
definition of what constitutes a Portuguese national revival will change.
The future of Portuguese Africa will profoundly influence the future
of tiny Portugal. Although significant liberalisation did not immediately
follow the installation of Dr Caetano as Prime Minister, reforms and
improvements occurred in Portugal which led some to believe that the
post-Salazar era would bring monumental changes in due time.[34]
Whoever governs Portugal in the 1970s will be obliged to reassess the
condition of Portugal, the poorest and least-advanced of Western
European countries. Besides integrating the elite and the masses, any
Portuguese leader would be able to effect true change only through a
re-interpretation of the three traditional policies of national revival:
authoritarianism, colonialism and nationalism.

African Kingdoms of Angola

The earliest inhabitants of Angola were probably Bushmanoid types,
ancestors of the few remaining present-day Bushman in south Angola.
Little is known of the prehistory of Angola, despite the fact that archae-
ologists have studied numerous stone artifacts in north-east Angola.
The lack of fossil evidence in the Lunda region of eastern Angola
makes it difficult to determine the identity of early Angolan man.
J. Desmond Clark, the eminent archaeologist-anthropologist, has done
field work in north-east Angola and is not entirely convinced that the
Bushman was the first human inhabitant of Angola.[35]

In ancient times it appears likely that the major centre of early cultural
activity in Angola was in the north-east, the site of diffusion of an
'equatorial forest culture', the Congo river basin. Many of the ancestors
of the present-day Bantu populations of Angola migrated to Angola
from the north and east and settled in north and central Angola. They
were hunters and gatherers who sought open country beyond the rain
forests of the Congo. In northern Angola they found open savannah
country, well-watered and with a rich fauna. For many of these early
hunters, Angola became a school of cultivation and cattle-keeping;
what they did not learn for themselves came to them from migrants
bringing cattle and cultivation techniques to Angola by 1600. The
picture that emerges of Angola before the arrival of the Europeans is
that of a fairly thickly populated country, especially in the open

19

grasslands between the rain forest of the Congo and the Kalahari deserts. At first, the peoples of Angola were not organised in what Bohannan has called 'state' societies.[36] In these 'stateless societies' there was little centralised authority and few societies had kings or chiefs or even well-defined village heads. Primarily nomadic, these early hunters could not resist the invaders—both white and black—who began to dominate Angola after 1300.

The pre-European history of Angola is one of the least known histories of tropical Africa. For the historically-minded visitor to Angola who observes the host of physical evidence of early history, this is surprising and frustrating. Portuguese historians, with access to Angola for nearly five centuries, have done most of their research in their own colonial history in the territory. One can count on the fingers of one hand the professional studies of early African history by Portuguese scholars; thus, the early history of Angola lies as a great opportunity and challenge to the interested student. In the caves, within the Mossamedes district, with their Bushman paintings, in the tool-strewn ground of the plateau, in the countless monoliths dotting the countryside of Angola from Dembos to Sá da Bandeira, and in the stone walls and monuments on hillsides, the historian will find written the unknown portion of the Angolan past.

The history of the Bantu migrations and the establishment of Bantu states in Angola form the background to the coming of the Portuguese in the late fifteenth century. The Bantu peoples, who today inhabit about one-third of the African continent, historically have shown a 'capacity for explosive expansion'.[37] From nuclear areas in eastern Nigeria, and later from Central Africa, the Bantu migrated southward after 1000 AD. Between 1300 and 1600 this Bantu diaspora directly influenced Angola, and Bantu migrants invaded the territory from the north and east. Probably the earliest Bantu kingdom in Angola to define its civilisation and achieve marked unity was the Kongo kingdom. Located astride the lower Congo river, with its capital city of Mbanza Kongo south of the river, the kingdom was founded in the fourteenth century. The kings of Kongo became absolute sovereigns, whose domains came to be divided into six provinces. Sixteenth-century descriptions suggest that the king, the *Mani Kongo*, or 'lord of Kongo', lived in a sumptuous palace with many servants and slaves and enjoyed music played by drummers and men with ivory trumpets.[38] The power of the kings was based primarily on their possession of slaves, an army, cloth woven by the Bakongo people and cowrie shells (*nzimbu*) found along the shore of Luanda island and elsewhere. From the valuable palm tree the people of Kongo obtained oils, a sap for alcoholic bever-

2. Major historic kingdoms of Angola

ages and materials for weaving their palm cloth. The ruling Kongo dynasty probably originated in the north, across the Congo river, in a small kingdom of Bungu.[39]

It is said that one of the younger sons of the Chief of Bungu, seeking his fortune, crossed the Congo river and consolidated his authority over small kingdoms to the south by means of war and marriage. The Kongo kingdom came to control about one-eighth of what is now Angola, but its authority on its frontiers was not absolute. Although the Kongo kingdom held the kingdom of Ndongo in Angola as a tributary, the strength of Kongo mastery is uncertain, beyond control of the original six Kongo provinces. In the fifteenth century, the Kongo became an African repository of European influences and ideas but the effect of European influence soon weakened and eventually destroyed the unity of the kingdom. Despite the degeneration of the Kongo domain, one factor remained intact in the minds of many of the descendants of the Kongo founders: the royal kingship centred on the capital, renamed São Salvador by the Portuguese. Through centuries of crisis alternating with neglect and isolation, the Kongo kingdom kept its principal tradition of kingship. Even after the final destruction of Kongo independence in the nineteenth century, the idea of the kingship endured. In the 1950s and 1960s the Kongo kingship, and the idea of an historic kingdom of importance, lived on in the minds of a number of African leaders and influenced politics in modern Angola as well as in Congo-Kinshasa.

Immediately to the south of the Kongo kingdom lay the Mbundu kingdom of Ndongo. The king of Ndongo was called N'Gola, the origin of the word 'Angola', as rendered later by the Portuguese. The Ndongo kingdom, as it was found by the Portuguese in the sixteenth century, was of more recent origin than the Kongo state. Originating in Central Africa, the leaders of Ndongo had founded a small kingdom north of the Kwanza river in Angola by about 1500. According to Birmingham,[40] three types of Mbundu peoples composed the Ndongo kingdom of 1500: hunters from Central Africa with no iron-making knowledge; a people with considerable iron-working skill; and other hunters, probably also from East-Central Africa, who brought with them the unifying knowledge of a sacred kingship or monarchy. By 1500, then, a strong monarchy ruled Ndongo, centred on a capital at Kabasa, north of Ambaca in Angola. The growth and destruction of the power of Ndongo was directly influenced by the arrival and expansion of the Portuguese invaders from the Atlantic. One of the great truths of Angola history is the almost simultaneous expansion of the Bantu kingdom of Ndongo from Kabasa to the Atlantic and the Portuguese expansion from an Atlantic beachhead inland towards Kabasa and up the Kwanza.

In spite of the obvious diversity of the cultures of the Bantu peoples of Angola, several common denominators emerge. Nearly all the principal states established in Angola by 1600 possessed iron-working, cloth-weaving, sacred kingship and a desire to trade among themselves or with strangers. Historians have been fascinated by evidence that these Bantu states had cultural traits that originated in areas thousands of miles away.[41] For the history of Angola, the important fact that emerges from even a partial acceptance of such cultural influences is that the Bantu peoples and their states were dynamic and ever-changing. Their historic and present mobility over tropical Africa suggests the possibility of their taking or receiving such cultural influences from as far away as Rhodesia or the Nile valley. How it occurred and how much independent cultural development of the traits involved in the debate there was, is still a mystery. The student of Southern-Central Africa, however, will note the resemblances between the human use of prominent land forms, stone-building and the shape of constructions from Rhodesia to central Angola. And, though the elliptical shapes of the Rhodesian ruins may not be exact replicas of shapes of the Bantu thorn kraals and houses of the great Angolan plateau, the similarity is too close to be dismissed. The possible connection between Egyptian ancestry and Angolan cultures is yet another question, also complicated by the fact that the early peoples of Angola did not, of course, leave written records.

While the Mbundu kingdom of Ndongo was concentrated in the territory between the Dande and Kwanza rivers, to their east and south they bordered on neighbouring kingdoms. Influences from Ndongo filtered into their neighbouring states, but the chief cultural factor in these neighbouring states was again the Lunda-Luba complex and the numerous migrations of refugees from that area of Central Africa. During the sixteenth century, several waves of peoples burst into eastern and central Angola and by 1600 some groups had reached the Atlantic. The kingdom of Kasanje, composed of the Imbangala, originated in the Lunda-Luba states in Katanga and became established north and east of the Kwanza, in the Kwango valley, between 1540 and 1600; they raided Ndongo after 1540, and perhaps reached the Luanda area before 1576.[42] After 1600 the Imbangala settled down in the Kwango valley, where they became tenacious middlemen in the trade between Lunda and the Portuguese on the Angolan coast. The Imbangala opposed Portuguese penetration and trade monopoly of the interior, and until 1911–13, when the Kasanje kingdom was finally

23

militarily subdued, the Imbangala remained a major factor in the history of eastern Angola.

As a chief progenitor kingdom and cultural influence of many Bantu states in Angola, the Lunda-Luba complex of Katanga had its origins in the savannah country of Katanga. The Luba invasion from central Katanga transformed the Lunda into a more dynamic state which periodically sent out groups of hunters into Angola. From this area came the Jaga peoples, who invaded Angola in the 1560s. Nomadic, cannibalistic and ruthless, the Jaga peoples attacked the Kongo kingdom and Ndongo and became embedded in various sections of central and eastern Angola. Certain Jaga customs remain among the Ovimbundu and certain peoples on the plateau. The Jaga have been identified with the Bayaka people who today inhabit the Kwango valley in Congo-Kinshasa.[43]

In the late nineteenth century, the Lunda peoples of eastern Angola and Katanga were attacked by a rival people, the Chokwe. Although the Chokwe did not develop a strong centralised kingship, their organisation and aggressiveness profoundly influenced the course of Angolan history. During the middle of the nineteenth century they became trading middlemen in eastern Angola and obtained guns from other trading Africans, the Ovimbundu of Bié; by 1900, they had destroyed the Lunda kingdom. Certain Chokwe oral traditions tell that their people migrated from near Lake Victoria in Central Africa, while others suggest their origins were in the Upper Kasai region.[44] The Chokwe were a largely matriarchal society. They were influenced by the Lunda-Luba kingdoms. Chokwe expansion north and west into Angola resulted in their capture of Mussumba, the capital of Lunda, in the 1880s. The expansion of Lunda-Luba culture since 1500, then, was in part replaced, during the last century, in eastern Angola by the rapid expansion of Chokwe language and customs. By means of war, trade, marriage and alliance, the Chokwe have impressed their culture on a number of peoples of north-east and east Angola. In the end, the African people which was able to obtain the greatest supply of European arms and goods and exercise its authority in trade monopoly was destined to conquer its neighbours.

Perhaps the most successful traders of the Angolan interior were the Ovimbundu peoples. The Ovimbundu consolidation, like those of the Imbangala and Chokwe middlemen, is of comparatively recent origin. Between 1500 and 1700 the Ovimbundu peoples moved in waves into Angola from the north and east on to the Benguela plateau. Their unified existence as a people composed of some twenty-two kingdoms did not achieve definition until the eighteenth century, when Ovimbundu kings of Bié, Bailundo, Ciyaka and others asserted their sovereignty over a large section of the plateau east of the Portuguese town of Benguela. Like many of the other centralised kingships in traditional Angola, the system featured a king who combined many functions in his person. He was at once high priest, rain-maker, chief hunter, diplomat, judge, diviner and royal personage. Although the Ovimbundu kings were usually considered divine and some inherited their thrones from their fathers and uncles, there was a considerable exercise of popular democracy. The king's councillors, usually respected elders, chose the successor to a deceased monarch and at times profoundly influenced decision-making. The apogee of the Ovimbundu king was in the late nineteenth century, when the Ovimbundu trade monopoly in Central Africa fed the royal coffers as never before. After the Portuguese conquered most of the Ovimbundu states with military expeditions between 1890 and 1902, the kings became more symbolic than real. Childs, an American missionary with several decades of experience among the Ovimbundu, described the Ovimbundu monarchs of the 1940s as 'hardly more than living museum pieces'.[45]

While the entire Ovimbundu group was never united under one king before the Portuguese conquered the plateau, some thirteen out of twenty-two kingdoms emerged as powerful entities. Throughout the Benguela plateau were found great rocks, out-croppings of granite and sandstone, monoliths which were used as royal habitations, sacred temples, fortifications and shelters by the Ovimbundu. Like the Dembos, the Ovimbundu made military use of the great rock formations; the Ovimbundu also constructed walls made of shaped fragments from these monoliths. Dozens of these now-ruined walls, built probably during the last three centuries, remain on hillsides and hilltops on the plateau. This writer observed the ruins of such a wall, several kilometres in length, and from four to six feet in height, on a hillside near Jau, in Huila district, in 1966. While a recent Portuguese study suggests that these Ovimbundu walls[46] are connected neither with the Zimbabwe ruins nor with the Ovimbundu but are from 'Mediterranean peoples', African oral tradition suggests that they are of recent African origin (although other walls may be buried beneath the surface). The Ovimbundu were observed building such stone walls in the nineteenth and twentieth centuries. Nganda, north of the present-day town of Vila Robert Williams, was the great rock capital of a Wambu kingdom, one of the thirteen major Ovimbundu states.[47] The walls and the great rocks of the Ovimbundu played an important role in the history of this region of Angola, a history only now being uncovered. To the Africans such stone works of man and God signified royal and divine acts, while

25

to the Portuguese they were fortified obstacles to their expansion of authority on the plateau.

The Ovimbundu entered a new era after 1902–03. Their various kings were directly or indirectly appointed by the Portuguese authorities and experienced significant European influences. Childs shows how influences of language and taste have affected the Wambu kingdom. With the recorded twenty-ninth king of Wambu, the African name was replaced by a Portuguese name. Yet Ovimbundu language influence remains important in Angola and today this tongue is widening its radius of influence.

All of the Bantu peoples of Angola have mixed and intermarried with one another. Some groups have been more dominant and influential than others: certainly, the Ovimbundu, the Chokwe and the mysterious Jaga. The Ovimbundu from the Bié (Viye or Bihe) area achieved the distinction of being Angola's foremost traders and long-distance trader-merchants. The nineteenth century was the heyday of Ovimbundu trade monopoly from Benguela to the Upper Zambezi. Ivory, wax, dye weed, slaves and wild rubber were the chief commodities traded by these men, called *Mambari* by the Barotse of Zambia. Ovimbundu trade caravans ranged from Benguela and Catumbella, a town well-located for the caravan trade, to the plateau and soon out-competed other African peoples as well as Portuguese *sertanejos*. The greatest period of their hegemony was during the rubber boom, 1874–1916. One Ovimbundu trader in the employ of the Portuguese *sertanejo* Silva Porto, called Domingos Cakahanga, made a successful transcontinental journey from Benguela to the mouth of the Rovuma in Mozambique. With the wars, famines and epidemics of the 1902–16 era, the Ovimbundu lost out as the chief traders of the central plateau. New factors— such as the railroad built from Benguela to Katanga, the frontier with the Belgian Congo and Northern Rhodesia, Portuguese control, the end of the rubber boom—undermined their position. Their travelling urge still pulsed, however; today, some adult males continue to migrate to the mines of South West and South Africa.

The last African kingdom of major importance in Angola yet to be discussed is that of the Kwanhama, a tribe of the Ambo group, in the Bantu-speaking group. The Kwanhama inhabit arid country east of the Kunene river, adjacent to the frontier of South West Africa. Early in the nineteenth century the Kwanhama consolidated a unified state under King Aimbiri (1805?–54). Recently, an Angolan scholar compiled an interesting history of the Kwanhama, describing them as 'the most evolved [advanced] Negro tribe of Angola'.[48] The king was not considered a divine person, but after death he was worshipped as a divine ancestor. In the Kwanhama court, the royal jester or buffoon was said to be a Bushman. When the Kwanhama came into contact with the European traders, King Aimbiri sought European trade, but was opposed by the Kwanhama poet-prophet, Sisaama, who predicted European domination would follow Aimbiri's allowing European traders to come. This African Cassandra, preserved in the oral tradition, interpreted the subsequent death of Aimbiri as a result of European influence.[49] Later Kwanhama kings gained more territorial power and obtained repeating rifles from Portuguese and German traders. Kwanhama prowess in war was greatly feared by the Portuguese, especially during the uncertain years preceding the First World War. Only after 1915, when Portugal invaded Kwanhama country with a large army of over 5,000 troops, did the tribe suffer final defeat and conquest. Rather than live under Portuguese rule, however, certain Kwanhama groups crossed into South West Africa. The last independent Kwanhama king, Mandume (1911–17), rather than surrender, fled to South West Africa, where he was later killed. King Mandume was the last truly independent king of the remaining traditional African states of Angola.[50]

2. Black Mother and White Father

The public good was never looked after here, and I believe that the country was ruined more by its lack of order than by its climate.   Captain-General Francisco Sousa Coutinho to his successor in Angola, 1772.

THE KONGO KINGDOM AND MUENEPUTO, 1482–1575

In 1482 the Portuguese navigator Diogo Cão discovered the mouth of the Congo river and came into contact with the largest Bantu kingdom in West Central Africa: the Kongo kingdom. Cão returned to Portugal before mid-1484 and brought back with him four Bakongo whom he wished to teach the Portuguese language so that relations between the two kingdoms could be established. The Portuguese had come into contact with an African state which, except for the possession of military and naval technology, was not unlike the kingdom of Portugal. When Cão touched the Congo banks, his home country was still in many ways a medieval kingdom. That intrepid stay-at-home navigator, Prince Henry of Aviz, had been dead only twenty-two years, and Portugal had been in existence as a separate polity for barely 300 years. The Kongo state was probably half as old as Portugal but, in terms of population, the manufacture of certain crafts, such as cloth and statuary, and a sense of sovereignty, Kongo was quite similar to Portugal.

The Kongolese welcomed the white strangers, accepted their priests and seemed eager to learn their ways and adopt their religion. The Kongo king, Nzingo a Nkuwu, was lord of a thickly-populated Bantu kingdom which had vassals on both sides of the Congo river, perhaps as far north as what is now the Cabinda Enclave and as far south as the island of Luanda, the present site of the capital of Angola. The Mani Kongo who met Cão's men were converted to Christianity and the king was baptised in May 1491 with the name of Dom João I. Kings of the Kongo have taken Portuguese Christian names as titles ever since.

The Portuguese enjoyed fairly peaceful relations with the Kongo state from this time until after 1575 when the Portuguese shifted their concentration of effort to the south, to Angola. Portugal followed a policy of peaceful diplomacy and recognised the Christian Kongo kings as sovereigns equal, in theory at least, to the kings of Portugal. The ideal was to create a Christian and commercial community in this part of tropical Africa without force or conquest. Immediately, however, contradictions and conflict appeared and were to bedevil Kongo-Portuguese relations for the next four centuries before Kongo was finally conquered by Portugal. The two kings carried on an interesting correspondence in letters. The king of Portugal expressed humane and wise opinions in his letters, but his Portuguese subjects did not impress the Bakongo with the same virtues. Portuguese traders soon entered the Kongo kingdom and sailors and slave-traders followed. As early as 1500 the king of Kongo became anxious about the actions of Portuguese. While he might complain about these evils in his letters to Portugal, or to the Pope, the Portuguese monarch could actually do little to enforce a just policy in Kongo or to redress the grievances of his Christian brother. From thousands of miles away, Lisbon found that the best intentions and finest plans could mean nothing.

Other contradictions appeared. Succession to the Kongo throne was always a difficult time of competition among eligible royalty. King João 1 died about 1506. His eldest son was a strong partisan of the Portuguese but he met Bakongo opposition to his candidacy. A bastard son, Nzinga Mvemba, independent and strong-willed, succeeded in getting elected by a group of nobles, only after a civil war had troubled the state. The bastard son became a Christian and was baptised as King Afonso 1 (1506–43?). He was perhaps the most important king in Kongo history, from the point of view of both the African and the European. He received a Portuguese education but he remained an independent king who put the good of his people above European demands and actions. In the history of acculturation in Angola, he was the first true *assimilado*, or African acculturated to Portuguese values and customs. Like many *assimilados* brought up in Angola and Kongo in the succeeding generations, he was initially optimistic about the chances of a fruitful relationship with Portugal.

Dom Afonso was a good Christian and an intelligent leader. He urged Portugal to send artisans and craftsmen to Kongo to teach his people, and Portuguese priests soon began to advise him and to play a role in Kongo politics. During his reign he sent one of his sons, baptised Henrique, to study theology in Portugal; in 1518 Henrique became the first black African bishop of the Roman Catholic Church. He was the first Bakongo of consequence to receive a formal Portuguese education for the priesthood outside of his country, a tradition that was

29

maintained intermittently up until the end of the nineteenth century. Though the Kongo elite's devotion to the Christian religion was never doubted during Afonso's reign, the Portuguese came to realise that the Mani Kongo were opposed to Portuguese activities which appeared to be anti-religious: especially slave trading. Slave trading activities eventually ruined the friendly relations between Portugal and Kongo and hopelessly undermined the strength and stability of the Kongo kingdom itself.[1]

Dom Afonso, like Henrique, was caught between two worlds and two cultures. Though he was an African, Afonso to some extent resembled a Portuguese in culture. He must have felt the pulse of Bakongo opinion about the Portuguese strangers around him. In doing so, this early Kongo king experienced perhaps the strongest force in his kingdom: the spirit of independence, of rebellion when aroused, of the African jacquerie which could break out under the pressures of foreign intervention. The Kongo people came to oppose the Portuguese presence just as the Portuguese countryman opposed the intruding Spaniard or Frenchman in Portugal. Those members of the Kongo elite, such as the major chiefs and relatives given the European titles of duke, marquis and count, or *assimilados* who were beholden to the Portuguese for support and education, had occasion to feel the wrath of the Bakongo peasants. The Kongo elite invariably found themselves caught between concern for their own positions, aided by Portuguese support, and the natural enmity of the Kongo people, threatened by foreign intrusion. This dilemma persisted for four centuries and in some ways continues today. The masses of Kongo, then, long after the Kingdom enjoyed stability and importance, constituted a vital factor in the relations between Angola and Kongo.

The Kongo court was consciously modelled on the Portuguese court, even down to the details of dress, food and manners. Churches and cathedrals were constructed so that by 1600 the capital of Kongo, named São Salvador in Portuguese, supposedly had twelve churches. After Dom Afonso's death about 1543, relations between Portugal and Kongo became strained. The Portuguese shift of interest to the south, to the Angola coast, and the growth of the slave trade were responsible for this change.

The remainder of the history of relations between Kongo and Portugal is melancholy. Portuguese slave trading grew in intensity. The port of Mpinda, in Kongo territory, was the scene of the first important slave trading and export of slaves in the region. By 1550 Portuguese ships were taking African slaves at the rate of some 8–10,000 a year to the sugar plantations on the islands of São Tomé and Príncipe and to Portuguese plantations in Brazil. Kongo was adversely affected by the growing trade in human beings. The loss of thousands of young adult males and the enmity and poison of warfare to obtain the slaves from surrounding peoples infected the Kongo and brought certain political consequences: a decentralisation of authority, civil wars among the Kongo provinces, and a neglect of administrative, artistic and economic functions for the sake of the slave trade. The Kongo kingdom was in full decline by 1600 and the enmity of the Bakongo towards the Portuguese seemed to grow in proportion to the decline.

Open warfare between the Kongo and the Portuguese followed. When the Dutch captured Luanda in 1641 and for seven years held the coast of Angola, the Kongo kingdom, though remaining Catholic in religion, allied with the Dutch invaders against the besieged Portuguese remaining in Angola. An iconoclastic symbol of their Dutch alliance was the placing of images of the heretic Calvinist Dutchmen even on the Catholic altars in São Salvador churches.[2] In one of the more important battles of African history, at Mbwila, on October 29, 1665, a Portuguese army severely defeated the Kongo army. With about 350 Europeans and over 3,000 African bowmen, the Portuguese *mestiço* commander, Luis Lopes de Sequeira, defeated the Kongo king, killed him and returned to Luanda in triumph. One grisly trophy of victory, the king's head, was preserved in a tiny chapel on Luanda bay, the *Igreja de Nazaré*. The battle was more tastefully commemorated within the church in a large panel made of Portuguese blue and white tiles, the *azulejos*. Mbwila effectively dissolved the remnants of Kongo ability to challenge the Portuguese in conventional battle. The Bakongo, however, despite their defeat, became adept at guerrilla warfare. They broke up into warring, rival states vying for position in a decaying São Salvador. And though Portugal might periodically try to revive the Kongo power through diplomatic and military aid, the Kongo kingdom never recovered from this defeat of 1665.

The twilight period of Kongo importance came in the eighteenth and nineteenth centuries. However, a connection with the Portuguese in Angola persisted. The necessary presence of European priests at the coronation ceremony of Kongo kings became a significant convention by the eighteenth century,[3] and the Kongo elite depended upon the Portuguese for supplies, arms and wines throughout the nineteenth century. Portugal still held some esteem with the São Salvador kings, who managed to use this connection for political and economic ends in the nineteenth century. Some reminder and imprint of Portuguese culture and influence remained around São Salvador: knowledge by a few scribes of the Portuguese language, a faint idea of Christian concepts and symbols, European titles, and a desire to retain the Portuguese connection by means of sending gifts of slaves and ivory to the governors at Luanda and expecting, in return, Portuguese aid similar to that sent to the original Dom Afonso I in the sixteenth century: arms, supplies, trinkets, clothes, robes and European missionaries. Many of the Kongo kings between 1665 and 1884, when the Kongo monarch King Pedro VI inadvertently signed a treaty of protection with Portugal, considered the Portuguese aid a key factor in enhancing their positions within their own kingdom. This idea conflicted with the spirit of Bakongo independence, exhibited by the peasantry each time any significant number of Portuguese attempted to remain in São Salvador or intervene in Kongo affairs. The power of popular rebellion rose to a high point in the 1859–1914 era, after the Portuguese decided to conquer and annex Kongo as a northern district of the Province of Angola.

By the time the Portuguese decided to concentrate their efforts to the south, the Christian experiment of the Kongo was little more than a memory. The Kongo remained a loose group of states troubled by poverty and instability. By educating now and then a Kongo prince, a custom that lasted into the late nineteenth century, the Portuguese created an elite which had uncertain allegiance from Bakongo or European. If the elite in São Salvador at times became puppets of Luanda, the Bakongo masses would have none of it and would rather murder such alien *assimilados* than risk Portuguese control. This situation changed in the middle of the nineteenth century with a new development in Portuguese policy: the determination to secure coastal trade by means of controlling once again the Kongo interior. The attempt to enforce this policy drew the Kongo again into the limelight of Afro-European conflict and pointed up the persisting contradiction between a tiny elite that clung to European support from afar and a hostile peasantry intent on ridding the country of all the white strangers of *Mueneputo*, Portugal.*

A PATTERN IS SET: THE PORTUGUESE CONQUER
ANGOLA, 1575–1675

The Portuguese decision to move south from Kongo to the kingdom of N'Gola, an African king of the Ndongo kingdom of Mbundu, requires explanation. Why did Portugal decide to change its approach from

* The common name for 'Portugal' or 'The Europeans' in this region became *Mueneputo* or *Maniputo*, an African amalgamation of *Mani*, or 'Lord', and *Puto*, or Portugal. This term could be employed by Kikongo and Kimbundu-speaking peoples.

Christian co-existence in the Kongo to military conquest in Angola? David Birmingham suggests[4] that the poor quality and low quantity of Portuguese trade cloth used in the slave trade barter prompted the Portuguese to turn to warfare to obtain slaves. The warfare involved two processes: by direct capture, common in the early years, and by means of forcing African vassal or client chiefs to sell slaves to the Portuguese traders at favourable prices.[5] Additional reasons included the hostile attitude towards the Portuguese of the N'Gola of Ndongo, the religious justifications given by the Jesuit priest, Father Gouveia, the support of Paulo Dias de Novais with powerful patrons in Portugal, the consequences of the Jaga attack on the Kongo and the subsequent Portuguese victory over them, and the jingoistic impulses of the disastrous reign of King Sebastian of Portugal (1568–78).

The old cliché of 'God, Gold and Glory' cannot fully explain the lure of Angola for the Portuguese. Equally important is the fact that Portugal became involved in African land politics and this involvement drew Portugal into Angola. Despite superior Portuguese military and naval technology and the support of an aggressive and militant Church, the Portuguese did not sweep the African peoples before them. They were forced by their own weaknesses to seek African allies in war and in slaving, to use African methods—armies of black bowmen were as effective as unreliable arquebus squads after the first traumatic discharges—and to become Africanised. The military plan to forge a *conquista*, or land conquest, inland from Luanda island committed an essentially maritime people to a land campaign they could never finish.

The maritime tradition of Portugal also helps explain the attack on Angola. The Congo river, or *Rio Poderoso* as early Portuguese maps called it, proved a great disappointment to the navigators who hoped to find a fluvial corridor to the heart of Africa or to the opposite coast, to join up with other Portuguese settlements in the Zambezi valley, established by 1550. The Congo was navigable by regular vessels for only ninety miles and was then blocked by rapids. The Portuguese hoped that the smaller and less turbulent Kwanza river, south of Luanda, would provide the desired corridor to the interior. Later Portuguese chroniclers like Cadornega lyrically praised the utility and beauty of the Kwanza. Reports of silver and gold mines inland from Luanda attracted the metal-minded Europeans and they saw the Kwanza as a path to wealth and fortune. Moreover, the Portuguese found the Kongo kingdom hot, humid and sickly and they longed to find an inland plateau with cooler air and no fevers.

Then, too, ignorance of the interior geography of Africa encouraged

33

the vain hopes placed on the Kwanza corridor. Rumours and reports from traders in Ndongo suggested that the continent was not wide at that point and that perhaps only 100–300 miles separated Angola from Mozambique. If Portugal could only get beyond Ndongo, they thought, they might soon run into the Indian Ocean on the other side. Instead, their probings and explorations penetrated a vast hinterland, seemingly endless. The actual distance between Cambambe on the Kwanza river and the Portuguese towns on the Zambezi was over 1,000 miles, an area not accurately mapped or known until the great journeys of Dr David Livingstone in the 1850s, and not personally known to scientific Portuguese explorers until the 1884–85 journey of Capelo and Ivens.

The first Portuguese contacts with Ndongo kingdom were commercial. Portuguese traders from São Tomé and Kongo established themselves on Luanda island and on the mainland. No one knows when they first began this trade with the Mbundu but it is certain that a lively trade was in progress by 1550. The Mbundu peoples and their neighbours viewed the white strangers with some alarm at first because they could not comprehend the nature of European ships. Early oral tradition of the Pende peoples tells of the first contacts near Luanda: 'The white men came yet again. They brought us maize and cassava, knives and hoes, groundnuts and tobacco. From that time until our day the Whites brought us nothing more but wars and miseries.'[6] Mbundu on the island later named Luanda believed that the strangers were travelling on the Atlantic on white birds and that the sails were white wings. Hence, one Kimbundu term for Europeans was *Ndele*, or *Mundéle*, from *Muene ua ndéle*, or 'masters of the white birds'.[7] The Portuguese learned that the islands off the coast and the hinterland were formally tributary to the Mani Kongo. The islands were full of small cowrie shells, *zimbo* or *buzio*, as they came to be known, considered valuable currency by the Africans. One island in particular constituted the currency treasury of the king of Kongo: *Luandu*, or Luanda as the Portuguese called the island and later the town they founded on the opposite mainland, meant a 'tribute' or 'tax' of cowrie shells.[8]

In 1520 several Portuguese were ordered by royal decree to visit and to convert to Christianity the N'Gola of Ndongo. Little is known of the accomplishments of that mission but soon the Mbundu near Luanda were trading slaves to the Portuguese. For the succeeding fifty-eight years Afro-European relations were fairly peaceful, but as the Angolan hinterland became established as a great slave factory for Portugal's empire in the South Atlantic a new pattern emerged. Another Portuguese mission to the N'Gola set out in 1560, led by the grandson of the navigator Bartholemeu Dias, Paulo Dias de Novais. Unlike the king of Kongo, the N'Gola was not interested in Christianity, and wanted only material goods from the Portuguese. He refused to allow the preaching of the gospel in his kingdom and treated the mission with disdain and cruelty. Dias remained a prisoner of the N'Gola until 1565, whereupon he returned to Portugal to attempt to get his king to sponsor an expedition to conquer Ndongo by force of arms.[9]

The Portuguese undertook to conquer Angolan territory, and Paulo Dias, the first of many Portuguese *conquistadores*, was appointed in 1571 hereditary proprietor of a colony that stretched from the mouth of the Kwanza south for about 170 miles. The charter demarcated no eastern frontiers to this tract, or to the colony of the crown between the Dande and Kwanza rivers, over which Dias was governor, or captain-general. His charter resembled those given to Portuguese *donatários* in Brazil. In his private colony, Dias was obliged to 'plant', within a period of six years, one hundred European couples and set them up as farmers. But, by the time of his death in Angola in 1589, he had failed to fulfil his obligations: not only had he failed to establish a hundred couples, but he had conquered no portion of his own private domain south of the Kwanza. Thus, from the very beginning, European colonisation in Angola was off to a false start.

The reasons for the failure were ill omens for the future. Birmingham gives four reasons,[10] to which a fifth may be added: (i) high mortality from tropical disease; (ii) African hostility; (iii) an arid climate on the Luanda coast, making it unsuitable for agriculture; (iv) the slave trade's domination of all activity; (v) the inferior quality of the European 'colonists' Dias brought with him to Angola. The powerful combination of these five factors shaped the fate of many a Portuguese enterprise in Angola from then on and moulded the colony in a pattern.

Dias's expedition of over 400 Europeans arrived at Luanda island in early 1575 and within a year he had established a small settlement on the upper slopes of bluffs overlooking Luanda bay. This was the nucleus of what came to be the city of Luanda, the capital of Angola. Having established a beach-head, he began to move inland towards the south-east and the capital of Ndongo. In 1579–80 the Portuguese war of conquest began in earnest. The Spanish conquest of Portugal in that year did not delay or halt the Portuguese campaign and Phillip II, ruler of Spain and now of Portugal, dispatched reinforcements to aid Dias's progress. Malarial fevers took more lives than African arrows and spears: one historian estimated that nearly 2,000 European soldiers died, mainly from disease, in the campaign in Angola, 1574–94. Rarely during the first century of Portuguese occupation did more than 1,000

35

Europeans reside in Angola but the Portuguese soon added to their numbers and their allies by means of miscegenation. In effect, a new class and kind of Angolan appeared with the Afro-Portuguese *mestiço*, or mulatto—given many names in the Portuguese language, such as *pardo* (brown), *fusco* (tawny), *mulato* and *mestiço*.* Before long, these men were participating in the Angolan wars as Portuguese soldiers and leaders.

In his fourteen years of military campaigning, Dias established the pattern of Portuguese control which lasted for centuries. He constructed a line of fortresses, called *presídios*, inland from the coast and up the Kwanza valley. By 1589, despite defeats by large African armies, Dias had managed to set up nearly half a dozen *presídios* on or near the Kwanza and Lukala rivers. Military expansion proceeded but civilian colonisation involving more than subsistence agriculture was non-existent. The hinterland of Luanda was called, in Portuguese legal terminology, a *conquista*, a term which later came to mean 'kingdom' or 'domain'. A *conquista* by Christians implies the existence of heathen or infidel people, and the manner of the Portuguese conquest and the nature of their administration was especially Iberian and medieval. As in the *reconquista* of the Iberian peninsula by Spanish and Portuguese crusaders, the Portuguese in Angola were essentially a military-commercial caste, penetrating African territory by a series of *conquistas* or islands of control. When the Portuguese obtained African allies in the campaigns, they brought them into a paternalistic system of sub-servience, called *vassalagem*, or vassalage. While the Portuguese would recognise the status and influence of nearby African chiefs, or *sobas*, and sometimes bribe or threaten them, the *sobas*, in turn, were obliged to ally themselves with the Portuguese.

Variations of this system remained in Angola until the twentieth century. The *sobas* who signed formal treaties or made oral agreements were obliged, in theory at least, to aid their Portuguese allies in military campaigns, in carrying trade goods and in procuring slaves. The system grew out of Portuguese weakness in numbers, their traditions in the Iberian milieu and the fragmentary nature of the African political systems. The system of *vassalagem*, or what a Portuguese scholar has recently called, 'Luso-African feudalism',[11] was based on the fact of Portuguese insecurity. Although many African chiefs were called 'vassals', many of them were more reluctant allies than vassals. The

---

* *Mestiço*, or 'mixed one', is a person born of parents from two races. A Portuguese law in 1684 decreed that there could be no distinction between whites, *mestiços* and free negroes in the Angolan army; merit was to be the only basis for promotion. See C. R. Boxer, *Portuguese Society in the Tropics*, Madison 1965, pp. 134–5.

sheer weight of numbers, or 'that mass of heathen', as Cadornega called the African majority,[12] represented the foundation for African power and Portuguese defensiveness.

From an early date, the pattern of Portuguese administration was set. The tradition was established that African 'vassals' would pay tribute or taxes to the Portuguese. Tribute may have begun as early as 1600 in the form of a religious tithe, or *dizimo* ('tenth tax'), which soon lost all religious connotations. The tax could be paid in several ways: in slaves, ivory, use of porters, or (later) in currency. There was great variation in the amount of *dizimo* collected in the Portuguese-controlled areas of Angola; sometimes the tax revenue was significant, while at other times it amounted to little more than a nominal tribute paid by a few chiefs. By about 1790, some thirteen towns and *presídios* paid *dizimo* to the treasury.

Eventually, the Portuguese administration formalised the vassalage relationships by requiring the signing of treaties or 'acts' of vassalage. Although one of the earliest regular vassalage treaties dates from 1838, it is clear that chiefs signed such treaties as early as the seventeenth century. An early example was the harsh peace treaty enforced on the Kongo kingdom in about 1650. Another tradition became established: the organisation of African mercenary or auxiliary armies which fought for the Portuguese—the *guerra preta*, or 'black war'. By the early seventeenth century, this had become an established institution, involving the gathering of African forces by a chief or sub-chief and joining these units with the European troops in a campaign. At first the *guerra preta* operated in a rudimentary manner with no regular pay, only booty, and with little structure or leadership, but soon it became invested with the trappings of an irregular African army. Invariably, African officers led the *guerra preta* into battle: one 'António Dias Muzungo', an African, was the first captain-major of the Angolan *guerra preta* from 1620 to 1630.[13] The ability to raise a reliable African auxiliary army helped assure the Portuguese survival.

After fourteen years of warfare, Paul Dias de Novais died in 1589, having failed to conquer the Ndongo kingdom. As a *conquistador*, he could not claim the success of Cortez in Mexico who, in 1519–21, conquered a land area larger than that of Angola and caused the collapse of the Aztec political system. Though Dias had founded several forts to the east of Luanda, he did not control the country around the forts. His successors faced the force of Bantu military strength and made slow progress up the Kwanza. In 1604 the Portuguese built the *presídio* of Cambambe, at the limit of navigation on the Kwanza. No silver mines were located. During the first half of the seventeenth century, the Portuguese met great opposition in the form of both African and European threats: the Bantu and the Dutch, who took Luanda in 1641 and held on until 1648. When the Dutch evacuated Luanda, on August 15, 1648—today an annual Angolan holiday—there began the work of reconquering what had been lost under the brief Dutch occupation.

During the next generation, the Portuguese fought many wars in their conquest of what came to be known as the 'kingdom of Angola', between the Kwanza river and the Kongo kingdom, and inland about 150 miles. As the Dutch inspired many tribes to attempt to throw out the Portuguese and did not tax the Africans, the Portuguese faced a formidable task. The Angolan wars which followed present a bloody chapter in history. Governor Salvador Correia de Sá e Benavides, who had recaptured Luanda from the Dutch after a spectacular arrival from Brazil, ruled Angola for four years, 1648–52. He laid the foundations for the Portuguese destruction of the neighbouring African kingdoms of Kongo, Ndongo and Matamba and for the revival of the slave trade to Brazil. After the Kongo kingdom was dictated a harsh treaty which included tribute to help meet the costs of reconquering Angola, the Portuguese turned to Libolo, south-east of Cambambe, where the Portuguese sustained at least one serious defeat.

As the Portuguese consolidated their hold on the Kwanza valley, they attempted to increase their profits in the slave trade. Levying a slave tribute to the Portuguese was one duty of the vassal chief. The great lesson learned in this era was that Portugal could not extract profit from the system without the co-operation of African states. Angola became a great 'Black Mother'. Conservative estimates of the total number of Africans shipped from Angola as slaves over the centuries range from two to three million. Perhaps four million is a more realistic estimate. This excessive number helps to explain the small population of Angola today. The following is a table of estimated annual slave exports from Angola from the beginning of the Angolan trade to the end of the Atlantic slave trade. The table does not take into account the thousands of Africans shipped as virtual slaves to the islands of São Tomé and Príncipe during the nineteenth and twentieth centuries.[14]

Year	Number per year
1536	5,000
1576	10,000
1612	10,000
1641	14,500
1710	3,500
1736	12,200

Year	Number per year
1765	17,200
1790–91	16,100
1820	10,000
1840	15,000
1850	5,000 (?)
1860	1,000 (?)

Besides the annual drain of human beings from Angola, another pattern was set: the Portuguese treatment of 'rebels'. A Mbundu chief, Kabuku Kandonga, a Portuguese ally, negotiated with a rebel chief and in 1653 the Portuguese lured Kabuku Kandonga into a meeting, captured him and then sent him to exile in Brazil.[15] The deportation of Africans, whether chiefs, *civilizados* or leaders, to other Portuguese colonies in America, Asia and Africa became a common pattern. Not a few of them, however, were eventually returned to Angola after their exiles.

After the 1665 defeat of Kongo, there remained three major African independent kingdoms in north-central Angola: Kasanje, Ndongo and Matamba. The irrepressible Queen Nzinga, clearly one of the most remarkable women in Central African history, reigned from 1624 to 1663 over the Matamba kingdom. As the 'Black Mother' of Matamba, she acquired a fearsome reputation as a shrewd negotiator, fierce warrior and merciless competitor. Rising to the throne of Matamba supposedly by murdering her rivals (including her nephew, and then consuming his heart), Nzinga flirted with Christianity but was never actually converted. In 1656 she signed a peace treaty with the Portuguese Governor of Angola and kept the peace until her death in 1663, at the supposed age of eighty-one years. Conflict with the Portuguese increased in Matamba until about 1674–76 when the Portuguese managed to have placed on the throne of Matamba a chief favourable to their interests, as they had done previously in Ndongo. As became the custom, the Portuguese officer was allowed to reside in the king's capital to watch over trade activities.

In Ndongo, the puppet king, Ngola Ari, died in 1664 and was succeeded by Dom João, or Ngola Ari II, a man who was not partisan to Portuguese interests. A serious war developed by 1669, as the Portuguese prepared to take the Ndongo capital at Pungu a Ndongo (later renamed Pungo Andongo), a rock fortress of large sandstone monoliths rising above a plain. Heavily supported by *guerra preta*, the Portuguese mounted an attack. A siege of three months reduced the African garrison and the Portuguese founded a European *presídio* among the rocks of Pungo Andongo.[16] This fortress was long considered the furthest inland, furthest eastward, Portuguese settlement in Angola.

In the hinterland, up to perhaps 120 miles further east, there were a few scattered Portuguese *feiras,* or trading market-posts. In the seventeenth century the Portuguese established a *feira* at the court of Kasanje, another kingdom located west of the Kwango river or some 300 miles east of Luanda. Portuguese and *mestiço* traders from the *presídio* of Mbaka were travelling that far east regularly by the mid-seventeenth century. In the hinterland of Angola, though the Portuguese had little military power and had to rely on African armies, their trade influenced African activity well beyond the reach of cannon shot from their tiny fortresses. By 1675, then, the Portuguese had subdued the major native powers within a radius of 150 miles east of Luanda and the lower Kwanza.

In expanding southward, the Portuguese searched for new ports and entrances to the interior: in 1617 they established a settlement at the bay of Benguela, that became the nucleus and base for another 'kingdom' in the interior. Benguela was isolated from Luanda and at times was almost independent in action. Yet no immediate interior penetration followed the founding of Benguela as happened in Luanda: not until 1685 did the Portuguese found two settlements at Caconda and Quilengues on the plateau east of Benguela, and these stations were soon abandoned due to their isolation, African opposition and the climate.

With the failure to discover an easy route to the interior or to reach the *contra-costa* ('opposite coast'), the destruction of the political strength of the Bantu kingdoms in north-central Angola, the failure to find gold and silver mines, and the establishment of the system of slave trading through African states on the periphery of Angola, Portuguese expansion to the east halted. By the end of the seventeenth century, a handful of Portuguese officials and traders—2,000–4,000 in all—and the *mestiço* sons they produced settled down to build a commercial kingdom founded on the supply and demand for African slaves across the Atlantic. Until 1720, even the captains-general were allowed to trade to augment their meagre salaries. Trade dominated all. The first two and a half centuries of the Portuguese presence in Angola was the era of the slave trade and the major political goal of any administration was to preserve a Portuguese monopoly over that trade.

THE MONSTERS OF INIQUITY

The Portuguese contact with Angola virtually began with war and some believe it may end with war. Until 1575, it is true, Portuguese relations with Africans were mainly peaceful. But from 1579, Portugal's new policy, penetration of Angola, was initiated with a military campaign which set off a series of wars lasting a century. But warfare did not end in the late seventeenth century: on the contrary, it became the rule rather than the exception for nearly every year from 1579 until 1921. Unpublished documents in Portuguese archives show that during those three and a half centuries scarcely five years went by without at least one Portuguese military campaign somewhere within the frontiers of what is now Angola. Rare years of peace came in the eighteenth century, with a few years in the early nineteenth century, and the brief recent era of 1921–61. Another war began in 1961.

Besides the military activity, a second important characteristic of the Portuguese presence has been the authoritarian, hierarchical nature of government. From the days of the first governor, Captain-General Paulo Dias de Novais, there has been Portuguese control of a part of the Angolan population—broken only by the brief interlude of the Dutch conquest of 1641–48. There has followed a long, continuous line of Portuguese governors; today the list numbers about two hundred, covering a span of about four hundred years, or about thirteen generations. The very longevity of this Portuguese presence and the fact that it has been unleavened except for a few brief periods of unusual change and peace may well startle the unprepared observer.

To argue the question of who began the wars may lead to the equally controversial question of what is a just war. Portuguese jurists and clergymen argued this when in 1571 Paulo Dias de Novais received his charter from the king of Portugal. Assessing the justification for four centuries of Angolan wars, however, is not as vital to the understanding of Angolan history as is the realisation that these wars created a certain atmosphere of feeling. By their very nature, wars are tragic and participation in them for whatever reason tragically affects all participants. Wars for slaves, alliances and provocations wrought a certain pattern of response and counter-response, and a sense of moral crisis and reaction to that crisis which touched many persons of all races. In the nineteenth century some referred to 'a moral deficit', others to 'the empire of immorality'. Though intangible in conception, this moral crisis influenced the course of government, race relations and many varieties of human interaction.

The moral crisis cannot be dismissed as a myth, the creation of liberal do-gooders, a stab in the dark of a foreign observer, or perhaps the idea of an inspired man of literature. Angolans of all colours and positions from the sixteenth century onwards have discussed this crisis. The history which follows better describes this phenomenon than a parade of judicious quotations, but an excellent introductory illustration is the

following anonymous poem by a seventeenth-century Portuguese writer,
the first known piece of Portuguese poetry written in Angola, found in
Cadornega's history.[17] Cadornega called the poem 'a little sarcastic',
surely a critical understatement.

> There is in this turbulent land
> a storehouse of pain and trouble,
> confused mother of fear,
> Hell in life.
>
> Land of oppressed peoples,
> rubbish heap of Portugal
> where she purges her evil
> and her scum.
>
> Where the lie and falsehood,
> theft and malevolence,
> selfishness,
> represent vain glory.
>
> Where justice perishes,
> for want of men to understand it,
> where God must be sought
> to achieve salvation. . . .
>
> From his throne God casts upon us,
> with cruel and bloody war,
> with the power of the land
> and pestilence,
> hot and malignant fever,
> which in three to seven days
> places beneath the ground
> the most robust.

The poet who wrote these lines wrote about what he observed in the
Luanda hinterland and the lower Kwanza. War and climate dominated
all. It is symbolic that the first known Portuguese poetry written in
Angola is not an epic of glory to the *conquistador* or to Portuguese
national heroism, but rather a bitter commentary on the evils of life in a
land of adversity. In their oral tradition, African informants would
paint much the same picture of 'wars and miseries'.[18]

A detailed social history of early colonial Angola would be difficult to
produce today, but what little historians do know suggests an interesting but alarming picture. In the area of race relations, first of all, it is

important to learn how the prevailing attitude of the Portuguese, the dominant racial group, though in the minority, developed. The predominant European feeling was what a recent analysis termed 'conscious white superiority'.[19] The feeling was based in part on the idea that the Negro was legitimately enslaved since, it was alleged, he was inherently inferior to the European. Until new evidence appears, the histories written by the *morador* (settler) António de Oliveira Cadornega and by a number of priests and soldiers who visited Angola remain the heart of the evidence that this prejudice was pervasive.

What encouraged this racial prejudice against the African? In the early period, when Catholic proselytising in the interior and church-building in Luanda were at their zenith, antipathy towards the heathen was certainly one factor. To even the less-than-devout Portuguese the Angolan Negro seemed to have no recognisable religion, though, viewed in perspective, many of the Mbundu or Bakongo superstitions were not very different from the traditional Portuguese peasant beliefs, some of which persist to this day. More important than the Christian militancy, perhaps, was the force of social competition and simple fear. Blacks greatly out-numbered whites: the ratio of black to white in Portuguese settlements was never less than 10 to 1, and sometimes more. The Portuguese have always been acutely aware of their small numbers, surrounded by countless *indígenas*. Moreover, the martial power of the African—despite his defeats in conventional warfare—was always evident, murders of masters by slaves were not uncommon, and sexual and physical competition complicated relations. It is not improbable that some of the racial prejudice arose from a guilt complex in Portuguese who reacted to the shameful treatment of the African slave. Prejudice was also encouraged by the fact that most of the Portuguese were from the lowest social strata in Europe. The social mobility and prestige of the poor white, the *degredado*** and the petty trader were in an inverse ratio to the status of the African, and to the extent that the 'petit blanc' could keep the African down, he remained one step higher on the ladder.

In the Portuguese settlements, especially in Luanda, colour and race became an index of stratification. By the middle of the nineteenth century, Luanda society was divided into what a contemporary almanac called racial 'castes'. There was the top caste of *brancos* (whites), then the *pardos* or *mestiços* (mulattoes), and, finally, the lowest caste, the *pretos* (blacks or Africans).[20] Although little racial segregation existed, there was a social and economic set of distinctions—tied to colour—in

---

* The Portuguese word *degredo* means 'exile, banishment, deportation'. Thus a *degredado* is a deportee, exile or transported convict.

society. Sub-castes existed within each caste: Portuguese officials and officers, for example, snubbed lowly *degredados* and petty traders, and sometimes refused to associate with them. Nevertheless, the down-trodden of Oporto or Lisbon might, in Angola, lord it over the lower 'castes' of blacks and *mestiços*. In this way, colour became a status symbol at an early stage and continued to act as such in the nineteenth and twentieth centuries. Just as important in Angola, however, were wealth and its display. The superior feeling and consequent behaviour of the poor white, then, were in large part a reaction to previous deprivation in Portugal, a hatred for the strange surroundings in a hostile Angola, and the unique opportunity in the colonial setting to become what it was impossible to become in Europe.

Luanda became the not-so-safe haven for the class Silva Correia called 'the monsters of iniquity',[21] the flotsam and jetsam of the Portu-guese-speaking world. That they exploited tropical Angola is not so surprising as is the feeling of intense competition with Africans and *mestiços*. The few Portuguese with more advantages and wealth, on the other hand, were rarely in such close contact with the African; they expressed prejudice, but it was a less intense attitude. It would be a mistake, however, to believe that the development of a substantial upper class of whites in Angola would have eliminated prejudice: it would merely have entrenched it in another manner. Nevertheless, the Portuguese race prejudice was neither better nor worse than other such European feelings in the colonial world. What was remarkable in the Angolan case was the unique set of economic and social ills which gave rise to the prejudice and the *falta de justiça** toward the African majority.

Despite the harsh conditions, Angola represented another chance for the deserter and trimmer. What had been a sense of inferiority in Portugal was transformed into superiority in Africa. Impoverished Portuguese would put on airs in ostentatious domination of Africans, in acquiring quick fortunes, such as the *degredado* or *morador* (settler) living in seventeenth-century Luanda, using his trading fortune, surrounding himself with black servants and concubines and affecting the ways of a Portuguese noble. A century or so later, in different circumstances in the interior, another poor white, António da Silva Porto, the famous *sertanejo*† of Bié, was enraptured by his sense of superiority as the head of an African trading community. We observe

---

* 'Lack of justice', a term frequently used by critics of the Angolan scene.
† *Sertanejo* means a 'person living in the hinterland or backland'. In nine-teenth-century Angola, the term came to mean a Portuguese trader who travelled from the coast to the interior.

his feeling of social triumph—the reaction of a poor boy from Oporto who came from hardship in Portugal and Brazil to Angola to make his fortune and retire to Portugal as he returns to his village after a success-ful trading journey into Central Africa. Cheered and applauded by African villagers on the way in, and given a sign of Ovimbundu respect, to the trader it was a dream-like royal progress. Filled with emotion, he described this bush encounter in his diary as a high point in his career.[22]

Angola suffered from the transplanted ills of Portugal and its people. The low social status of many Portuguese aided in the generation of racial prejudice and social conflict. To the consequences of a slave trading economy was added Portuguese underdevelopment. Thus, African advancement was doubly difficult. Angola's role as a dumping ground and place for social opportunity for the *degredados* and peasants of Portugal conflicted with the desperate need of the African for social solutions of his own. Without a strong and resourceful government in Luanda, the struggles of these two submerged groups would be con-stantly destructive.

Angola acquired the reputation of a land of exile superimposed upon a slavocracy. By 1660, the *degredado* pattern was established. Positions in the army, police, trading, skilled trades and tavern-keeping world that were not filled by Africans were taken by the convict. Rarely could the convict be restricted to any one prison, town or region; until the twentieth century, when control was intensified, the *degredado* would turn up anywhere in the colony. Not all were felons and gypsies; some were bona fide political exiles, including a few Brazilian men of letters. Nor were all the *degredados* Europeans for eighteenth-century records suggest that some were of African ancestry;[23] their numbers added to the growing community of Angolan-born *mestiços* who by 1778 out-numbered the Europeans by over 2 to 1. As Cadornega's anonymous poet so well described in the seventeenth century, the colour of the offspring of the Portuguese male and the African female grew darker and darker over the generations. Exile, slavery, malaria and miscegena-tion formed the essence of old Angola.

TRADE ON THE NORTH COAST, AND IN THE INTERIOR,
1675–1836

In the late seventeenth century, the Portuguese shifted their attention from inland penetration to the conquest of the coast of Angola, from Luanda north to beyond Cabinda, sometimes called *a costa do norte*, or the 'North Coast'. A number of factors encouraged this policy: the loss of the Mina coast in Guinea by 1642, the increasing competition from Dutch, French and English shipping and trading on the north coast, and the attractiveness of the coast as opposed to the interior of Angola as an area of immediate fortune-hunting. This policy, like so many of the other Portuguese policies, was founded on the poverty and weakness of the mother country. The poor quality of Portuguese trading goods in Angola, 'such sorry goods', as the Dutch factor Bosman described them in the 1690s,[24] meant that other European competitors in trade invariably had a great advantage over their Portuguese counterparts. Not only was the Portuguese trade monopoly of Angola threatened after 1670, but sovereignty was in jeopardy.

Foreign competition on the coasts of Angola and Congo reduced the number of slaves Portugal could export to Brazil. An economic dependency of Brazil, Angola could not afford to lose the basis of its revenue which paid for supplies, food and aid from Brazil. From Benguela to Cabinda, Dutch, French and English ships were buying slaves from Angolan chiefs right under the noses of Portuguese authorities. In plans of 1723, 1758 and later, the government proposed building new fortresses at key trade points in Cabinda, Molembo and Loango. Little was done until 1759, when the Portuguese built a fort and established a new *presídio* at Encoge (Encoje), which was situated on a well-travelled trade route from the interior to the Congo coast. The Portuguese strategy was to control the African trade closer to its source, before the goods reached the coastal ports north of Luanda. Encoge became the northernmost Portuguese station—only intermittently garrisoned, of course—until the mid-nineteenth century. But the establishment of this post did not accomplish the Portuguese objective. Foreign *contrabanda* continued largely unchallenged and became the major preoccupation of the Portuguese administration for over a century. Even the enlightened Governor Francisco Sousa Coutinho (1764–72), one of the few genuine Iron Surgeons to occupy the governor's palace in Luanda, was forced to turn his attention to the problem—which also affected the coast south of Luanda—and he founded the settlement of Novo Redondo, between Luanda and Benguela, to intercept English ships.

Although the coastal contraband problem was Portugal's chief concern during most of the eighteenth century, a few probes were made into the Central African interior. Sousa Coutinho believed Angola would be enriched only if Portugal could find and secure a route to Mozambique to tap what he considered was 'the stream of gold' (yet another Eldorado) from the Zambezi valley; furthermore, this energetic governor urged Portugal to expand inland into Central Africa in order to prevent the Dutch, then in control of the Cape region of South

Africa, from extending their authority northward to the Zambezi and cutting off Portuguese control between Angola and Mozambique. As a part of his programme, Sousa Coutinho sponsored the establishment of European colonies on the Benguela plateau, in a cooler and healthier climate.

However, the pull of the coastal trade and the threat of *contrabanda* drew attention from such plans of internal expansion. In 1783 the Portuguese launched an expedition to Cabinda port to build a fortress. The Portuguese army under Pinheiro Furtado was defeated both by malaria and by a French fleet under Marigny; in 1784 the garrison surrendered to the French and destroyed their half-built fortifications. By the Convention of Madrid (1786), England, France and Portugal agreed that Portugal would recognise freedom of slave traffic for all European nations north of the Congo river, and, in return, France promised not to trade with Angolan ports south of the Congo. Portugal was left weakened and frustrated in its attempt to control trade north of the Congo.

After their failure at Cabinda, the Portuguese turned to the south coast. The Baron of Mossamedes (1784–90), the governor, realised the power of European and African resistance in the north and in 1785–86 sent expeditions to the south to explore. The bay near the mouth of the Bero river, nearly 200 miles south of Benguela, was explored and named 'Mossamedes' after the governor. Again, trade preceded the flag. Although the village of Mossamedes was not established until much later, in 1840, these first exploring parties found European traders bartering with the local Africans. As Mossamedes was on a stretch of desert coast, the explorers reported that it would be a healthy location for European settlement. But, although the mosquito was rare, the later settlers were to find the lack of fresh water at Mossamedes as dangerous an obstacle to settlement as the diseased insect.

As a result of the Mossul war, in 1788–90, the Portuguese control of Angola was again threatened by European competitors and African hostility. Only fifty miles north of Luanda, English vessels traded in slaves and sold arms and powder to African tribes. An African leader called variously by the name of Maniquitungo ('Lord of Quitungo') or the Marquis of Mossul, who had been friendly with the Portuguese authorities, controlled what became the port of Ambriz (Quitungo) and enjoyed a roaring trade with English and French merchants, to the anger of the governor at Luanda. When the Portuguese and the army of Mossul came to blows in 1788–90, the Portuguese lost the first battles; Africans slaughtered Europeans as close to Luanda as the Bengo river, and for a short period Luanda was threatened with an invasion. In late

47

1790, however, the Portuguese began to win and the African leader was obliged to hide for safety aboard an English vessel at Ambriz. Taking advantage of their victory, the Portuguese built a fortress near Ambriz. Although English and French pressures again won the day and Portugal was forced to destroy the fort in 1791, the Marquis of Mossul, now defeated in the field, came to Luanda and submitted to *vassalagem* in 1792. This document, supposedly signed by the repentant Maniqui-tungo, was later used as evidence for the Portuguese case in the 1855 occupation of Ambriz.

Until 1836, when new changes began to work in Angola, the colony was little more than a 'commercial-military factory'.[25] A gradual expansion of Portuguese trade into the plateau area of Angola and beyond became more important, but at first little more than increased slave trading resulted from this initiative. Large-scale European colonisation and plantation agriculture, as developed in Brazil, did not take place in Angola for a number of reasons already discussed. Although the history of Silva Correia stated confidently that 'the extension of the Conquest [of Angola] increases day by day, encouraged by trade',[26] the fact that trade dominated all other endeavours and that the trade was mainly in human beings could not help but stunt the country's development. Accompanying the horrors of war, raids and depopulation in the slave trade, came the ill effects of the commodity for which African slave dealers eagerly exchanged slaves: Brazilian rum, *geribita*.

The African consumption of Brazilian *geribita*, or *cachaça* or *aguardente*, was especially important in the period 1660–1830. For over a century and a half, rum or brandy from Brazil was the most valuable trade item the Portuguese had. Its effects were readily appreciated by observers in Angola: the ruin and degradation and sometimes the death by poisoning of many Africans who consumed it and the discouragement of a rum industry in Angola. Thus, on several occasions, there were petitions of Angolan settlers through the *câmara municipal* to ban the sale of Brazilian rum in Angola. When a rum industry began in earnest in Angola after 1840, based on coastal sugar plantations between the Bengo river and Mossamedes, it was alternately encouraged or opposed by governors depending on their views of the effects of rum on the African population. The question of the importation of alcohol continued into the twentieth century. The European rulers of Angola frequently asked such questions as: Does such importation benefit Angola? How does it affect the people? When Angola became self-sufficient in rum production in the nineteenth century, the answers to these queries could be subordinated to the economic interests of European manufacturers.

In the period 1800–36, Angola passed through a stage of transition. Three developments threatened irrevocable change for the colony: the further weakening of Portugal by the Napoleonic invasion (1807–11) and bloody political disputes (1820–45); the independence of Brazil (1822); and the gradual abolition of the African slave trade (1810–36). Marked for eradication, the slave trade was the most important source of revenue of the Angolan economy. In treaties signed with Britain in 1810, 1815 and 1817, the Portuguese government promised to limit the slave trade and gradually to abolish it in Portuguese Africa; but well before 1836, the slave trade in Angola had decayed. The reasons for this decline in slave exports and for the decrease in profits from the trade may be found both in Brazil and in Angola. Due to the decrease in Brazilian prosperity after 1750, with the exhaustion of the gold and diamond mines, plantation owners demanded fewer slaves from Angola.[27] Silva Correia argued in the 1790s that Angola could not expand slave exports until a new receiving port was opened in Brazil.[28] In Angola, the factors of foreign *contrabanda* and competition and Portuguese poverty tended to discourage a larger export business. The degeneration of the slave trade, well before the abolition decree in 1836, can be explained also by a vicious circle of poverty and lack of development. Depopulation from the slave export helped cause a shortage of labour to man industrial and agricultural pursuits, which resulted in a greater dependence on Brazilian aid and markets. With few slave markets outside Brazil, and with those markets being satisfied by foreign interlopers, the Portuguese in Angola were thus caught in a hopeless bind.

Yet another factor limited the export of Angolan slaves after 1750: the Africanisation of the Portuguese slave trade. By the middle of the eighteenth century, very few European traders were able to participate in the slave trade exchanges in the interior of the northern part of the country. Besides being forbidden by laws and decrees to travel inland beyond a certain point such as Pungo Andongo, the Portuguese merchants knew that the tribute costs of crossing non-vassalised chiefs' lands and the prices of slaves rose considerably when Europeans were present. Moreover, journeys like this were dangerous and Europeans were few. Increasingly after 1700, therefore, the Portuguese hired African and *mestiço* agents, called *pombeiros*, *aviados* or *feirantes*,* who went inland and transacted the business formerly supervised by Europeans. By 1800, most of the middle men, agents and dealers

---

* *Pombeiro:* 'one who went to a *pombo*', or slave fair or market in the interior. *Aviado:* agent representing Portuguese merchants in the bush. *Feirante:* 'merchant' or 'one at a *feira*', or trade fair.

49

beyond the frontier were non-Europeans. Silva Correia attributed a cause of the degeneration of the trade to the poverty of the black agent and his consequent cheating of his boss. By pocketing a good portion of the trade goods to be exchanged for the slaves, the *pombeiro* acquired the means to extract himself from debt to the Europeans, but, as a result, could produce fewer slaves at the coast. In the early 1790s, Captain-General Vasconcellos complained that the trade had been ruined by African agents who cheated their bosses after getting deep into debt. Commander William Owen, on his brief visit to Luanda in 1825, spoke with Portuguese merchants and confirmed this analysis of the reduction of the export business. But the indebtedness of the *pombeiro* and his independence in the bush cannot fully explain the new development. Certainly, the behaviour of the *degredado* discouraged the smooth operation of the system. Furthermore, the behaviour of the *pombeiro* in cheating the European merchant was both an imitation of European methods and yet another instance of African resistance and the progressive Africanisation of the Portuguese area of Angola.

By the 1830s, Angola had reached a new stage of weakness. What two and a half centuries of slave trading and wars had begun, new crises in Portugal helped to complete. The trade corrupted all that it touched. What slight progress towards viable agriculture that existed in 1830 was largely the work of a few Brazilians, and their numbers began to thin after the 1822 independence of their homeland. Only one Portuguese merchant of consequence worked in Angola and the remainder of the business community was Brazilian. To the handful of *colonialistas* in Lisbon, Angola did not seem a viable possession. To a number of Africans, it seemed possible that the Portuguese hugging the coast might soon be panhandled out of business or even driven into the sea. To other observers of the era, it seemed that Angola, the tormented child of a black mother and white father, might not survive the new century.

1. Prince Nicolas of Kongo (1830?-1860), on the occasion of his audience
with the Queen of Portugal in 1845

2. Portuguese missionary and his African charges, in military uniforms, Southern Angola, late 1880s

3. A Barren Sovereignty Expanded

The interests of Portugal would be far better consulted by developing the resources of the vast territories which she already possesses in Africa, than by seeking to extend a barren sovereignty over future tracts of country on that Continent, which can only be acquired by violence and bloodshed.

Lord Russell to Count Lavradio, Portuguese Ambassador to England, 1860.

THREE PHASES OF PORTUGUESE EXPANSION IN THE NINETEENTH CENTURY

By 1891 the shape of present-day Angola had been delimited by frontiers and Portugal possessed a territory of over 480,000 square miles. By 1921 possession had been safeguarded by Portugal by means of colonial investments, the Anglo-Portuguese alliance treaties, military campaigns and administrative measures. Portuguese expansion into the interior was not a strictly progressive development over a century, nor was it a gradual accumulation of strength. It occurred in fits and starts, including one period of expansion, a 'pre-Scramble', from 1840 to 1861, which profoundly influenced later Portuguese expansion once the true 'Scramble' began about 1880. This early colonial revival in the nineteenth century has been neglected by historians but, when analysed, it can help suggest the background for Portuguese expansion later in the century and the shape of the largely coastal Portuguese presence in Angola.

Portuguese expansion of control and sovereignty in Angola in the nineteenth century falls into three major phases. First, there was an era of initial expansion, which coincided with the gradual abolition of the Atlantic slave trade, 1836–61. Next, there was a second period of comparative withdrawal, a wave of anti-imperialism in Portugal and concentration on the coast of Angola, following the pre-1836 pattern, from 1861 to about 1877. Finally, the third period of expansion on to the plateau from 1877 to 1891 falls generally within the well-known period of European expansion in the rest of tropical Africa.[1]

51

The First Phase, 1836–61

The early expansion policy in Angola was conceived largely by one man, the liberal Portuguese statesman, the Marquis Sá da Bandeira (1795–1876), Minister of the Navy and Overseas in 1835–36. To this brilliant Portuguese leader, the abolition of the slave trade and eventually of slavery in Portuguese Africa were the essential prerequisites of economic development. But what revenue could replace the slave trade in an Angola without agriculture or industry? His answer was a plan to raise new revenues from two sources: increased taxation of the African population and increased customs revenue from ports and harbours in Angola. To create new revenue to fill the vacuum left by the old but now illegal slave trade, he planned to expand Portuguese sovereignty in Angola and, indeed, in all Portuguese Africa.

On December 10, 1836, the Portuguese government, after long negotiations with and pressures from its ally, Britain, issued a royal decree abolishing the slave trade in Portuguese vessels in Portuguese Africa. The trade did not collapse immediately: as late as 1843–44, about two-thirds of Angola's annual revenue derived from the traditional slave trade duties imposed at ports. By 1847, however, the Atlantic trade and its revenues were coming to an end in Angola. Vigorous protests by Portuguese settlers and traders as well as by African chiefs had followed the controversial abolition decree, but, despite a few lapses by subordinates, the governors-general attempted to enforce it. However, it was the Anglo-Portuguese Treaty of July 1842 that put 'teeth' into the 1836 decree by declaring that henceforth slave trading in Portuguese vessels would be considered piracy at sea and punished accordingly. The treaty provided for an Anglo-Portuguese or Mixed Commission and Court of Arbitration for captured vessels at Luanda. For Angola, this was the beginning of a new era of change and contact with the outside world. With the Mixed Commission and Court of Arbitration came new diplomatic and business contacts. In 1844, Angola's ports were officially opened to foreign trade.

Sá da Bandeira's plan for expansion was fraught with difficulties and only slowly carried out. In 1838, in order to stop the perennial foreign contraband activities north of Angola and to increase Angolan customs revenue, he ordered the occupation and annexation of the ports of Ambriz and Cabinda: however, the Portuguese did not execute that plan until 1855 in the case of Ambriz and 1883 in that of Cabinda, and even then they met opposition from Britain and France. Britain's policy on Portuguese expansion north of Luanda presented a paradox: to Portugal, the ending of the slave trade could not be achieved without

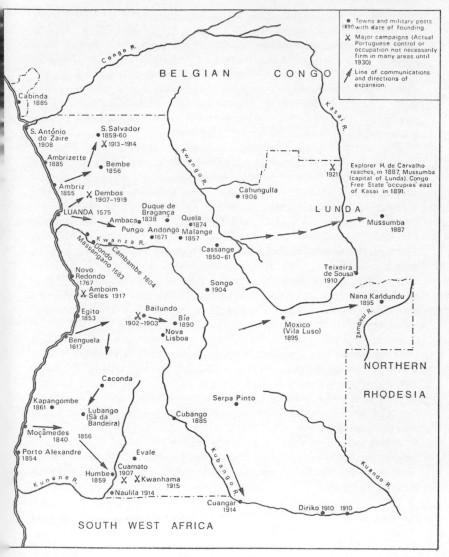

Towns and military posts with date of founding.

Major campaigns (Actual Portuguese control or occupation not necessarily firm in many areas until 1930)

Line of communications and directions of expansion.

BELGIAN CONGO

Cabinda 1885

S. António do Zaire 1908

Ambrizette 1885

Ambriz 1855

LUANDA 1575

S. Salvador 1859-60
X 1913-1914

Bembe 1856

X Dembos 1907-1919

Duque de Bragança 1838

Ambaca 1838

Pungo Andongo 1671

Quela 1874

Malange 1857

Cahungulla 1906

LUNDA

Mussumba 1887

Explorer H. de Carvalho reaches, in 1887, Mussumba (capital of Lunda). Congo Free State 'occupies' east of Kasai in 1891.

X 1921

Massangano 1583

Dondo

Kwanza R.

Cambambe 1604

Cassange 1850-61

Songo 1904

Teixeira de Sousa 1910

Novo Redondo 1767

Amboim Seles 1917

Egito 1853

Bailundo
X 1902-1903

Bíe 1890

Nova Lisboa

Moxico (Vila Luso) 1895

Nana Kańdundu 1895

Zambesi R.

NORTHERN

Benguela 1617

Caconda

Kapangombe 1861

Lubango (Sá da Bandeira)

Serpa Pinto

Cubango 1885

RHODESIA

Moçâmedes 1840

1856

Porto Alexandre 1854

Evale

Cuamato 1907

Humbe 1859

X X Kwanhama 1915

Naulila 1914

Kubango R.

Cuangar 1914

Diriko 1910   1910

Kuando R.

Kunene R.

SOUTH WEST AFRICA

3. Portuguese expansion in Angola

extension of sovereignty, but this was anathema to Britain, since Portuguese expansion (and the accompanying customs duties) would inevitably curtail the freedom of trade then enjoyed by British merchants. Thus, British policy, especially during Lord Palmerston's tenure of the Foreign Office (1839–46), and later during Lord Russell's, discouraged the expansion of Portuguese sovereignty over the small ports of Ambriz, Kissembo, Ambrizette and Punta da Lenha in the Congo estuary, while applying continued pressure to abolish private participation by Portuguese in the slave trade.

The first period of Portuguese expansion began in 1838 with the military conquest of a new *presídio*, Duque de Bragança, some 50 miles east of Ambaca. The Portuguese government at the same time encouraged new industry in Angola and authorised the establishment of a company for exploiting petroleum east of Luanda; this project soon collapsed with the death of its chief, the Swiss Doctor Lang. In response to African rebellions and attacks on Portuguese settlements, the Portuguese extended formal control well east of Duque de Bragança, to Kasanje fair in 1850–51. Portuguese colonisation expanded south of Benguela in 1840, when the town of Mossamedes (Moçâmedes) was established on the arid coast north of the Kunene river, thus initiating a new European foothold on the coast from which later exploration and colonisation would emanate.

During this first phase of expansion, Luanda played a major role as a base for the penetration of the Angolan hinterland. Benguela, a smaller and less-developed town, acted as a base for the free-ranging *sertanejos* and *pombeiros* of central-south Angola as they traded from the Kunene to the Okavango (Kubango) and from the Bero to the Zambezi and sometimes beyond. The hinterland of Luanda, within a radius of 150 miles, was the most developed agricultural region. Here began the plantations, or *arimos* and *roças*, of coffee and sugar in the 1830s and 1840s, soon to be complemented by a rum and brandy industry, sisal-growing and the ubiquitous manioc flour (*fuba*) industry, peddled by *fubeiros* in coastal Angola. But trade, not agriculture, obsessed the Europeans as well as the Africans and the flourishing contraband trade, dominated by Americans, Britons and Frenchmen, turned the attention of Luanda mainly northward rather than inland.

Led by Sá da Bandeira, the *Conselho Ultramarino* (an official body in Lisbon which planned colonial reform and expansion) and the remarkable but embattled regime of Governor-General José Rodrigues Coelho do Amaral (two terms: 1854–60; 1869–70), the Portuguese began a scheme to control northern Angola by military campaigns and to dominate the coast from Luanda to Cabinda by occupying ports and applying Portuguese customs duties on all trade. Portuguese army and navy units occupied four key towns, three of them inland in or near the Kongo kingdom: the port of Ambriz (1855), Quiballa (1856), Bembe (1856) and São Salvador (1859–60), the old capital of the kingdom. Due to British (and at one point, American) naval and diplomatic pressures, the Portuguese failed to occupy other key trade points on the north coast, such as Kissembo, Ambrizette and Punta da Lenha. During 1855–61, the Luanda administration began a copper-mining operation, financed by British and Brazilian capital, at Bembe (Congo district), dispatched army expeditions and fought campaigns with local African powers in an attempt to achieve political and economic supremacy in the lower Congo region, the north coast and the Kwanza valley. Although many of the campaigns seemed fruitless, and the British complained that further expansion would lead to little more than 'a barren sovereignty', as Lord Russell put it in 1860,[2] the ultimate object was to make Angola more prosperous, assert Portuguese control and carry out Sá da Bandeira's plan to replace the slave-trading economy of Angola with new development.

Governor-General Amaral, as a less successful Portuguese version of Faidherbe in French Senegal, made a great effort to expand Portuguese dominion in Angola. His industrious administration of 1854–60, preceded by his encouragement of expansion while governor of Benguela, is an important watershed in the century. Lacking a powerful navy or merchant marine with which to subjugate Africans along the coast or to neutralise British forces, Amaral tried to dominate African trade routes from the interior to the coast by means of occupying the interior immediately behind the desired ports. Earlier, in 1846, the British authorities had refused to recognise Portuguese claims to the coast north of Ambriz; British officers prevented formal Portuguese occupation on several occasions.[3] Thus, by 1860, Amaral's regime had failed to occupy the Congo mouth or any port north of Ambriz, and the Portuguese measures to increase revenue by occupying Bembe, Quiballa and São Salvador in Kongo and Kasanje in the east, as well as several stations on the southern plateau, were counter-productive as they aroused African hostility. An expeditionary force of 700 European troops dispatched from Lisbon in 1860, over half of whom died of malaria and dysentery within a year, was powerless to quell the African rebellions prompted by Portuguese expansionist activities.

Whatever slight sovereignty Portugal was able to exercise from Luanda over the north of Angola in the period 1855–65 was rapidly undermined, as the province could not afford the expense of Amaral's military campaigns. Indeed, his operations at Ambriz and Kongo had to be partly subsidised by a loan from an ex-slave trader, the Brazilian merchant F. A. Flores. Although an 1856 law significantly raised the African hut tax (*dizimo*) in Angola, for the first time demanding from Africans currency or trade goods instead of slaves, the tax was a great miscalculation. Thousands of Africans refused to pay it and either took to arms or migrated beyond Portuguese jurisdiction. By 1861 large sections of northern Angola were again depopulated by migrations and wars. By 1870 São Salvador and Kasanje were evacuated by the tiny Portuguese garrisons; Bembe and Quiballa were abandoned within the next three years. Deadly disease, rough terrain, poor communications, Portuguese weakness and African enmity ultimately doomed the Portuguese ambitions, and Amaral himself admitted that his resources could not support Lisbon's plans. In 1869 Amaral returned for a second term and admitted his tactical mistakes: 'The object we really had in mind was to achieve the domination of the coast by the occupation of the interior.'[4] For an officer of what had been, in the early sixteenth century, the supreme maritime power, this was indeed a desperate scheme. Portugal had neither the ships nor the men sufficient to oppose British obstinacy.

The 1855–1860 venture had exhausted the wretched resources of Angola, and Portugal was again obliged to subsidise the budget. Impoverished further by wars with the Dembos, Bakongo, Mbangala and Mbundu, weakened by African migrations and a serious smallpox epidemic, without new revenue to fall back on, Angola emerged from the first expansionist phase with little strength to continue expansion and only slight economic development. As of 1861, African traders and warriors rather than the Portuguese controlled most of the interior of Angola, and Portugal was as yet impotent to change the situation. During the period 1855–75, financial and development programmes in metropolitan Portugal preoccupied Lisbon and drew strength from Luanda. As the King of Portugal, Pedro v (1853–61), wrote to a minister after learning of the disasters of 1860 in Angola, Portugal could expand in Angola only at the expense of 'weakening the metropolis in favour of the colonies'.[5] Thus, after 1861 Portuguese policy in Angola favoured coastal concentration, administrative centralisation and withdrawal of frontier garrisons and commitments.

The Second Phase, 1861–77

Governor-General Sebastião de Calheiros e Menezes was in Angola for only a year or so, 1861–62, but he had a profound impact on Portuguese policy for Angola throughout much of the remainder of the century. His ideas are found in his report of 1861 (published in Lisbon in 1867);[6] they laid the basis for a halt to interior expansion, withdrawal to the coast and a rigid labour policy. Frontier garrisons were gradually withdrawn to cut expenses and expansion on the plateau was discouraged. Since the new towns of Ambriz and Mossamedes did not pay their way, Calheiros suggested Portugal concentrate its efforts in the part of Angola between the Dande and the Kwanza, the area where in 1854–55 Dr Livingstone had noted Portugal was strongest in imperial authority.[7]

The Portuguese generally followed a policy of coastal concentration from Calheiros's administration until after the arrival of the first scientific exploration expedition dispatched by Portugal, the journeys of Capelo, Ivens and Serpa Pinto, 1877–79. Portugal's record of colonisation and agriculture and general economic development remained extremely weak during this transition period, but did improve slightly. However, trade remained the great concern of all Europeans and of most Africans in or near Portuguese settlements. With such attention paid to a barter trade for ivory and wax, and with the continuation of internal slave trading, it is little wonder that the economy did not change rapidly. Portuguese military power declined in this phase. Lisbon could not afford to send significant detachments of European troops and the well-entrenched custom was that African auxiliaries filled the ranks for bush campaigns. But the wars, migrations and epidemics of 1850–65 had ruined this traditional arm of Portuguese power: units of *guerra preta*, made up of the *empacaceiros*,* had been severely decimated and dispersed by 1865. They had deserted by the hundreds during the earlier expansionist phase, and the migration of tribal Africans away from the Portuguese tax collectors continued throughout this later era.

The British navy and Foreign Office persisted in discouraging Portuguese claims to the north coast up to Cabinda. To the merchants and governors of Luanda, the occupation of *a costa do norte* was a point of national honour, a rallying cry of patriots, and not a question of the slave trade or free trade. To the Luanda traders, always an important opinion group and lobby in the administration of Angola, the prospect of controlling the Congo mouth was highly attractive. The Portuguese, they hoped, would be able to enjoy the profits being taken by British, Dutch, French and American merchants. In 1865, five prominent merchants of Luanda sent a petition to the Ministry of Navy and

* *Empacaceiro* derives from the word *empacaça*, or 'Angolan buffalo'; in early colonial Angola, African hunters stalked these buffalo for the Portuguese. Thus, Africans hired and paid by the authorities for duty as soldiers, mailmen, porters and policemen came to be called *empacaceiros*.

Overseas in Lisbon requesting a colonial deal with France in order to achieve the long-proposed Portuguese take-over of the coast. In exchange for Portuguese Guinea, sandwiched between French Senegal and the scattered settlements of French Guinea in West Africa, they proposed that France should support Portugal's old claims to the Congo coast, against the official British policy. The coast, the merchants believed, represented wealth for the colony, while the interior was only a burden. They included in their proposal the coast down to the Kunene river. Their petition read in part: 'We will not have to conquer anything towards the interior; it is sufficient to occupy the principal places of the coast. All the commerce of the interior natives will unfailingly come there to be exchanged for by Europeans. This very important occupation will cost us merely a small cession, whereas enormous advantages will redound to us.'[8] The merchants' plan came to nothing, but its existence suggests the persistence of the coastal and maritime orientation of Portuguese expansion in Angola. However, British policy on Portuguese coastal expansion remained adamant until the late 1870s.

There was little expansion in southern Angola during this phase. Though Mossamedes survived—largely unaided by Luanda—droughts and African attacks, little colonisation took place on the plateau. The location of the capital at Luanda, in the northern quarter of the long coastline, hindered an even colonisation of the littoral. Overland travel between Luanda and Benguela, and between Benguela and Mossamedes, was dangerous and often suicidal. Sea travel was the safest means of transportation since there were large areas where African groups were independent of any Portuguese control and would attack European travellers. Indeed, Kisama country, south of the Kwanza, a *bête noire* of the Portuguese since the days of Paulo Dias, continued to be independent until after 1920.

The abortive attempt to occupy the Congo coast and secure new posts on the frontiers from Kasanje to Kunene had aroused the African countryside against the Portuguese. Though a contemporary observer, writing in 1875, noted some economic progress in Angola since 1866, he also asserted that, except for small regions near Luanda and Benguela, the Portuguese had little control over the hinterland.[9] Continued rebuffs to Portuguese authority and new criticisms by foreign travellers and humanitarians after 1870 became challenges to which the Angolan administration began to respond.

The Third Phase, 1877–91

In this final phase, there was a renewed enthusiasm for interior expansion, accompanied by the traditional coastal interest. With the passing of Sá da Bandeira from the scene, a new colonial movement began. Its origins may be dated from the establishment in 1875 of the Society of Geography of Lisbon, a private organisation of soldiers, statesmen, geographers and academics whose colonial enthusiasm and action galvanised Portugal's colonial programme. Outstanding colonial thinkers, such as Luciano Cordeiro (1844–1900), writer, founder of the Society of Geography and later Portuguese delegate to the Berlin West African Conference, João de Andrade Corvo (1824–90), Foreign Minister and Minister for Navy and Overseas in the 1870s, Manuel Pinheiro Chagas (1842–95), Minister for Navy and Overseas in the mid-1880s, and others, urged Portugal to renovate the colonial effort in Africa with a new programme of spending on economic development and campaigns of occupation. Echoing earlier criticisms by Sousa Coutinho and Coelho do Amaral of the 'economising' of former governors of Angola, these activists deplored Portuguese conservatism in failing to invest in the African territories.

What motivated the new generation of colonial activists in Lisbon? These patriots appreciated that Portugal was the oldest colonising power in Europe and were appalled at its current weakness in Africa. To them, the development of Portuguese Africa promised a new age of Portuguese prosperity and prestige in Iberia and Europe. In the late nineteenth century, imperial expansion became a new idea for renovating Portugal. In 1879, a colonial enthusiast argued the ultimate justification for the risky business of colonial expansion: 'In the Council of Nations, Portugal should be principally esteemed a colonial power. Only the colonies can give us in Europe the influence and position which otherwise would be denied us so justifiably because of the narrow boundaries of the metropolis, and its situation in the peninsula.'[10] This sentiment became more than colonial rhetoric among the Portuguese intelligentsia; it was echoed again and again in the twentieth century. Portuguese nationalism became closely tied to imperialism.

Although Lisbon-based colonialists might dream of empire, the reality was depressing—depressing enough to turn Governor-General Alexandre de Almeida e Albuquerque from thoughts of plateau expansion: 'Following my illustrious predecessors, I will tell your Excellency that the expansion of the province into the interior is an evil without compensation . . . for the major settlements are like so many other islands drowned in a limitless native ocean. . . . It is sadly necessary to confess that our empire in the interior is imaginary.'[11] When the national expedition of Capelo, Ivens and Serpa Pinto arrived in Angola in 1877 to explore Central Africa as far as Mozambique, they found that Governor Albuquerque offered little help and was anti-expansionist. His attitude dampened the hopes of the three officers, who eventually split into two separate expeditions, with Capelo and Ivens exploring north-central Angola to the Kwango river, and only Serpa Pinto managing to cross the continent, emerging at Durban in 1879. The rather mediocre results of this scientific-political expedition were the result of a helpless Lisbon, an indifferent Luanda, the personal bickering of the Portuguese explorers and little or no Portuguese control of the Angolan plateau. Later, as the colonial fever increased among the Portuguese, more funds were devoted to scientific expeditions in Africa; later expeditions, such as those of Henrique de Carvalho (1884–87) and the second journey of Capelo and Ivens (1884–85), were more successful.

Governor-General Francisco Ferreira do Amaral (1882–85) was a more enthusiastic expansionist than his predecessors, but in 1884 he explained to Lisbon why the Portuguese were in a weak position in Central Africa:

> One of the reasons why our rule today in the interior is weak is because the *concelhos* of the east were abandoned . . . because the expense they incurred could not be covered by ordinary means, and we had to choose awaiting the natives on the coast rather than proceeding to civilise them in the interior. Following this policy came the foreign explorations and designs obliging us to change our tactics, and now it is imperative that we move toward the east and reconquer what we possessed.[12]

In 1881, Júlio de Vilhena, Portuguese Minister of the Navy and Overseas, presented a plan to establish inland stations between Angola and Mozambique, in order to fulfil the old dream of a coast-to-coast empire. The stations would be military and political outposts, acting as nuclei for European settlement and civilisation. The Portuguese did not follow this plan: with the exception of the work of Henrique Dias de Carvalho in eastern Angola (Lunda), the occupation of the plateau was pitiful. Had that plan been followed, had the 1840–60 'proto-Scramble' been pursued, Portugal today would possess much of what is now Rhodesia, Malawi and Zambia, and part of southern Congo. Traditional obstacles stood in the way: lack of manpower, climate, disease, poor organisation and African opposition to entry into the interior. Yet, despite the lack of practical achievement east of the Kwango river or west of the town of Zumbo on the Zambezi, Portuguese explorers, like Serpa Pinto, Capelo, Ivens, Cordón, Paiva de Andrada, Cardoso, Carvalho and others, did transmit a lot of knowledge about Africa to

Portugal and criticised the lack of Portuguese power in Angola and Mozambique, thereby supporting the earlier criticism of the British explorers like Cameron, Young and Livingstone. A new awareness of the need to develop Angola and to eradicate the horrors of the slave trade and slavery still operating in the interior was publicised by the writings of these Portuguese patriots.

In the Scramble for Africa, Portugal attempted to make up for lost centuries. At the Berlin Conference, 1884–85, and during the 1890 crisis of the British 'ultimatum' over Nyasaland and Rhodesia, Portugal tried desperate last-minute measures to grab territory it felt entitled to by virtue of discovery, exploration and the beginnings of effective occupation. The two most disputed areas were the Congo mouth (both banks) and the Shiré river highlands in what is now Malawi. Both attempts, made beyond the eleventh hour through diplomatic and military moves, were failures and rival powers took some or most of the territory. At the Berlin Conference, Portuguese delegates were given their first ultimatum and were forced to back down after an abortive expedition to occupy several ports on the right bank of the Congo. Portugal was awarded a portion of the left bank of the Congo as well as the Cabinda Enclave, but only on the sufferance of Britain, France, Germany and King Léopold. In January 1890 came the British ultimatum, a setback which has become an emotional issue in Portuguese history. Portugal was forced to withdraw expeditions from Nyasaland and Rhodesia or face British naval demonstrations at Lisbon and Mozambique.[13] The political repercussions of these events were important and played a role in the fall of the Bragança monarchy two decades later.

Despite the real and imagined losses of territory in the Scramble, Portugal did well to retain the large area it possessed. Portuguese lack of means was not the only factor. As shown above, policy was also a culprit, for in any given Portuguese enterprise determination and energy, if applied, frequently overcame obstacles. Centuries of concentration on coastal expansion, a short-lived policy of withdrawal and an all-pervasive monopolist economy hurt Portuguese chances of opening up Central Africa. For much of the nineteenth century, the Anglo-Portuguese alliance had seemed a curse to the Portuguese. But in 1899, after the emotional upsurge following the ultimatum had subsided, Britain and Portugal reaffirmed the ancient alliance in the Anglo-Portuguese Secret Declaration, which pledged Britain to protect Portuguese Africa against 'future as well as present enemies', and this helped Portugal to consolidate its hold on the African territory it possessed after partition.

Portugal's claims at the Congress were consistent with earlier claims in the mid-nineteenth century. Claims for Angolan territory were similar to those made in the report of Governor-General Calheiros in 1861: the coast from 5° 12' to 18° south latitude. After the partition treaties of 1885, 1886, 1891 and 1894, the coastal limits of Angola (including Cabinda) were from 5° to 17° 25' south latitude.[14] In treaties with Britain, France, Germany, Belgium and later with the Union of South Africa, between 1885 and 1926, Angola was delimited both on maps and on the ground. In 1905, the frontier between Northern Rhodesia and Angola was worked out by the decision of a mediator, the King of Italy. The final delimitation of Angolan frontiers took place in 1926 with the agreement between Portugal and the Union of South Africa over the Angola-South West Africa border. Despite the grumblings of some colonial thinkers and lingering *saudades* (nostalgia) that Portugal might have taken all of Central Africa, many Portuguese considered it little less than a modern-day miracle that Portugal retained vast Angola. By the end of the nineteenth century, less than *one-tenth* of the territory acquired by the belated Portuguese expansion was effectively controlled or occupied. A mighty task of consolidation remained.

ECONOMIC PROBLEMS OF THE NEW ANGOLA

By the late nineteenth century, Sá da Bandeira's plans for economic reform and development had still not been fulfilled. Although the Portuguese ran what might be called 'a young colonial administration',[15] the revenue came largely from artificial sources: customs duties on trade, the African hut tax and other taxes. While public revenue doubled between 1843 and 1860, expenses tripled, and the same trend continued after that date. As yet, Angolan agriculture was very weak and there was virtually no industry. The reasons for this failure to develop are not difficult to find. Generally, Angola lacked capital, know-how and sufficient labour to bring rapid development, and, without these essentials, the slave trade economy could not be reformed. The government's protective duties were usually an excuse for a policy rather than an element conducive to development. Although Portuguese reformers knew Angola needed money, men and technology, they could not produce them until the first quarter of the twentieth century. Until that time, Angola remained largely a province for Portuguese petty traders.

A key problem of the Angolan economy has always been labour: how to prevent the export and migration of labour, and how to organise the available labour. Governor-General Calheiros, in 1861, laid the basis for future labour policy. In 1858, Portugal had passed a compromise decree under which slavery was to be abolished gradually in Africa over the next twenty years (by 1878); those marked for emancipation were called *libertos*. Calheiros observed that while Angola suffered a labour shortage on the new farms and plantations, and a constant dearth of porters, the freedmen, instead of working within the European sector, tended to drift away beyond the frontiers or into vagabondage. He concluded that free labour was an impossibility in Angola; the government could not allow the *libertos* to become truly emancipated, as they would not willingly work for wages. His thesis was fully supported by the European settlers: 'European agriculture in Angola, in colonial products, is impossible without forced labour. . . . Free black labour, given to the whites for payment . . . is, at least for now, a dream.'[16] Forced porterage, theoretically abolished in 1856, continued, as did slavery. In short, the old system of the slave labour economy continued in new guises. There were new terms: *liberto* or *serviçal*; the 1878 labour code and the 1899 regulation stated that *libertos* were free, but contained vagrancy clauses which, in effect, echoed Calheiros's 1861 message, that African vagrancy justified forced labour. Then there was the *curadoria*, or government office established early in the republican period, whose function was to procure African labour for European enterprises, an outgrowth of the late nineteenth-century practice of Portuguese officials obtaining labour in a regular manner for European planters in remote districts. The labour shortage, always a reality but always the centre of controversy as to its real causes, continued to be a key economic weakness and a major humanitarian issue.

But there are no simple solutions to Angolan problems, only simple explanations and good intentions. Although certain Portuguese farmers and proprietors were cruel, it is clear that many were not.[17] Even the most popular *roceiro** periodically had African workers desert or quit: to the African, labour for the European was never an unmixed blessing, and the African cultural milieu encouraged a non-Portuguese view of time and labour. There were other explanations for the perennial labour shortage: the generally sparse population of Angola, disease, climate, warfare and an unevenly-distributed population. A major reason was the heavy African migration out of the Portuguese-controlled section of Angola to escape taxes and, of course, more forced labour. Until the economy eliminated its forced labour base, little lasting progress was possible, but vested economic interests often thwarted its abolition. Few Portuguese statesmen understood the situation better than the

* A *roceiro* is a farmer or plantation owner in Angola (from *roça*, farm, plantation, in Angola and São Tomé).

Marquis Sá da Bandeira who, in his 1873 swan song of liberal criticism of conditions in Portuguese Africa, wrote words that were equally valid in the mid-twentieth century: 'Without the complete abolition of forced labour, it will not be possible to establish in our colonies a durable system, to bring them to prosperity.'[18]

At an early stage, the Portuguese authorities realised the African hatred of taxes. The 1873 abolition of increased *dizimo* (African hut tax) was a direct, if belated, response to African rebellions against it, especially the Dembos War (1872–73). This was neither the first nor would it be the last time Portugal responded to rebellion. The rationale behind the 1873 reform was pragmatic as much as if not more than humanitarian. It was argued that the 1856 *dizimo*, rather than encouraging Africans to work to pay the tax, actually caused the depopulation of Angola. To continue it would mean the ruin of the labour policy.[19] Colonial stability was always a justification for solving an economic problem with an unpopular but realistic decision.

Though labour was always a crucial issue, the need for more capital, more European colonists, technology and basic utilities was also paramount. During the century following the abolition of the slave trade, Angola moved from the age of the African porter and trader to the age of the railroad and banker. It was not a smooth transition. While monopolies built empires, between the peasant and the banker there was a great gap in the economic system: the ordinary Portuguese inhabitant of Angola was not a farmer or industrialist, but a petty trader, a *sertanejo* (store-keeper), whose ambitions were limited to owning a *taberna* or store. Capital in such a system was always scarce.

Despite the sporadic nature of the incentives, agriculture did increase its hold over coastal regions after 1840. The cultivation and export of crops introduced from the Americas in the early nineteenth century— coffee, sugar and cotton—increased on European-owned plantations north of the Kwanza as well as near the coast at Benguela and Mossamedes. The export of coffee from northern Angola increased four-fold between 1860 and 1872. Introduced about 1830 in Cazengo, Cuanza-Norte district, coffee rapidly became a major cash crop which later competed with coffee from the Portuguese islands of São Tomé and Príncipe. Sugar was grown to make rum and brandy, an industry which reached a peak between 1870 and 1900. Wild rubber from eastern Angola became a boom crop in the same period, but after 1900 declined in importance.

In the interior of Angola, the economics of trade decided the fortunes of African peoples and the handful of European *sertanejos* who traded with them. There were two major trade routes: from Lunda kingdom through the kingdom of Kasanje of the Imbangala (the middlemen) to Malanje and on to Luanda; and from the upper Zambezi and the Bié plateau to Benguela. Controlled increasingly by African middlemen during the nineteenth century, both trade routes fed the economies of the chief towns of Luanda and Benguela with supplies of ivory, wax, slaves (before 1845), orchilia weed (dye material) and, later, rubber.

Although historians have recognised that any history of Angola must be an economic history (for trade determined most movements), this thesis must be qualified by the social and psychological significance of trade for its participants. The trader's life in the interior, *a vida sertaneja*, had, in the words of Silva Porto, an attraction beyond the lure of wealth. Trade, yes, but social status as well attracted that proud native of Oporto and many of his colleagues. Silva Porto lived like an African, with several African wives, in an African village and, for nearly fifty years, traded in Bié on the Benguela plateau. As noted earlier (page 44), he prized his status as the paternalistic chief of an Ovimbundu trading community. Despite his own extraordinary role as a patriot, explorer, trader and agent of Portuguese authority and culture, the history of his trading fortunes is a microcosm of the fortunes of many European *sertanejos* on the Bié-Benguela trade route in the nineteenth century. Settling permanently in Bié by 1845, Silva Porto had, by 1869, lost several trading fortunes through the decrease in supplies of ivory and wax in the interior, the rising prices of trade goods, the increasing tribute demanded from chiefs whose territory he travelled through on his trade journeys and the numerous African fines (*mucanos*), sometimes arising from accusations of witchcraft, which ate away his profits. Fed up with these misfortunes and the gradual Africanisation of the plateau trade by aggressive Ovimbundu, he left Bié and bought a farm near Catumbella, where he struggled as a cultivator from 1869 to 1879. But he could not resist entering trading again, and in 1880 he made another long journey into Central Africa with an Ovimbundu caravan. Again he made little wealth and complained continually that he was poor and that Portugal should send armies and scientific expeditions to conquer and control central Angola. Continual failures in trading expeditions due to African *mucanos* and tribute and competition from *pombeiros* led him to consider retiring to Portugal. This ambition became an obsession with him as early as 1860, but his own modest means, his love of the trading life and his obligations in Bié kept him in Angola. Whenever he considered leaving for Portugal, his social status as a trader, not his economic wealth, always made him reconsider. In 1882 he wrote in his diary: 'In the land of the blind, the one-eyed are king. As poor as I am now, if I retired to Portugal today, I would amount to nothing ['Zero']; on the other hand, I am who I am around here as long as I possess one piece of trade cloth.'[20]

Ovimbundu trading acumen and agressiveness ruined many a Portuguese *sertanejo* in the 1840–90 period. As the chief and his elders, the *pombeiro* and his caravan leaders, understood the prosperity to be had, the goods that could be bought (especially clothes, guns, rum and trinkets), they would stop at nothing—a tendency learned well from their Portuguese teachers—to win a trade advantage. Soon the *sertanejo* who, during the 1840s, enjoyed profits from the Benguela-Bié trade was hard pressed by new demands for tribute (in trade goods) from chiefs, higher prices for the goods along the way, numerous fines and penalties for the least excuse, a decrease in the supply of ivory and wax, accusations of witchcraft, extra charges when porters died and relatives required compensation in trade goods, the adulteration of traded wax by means of inserting rocks within the wax before weighing and many other vexations. As a result, by 1885 the plateau trade was largely controlled by the Ovimbundu middlemen and the Portuguese *sertanejo* was either out of business or impoverished. The increasing control of the plateau trade by the Ovimbundu had a number of interesting by-products. Silva Porto claimed in his diary that the Africans had ruined the trade after they took it over by unwise business practices, indebtedness and impulsive exploitation. But in 1885, Silva Porto noted that one Ovimbundu, with the adopted name of D. Pedro António Camgombe,[21] was the first African to become a *sertanejo*, or a trader with considerable capital, thus indicating a watershed in the Ovimbundu acquisition of the trade monopoly and their achievement of growing prosperity in the system first introduced to them by the Portuguese *sertanejos*, probably in the late eighteenth century. The Ovimbundu domination of the trade by 1885 had other ramifications. Portuguese traders were forced to penetrate further into Central and Southern Africa to seek new markets and supplies; Silva Porto admitted that his trips to Katanga were so motivated.[22] Furthermore, the Ovimbundu introduced new commodities and new ideas wherever they traded: they introduced the cultivation of cassava to Northern Rhodesia,[23] and first sold guns to the tribes east of Bié, especially to the Chokwe who used the guns to conquer the Lunda kingdom.[24] And it was the Ovimbundu middlemen who, after 1860, appreciated and first brought back wild rubber from eastern Angola which soon developed into a boom item, a trade commodity whose value *sertanejos* like Silva Porto were slow to comprehend.[25]

Other peoples took full advantage of their geographic position and their trade acumen and aggressiveness. The Chokwe expanded, after

1870, by means of trade and so did the Imbangala of Kasanje, who acted as middlemen between Luanda and Lunda. But it was the Ovimbundu take-over of the plateau trade and their near absolute paramountcy in politics east of Benguela which laid the cornerstone of Portuguese paramountcy on the Benguela plateau. Since 1850, Silva Porto had written to influential friends and officials in Luanda and Lisbon that Bié had to be conquered militarily. Ovimbundu trade dominance by 1885 only confirmed his fears and angered him to distraction; his poverty and his disregarded pleas for Portuguese authority were insults to the national honour. His suicide in March 1890 coincided with the end of Ovimbundu hegemony. For, although it was not until 1902–03 that Portugal controlled the heart of Ovimbundu country by means of a military campaign, or until 1911 that the rubber boom collapsed and a serious famine in eastern Angola undermined the Ovimbundu trade prosperity, the insults of Chief Ndunduma, the ravages of the rum trade and complaints of resident officials, who dared not exercise authority beyond their doorsteps in Bié, together provoked a reaction from the Portuguese government which resulted in the end of African independence.

The Africanisation of the plateau trade in nineteenth-century Angola, like the Africanisation and foreign control of the coastal trade in the eighteenth century, represented a provocation to Portuguese imperialism. It showed how the African, especially certain groups, could acquire European tastes and skills and still act independently of European authority. To the great plateau middlemen, the Ovimbundu, the Imbangala and the Chokwe, the imposition of European rule by 1914 was as much a blow against their economic prosperity as it was an insult to their political freedom. The drawing of frontiers and building of forts put an end to the classic era of African trade, when trade monopoly determined the fortunes of African peoples and their first bush tutors, the ubiquitous *sertanejos*.

Angola experienced a short boom period in the 1890s with the exports of rubber and new crops. The country's trade value increased by nearly 100 per cent between 1890 and 1898, but the prosperity was not sustained. According to an astute English contemporary who knew Angola in the late 1890s, Angola would develop rapidly only with 'plenty of capital, moderate taxes and low duties'.[26] As the colony at that time received little of this consideration, the economy remained stagnant and highly dependent upon foreign capital, Portuguese subsidies and monopoly enterprises brought in to solve specialised problems.

Transportation loomed as a perennial burden. Angola had hardly any roads as late as 1921 and agricultural produce from the interior required costly transportation by porter or Boer ox-cart to the coast. In 1854, Livingstone suggested the building of a railroad from Luanda to Kasanje, and there were dozens of such plans in succeeding decades. Steam navigation in Angola began in 1866 on the Kwanza river, financed by a prosperous Portuguese-American, A. A. Silva, from Massachusetts. Only in 1886 was the first foot of railway track laid, from Luanda to Ambaca, and the line did not reach Malanje until 1919. Next, beginning in 1903, came the Benguela railway, built by British-South African capital and know-how, which did not reach the Belgian Congo border until 1928. The third important railroad line, from Mossamedes, was suggested by Capelo and Ivens in their 1886 book but was begun only in 1904 and reached the plateau town of Sá da Bandeira in 1923. Largely financed by foreign capital, supervised by foreign engineers and worked by masses of Angolan labour, these railroads opened up the Angolan plateau by the mid-1920s, stimulating European colonisation, mass employment, surveys of mineral resources and general development. The coming of the railroad to the plateau effectively brought economic Angola into the nineteenth century. How to move on into the twentieth was another problem.

CREOLE LUANDA

In the nineteenth and early twentieth centuries, Luanda came into its own as the only town with any modern amenities and as a home for a unique creole culture.[27] Although as late as 1924 Luanda was described by a critical Portuguese as *cidade porca*, 'pig city', it remained for many years, in the words of Mary Kingsley, the 'only city' worthy of the name on the coast of West Africa. Its population growth was not significant, however, until after 1940. The following figures indicate the city's modern growth.

1846	6,000
1866	15,000
1900	20,000
1930	50,000
1940	61,000
1950	141,000
1960	224,000
1969	300,000 (estimate)

Because of its size, amenities and role as the site of the colonial government, Luanda became the dominant cultural, political and economic centre. It remained the capital, except for a brief period in the 1920s when Norton de Matos made centrally-located Nova Lisboa the capital. Obtaining European amenities for the city was no simple matter in a bankrupt colony populated in part by convicts. One overwhelming problem for centuries was a fresh water supply. In 1645, the Dutch invaders began a canal to pipe fresh water from the Bengo river to Luanda, but the project languished after the Dutch departure and there was no regular fresh water supply (the traditional solution was arranging for barges of water barrels to haul water from the Bengo) until 1889, when a Belgian company completed the canal.[28]

Other important innovations included the first public library (1873); the first telegraph service and regular police force (1877); a city hospital (1883); a slaughterhouse (1887); a stagecoach service (1891)—previously the main mode of transportation was by African-powered hammocks; illumination of city streets by peanut oil (1839–76), by petroleum lamps (1876–97), by a brief gaslight era (1897–1900), by petroleum again (1900–38), and finally by electric light.[29]

How did the Luandans entertain themselves? Public entertainment became organised only in the nineteenth century with the weekly band concerts at the governor-general's palace in the upper city and with the organisation of several music societies, such as the Philharmonica Africana in 1889. The first bullfights, with bulls imported from Portugal, were held in Luanda in 1867. The most common form of daily entertainment for all races in Luanda was apparently gambling in the ubiquitous *tabernas* of the lower city. The drinking of locally-brewed rum and brandy was also always popular.

Creole Luanda had its own African entertainment and social life which always attracted visiting or resident Europeans. As the city developed, the majority of the population was black African—labourers, slaves, servants, stevedores, skilled tradesmen, market pedlars and artisans. Largely Kimbundu-speakers, these Luanda Africans included the skirted fishermen of Luanda island, who for centuries provided the city with a daily supply of fresh fish, and the Cabinda crewmen of ships. Pre-1920 Luanda was an African city with a few elements of European life. Africans lived in all parts of the town and built groups of thatched huts close to the harbour, on the islands and in the upper city. While there were a few European streets in the lower city, *a cidade baixa*, with some churches and houses, much of that area was dominated by African living quarters. Nearly all the churches of Luanda were built in the period of the slave trade prosperity in the seventeenth century. African *bairros*, or neighbourhoods, with such Kimbundu names as Bungo Quipacas and Maianga, made up most of the city. In the twentieth century, African Luanda changed radically as masses of African dwellings were cleared out of the lower city and Africans came to live in the *musseques* ('sandy places') behind Luanda, a vast slum district of huts which by the 1960s was inhabited by several hundred thousand Africans. In 1922, when High Commissioner Norton de Matos cleared out one section of African huts from a European residential area,[30] a contemporary observer in Luanda called this proper social hygiene. In its residential pattern, creole Luanda became Europeanised.

The creole culture also underwent Europeanisation. In 1873, Luanda was chiefly an African town, patrolled by African police, protected by an African army, repaired and waited on by African workmen; it was recorded in that year that the governor-general himself was set upon and beaten up by an unknown group of African assailants. The creole culture was a blending of Portuguese and Kimbundu elements. There was a fairly relaxed racial atmosphere, a certain harmony—despite periodic violence—and some of the Europeans participated in some of the African customs. Two Angolan *assimilados*, J. D. Cordeiro de Matta and M. A. Francina, recorded local Kimbundu language and traditions, and wrote poetry in Portuguese. While the educated *assimilado* wore Portuguese clothes, traditional dress was most common for the masses. In music and the dance, creole Luanda was most expressive—as also were, to a lesser extent, Benguela and a few other towns. Kimbundu dance and music produced the *massemba*, a group dance still popular in Luanda on festive occasions, which also attracted the Portuguese. The institution which typified the special creole mixture was the annual celebration of *carnaval*, the Roman Catholic festival of dancing and processions lasting several days. The *carnaval* of Luanda originated as early as the seventeenth century in religious festivals and saints' days. Soon the African population were joyfully participating in the dances and processions, and eventually the festival became a vigorous creole institution, dominated by African dancing. As early as the 1870s, dancers and musicians from the African quarters were creating for each *carnaval* new songs and dances which would satirise or characterise life in Luanda—an important part of the celebrations was always African mimicry of European dress and manners.

Though Africanisms in the dance, in everyday language in Luanda, and in witchcraft and the use of drugs survived in the mid-twentieth century, by the 1920s Luanda *carnaval* began to lose its original, relaxed creativity. Its waning as a creole expression of African integration blended with independence, as a safety valve for an impoverished and over-worked population, remains something of a mystery. As early as 1920, Europeans had criticised or even openly opposed it. Stricter control of the population, more European immigration and a process of

Westernisation may be responsible. In any event, the Luanda *carnaval*, in 1880–1910[31] a dynamic counterpart of the more famous *carnaval* of Rio de Janeiro, was a dying institution by the mid-twentieth century. Although by then Luanda was becoming, in many ways, an Angolan version of a Portuguese city, it did retain something of the old cosmopolitanism of coastal West Africa, a creole culture which survived in the older resident population born in the country. In 1967 and 1968, a creole *carnaval* in the streets, restricted following the 1961 violence in Luanda, again was celebrated.

THREATS TO PORTUGUESE SOVEREIGNTY: THE BOERS IN SOUTH ANGOLA

In the late nineteenth century, as the Portuguese were partitioning the territory and planning to consolidate their authority, several foreign elements established themselves in Angola: trek Boers, who settled in southern Angola; German explorers, agents, businessmen, soldiers and traders, who were active in southern Angola after 1870; and foreign Protestant missionaries, who established missions, hospitals and schools, beginning in 1878. Each group at various times disagreed with the Portuguese authorities over questions involving sovereignty and national control. It is important to understand the nature of these foreign threats, real or imagined, and to determine how the government reacted to them.

The 'Thirstland Trekkers', having journeyed for five years across South West African deserts from Transvaal, first appeared across the Kunene in late 1879. They came at a time when the Portuguese needed help against hostile independent African tribes in south Angola and against threats of British expansion from the coast of South West Africa. Though by 1885 Germany, and not Britain, was paramount in South West Africa, the African threat remained. At first, relations between the Portuguese authorities and the trek Boers, led by Jacobus Frederick Botha, were good. The Portuguese admired their new guests for their ability as fierce bush fighters against African tribes, their great ox-carts which were used for cargo transportation, and their talent at building roads in the back country. Despite the fact that they knew of the nomadic ways of the new arrivals, the Portuguese at first believed that the Boers would settle down and become master farmers and prize cattle graziers. For their part, the Boers were eager to find well-watered farm and grazing lands far from the reach of British authority. To them, the plateau country of south Angola, from the Kunene to Bié, was a promised land, a haven from the thirstlands of

South West Africa and Transvaal politics. Since both Boer and Portuguese hated and feared the influence of London and Cape Town, the expedient alliance seemed bound to prosper.

Boer-Portuguese relations in Angola passed through two stages: a symbiotic, successful period (1879–93), followed by a stage (1893–1928) of growing suspicion, mutual recriminations, misunderstandings and a final major exodus of several thousand trekkers back to South West Africa in 1928. The first period was marked by Boer success as bush fighters in numerous pacification campaigns. They crushed African rebellions and cleared the way for Portuguese authority. Their ox-carts and new roads worked a transportation revolution, allowing trade in farm goods to flourish as never before, and, before the Portuguese garrisoned settlements on the plateau with regular European units, the Boers acted as auxiliaries and fierce mercenaries. In the early years of the Boer settlement, the 'African Dutch' were well rewarded by their Portuguese hosts. During 1880–82, the heads of families of the first trekker community received choice acreage at Humpata, north of Sá da Bandeira. Formed into the *colónia de São Januário,* the Boers were given free lands, freedom of religion, freedom from Portuguese taxation for ten years, freedom to use their own language, and their own municipal representatives, all in return for accepting Portuguese sovereignty.[32]

The relationship soured as both parties played true to character. The Boers soon became restless: some migrated back to South West Africa, or north and east into the Congo; others disdained sedentary farming and raided nearby herds owned by African tribes. As early as 1884, the Portuguese hoped to neutralise the nomadic Boers by allowing the settlement near Humpata of about a thousand *bastaards,* a nomadic group of South African mulatto renegades. In 1885, the Portuguese subsidised the settlement of Madeiran colonists at Lubango, as a buffer to nearby Boer presence. When this did not succeed, the Portuguese sought new means to control their independent guests. They planned the cultural assimilation of the Boers, devout Calvinists speaking Dutch or Afrikaans. The government dispatched Portuguese priests and schoolteachers in an attempt to win the Boers to full rather than nominal Portuguese citizenship. When most Boers refused to send their children to Portuguese schools or to become Catholics, when their nomadic tendencies, their reckless hunting, their fanatic love of others' cattle herds and their occasional cruelty towards Africans became known, their popularity greatly declined. A modern Portuguese historian has criticised the Boer colony, 'which produced nothing, took over the best lands, and kept them almost completely uncultivated'.[33] A good portion of the Boer community moved away from Humpata, trekked to remote tropical oblivions, and became, in effect, a poor white class. Remnants of the community were observed in 1957 by a Portuguese who described many as 'regressive'.[34]

Boer ideas of political independence frightened the Portuguese. Disdaining Portuguese authority, the Boers acted as a law unto themselves. In 1907–09, the government of Governor Paiva Couceiro, who sincerely hoped to assimilate the Boers, deported one Joubert Pienaar for his alleged conspiracy to establish an independent Boer republic in the Huíla district, and later, in 1914, other Boers were accused of conspiring with the Germans against the Portuguese during the German operations in south Angola. Paiva Couceiro's plan to deal with the troublesome cattle-keepers involved surrounding them with Portuguese schools, teaching them Portuguese, limiting their land titles and preventing the further migration into Angola of new Boer communities, in order to save the remaining plateau land for Portuguese colonists. It was their failure to get clear title to their farmlands which prompted most of the Boer community to leave Angola in the treks of 1910, 1911 and 1928. As the Portuguese authorities increased bureaucratic and national control over the lands, many misunderstandings had arisen. In 1928, much of the remaining Boer community packed up, mounted trucks sent from South West Africa and left Angola;[35] by this time the community had grown from 300 in 1879 to more than 2,000. Although some Boer families remained behind, most left Portuguese territory and settled in South West Africa. Thus ended the settlement of an anachronistic community whose usefulness to the Portuguese government had ended by the second decade of the twentieth century.

German Activities in Angola, 1870–1915

Although the most serious German threat to Portuguese rule in Angola was over by 1915, that threat marked the only time since the brief invasion of the Dutch in the seventeenth century that foreign armed forces intruded on to Angolan soil and defeated the Portuguese. The German presence remained after the First World War in the form of immigrant German farmers, some of whom introduced the sisal crop to Angola, and businessmen in south Angola—a prosperous and efficient community, the largest non-Portuguese European community in Angola. In the 1960s there was even a German school at Benguela.

Of all the foreign threats, the pre-1915 German activities involved the most intense planning and conspiring for future control in Angola. Although the Portuguese tended to exaggerate foreign threats, their fears were in part justified in the case of the German government and

73

certain German business interests during 1880–1915. Fortunately for the Portuguese—and probably for Angolans in general—German plans for control or conquest of Portuguese West Africa did not materialise. By the mid-twentieth century, relations between Germans and Portuguese in Angola had markedly improved.

In 1886, Germany signed an agreement with Portugal delimiting the Angola-South West Africa frontier. Since neither party could agree on a definite border—Portugal wanted a frontier at the latitude of Cape Frio, while Germany desired a more northern frontier at the Kunene— in 1909 they marked off a seven-mile wide neutral zone, which, in theory at least, remained in existence until the First World War. German negotiations with Portugal's ancient ally, Britain, were equally vague and were conducive to misunderstanding. In the Anglo-German secret agreement of August 30, 1898, Germany was to acquire Angola as an 'economic sphere of influence' (except for a British sphere in central Angola including Luanda) if the Portuguese government defaulted on repaying loans from Germany and had to offer Angolan customs duties as security. Portugal was quickly informed of the secret contents of the document, and, with the signing of the 1899 Anglo-Portuguese Secret Declaration,[36] which pledged Britain again to protect Portuguese Africa from Portugal's enemies 'future as well as present', the 1898 agreement seemed to be neutralised. Since Portugal obtained subsequent loans mainly from Britain and France, Germany's lever for putting the 1898 agreement into operation, seemingly strengthened by a 1913 revision, was never used. Thus, despite the much feared secret agreements of 1898 and 1913, Portugal found some support from Britain to safeguard Angola from Germany.

In exploration and economic penetration, German activities were far from negligible. In the 1870s and 1880s, Portugal feared the creation of a German territory in east-central Angola. Well-equipped and efficient German expeditions and explorers like Lux, von Wissmann and Pogge, entering from northern Angola, penetrated earlier and further into Central Africa than did their Portuguese competitors. In the 1880–1914 period, German merchants and their agents purchased land in the Portuguese Atlantic islands and later in south Angola, established farms and invested in colonial companies such as the Mossamedes Company, founded in 1894. German representatives, like the German consul at Lubango (Sá da Bandeira), Herr Schöss, invested in projects and investigated conditions in the colony as early as 1900, and he is reported to have conspired in 1914 with Germans in South West Africa to take Huíla district for Germany and declare himself the new Governor![37] In two periods especially (1898–1903 and 1912–14), colonialists in Germany organised an *Angola Bund* and wrote articles in the German press suggesting the annexation of south Angola.

German interest in obtaining a convenient port as an outlet for the copper mines at Otavi, South West Africa, led to further plotting and pressures. Between 1898 and 1903, the German government and several German colonial cartels in South West Africa brought pressure on Portugal to grant, first, a German railroad concession to build a line linking a south Angola port (Baía dos Tigres or Porto Alexandre) with the Otavi mines, and, then, the cession of an Angolan port to German territory. Portugal refused to be moved, delayed its decision and finally outwitted the Germans by proposing that Portugal rather than Germany should build a line to Otavi. Such a concession was refused by the Germans, and the 1903 railroad concession to Robert Williams, backed by British-South African capital, for the Benguela railway, plus the 1903 decision of the Germans to develop Swakopmund as the port for the Otavi mines, effectively thwarted pressures for further concessions in south Angola.[38] Although a new campaign was mounted by the German press and colonial organisations in 1912–14, the German economic threat to Portuguese sovereignty in Angola amounted to little until the opening of hostilities in the First World War.

From 1900 to 1914, the neutral zone between the two colonies was the scene of frequent German probes, raids and minor border violations. Neither party knew the exact extent of its opponents' jurisdiction in the zone, which was neutral in name only. The thin line of Portuguese forts built by Roçadas and João de Almeida in 1906–10, was no guard against German aggression and African tribal hostility in the Kunene and Kubango valleys. Germany increased the pressure, by means of missions in the zone, sales of new repeating rifles to the fierce Kwanhama peoples who straddled south Angola and the northern section of South West Africa, encouragement of African rebellions against Portugal, contacts with the Boer trekkers, liaison with Germans in Lubango and Mossamedes and plans for a takeover of what the Germans considered prime farm land compared to the arid lands in their colony. German secret war aims of September 1914, revealed only after the Second World War, clearly suggested the role of Angola as a western part of a German Central Africa, to be annexed as part of the spoils of an expected victory.

German military performance on the ground in Angola was brief and indecisive. Although Germany and Portugal were not, at that stage, at war in Europe, hostilities between their forces were sparked off by an incident at Naulila, near the Kunene, in October 1914, where three German nationals were killed by Portuguese gunfire after a misunderstanding.

Determined to avenge German honour and assert their power in south Angola after the Portuguese internment of German nationals at Luanda, several German expeditions set out from South West Africa and invaded Angola. At the same time, Portugal dispatched a force from Lisbon. Although Germany and Portugal were not officially at war until 1916, the Portuguese administration declared a state of siege in Angola in 1914. German forces burned five small Portuguese posts in southern Angola, and then, after a gruelling march of over 500 miles, a German force of 490 Europeans and 150 Africans, with two machine-guns and small cannon, attacked a Portuguese force at Naulila on December 18, 1914. The Naulila affair was a short but hard-fought battle which resulted in heavy losses for both the Germans and the Portuguese. While German casualties are not definitely known, the Portuguese lost at least 69 dead, 76 wounded and 37 prisoners. Before they abandoned Naulila and returned to their colony, the Germans hanged six African prisoners—an incident which later prompted several Portuguese historians to attack Germany on the grounds of atrocity and racial viciousness.[39] The German aggression against Angola was limited by the geography and climate of their own colony and by superior forces sent from South Africa: by May 1915 the isolated German troops in South West Africa surrendered to South African units. Portugal officially declared war on Germany only in 1916. With the defeat of Germany's African allies against the Portuguese in south Angola by late 1915—the work of a large expedition from Portugal and new African recruiting in Angola—the Portuguese had wiped out the final consequences of what had been the boldest direct threat to Angola by a European power in modern times.

CATHOLIC AND PROTESTANT MISSIONS IN ANGOLA, 1878–1921

To the mass of Angolans, the coming of foreign Protestant missions in the last quarter of the nineteenth century signified greater opportunity for more Western religion, education, materialism and medicine than experienced before, under Roman Catholicism. At the same time, the new missions brought ideas which tore the African from absolute allegiance both to his own traditional society and to Portuguese authority. To be sure, the conflicts which arose in Angola after the coming of Protestant missions occurred in various forms and intensities in the rest of colonial Africa, but in Angola the struggle between the government authority and certain Protestant missions was remarkable for its bitterness and continuity. To the Portuguese authorities, and often to settler opinion as well, the Protestant mission could be a foreign threat as dangerous as those of the Boers and Germans, only more subtle and insidious. Instead of threatening Portuguese sovereignty with capital and force of arms, the missionaries brought new ideas and foreign religions. They constituted no real threat to the loyalty of European settlers in Angola, but they did pose a threat, both real and imagined, to the loyalty of Africans. The arrival of the first English Baptist missionaries in northern Angola in 1878 began a new era. Conflicts between the Portuguese and the newcomers and their successors would become the most controversial of questions during the next three generations.

Angola experienced Protestant missionary activity considerably later than most Western African territories. When Protestants entered the Angolan field, they found the Catholic Church and mission movement, with three centuries of work behind them, weak and largely confined to the towns of Luanda and Benguela. Rather than remain on the coast, most of the Protestant missions settled at posts well in the interior. At first, therefore, they encountered little Portuguese authority, little Catholic influence and a mass of Africans in large part untouched by Western ideas or influenced only by an ancient trade with the Portuguese. To many proper Victorian missionaries in late nineteenth-century Angola, alcoholism, the slave trade, slavery, duplicity and extortion rather than Catholicism and Portuguese culture characterised the previous outside contacts of most Angolan peoples. Then, too, the Protestants believed they were witnessing both in the bush and in the town a profound moral crisis in a disintegrating African society.

The following is a list of the early efforts of the Protestant missionaries in chronological order, including (when known) the first location of the mission.

English Baptist Missionary Society, 1878—S. Salvador, Kongo
American Board of Commissioners for Foreign Missions (Kongregationalist), 1880—Bailundo
American Baptist Foreign Mission Society, 1882
Methodist Episcopal Church, 1885—Luanda
United Church of Canada, 1886—Bailundo
Christian Missions in Many Lands, 1889
The Plymouth Brethren, 1890—Bié
Mission Philafricaine, 1897—Caluquembe
Angola Evangelical League, 1897
Christian and Missionary Alliance, 1907
South Africa General Mission, 1914
Seventh Day Adventists, 1924—Cabinda

From the beginning, each group in Angola had a different view of the intentions and role of the Protestant mission. To the African, the foreign missionary often became, at best, a friend to African self-development and self-assertion or, at worst, a benevolent neutral. To the Portuguese administrators and local traders, the missionary threatened Portuguese authority and traders' profits; however, in the pre-1920 period, in general, the missionary was treated by Lisbon and sometimes by Luanda with politeness as a foreign guest. The missionary himself felt his role was to convert to Christianity, to educate and to minister medicine to the African population in the 'dark' regions untouched by the light of his faith. Only a few were actively anti-Portuguese.

For two decades there was relatively little conflict concerning missionary activities. But, as early as 1882, in anti-Protestant articles in the Luanda press, and in 1903, in a decree which required the teaching of the Portuguese language in mission schools in Bié-Bailundo, signs of later contention appeared. The role of the Catholic Church and mission in Angola complicated amicable relations between the authorities and the Protestants. Virtually no Portuguese Catholic missions were in the Angolan interior until 1881–87, when men such as Father António Barroso, at São Salvador, Kongo, and Father J. M. Antunes, in south Angola, established missions and schools far from the coast. The only other Catholic missions of consequence in the interior belonged to the Holy Ghost Order, mainly from France and Alsace, established in 1865. The work of this Order was and is impressive but was limited to southern Angola. The Portuguese missionary revival in the 1880s, led by the actions and writings of Barroso and Antunes, coincided with the colonial expansion and military campaigns in the interior and even encouraged them. The writings and speeches of Barroso[40] stressed that the Portuguese Roman Catholic missionary (the two adjectives were synonymous in his mind) had a dual role to play: to civilise or educate the African, and to 'nationalise' him, or make him into a loyal Portuguese. To Barroso, Protestant missionary activities were threatening and he emphasised to his government friends that the Portuguese missionary in Angola could be useful for his opposition to 'foreign propaganda' which might infect the African.

Though the Catholic missions might resent the Protestant missionaries' early successes, their greater resources and energy and the proliferation of bush schools and their attraction for African students, and though the Catholics did at times complain and influence the Portuguese authorities to upset Protestant projects, the authorities both in Lisbon and in Luanda were generally neither anti-missionary nor anti-Protestant for most of the early period. Though many governors and ministers had their suspicions and fears of the usually better-equipped and more wealthy foreign missions, at the time the government could exercise little direct or indirect control over missions in the remote interior. Moreover, the imagined legal force of the international treaties of Berlin and Brussels, the Anglo-Portuguese conventions and the First World War limited Portuguese restrictions on Protestant freedoms. Nevertheless, Portuguese xenophobia, a recurring national characteristic in times of stress, did affect relations, and even the French and Alsatian personnel of the early Holy Ghost mission in south Angola came under some Portuguese criticism before 1900.

There were certain incidents in the early period which provided fuel for later Portuguese fears and suspicions and which foreshadowed troubled days in the 1960s. When, in 1890, the Portuguese *sertanejo* in Bié, António da Silva Porto, committed suicide under mysterious circumstances (wrapping himself in a Portuguese flag and blowing himself up with kegs of gunpowder), nearby Protestant missionaries nursed him in his last moments; later, during an African rebellion, they negotiated between African rebels and the authorities. As a result, certain Portuguese in Bié began a whispering campaign about the missions. In 1908, the Reverend Wesley M. Stover of the American Board of Commissioners for Foreign Missions in Bailundo was expelled for certain actions, including alleged connections with African rebels in the 1902 Bailundo rising—probably the first time a Protestant missionary had been arrested in and deported from Angola.

The Bailundo rebellion in 1902 illustrates some aspects of the early conflict between the Protestant missions and the Portuguese. Between April and August 1902, the greater part of the districts of Bié and Bailundo came under the control of a moderately well-organised African rebellion which was inspired by the idea that the Portuguese were very weak militarily and that they could be driven out of the country. The targets of African hostility were local traders and tax collectors, not all of them Europeans, whose extortions and cruelties in the rum and slave trades aroused a united response of violence. Portuguese traders and local officials resented the fact that no Protestant personnel or buildings were harmed by the rebels while Portuguese facilities were destroyed. Before the rebellion was crushed by Portuguese expeditions in late 1902, over two dozen Europeans had been killed and several had committed suicide rather than suffer tortures designed particularly to remind the victims of their role in the slave trade: at least one European was paraded in irons. This explosion was the result of years of sufferings, with very little opportunity for direct

79

Angola

African protest on the plateau. An exception was a case documented by the Englishman James Johnston,[41] who reported the 'grim satire' perpetrated by Africans on the wayside grave between Benguela and Bailundo of a slaving *pombeiro*: twenty slave shackles were stuck prominently at the head of the tyrant's burial spot. To Johnston, the contrast between this silent protest and the respectful treatment of a non-slaving *pombeiro's* grave was instructive.

A second serious incident involving a Protestant mission was the arrest and imprisonment in 1914 of the Reverend J. Bowskill of the Baptist Mission in São Salvador, Congo.[42] Bowskill attributed the 1913–14 Bakongo rebellion, in which he became involved as a mediator and interpreter, to the African reaction to higher taxes and increased forced labour recruitment for Cabinda. Again, local officials and their partisans were to blame, rather than Lisbon and Luanda. Bowskill was soon released but some authorities remained antagonistic towards Africans connected with the Protestant missions, despite the fact that the rebel leader was a Catholic chief. In both the incidents, of 1902 and of 1914, the Portuguese accused the foreign missions of fomenting disloyalty among their African charges. This accusation and official and unofficial methods of combating the real or imaginary threat with regulations, restrictions and off the record violence were implicit from the beginning of the Protestant question. Although it was often fed by rumour, the recurring conflict did have some basis in truth. The African experienced a certain amount of *de-nacionalização* by the very nature of his contact with foreign Protestant missions which encouraged independent African-run churches.

In the early days the Protestant mission served as educator, minister, doctor, father figure, even supply centre and repair shop. Most missions taught religion and general education in the local vernacular. After learning Kimbundu or Kikongo, missionaries translated the Bible into these languages and compiled dictionaries for general use. Often Protestant missionaries could converse in the African language of a remote district while the Portuguese *chefe de posto* knew little or nothing of it. After 1906, the Portuguese colonial service created schools which included African language study. The language question went beyond the problem of knowledge of local dialects and became associated with Portuguese nationalism and official policy.

The Portuguese policy towards Protestant missions gradually became more restrictive during the early years of this century. As early as 1903, missions in some regions were required to teach the Portuguese language. The important watershed era was during the last eight years of the first Portuguese Republic, 1918–26. The republican government had at first offered to help subsidise Protestant missions, in an attempt to undermine Catholic missions in Angola. Later, however, there was a pro-Catholic reaction and pro-clerical regimes began to shift their support back to the Catholic Church by means of subsidies and legal agreements. Small subsidies to the Catholic missions began in 1919. In 1921 the High Commissioner of Angola, Norton de Matos, issued his famous Decree Number 77, which forbade the teaching of native languages in missions, except under certain circumstances. Missions were obliged to create Portuguese language programmes for Africans and all books published in the native language had to contain a Portuguese translation. The Protestants tended to resent the decree, but the Portuguese believed it would help control foreign activities and play a vital part of the programme of civilising and 'nationalising' Africans in Angola. It was a logical development of the Portuguese belief that knowledge of Portuguese language was the most vital expression of Portuguese sovereignty and culture in Africa.

By 1930, Protestant missions in Angola had achieved a considerable amount of educational progress, considering the means at their disposal. As the new regime in Portugal put its full support behind the Catholic Church as an educator and agent of Portuguese culture and nationalism, there was less co-operation between the Catholic and Protestant missionaries. More than Catholic antagonism toward Protestant activities,[43] however, the roots of the conflict were in the struggle between missionary humanitarianism concerning treatment of the African and the Portuguese sense of nationalism and insecurity. Thus, there was relatively little open conflict in the years 1878 to 1960, but the makings of later confrontations were at work.

ANGOLA IS OUR HOUSE

Military conquest of the interior was completed between the years 1890 and 1930. By the latter year, the flames of African traditional rebellion had been stamped out. To the Portuguese, proof of their possession and a hint of control indicated a glorious transformation of the nation. The rise of a regenerated colonial mystique in Portugal contrasted with a growing African eagerness, especially after the First World War, to acquire a European education and certain material possessions.

The Portuguese leadership who served and worked in Angola in succeeding decades became colonial mystics and optimists. The much-criticised 'colonial pessimism'[44] of the previous century evaporated, and what the famous 'generation of 1895' began in campaigns against

81

Chief Gungunyane in Mozambique, their colleagues finished in 1919 in Dembos and in 1915 in Kwanhama. This growing colonial preoccupation was often expressed in the recalling of the symbols and precedents of the glorious era of the Portuguese discoveries. Much of this was a response to the inglorious recent past in Portugal and, perhaps, to the musings of Portuguese afflicted by what Miguel Torga later termed 'moral anemia' (see chapter 1, pages 14–15). Naturally, they believed that Portuguese Africa was a chance to redeem Portugal, an opportunity to relive past glories and to regain lost prestige. Writers involved in the neo-colonial fever have drawn analogies between the virtues of Portuguese soldiers in modern Africa and those of medieval crusaders fighting the Moors. The infidels in Angola were, of course, Africans.

The colonial mystique remained entrenched, despite democratic, egalitarian and even socialist doctrines in the air during the republic (1910–26). Even so well known an academic as Professor Bento Carqueja of the University of Oporto could write in 1920: 'In the colonies is the surest security of our national autonomy, the most solid guarantee of our prosperity.'[45] Nor were the Portuguese thinkers alone in believing or professing to believe that Portuguese Africa provided Portugal with desperately-needed prestige and potential wealth. An editorial in the *Cape Times*, Cape Town, in 1928 suggested that Portuguese Africa was a guarantee of 'any permanent and expanding national prosperity for which Portugal may hope', and that, although Angola and Mozambique were then undeveloped and, in effect, 'costly hobbies', the future held promise.[46] The idea persisted of Angola as a sort of national saviour of the modern era. It was an imperial dream, nourished as in the past by nationalism and an inferiority complex. The dream stood behind the Portuguese during the saddest hours of national crisis.

Characteristically, the Portuguese leadership as well as the settler intelligentsia were very jealous of their sovereignty over each acre of Angolan soil. Any hint of foreign colonisation on Angolan soil brought immediate reactions. Two representative study missions visited the attractive Benguela plateau in the early twentieth century: the first in 1913, seeking a place for a Jewish national home;[47] the second in 1923, sent out by the Italian government. The Portuguese government discouraged both schemes from getting beyond the planning stage. There was a brief panic when Luanda newspapers learned of a rumour that one million Italians would be planted in Angola.[48] Italian newspapers began the story—fed perhaps by the enthusiasm of the new Fascist regime in Rome for the idea of the colonisation of Africa. The

3. 'Multiracial Society, Southern Angola, 1884'

4. View of Luanda, 1880-1890, showing 'African quarter' in the foreground

5. View of Luanda in the mid-twentieth century

scheme was hotly rejected by Portuguese Angolan writers, who, true to their custom, turned to Lisbon when a foreign threat appeared.

Portugal, it is true, now owned Angola, but it did not *control* Angola upon receipt of title. Portugal still had to put its own house in order. Centuries of neglect, poverty, isolation and misgovernment in metropolitan Portugal could not so easily be undone. Until well into the twentieth century, Portugal could not control many Europeans who claimed to be Portuguese citizens and whose actions fomented African rebellions then as they had in the days of Silva Correia (see page 44, above).

The fact of possession impressed many in Angola and in Portugal. To that latter-day *Velho do Restelo*, that Doubting Thomas of pre-Ultimatum Portuguese colonialism, the writer J. P. Oliveira Martins, the prospect of Angola under real Portuguese sovereignty—even the most barren—totally arrested his pessimism about the Portuguese future in Africa. He was now prepared to acknowledge that Portugal owned Angola. As he wrote in 1891 in a Brazilian newspaper: 'Small or large, good or bad, Angola is our house.'[49]

4. Angola is Whose House?

'How has Angola benefited under Portuguese rule?'
José de Fontes Pereira, 1882.

ENEMIES WITHIN AND WITHOUT

On April 8, 1882, in a weekly Portuguese newspaper published in Luanda, the following editorial passage appeared:

> How has Angola benefited under Portuguese rule? The darkest slavery, scorn and the most complete ignorance! And even the government have done their utmost to the extent of humiliating and vilifying the sons of this land who do possess the necessary qualifications for advancement. . . . What a civiliser, and how Portuguese![1]

The writer was not a Portuguese liberal from Lisbon, or an English humanitarian or newspaper correspondent or even a Protestant missionary, but José de Fontes Pereira (1823–91), an *assimilado* lawyer, born in Luanda, the product of Portuguese assimilation and miscegenation, an educated *mestiço*. The message of the journalist seemed to belie the traditional Portuguese assertion to foreign and domestic critics that they brought to Africa a progressive civilisation.

How was such an attack possible? The editorial was published uncensored because the current Portuguese political system featured a constitutional monarchy, liberalism and certain civil liberties. In fact, from 1870 to 1926, the press in Portugal and Angola was relatively free, with only occasional instances of official censorship by the government, and the handful of Angolan *assimilados* and Europeans used the colonial press as a forum for grievances and ideas, a vehicle to bring reform. Unfortunately for future generations, the free press tradition did not survive the 1920s. Instead of bringing reform, most of the hypercritical writing brought harsh official reaction. Political chaos and anarchy paralysed the state. But the fact of native Angolan criticism, publicly stated for all to see, was not forgotten. Three generations ago, educated Angolans were attacking Portuguese rule, using many of the same words and themes as those used in the middle of the twentieth century by a later generation of Africans. The basic fact of such criticism could not be forgotten or erased from the record. Angolan *assimilados*, largely isolated from outside contacts and pressures, attacked the bases of Portuguese presence in their land, and, although they represented only a handful of people in a few coastal towns, they spoke out using a devastating perspective: the view of European rule *from within*.

Throughout the modern history of Angola, threats to Portuguese power have come not only from without, from foreign sources across seas and frontiers, but from within. These internal threats present a far from simple picture for the record suggests the interplay of many perspectives and interests. A history of Angola with only the view of Lisbon or only the interest of Africans in mind cannot present a complete picture of the complex of competing interests of Angola's varied peoples. As has been seen already, a natural conflict developed between the government in Lisbon and officials in Angola. Moreover, European traders and farmers rarely saw eye to eye with Lisbon on what was considered to be Angola's best interests. Other strong opposition to Lisbon came from the Angolan elite as well as from among tribal Angolans. The conflict of interests was not limited to economic matters, despite the largely economic nature of settler grievances. On the contrary, conflict was inherent in nearly every phase of administrative action: in law, education, industry, agriculture, politics and transportation. To the protagonists, the ultimate question was: 'Who will control Angola?' Does Portugal control Angola's fate, or do the *colonos*, or the *assimilados* or the *indígenas*? That question has never been fully answered to the satisfaction of all parties concerned.

In surveying Angolan history, it is important to realise that Angolan politics have rarely received much attention while native policy, forced labour and economics have been emphasised. Nevertheless, despite the obscurity and the neglect of the subject by Portuguese historians, there is a distinct continuity and substance to the protest and nationalism of nineteenth- and twentieth-century Angola. Angolan resistance to Portuguese rule, whether by African, *mestiço* or white settler and whatever its form, has a considerable history. Much of the resistance was fragmented, localised and poorly organised, but it did exist. If Portugal survived, it was due largely to Portuguese persistence and the availability of African allies to defend Angola against African and European enemies 'within and without', as one governor in the 1790s put it. For nearly every African who opposed Portugal, there have been others who have done nothing, remained neutral or been actively pro-Portuguese. But the fact of Angolan resistance remains.

This chapter will survey the first stage of modern Angolan protest and nationalism from 1822 until 1910. It is a story charged with emotion, obscured by rumour and threaded with biased accounts. But the record of actual resistance—however hopeless and hare-brained it may seem—speaks for itself. The history of Angolan self-assertion during the last century and a half is not merely an Angolan phenomenon; the resistance of the Fontes Pereiras and Franques is also part of the larger story of the rising consciousness of the darker peoples of the world and their struggle for dignity and self-fulfilment.

The origins of modern nationalism in Angola are found in the nineteenth century. There were several variants of nationalism, however, which were reflected in the conflicting interests of the respective groups involved. If nationalism is defined as a modern expression of group identity and of grievances against foreigners or outsiders using Western techniques or adaptations of them,[2] then nationalism in Angola was first expressed in the form of army mutinies of Angolan troops in the seventeenth century and by European separatist movements in the early nineteenth century. The protest activities of Angolan *assimilados* in the towns represent a form of nationalism with roots in the pre-1880 era. Although there were innumerable African rebellions against Portuguese rule, beginning in the sixteenth century, few uprisings showed signs of modern nationalism, with the possible exception of the organised risings in the Kongo kingdom sparked by Bakongo jacqueries and sometimes led by Bakongo *assimilados*. Most African risings enlisted the support of no more than one locality and had no plan beyond ridding the country of the European strangers. Territorial nationalism arose when Angolans, no matter what the ethnic group or race, protested and resisted in a collective manner across lines of race and culture and identified with Angola rather than with Ambaca, Benguela or Kongo. In nineteenth-century Angola, three groups participated in nationalistic activities: the rebel Bakongo princes and chiefs and their followers; European settler movements; and Angolan *assimilados* or *civilizados*. Some of their descendants continued these activities into the twentieth century.

BAKONGO NATIONALISM

Before the rise of modern nationalism in Angola, a kind of 'micro-nationalism' or 'ethno-nationalism' operated in the Kongo kingdom. An early expression of discontent was found in letters from the kings of Kongo to the kings of Portugal and to the popes, protesting against the slaving activities of Portuguese merchants at Luanda and São Tomé from the sixteenth century onwards. By far the most common form of protest, however, was armed rebellion. In the activities of Kongo princes in the nineteenth century, new forms emerged. The most significant early version of African nationalism is found in the activities of two Westernised princes of Kongo, Dom Aleixo (Alexus), and Dom Nicolau (Nicolas) of Agua Rosada e Sardonia.[3]

Prince Alexus was a brother of the King of Kongo and received some Portuguese education: he was a beneficiary of the Portuguese tradition of educating certain Kongo princes for the Catholic priesthood. He became a rebel against Portugal when, in 1841, in Dembos territory, he urged an important chief to refuse to pay a new Portuguese tax. Alexus was captured and imprisoned by the Portuguese, and he remained in a Luanda prison dungeon from 1842 to 1856. The German traveller Georg Tams visited the prince in prison about 1845; he was told by Alexus, in good Portuguese, that the authorities had no right to imprison him, that they had no legal jurisdiction over his country and that he owed no allegiance to Queen Maria II of Portugal.[4] Alexus identified with the Kongo kingdom, not with Portuguese Angola. He died a natural death shortly after his release from prison.

Prince Nicolas (1830?–60) was a younger relative of Prince Alexus, perhaps a nephew, and was a son of King Henry II of Kongo, who ruled Kongo from about 1842 to 1857. Nicolas, like Alexus, was an *assimilado* with some Portuguese education. He was educated in Lisbon and in Luanda at the expense of the Portuguese government during the years 1845–50. Destined for the Church, Nicolas decided instead to enter the Portuguese colonial service in Luanda where he was promoted to progressively higher positions and met a number of foreigners who evidently became interested in him. Prince Nicolas is important in Angolan history because he was probably the first African of any importance to express nationalistic feelings using Western techniques. He became dissatisfied with his position in European society, yet he could not return to his native home in Kongo because he was already Westernised and because, by Kongo rules, he was ineligible for the kingship as he was the son and not the nephew of the King. Yet Nicolas was ambitious for a higher station in life.

A fateful series of events during 1857–59 brought Prince Nicolas not only notoriety with the Portuguese authorities but some fame with Africans and foreign agents in Angola. His father, King Henry II, died in 1857 and a violent succession struggle began in São Salvador. The Portuguese decided to support the African prince they considered the legitimate heir to the throne, Dom Pedro, the Marquis of Catendi, apparently a nephew of the deceased king's eldest sister. In 1859 Dom Pedro was crowned with Portuguese missionaries in attendance as King Dom Pedro V of Kongo. Portuguese army units supported his candidacy

and placed him on the throne, driving out the army of an African rival,
Álvaro Kiambu Ndongo.[5] From Luanda, Prince Nicolas protested
against the coronation of Dom Pedro, not by instigating armed rebellion,
in the African tradition, but by writing letters of protest to the King of
Portugal, to the Emperor of Brazil and to the Portuguese public in a
letter published in a Lisbon daily newspaper, *Jornal do Commercio*, on
December 1, 1859. The publication of his protest letter was the event
which ultimately resulted in his tragic death. Written in idiomatic
Portuguese, the letter argued forcefully in terms of the rights of the
Kongo kingdom and Nicolas's qualifications, because of his education,
for leadership of Kongo. He asserted that Portugal had no right to
claim that the Kongo kingdom or King Dom Pedro v were now 'vassals'
of Portugal under the coronation treaty of 1859: the state and king were
'ancient allies' and 'a friend and faithful ally' respectively, as stated in
previous treaties between Portugal and Kongo. The King and his
courtiers had signed the coronation document which implied that they
were vassals because they were ignorant of the Portuguese language and
misunderstood a key phrase. Nicolas took upon himself the status of a
prince of a free Kongo kingdom, to safeguard the interests of Africans
who did not have a Portuguese education. The most interesting and
perhaps crucial portion of his 1859 protest letter was his assertion that
the Marquis of Catendi, his first cousin, had been duped by Portugal
into signing the document and that this was 'an infraction of national
independence, well recognised by history and by the very government
of His Most Faithful Majesty and by all his representatives in this
Province'.[6]

The Governor-General of Angola learned of Nicolas's protest in
February 1860 and attempted to transfer him from a civil service job in
Ambriz, north of Luanda, to the remote southern town of Mossamedes.
The Brazilian and British consuls became involved in the affair, as they
helped Nicolas in a plan to escape from Angola and travel to Brazil for
further education. The fact that he planned to pay for his passage and
future education in Brazil by selling a number of family slaves to
European merchants near Ambriz suggests the ambiguous character of
his nationalist protest and plan. Was the Brazilian consul planning to
enter into an alliance with the Kongo kingdom? Did someone help
Nicolas write his famous protest letter, published in Lisbon? The
answers to these questions still remain mysteries, even to Angolan
historians. The story of Nicolas ended tragically for, in an attempt to
board a British vessel at Kissembo, north of Ambriz, he was murdered
by a mob of Africans who considered him a pro-European stooge, a

Westernised traitor to traditional African independence north of Luanda.[7]

Though he did not achieve his ambitions, Portuguese authority and strength in northern Angola were considerably weakened as a result of these events. The Governor-General failed to capture Kissembo in an attempt to avenge Nicolas's death and also to add customs revenue to the Angolan treasury, and a European expedition dispatched from Lisbon to pacify the Kongo region met strong African resistance and suffered from the Angolan climate and disease. Within a decade of Prince Nicolas's demise, the Portuguese writ north and east of Ambriz was nearly non-existent; the last Portuguese garrison was withdrawn from the Kongo capital in 1870 and not until after 1884 did the Portuguese have any real control over the Kongo region. Prince Nicolas's allegation that King Dom Pedro was ignorant of the Portuguese language was borne out in 1884 when the King, now old, apparently signed a document acknowledging Portuguese suzerainty over the kingdom: he believed that, by signing this document, he was merely thanking the King of Portugal for gifts. Nationalism in the Kongo kingdom, therefore, revolved about two different concepts and levels of consciousness: that of the Kongo royal elite, favoured by Portugal for centuries through gifts, religious privileges and special education; and the sense of independence of the masses of Kongo peasants and their lesser chiefs. Both groups continued to play significant roles in Angolan history in the twentieth century.

A fairly recent example of the persistence of the Bakongo *jacquerie* was the 1913–14 rebellion led by Tulante Álvaro Buta, a Roman Catholic minor chief near São Salvador. When the Bakongo peasants realised that the Portuguese-appointed King, Dom Manuel Kiditu, was controlled by European officials and would not prevent the increased forced labour recruiting in their district, they rose in a widespread rebellion which gathered Catholics, Protestants and animists under Buta's leadership. The demands made and the relationship between the rebel leader and the masses suggest the vitality of an organised sense of independence, largely unrelated to Western education[8]—a factor which again came into play in 1961. Buta demanded that the Portuguese secretary to the King be dismissed, that the King be deposed and certain hated individuals be exiled, that an end be made to official recruitment of workers for private enterprises and that no Bakongo be made to work outside the area of the Kikongo language. Later, when the Portuguese failed to keep truce agreements, Buta found himself pressured by the government to recruit porters for the campaign against the Germans in southern Angola. The popular Kongo reaction to this

Angola

development forced Buta to continue the rebellion to its tragic conclusion. It was known that Buta would have been killed by the peasants,
as their ancestors had done away with Prince Nicolas not two generations before, if he had given in to the European demands. Like Prince
Alexus, Buta ended up in a Luanda prison.

EUROPEAN RESISTANCE

African nationalism has not been alone or necessarily even the first in
the field of protest and resistance in Angola. In many ways, the early
political history of coastal Angola was the story of conflict between
Portuguese settlers and officials sent from Lisbon. There were many
European movements and conspiracies against Lisbon rule, beginning
at least as early as the seventeenth century. With the emergence of
liberalism and with constitutional battles in Portugal itself, Angola
experienced new and more complex influences of political and social
change. Liberalism caused a profound upheaval in Portugal and the
repercussions in Angola were equally serious, further complicated by
local issues and grievances, all of which in one form or another would
continue to trouble the territory well into the twentieth century. In
Angola, the issues of absolutist monarchy versus constitutional
monarchy, liberal versus conservative, clerical versus anti-clerical,
were complicated by the local question: how much did the Portuguese
government do for the European settlers? Moreover, such a question
was made more difficult by the nature of Portuguese rule, for the
frequent changes in Lisbon-directed personnel, especially the governors,
caused great variations in the approach to settlers' interests. Personality
conflicts with and the arbitrary action (or simple desperation) of one
governor one year could be followed by harmonious relations with a
popular man the next.

European separatist movements and independence conspiracies in the
nineteenth century flourished in Angola during Portugal's weakest
moments. Many events weakened Portugal's hold over Angola: the
Napoleonic invasions, 1807–11; the political civil wars, 1820–45; the
independence of Brazil, 1822. The first repercussion in Angola came in
February 1822, when an infantry regiment in Luanda mutinied against
the liberal government; it was promptly crushed by the Captain-
General. More serious rebellions followed. In 1823, soldiers and
settlers in Benguela banded together in a separatist revolt and rebelled
against Portugal. They voted to join with newly-independent Brazil in
the so-called 'Confederação Brazilica', a union of Angola and Brazil to
perpetuate the traditional slave-trade relationship between the South

90

Atlantic partners. The Luanda government called in reinforcements and defeated this revolt.[9] Economic interest invariably prompted much of the discontent, and the conflicts of the 1820s were only precursors of later revolts and conspiracies to rebel. Brazilian slave-trade interests encouraged such pretensions and as late as 1830 the governors of Angola feared the persistent rumour that Brazil would send a fleet to conquer Angola, the coveted Black Mother during more peaceful days. The Brazilian threat, however, never materialised: the major threat to Portuguese sovereignty came from within.

Even before the abolition treaty of 1836, African chiefs and some settlers organised resistance to the anti-slave-trading activities of the governors, and, in the 1830–45 era, there were a number of revolts in southern Angola. The administration was obliged to build stronger fortifications to protect itself against the attacks of the pro-slave-trade interests near Benguela; African chiefs could not comprehend the meaning of the new laws and the official attempt to destroy the economic foundation of the territory, the habit of over three centuries, and settlers were their ready allies in the conflict. Such was Portugal's fear of settler-African revolt on this issue that in 1838 it negotiated a treaty with Britain to guarantee British aid in case of a general revolt. Discontent against new taxes—no longer to be paid in slaves, of course— was added to the general resistance to abolition of the slave trade. The Dembos uprising in 1842–44 by chiefs inspired by Prince Alexus was one consequence, but other rebellions in southern Angola were the result both of resistance to the 1836 treaty and of anti-European feelings. The 1835–45 rebellion near Benguela of several Westernised Africans, blacks and *mestiços*, led by the brothers Ferreira Gomes, was more an anti-European rebellion than an anti-abolition uprising.[10] African tribal discontent had welled up to such an extent by 1860, after an abortive Portuguese attempt to expand occupation and control, that the retiring Governor-General was forced to write to Lisbon: 'The failure of the enterprise undertaken has broken our prestige. . . . It is necessary not to lose sight of the lessons of history. The island of Santo Domingo was no more advanced in 1802 than is Angola at present.'[11] He feared a general uprising throughout Angola and perhaps foresaw Portugal's suffering the fate of France on the island of Haiti.

Once the slave trade had finally been abolished, other local issues provided tinder for conflicts between Lisbon and Luanda. European settlers resented Lisbon's determination to abolish slavery in stages and to end forced porterage, and their hatred of Lisbon's liberal, humanitarian programme prompted settlers to organise Angola's first modern association with political functions: A Comissão Promotora dos

Angola

Interesses Comerciais da Província de Angola of Luanda, founded shortly before 1851.[12] The Comissão was a merchants' lobby dedicated to promoting the conservative opinions of Europeans involved in the old Angolan economy, based on revenues from the slave trade and slave labour. This originated a tradition of European organisation in Angola for economic interests rather than for ideology or 'party'. Out of the Comissão grew the more powerful Associação Comercial de Loanda, established in 1863-64 by the same economic interest group. During 1859-60, conflict with Lisbon came to a head as European settlers and African *assimilados* plotted to achieve an independent Angola. Exiles from Portugal, perhaps infused with republican propaganda, encouraged the movement which, according to a contemporary Portuguese observer in Luanda, envisioned 'utopian ideas of independence', including the liberation of Angola from Portugal by means of a republic joined with Brazil, or even, *mirabile dictu*, the offer of Angola as a colony to the United States of America![13] The latter idea was revived later in the nineteenth century by an aggressive Swiss-American consul, missionary and scholar, Heli Chatelain (1859-1908).

The 1859-60 plan came to nothing, but a number of successors followed in the next decades, again supported by republican, white settler and *assimilado* interests. Until after 1870, when Brazil's foreign interests became more American-oriented, there was always some Brazilian encouragement; after their country's independence, some Brazilian merchants, traders, entrepreneurs and teachers remained resident in or near Luanda,[14] and they played an important, even crucial, role in Angolan industry and commerce and culture, far out of proportion to their numbers. Dr Saturnino de Sousa e Oliveira, who lost his position as Brazilian consul as a consequence of his involvement in the Prince Nicolas affair in 1859-60, remained in Angola to become a noted teacher, pioneer linguist in Kimbundu[14] and physician in a serious smallpox epidemic. The Portuguese government was even more indebted in material terms to several wealthy Brazilian merchants, former slavers, including Francisco A. Flores, who made important loans to the government treasury and financed worthy projects.

Early nationalism in Angola was encouraged along its tortuous path by the emergence of a free private press.[15] The earliest printing press in Angola produced in 1842 the first publication, *Aurora*, an obscure literary journal which survived only a few numbers. The *Boletim Oficial do Governo Geral da Província de Angola*, first published in 1845, was the first continuous periodical; the weekly government gazette of Luanda, it has endured to the present (albeit with three parts instead of the original one). Between 1866 and 1899, at least forty-six journals

92

were published. To the culturally-deprived settler with some education, to the eager *assimilado*, to the ignorant but quick African apprentice, the Luanda press was a godsend, a forum, a sacred device, a focus of grievance and, above all, a pastime of no mean importance. Thus, Angolan nationalism was developed along more definite lines during the early press struggles.

The first private weekly newspaper was launched in 1866, with the publication in Luanda of *A Civilização d'África Portugueza*, edited by a European and interested in reform along the lines of European settler interests. It immediately came under fire from the Governor-General, who fined and chastised the first editor shortly after the first numbers; press criticism of the government and the question of press freedom were constant themes of Angolan history for the next two generations, and this early conflict was a harbinger of future clashes between editors and officials. European separatist ideas flourished in this atmosphere but the beginning of radical, pro-republican press activity came seven years after the appearance of the more moderate *Civilização*. In 1873 there came a new departure in Angolan journalism: the publication of *O Cruzeiro do Sul*, a radical sheet written by both Europeans and Africans, advocating republican solutions to Angolan problems and calling for sweeping changes. This was the beginning of a new era in the history of Angolan nationalism.

THE ANGOLAN ASSIMILADO

The more formal twentieth-century policy of 'assimilation' had its roots in a natural process of miscegenation and in traditions over three or four centuries of inter-racial contacts. By the first quarter of the nineteenth century, there had emerged a surprisingly large number of Africans and *mestiços* who were, in varying ways, assimilated to Portuguese culture. These Angolans belonged to a number of different groups: free negroes, sons of chiefs and kings, sons of Portuguese settlers and African mothers. Before 1900, their position in society depended not so much on race or colour as on their personalities and the amount of education they possessed. The laws of the liberal regime in Portugal after 1820 decreed that all the people of Angola were Portuguese citizens. Thus there were virtually no legal restrictions or obstacles to jobs, education or voting rights. The combination of racial mixture, Portuguese liberal legislation after 1820, habit, African initiative and the failure of the traditional Portuguese immigration policy was responsible for the position of the Angolan *assimilado*.

In Angola the *assimilado* group emerged from the processes of miscegenation and from the influence of the inland penetration of trade and culture from Luanda and Benguela. The sophisticated, European-dressed African bureaucrat of mid-nineteenth-century Luanda was not the only *assimilado* in the population. There was also the free negro from the interior who cultivated coffee in the Kwanza valley and who transported the crudely mined copper from Bembe mines to Ambriz; the Cabinda cabinet-maker and the stevedore on the Luanda wharfs; the *Ambaquista*, or civilised African from the Ambaca region, a jack-of-all trades in literary pursuits for illiterate chiefs or ignorant Portuguese traders, who in the 1840s was acquiring European dress and bribing Portuguese officials to avoid army service. Each of these groups spoke, and some read, the Portuguese language, albeit not always with perfect syntax or grammar.[16] Indeed, *Ambaquista* prose was the butt of a number of European 'ethnic' jokes.

Although the Cabinda and *Ambaquista* groups were significant early *assimilados*, they did not acquire much prestige or status in Angolan society beyond a small circle of sycophants. The urban Angolan *assimilado* was a different case; the acquisition of trade and literary skills in the larger towns enabled Angolans of all colours and races to advance themselves in society. Available statistics for the nineteenth century suggest that the African skilled worker dominated trades and services in Angola. In the 1820s and 1830s the majority of skilled workers in the Luanda area were free Africans, or privileged *libertos* about to be emancipated. The few Portuguese who went to Angola went there to trade or to become administrators—thus, who else but the African would make the wagons and repair the carriages? It is true that many of the European *degredados* (convicts) had various skills and crafts, including an occasional convict physician and numerous politicians, but many of these transported people preferred trading or tavern-keeping to other pursuits.

By the end of the nineteenth century there was a considerable *assimilado* population in Luanda and in the smaller towns of the hinterland and a few in Benguela. According to 1898 statistics, out of some 226 iron workers, 135 potters and 47 stone masons in and near Luanda, only a few were European; most of the 1,500 skilled workers in Angola at that time were African. *Assimilado* positions went beyond those of skilled trades. Perhaps the most significant *assimilado* political impact was in their growing predominance in the colonial civil service and in the Angolan army and police. By the turn of the century, the *mestiço assimilado* constituted a petty bureaucracy of its own, concentrated in Luanda and its hinterland. While African *assimilado* positions were limited in the eighteenth and early nineteenth century to trading and the priesthood—when the new Bishop of Angola and Congo arrived in 1853 he found that all five Portuguese priests in Angola were black—the government bureaucracy provided, by the mid-nineteenth century, the new entry into civilised society. The *assimilado* filled many positions and sometimes rose to achieve significant managerial positions. In 1900, in the Office of the Secretary-General, the second highest Portuguese post in Angola, some twelve out of thirteen of the employees were Africans, including the department supervisor. In the Treasury, Customs House, Post Office, Telegraphs, law courts and Governor-General's Office, Africans filled many jobs and drew regular salaries. Until after 1890 there were few legal or legislative obstacles to their advancement, and even when there were barriers, some *mestiços* and Africans would manage by initiative, self-education and drive to get good jobs. The most distinguished Angolan lawyer of the nineteenth century was apparently the *mestiço* advocate, E. C. de Lemos Pinheiro Falcão (1818–51); he was educated at Coimbra University in Portugal, and appointed as one of the Commissioners on the Mixed Commission and Court of Arbitration for the slave trade established about 1843 in Luanda. A famous, well-educated 'son of Angola', he was the offspring of a Portuguese father and an African mother, as was frequently the case with the Angolan *assimilado* of any consequence.

Pinheiro Falcão was not the only 'son of Angola' to achieve an important position. Though apparently no African was elected as deputy to represent Angola in the Portuguese Parliament until the twentieth century, there were at least two *mestiço* mayors of Luanda (*presidentes da câmara municipal*) in the period 1912–25, and quite a few *mestiços* were city councillors (*vereadores* in the *câmara municipal*). A number of *assimilados* were supervisors in civil service departments in Luanda and in other towns, including such well-known Angolan names as Mattoso da Camara, Salles Almeida, the Van Dunems, Africano Ferreira, José de Fontes Pereira, Arantes Braga, Carlos da Silva and Arcenio de Carpo, all of whom were journalists and news-paper editors on the side. In the nineteenth century most of the *assimilados* in this society were *mestiços*, who dressed as Europeans and spoke idiomatic Portuguese, and who were born in or near Luanda, Ambaca, Massangano, Icolo e Bengo, Malanje or similar towns north of the Kwanza. They were mainly Mbundu in origin but with a Portuguese father at some stage of their ancestry. While a few, like Prince Nicolas and Pinheiro Falcão, were fortunate enough to get an education in Portugal, most of them had only a few years of primary schooling in Luanda and were largely self-educated. Although most of them could speak the Kimbundu language of their home backgrounds, few could

95

write it, since written Kimbundu was little known and few grammars were available for study until the twentieth century. *Assimilados* were brought up on the Portuguese language and even the so-called African press that developed in Luanda after 1881 used very little Kimbundu and preferred to publish in Portuguese. There was another good reason for using the Portuguese language in the early *assimilado* weeklies: the editorials were written to convince Portuguese officials and settlers of the Angolan viewpoint, and, since few Portuguese officials could understand Kimbundu, publishing in that language was rather pointless. Practicality triumphed over cultural nationalism. The cultural pattern of the Angolan *assimilado* was almost exclusively and consciously Portuguese, and, in effect, *assimilados* were often black Portuguese.

Roman Catholicism was also characteristic of the early Angolan *assimilados*. As the Catholic Church was one of the few openings for the intelligent African before 1850, a number entered the priesthood. It was one of the few institutions in Angola which was interested in any kind of African education; a seminary was established in the capital in 1861 and in 1907 an enterprising bishop asked the government for permission to add a secondary school course, or *lyceu* (*liceu* in modern spelling). As with so many other activities in Angola, Luanda was the centre of the Catholic Church in the country and the site of the major chapels and churches and the cathedral. Until the regeneration of Portuguese colonialism after 1875, African priests were in the majority in the Angolan clergy. As late as 1910 several African priests, such as A. J. de Nascimento and Manuel de Moraes, were actively writing in the African press, giving voice to Angolan grievances and representing native interests.

Assimilado positions in the Angolan army were also especially significant. One Angolan, General Geraldo António Victor, the offspring of an Italian convict father and an African mother, achieved the highest military rank of any African in the history of Portuguese Africa and became a hero to Europeans and a folk and culture hero to the creole society of Luanda for his leadership and bravery in campaigns in Guinea and Angola. At least two Angolans in the nineteenth century achieved the rank of colonel in the first line of the army, while many chiefs and sub-chiefs fought in the second line, or *guerra preta*. African recruits, some by force and some by volunteering, constituted the greater part of the Angolan army during most of the Portuguese period under study. The ubiquitous African auxiliary serviceman, the *empacaçeiro*, was an *assimilado* with lesser rank, but like other *assimilados* his function was to aid Portuguese authority and conquest in Angola.

The nineteenth century and the first two decades of the twentieth saw the heyday of the *assimilados'* position in society. Never before and never again were they so confident of their role or so sanguine about their prospects under what they considered the inevitable victory of a republic in Portugal and consequent autonomy in Angola. A high point of *assimilado* hauteur is revealed in the 1889 editorial of the *mestiço* editor and journalist-functionary, Carlos da Silva, in which he asserts that the educated sons of Angola were then strong enough to 'assimilate' the Goanese community in Angola and to unite to protect Angolan rights.[17] Or was the *assimilado* zenith reached in early 1921 as African representatives were elected to the Legislative Council (Conselho Legislativo)?

In the late nineteenth century, new obstacles to the continued advancement of the *assimilado* began to appear. These grew out of the general revival of Portuguese colonial efforts in Africa after 1875, with new European immigration, stricter control of colonial affairs, new legislation and more efficient officials, and with metropolitan politics grafted on to those in Angola. Barriers to *assimilado* advancement provided grievances that added fuel to Angolan nationalism. An increase of European immigration from Portugal and the islands wiped out the numerical superiority these educated 'sons of Angola' had enjoyed up to 1890. Europeans began to move in and compete for jobs, and government policy, though claiming to practice no discrimination, began to restrict entry into certain jobs in the bureaucracy by raising educational requirements. Under a law passed before 1901, in order to qualify for the position of telegraphist, Angolans had to have certificates in the subjects of Geography and Latin—neither of which was then taught at that level in Angolan schools.[18]

Nor was this the end of restrictions. In 1911 a government decree set new educational requirements for entry into the lower ranks of the bureaucracy by requiring five years of secondary schooling; *assimilados* were naturally in trouble since there was no regular secondary schooling until 1919, when the first *liceu* (high school) was established in Luanda. In 1913, for the first time, Lisbon and not Luanda made most civil service appointments. Restriction of entry into the colonial service was a serious *assimilado* grievance since government service was the major occupation of the province at that time and since most rewards and remunerations derived from it. With the passing of High Commissioner Norton de Matos's 1921 law dividing the Angolan service into a European branch and an African branch (*quadro geral auxiliar*), the setback to Angolan advancement was nearly complete. The capstone was set in the 1929 statutes, which created the classification of the Angolan population into 'natives' and 'non-natives', the latter category composed of

Europeans and *assimilados*, the first official usage of the term. In creating the Angolan branch of the colonial service, the government set up a lower echelon of service, restricted the promotion of *assimilados* to the rank of first clerk, created a differential salary scale and prevented any competition between European and *assimilado*.

The *assimilado* deeply resented the rising racial discrimination which began to be especially noticeable in the late nineteenth century in Luanda social clubs. Racial prejudice was more openly expressed as more Europeans came to Angola and as the *assimilado* felt himself assailed by a rising tide of racial antagonism and racial conflict. Why were obstacles placed in the way of Angolan advancement? Was the motivation of the Portuguese settlers purely that of keeping down the African to safeguard his own position? Self-interest was one important factor, but certainly the sincere belief in the racial inferiority of the African reinforced it. A conviction on the nature of the African supported discrimination and prejudice and tended to dull considerations of morality. This was the background for the institutionalisation of Portuguese native policy in law and precedent. There is an indication of the origins of the *indigenato* system in the 1893 speech of a Portuguese member of parliament, Dantas Baracho, who had returned from a tour of Angola as royal commissioner for delimiting the border between Angola and the Belgian Congo. Baracho asserted that the African did not deserve citizenship rights under the Portuguese constitution, since he was inherently lazy, drunken and criminal, and he said that Africans should be banned from public offices, managerial jobs and positions in the army and police.[19] This startling speech was answered in a brilliant letter by the *assimilado* priest Father A. J. de Nascimento to the weekly newspaper, *Commercio d'Angola*.[20]

The *assimilado* position in Angola, endangered in the late nineteenth century, was undermined in the 1920s. It was only partially restored in later decades through the efforts of Angolan activists and protesters. In the conflicts of these years, the *assimilado*, whether African or *mestiço*, moved towards the role of mediator or racial middleman between the mass of tribal Africans and the Portuguese rulers. More often than not, the *assimilado* was loyal to Portugal but especially aware of the value of African culture and of his own kinship to African interests. He was torn between African tradition and Portuguese culture. In order to preserve or advance his position in society—far more privileged than that of his African peasant brother—he felt pressure to remain loyal to Portugal during African rebellions. He was, in the words of an Angolan *assimilado* in 1917, 'caught between two fires'.[21]

REPUBLICANISM, REFORMISM AND AUTONOMY

The generation between the rise of an African press in Luanda after 1881 and the coming of the first Portuguese Republic in 1910 was fraught with agitation and conflict. The crucible of Angolan nationalism in this era was the weekly newspaper, while its untested ideology was republicanism. This turbulent era threw up some extraordinary Angolan journalists and many remarkable editorials. The most revealing material came from the pens of a handful of *assimilado* protesters whose polemics stirred new ideas of Angolan independence and resistance to Portuguese policies. Although some writers were willing to go to any lengths to achieve their political dreams, the majority of journalists and political men remained loyal to Portugal, convinced that a new day of reform in Lisbon government would be inevitable with the arrival of a republic and the end of the dying Bragança monarchy. Angolan nationalism became increasingly republican throughout the nineteenth century and this political tendency encouraged *assimilados* to follow it as the holy grail of eventual emancipation and advancement.

The most important *assimilado* journalist of the nineteenth century was the *mestiço* lawyer and writer, José de Fontes Pereira (1823–91).[22] His fiery editorials struck terror in his opponents and he aroused the ire of not a few governors-general. He lost his job in the civil service on at least two occasions and suffered threats of death, imprisonment and ostracism during his active career of journalism (1870–90), during which time he wrote controversial articles for at least eight Angolan weeklies and four Portuguese journals. In the radical sheet *O Cruzeiro do Sul*, Fontes Pereira launched his vitriolic crusade against corruption, injustices and immorality in the Angolan system.[23] Sceptical, sarcastic and untiring in his research, this remarkable reporter espoused an Angolan brand of republicanism while, at the same time, urging general non-political reforms in the economy and government. His writings covered most of the great issues of modern Angolan history: forced labour, continuing slavery, inefficiency and corruption in the Portuguese colonial service, the impoverished economy, racial discrimination against Africans, the poor education system, the export of labour to the islands of São Tomé and Príncipe, and many other questions. The enfant terrible of the Luanda fledgling press did not restrict his attacks to government and laws, but bitterly assailed governors-general and their coteries.

To Fontes Pereira, the newspaper was not only a noble instrument for the expression of liberal opinion but also a weapon to expose inequities and sham. He was the first Angolan *assimilado* to develop radical criticism of Portuguese policies and to publish it in the Portuguese language. He conceived of a unified Angola under an expanded Portuguese domain in which native 'civilised' Angolans would eventually dominate society. As an *assimilado*, he identified with Angolans who had had a European education; to him, the *preto boçal*, the common term of the era for the pejorative 'raw native', was not yet a part of Westernised Angola, although his human rights had to be protected against the injustices of slavery and forced labour. Rejecting the post-1882 Portuguese system of traditional assimilation, Fontes Pereira placed his hopes on the new foreign missions being established in the Congo and in plateau Angola. Although he was a devout Catholic who attacked anti-clericalism, he saw in the Protestant missions new means for the advancement of Angolan *assimilados* and for the more rapid assimilation into civilisation of the masses of Angolan tribesmen.

After 1882 he gave up hope that the existing Portuguese system would bring adequate change. One of his most effective editorials, written for the African weekly *O Futuro d'Angola* on April 8, 1882, asked a question that has haunted Angolan nationalism from that day to this: 'How has Angola benefited under Portuguese rule?' This was shortly followed by similar attacks on the system of politics and bureaucracy which seemed to be robbing the *assimilado* of his rights and achievements. In an editorial on the subject later in that month, he jabbed at the lack of political and economic autonomy in Angola and the centralised Portuguese control.

> Generally considered as being outside the accepted social circle [of metropolitan Portuguese], the sons of the colonies are allowed a significant role only when the Portuguese need them to elect to Parliament that gang of rogues which the Government chooses to give it a vote of confidence; that mess of pastry-cooks which robs the official ministers of the action of justice. The sons of the colonies, moreover, possess no nationality because the government of the metropole and their delegates are those most interested in condemning them [the natives] as foreigners, depriving them of the exercise of the first public offices now filled by certain rats they send us from Portugal . . . they do not use their intelligence to civilise a people for whom they have no respect, and this is proved by the common saying that *'com preto e mulato nada de contrato'*! ! ! ['With mulattoes and blacks, no need for contracts.']²⁴

In 1882 Fontes Pereira suggested an organisation or league of Angolans to pursue political interests, and Carlos da Silva made a similar proposal in 1889, but no such organisation evolved until 1913, after the coming of the republic. Fontes Pereira did not live to see it; he died in 1891 at the age of sixty-eight.

It was an index of Fontes Pereira's radicalism that he actually suggested that Angola should be colonised by Britain or another colonial power better prepared than Portugal to 'civilise' Angolans. This unorthodox suggestion was the highest treason imaginable for an Angolan *assimilado*, the more so since he made the suggestion in an editorial during the 1890 'ultimatum' crisis when Portugal feared the loss of much of Portuguese Africa to an aggressive Great Britain. As a result, he lost his job in the civil service, was prosecuted by the government-general, and probably did not publish any more journalism. Within sixteen months of the publication of these inflammatory words, he was dead. The piece provoked a mob of some ninety Portuguese to march on the Luanda office of the African paper which published the article.

> . . . . It is not surprising that foreigners, understanding all this [Portuguese weakness], should try to take over Portuguese lands which are still preserved in a state of nature, or that they should take advantage of them as potential wealth in order to exploit them and to civilise the natives, making them useful citizens for them and for the rest of humanity. For our part, we would advise these foreigners not to waste time discussing in Europe matters which would benefit them in Africa; it is necessary for them only to address themselves to Africa's inhabitants, the natural lords of their own lands, and make with them all the necessary treaties of commerce and reciprocal protection. If the foreigners do this, they will be received with open arms for it has been proved that we have nothing to expect from Portugal except the swindles and shackles of slavery, the only means it has to brutalise and subjugate the natives! And with this conclusion, we declare that we trust neither in the good faith nor in the sincerity of the Portuguese Colonial Party, whose members are only crocodiles crying in order to lure their victims. We know them only too well. Out with them!![25]

As respected as he was by the *assimilado* community of Luanda, Fontes Pereira's last writings provoked severe criticism. Although many Angolans were also republican by persuasion, anxious to end the 'liberal despotism' of the Braganças, and in agreement about the 'swindles and shackles of slavery' under the Portuguese regime, few were willing to reject Portugal as a coloniser. On the question of ultimate loyalty to Portugal, the majority of assimilated Angolans were moderates, not radicals, and many sincerely hoped that change would come under Portuguese supervision.

The colonial mystique of the twentieth century had its intellectual roots in this era when military heroes as well as Angolan *assimilados* described what they believed was the peculiar talent of the Portuguese to civilise tropical Africa, to become integrated with African customs while bringing Christianity and enlightenment, and to allow the Angolan to advance to the colourful tune of the Luso-African (and later the Luso-Tropical) drummer. This belief is strikingly illustrated by the *assimilado* attacks on the treason of Fontes Pereira in 1890. Carlos da Silva, his *mestiço* colleague and editor, rejected his friend's views on the virtues of placing Angola under Britain, and he changed the title of his newspaper, 'The African Protest, or Cry', to a more gentle title, to placate angry Portuguese public opinion, 'The African Moderate, or African Civilization'.[26] A high Angolan *assimilado* official in the Post Office in Luanda, António de Paula Brito, attacked Fontes Pereira's allegations, calling him a traitor to Portugal and saying that only in the Portuguese regions of tropical Africa could 'a black raise himself to such a position' as both he and his adversary enjoyed in the Portuguese colonial service.[27] This was neither the first nor the last time that a loyal Angolan *assimilado*, on his own initiative, defended Portugal against a radical *assimilado*. The question of ultimate loyalty to Portugal in a crisis divided the *assimilado* community even at this early date; it was a factor which complicated the unity of *assimilado* political activity in Angola and which was further complicated by the atmosphere of Portuguese hyper-nationalism. Paranoic fears of foreign invasion and control periodically ravaged the *assimilado* communities as well as those of the Portuguese.

Despite his sudden retirement and infamy, Fontes Pereira was lauded in his obituaries as the 'dean of Angolan journalism' and as the 'most combated and most combative' of Angolan writers.[28] He was remembered and emulated in the next *assimilado* generation, though the Portuguese government considered him as just another in a long line of 'useless visionaries, detestable clerks' mentioned in 1885 in a governor-general's letter to Lisbon.[29] Yet, in the final analysis, his profound humanity and journalistic brilliance more than balance his obvious self-interest in the advancement of the Angolan *assimilado* and the utopian nature of his dream for Angola and Angolans.

Fontes Pereira's writings were not the beginning and end of Angolan journalism. Dozens of Angolans wrote and edited weekly papers in the 'free press era' from 1866 to 1922. Politics in Portugal, in this era of liberalism's testing time, help to explain why a great deal of radical and critical writing was published and read by a growing Angolan public. Until Angola was under full Portuguese control, effective censorship was difficult, and Angolans of all races stoutly defended their freedom of the press. Literacy in Portuguese was, of course, far from universal; many of the Portuguese were illiterate *degredados* and, before the reform of the educational system, only a handful of Africans could read the language. However, the press freedom before 1922 in Angola was not absolute: it was limited according to the moods and characters of the governors-general in the palace on the hill. Invariably, governors considered 'order' more important to the progress of Angola than 'freedom'; certainly, many writers tended to make licence out of freedom in their personal attacks. In reaction to the rising republican agitation and pressure both in Portugal and Africa, the government passed in the 1880s a series of progressively restrictive censorship laws. After the crisis of early 1890, the Lisbon government passed a severe censorship law in March 29, 1890, which increased official censorship and curtailed the freedom of the colonial press.[30] This, and laws passed under the Republic (1910–26) and followed up by the *Estado Novo*, institutionalised a long tradition of press censorship.

European separatist movements which fought for Angolan autonomy or even independence as a republic encouraged *assimilado* agitation. There was a certain interdependence between the two movements. Although European editors, including some Brazilians, began the free private press in 1866, Angolans were soon participating as reporters and eventually as editors and owners. The birth of European social clubs and professional groups in the 1860s and 1870s also encouraged African organisation. After some Angolans joined these first clubs, or were discriminated against in them, they moved to establish associations of their own. Many of the republican political activists among the European population were transients: exiled politicians who had failed to overthrow the monarchy, exiled felons and convicts, professional men with family or monetary interests in Angola and merchants. Their writing and organising for reform and republicanism and their masonic lodges inspired Angolan action in the same direction. Some African presses in the 1880s and 1890s were financed by European benefactors and were part of the general pattern of European control: the system that may be called the 'politics of patronage'. Like the *caçique* in historic rural Spain, the Portuguese *patrão** in Angola was a versatile boss in

---

* A modern dictionary definition in English of *patrão*, with alternative meanings: master; boss; employer; foreman; chief; landlord. Plural is *patrões*. From *The New Michaelis Illustrated Dictionary*, Vol. II, *Portuguese-English*, Brockhaus, Wiesbaden 1961.

business, industry and agriculture; he was close to government circles or even a member of a representative body. He might have an interest in one or more newspaper and the editorial line would reflect his opinion more than that of the city, town or region where it was published. Many Angolan newspapers were launched to discuss one particular crisis or question. In Angola more than in Portugal (where birth and background mattered more), the possession of *money* gave the *patrão* much of his power and influence.

In 1890–92 the Portuguese government was confronted with a budding conspiracy by a number of important European *patrões* in Luanda: they plotted to create an Angolan republic and to end control from Lisbon. The correspondence of the American consul, Heli Chatelain, outlines the progress of this abortive movement in 1891–92[31] and suggests that bankers and lawyers were involved and that public opinion in Luanda and in part of Lisbon believed Angola would soon achieve independence. The normal way of dealing with such threats was a government deportation order or the transfer of a civil servant out of the centre of the conspiracy to a remote area. Despite the fact that Portugal did not eliminate the grievances—lack of financial autonomy, *degredado* transportation to Angola, lack of attention to Angolan political interests, a less than successful negotiation over the Angola-Congo frontier, the labour question, and the recruiting of Angolan labour by Belgian agents—the plot failed to gather strength.

Portugal's policy of transporting convicts and political exiles to Portuguese Africa was, as we have observed, a constant factor in the history of Angola. Yet the residence of at the most a few hundred determined republican agitators and politicians in the 1890–1910 period in Angola was not enough to spark a revolution or a successful separatist revolt in Luanda. Even though the exiled republicans were active again, the decisive factor was politics in Portugal and the ephemeral but ultimately decisive government control of Luanda and Benguela, the centres of agitation.

However, pressures from European organisations did move Lisbon toward a policy of autonomy for Angola. Certainly, republican journalism and speech-making in Angola were behind the attitude, but the organisation fundamental to the movement was the Associação Commercial de Loanda, an organisation of Portuguese merchants founded in 1863.[32] From its establishment, this lobby-type group agitated for economic autonomy. An 1883 report from the Associação recommended autonomy for Angola; a pamphlet written by several of its members in 1902–03 called for administrative decentralisation and a manifesto later complained of the drain of labour from Angola to São Tomé. Rather than expressing liberal and humanitarian interests, this pressure group of European businessmen stated what they believed was best for Angolan interests—that is, European settlers' ideas. Most of the motivation was commercial self-interest, it is true, but some pamphlets did protest against the continued forced labour and slavery and the export of Angolans to São Tomé. For their efforts, some of these Europeans were jailed, tried and then released by the government. Other questions arose in the 1905–10 period, as settlers met, discussed and wrote pamphlets on the rum and brandy question, and several Europeans ran for deputy to the Portuguese Parliament using *autonomia* for Angola as a platform. On November 12, 1906, members of the Associação petitioned the Governor-General for autonomy for Angola in line with the decentralisation taking place at that time in British and French Africa. In effect, in the last years of the Bragança monarchy, the *patrão* and his circle were asking for self-government. Much of this campaign was supported by such ardent republicans as José de Macedo, deported from Portugal for his republican publishing, who established his radical weekly, *Defeza de Angola*, in Luanda sometime after 1900. In Macedo's crusade, the republican press, republicanism and humanitarian reformism went hand in hand, especially in the 1900–10 era; hence the attacks on slavery in plateau Angola and on the export of *serviçães* to São Tomé, as well as the criticism of Portugal's tight financial control over Angola.[33] In this way, the Angolan *assimilado* was led to believe that the victory of republicanism in Portugal would mean freedom and dignity for Angolans in Angola.

Along with republicanism came certain socialistic ideas. In the literature and activities of the period there was a trend towards secular charity and welfare organisations, as well as a tendency for *assimilados* to organise into political leagues and improvement societies to attack Portuguese settlers as 'false civilisers' and to assail the Portuguese economic policy as that of 'exploitation' of the black man and deliberate destruction of *assimilado* advancement. There had been suggestions in the African press in the 1880s that Angolans organise evening schools and training centres and league together to protect their rights. While little came of these ideas, the Associação de Beneficencia Pública was founded in 1909 in Luanda to help the urban poor with medical treatment and to repatriate indigent Portuguese settlers.[34] In August 1910 it was reported that this organisation distributed welfare to some 120 people, both Europeans and Africans.[35] However, the government discouraged these activities by insisting, under a law passed in 1895 in Angola, that all organisations of citizens had to register with the government and to submit their constitutions for official approval.

Even more remarkable than the budding organisational movement and republicanism in Angola was the significance of the publication of *Voz D'Angola Clamando No Deserto: Offerecida Aos Amigos Da Verdade Pelos Naturaes*, printed in Lisbon in 1901.* Essentially, this was an *assimilado* protest in the bitter tradition established by Fontes Pereira, an anthology of articles published in the Luanda press between 1889 and 1901, mainly by African and *mestiço* authors. Although it was ostensibly only a counter-attack by Angolans against the racial attacks of a settler newspaper, *Gazeta de Loanda*, it was far more significant than an ad hoc response to European racism and discrimination. It was also an angry attack on the very nature of Portuguese civilisation and on the character of the newly-arrived settlers, and it was a thorough defence of the character of the negro Angolan 'as a man like any other', and dared to state that Angola was the land of the black man.

Throughout two hundred pages of sometimes rambling articles, these angry *assimilados* produced an anti-thesis to the proponents of Portuguese civilisation. Four major points emerged. First, the concept of 'false civilisation' was developed. While the *assimilados* were eager to become 'civilised', Portuguese civilisation did not come up to the professed standards claimed by Portugal to typify their work in Africa. Instead, the African was being exploited in his own land. Portuguese civilisation in Africa seemed to have no future promise because Portugal brought a deprived culture and economy to Africa. While there was ignorance in Angola there was much illiteracy in Portugal itself, a point that had often been made by Fontes Pereira. In summing up the contribution of Portuguese civilisation, the writers asserted that:

> Portugal, having conquered this colony over 400 years ago, has done nothing for the progress of the country, neither in matters material, literary or moral . . . the people are brutalised, as in their former primitive state. . . . This is a crime of outrage against civilisation, leaving this very rich colony stagnant. . . . Only the negligence of its rulers can explain this state of affairs.[36]

The embittered writers questioned the concrete results of the growing Portuguese colonial mystique:

> These racial witch-hunts and other violences of the same order have convinced many tribes not to accept civilisation founded on the egoist policy of some European nations; because, surrendering themselves at first to the influence, the fluent word, of the missionary,

* The English translation is 'The Voice of Angola Crying in the Wilderness: Offered to the Friends of Truth by the Natives'.

speaking in the name of God and a society which presents itself as being full of sanctity and surrounded by virtue, the natives believed they had nothing to fear from the whites; but they soon see . . . ; moreover, so-called civilisation is nothing more than a series of theories without any practical importance.[37]

To them, civilisation seemed to mean little more than 'sacking, devastating, selling, torturing, killing. . . .' Secondly, the articles pointed out that, despite the fact that many Angolans were 'uncivilised', the Angolan was indispensable to the economy and without his hard labour not one ship could leave an Angolan port.[38] The exploitation of his labour gave him a real stake in the progress of the territory. Thirdly, there was a real difference between the Lisbon government, which passed enlightened laws, and the group of uneducated, ill-mannered Portuguese who had descended on Angola since 1870. They, not Lisbon officials, were the true enemies of progress in Angola since they were racist, backward and uncultured and attacked the *assimilado* both physically and mentally. These Portuguese settlers, 'petits blancs', part of Angolan fugitive society, came to exploit, to lust for blood, having been brought up in what the writers termed 'an authoritarian and violent way of life'.[39] While the black was the epitome of 'simplicity, submission and tranquility', *o povo Português* was 'vicious, criminal and bloody'. Crime statistics published by these *assimilados* suggested that, although Africans were in the majority, most crime in Angola was committed by 'the false civilisers'. African rebellions in the bush were interpreted as protests against civilisation and, when it came to submission to forced labour, the Angolan, they asserted, preferred the Portuguese jail in order to preserve 'his personality'.[40]

Finally, this remarkable polemic stated that despite the traditional policy of oppression mixed with occasional good intentions, the emancipation of Angola was inevitable.[41] It is not surprising that this heretical book was published in Lisbon rather than in Luanda. Written for official Portuguese consumption and for Angolan *assimilados*, it was probably the most penetrating written group protest in the history of Angola. Like a book published two years later—*The Souls of Black Folk* by W. E. B. DuBois, a negro American thinker whose ideas would later influence educated Portuguese Africans—*Voz D'Angola* was produced under the pressure of the most intensive racism yet seen in the Western world. Both books expressed a similar philosophy and protest on the treatment of the negro, but of the two the Angolan book was much more bitter.

Out of this stinging rebuke to Portuguese rule emerged among the tiny intelligentsia a collective sense of Angolan nationalism, of 'negro-ness' involving the Angolan personality, and the conviction that the *civilizado* could advance 'as a man like any other'. During the debate on the nature of the African (was he 'inherently lazy'? was he hard-working?), protests over forced labour and treatment of São Tomé *serviçães*, serious African revolts in the interior and rising republicanism, the revolution came. On October 5, 1910, Portugal's monarchy went into exile and a republic was established. To many Angolans aware of the outside world it appeared that a dawn of hope had come.

5. Angola and the Republic, 1910-26

What we want is that our rights be respected.

Afonso Baptista Franque,
Angolan nationalist, 1924.

TRANSITION OR TRADITION?

Despite three decades of republican agitation, many Angolans in Luanda were surprised by the events of October 5, 1910, in Lisbon. The boldest headlines yet seen in Luanda papers announced the news. Celebrations and cries of 'Long live the Republic!' filled the streets, and a holiday was declared in honour of the occasion. To the intelligentsia, it seemed that 'the people' had triumphed, a revolution had come. But had a day of great change really arrived? Despite well-intentioned plans and efforts, many of the republican policies were doomed to failure. For not only did the existing resources of Portugal fail to meet the challenges in Africa, but the failure of the republic itself, and the consequent authoritarian political reaction among the leadership, had a profound impact in Angola. It fell to the republic to finish the tasks of military conquest, expansion of authority and the implementation of a colonial policy, but tradition and vested interests set limits on its effectiveness, and, in spite of the hopes of ardent republicans and their foreign admirers in Angolan missions, no sweeping changes came before its demise in 1926. What did the republic attempt? Why did its laws become, in effect, the blueprint for legislation of the dictatorship after 1926?

Between 1910 and 1921, Portugal passed a series of important laws that brought certain reforms in politics, religion, education, labour and the economy. On forced labour, continuing slavery and the export of Africans to plantations in São Tomé and Príncipe, the republic's policies failed to accomplish much because of lack of resources in enforcing these laws, the resistance by the Angolan *patrão* and his settler partisans and the force of tradition. The first Governor-General of Angola appointed by the republic was Colonel Manuel Maria Coelho, who had lived several decades in Angola (from 1891 to 1896 as a republican political exile). Coelho tried to end forced labour and in

1911 he deported eleven Portuguese for this offence.[1] But he fought a losing battle and he resigned in disgust in March 1912. At the same time, a settler-trader coalition allied with influential men in Lisbon forced the dismissal of the Governor of Mossamedes, Carvalhal Henriques, who had acquired a reputation for opposition to forced labour. The issue of native labour, *mão de obra indígena*, became a cause célèbre which involved Portugal in national as well as international controversy with its rival colonial powers, Britain and Germany. The international debate between British humanitarians and Portugal has been thoroughly discussed elsewhere,[2] but it is worthwhile to mention at least the outlines of legislation and the discussions in the local press. In 1910 there was little free African labour in Angola outside Luanda and a few towns in the Kwanza valley and perhaps Benguela. The *serviçães* were treated like animals and economic booms such as that of rubber between 1880 and 1905 worsened rather than bettered their condition. Forced labour had been, in effect, institutionalised in the 1878 Regulation and further entrenched in the Regulation of 1899, which, according to Duffy, was the most thorough native labour code until 1928.[3] The 1899 code centred on 'the moral and legal obligation' to work. The republic passed a Regulation in 1911 that was virtually a copy of the 1899 law but did place new and more restrictive regulations upon the Portuguese employer: the term of contract was limited to two years, and there were new penalties for employers who beat their African workers. In 1914 the republic abolished all previous labour laws and a new law was instituted to reform the system. The republican legislation decreed that all Africans, except *civilizados*, had an obligation to work a specified length of time during each year. Later, laws were passed to reform private employment of forced labour: in 1921 such forced labour was, in theory, abolished by High Commissioner Norton de Matos. But, despite well-meaning legislation and a few official zealots in Lisbon and Luanda, labour practices continued largely as before. Foreign humanitarians hoped that the republic would start off on a different foot in the area of labour policy but their published observations tended to confirm their worst fears: forced labour under the republic was as bad as if not worse than under the ailing Bragança monarchy. Thus, books written in the last years of the monarchy—Henry W. Nevinson's *A Modern Slavery* (London 1906) and Charles Swan's *The Slavery of Today* (London 1909)—blended readily with the tunes of protest found in John Harris's *Portuguese Slavery: Britain's Dilemma* (London 1913) and Edward A. Ross's *Report on Employment of Native Labor in Portuguese Africa* (New York 1925), written during the republic.

Despite the continual attacks by *assimilado* journalists, the criticisms of liberal European residents and the growing influence of the foreign missionaries, the actual practice of dealing with African labour was not essentially reformed under the republic. The sophisticated *assimilado* of Luanda had no influence among Portuguese *patrões* in the interior farms and plantations and his protest went largely unheard; at this period, Lisbon had almost insurmountable difficulties in military pacification of the remote interior and could devote little attention to a matter which, even when Angola was under full control after 1930, aroused the most lethargic settlers to threats of rebellion. Furthermore, the forces of habit and day-to-day custom were slowly creating an atmosphere in which widespread exploitation of African labour flourished. Two factors encouraged this development: the natural increase of government control over the lives of Angolans, and the growing racism and racist philosophy of officials as well as settlers.

The republic succeeded in dragging the reluctant Angolan bureaucracy into the twentieth century. For the first time, regulation of all phases of life became fairly efficient, despite corruption, poverty and misinformation. Although Angola was given greater political and economic autonomy in 1914 and in 1920, the undercurrent was in fact in the opposite direction. Financial autonomy was placed after 1921 largely in the hands of Lisbon's envoys, the powerful high commissioners, and, if the settler got little satisfaction out of the much-vaunted autonomy transfer, the African peasant and labourer got even less.

The lives of the African masses became more *policiada* than ever; even the legislation and control under the decrepit Braganças could not compare with the explosion of laws, the *furor legislativo*, touched off by zealous Lisbon politicians.[4] Stricter control over Africans' movements, brought in during the 1900–20 period, was probably instigated with the best intentions: to safeguard African welfare in the face of settler exploitation. Tragically, the results of this new control undid the safeguards. An illustration is the introduction of the *caderneta*, or notebook containing a man's labour record, which had to be carried by all Africans except *civilizados*. As early as 1910 printers advertised in Luanda newspapers that *cadernetas* could be purchased by employers and employees.[5] The Lisbon attempt to regulate and watch over African labour was fruitless; the red tape falling upon the African not only failed to protect him from abusive employers but soon robbed him of his dignity as 'a man like any other' and led to his involvement with the Portuguese authorities when he forgot or neglected to comply.

European attitudes to Africans during the republic were largely the sum of Portuguese tradition but with an added element of racism from the Anglo-Saxon world. Not only was there an increase in the numbers of Portuguese immigrants to Angola, but also there was a rise in racial prejudice and a deterioration of race relations. When Norton de Matos arrived for his first term as Governor-General of Angola in 1912, he was struck by the harsh settler attitude toward Africans. Slavery and forced labour were supported by a substantial portion of the European population, made up chiefly of some 15,000 Portuguese. This attitude was not an entirely local phenomenon, for racist ideas had infiltrated from Europe. That better race relations were not possible in the Angola of 1912 was due, he wrote, to a new 'Germanic mentality' of racial superiority.

> Respect and affection for the coloured man disappeared; we became reluctant to consider him our equal; we allowed ourselves to be taken in by the opinion, which came to us from abroad, that a black man could never fully attain the level of our civilisation since, intellectually, morally, politically and socially, he was not our equal.[6]

He claimed that this new sense of racial superiority had neutralised even the Christian ethic. Discrimination and oppression were supported by the philosophy of pseudo-scientific racism: the negro was held to be inherently inferior. Judging by the tone and content of the *Voz D'Angola* (1901), discussed above (pages 106–8), this racial atmosphere went back at least two decades before the arrival of Norton de Matos. What was new was the intensity of feeling of racial superiority, not the philosophy supporting it, for Portuguese could easily turn to the writings of Oliveira Martins and António Enes, or as far back as Cadornega in the seventeenth century, for attacks on the negro character and for an abhorrence of miscegenation. Though Norton de Matos was careful to explain (and in doing so, to oversimplify) the non-Portuguese origins of early twentieth-century racism in Angola, he himself became as infected with it as others, and in his *Memórias*,[7] published in the 1940s, he attacked miscegenation; he remarked at the small number of *mestiços* recorded in the 1940 census and wrote: 'I am convinced that in Angola no one wants to be considered a *mestiço*.'[8]

The racist feelings of Norton de Matos and of a host of other officials connected with Angolan affairs cannot be explained solely in terms of their imbibing a foreign racist philosophy or even a homegrown variety. Other factors that encouraged the growth of anti-negro sentiment were Portuguese nationalism and cultural chauvinism and hostility towards the political activities of Angolan *assimilados* during the turbulent period, 1910–26.

The record of the republic up to 1921 was also very poor in such matters as finance, development, education and health, despite the best intentions and efforts of some eager reformers. In the area of military pacification, as shown in chapter 3, most of the campaigns and the pioneering of communications were over by 1921; despite sporadic revolts in Congo (1914–15) and at Massangano (1924) and unrest in the remote eastern districts of Moxico (where, until the 1930s, Portuguese authorities did not dare collect taxes nor venture far from their primitive forts—and where the scattered populace was not honoured by a visit of the governor-general until 1958) the job of pacification, supported by *assimilados* from Fontes Pereira to Assis Júnior, was essentially done.[9]

Administrative changes were along the lines of transition from traditional military government to civil government. A process of reorganisation in Angola during 1911–13 put into practice ideas of such colonial leaders as António Enes, Mousinho de Albuquerque and Eduardo Costa. The colonial laws of 1914 and 1920 gave considerable financial and local political autonomy to Angola, but the conflicting interests groups in Angola enjoyed only a modicum of new freedom, as most of the new power was devolved on the highest Portuguese representative in Angola—the governor-general. They were granted the power long sought by their predecessors in the nineteenth century. The zenith of this republican policy came in 1921 with the creation of the high commissioners, with quasi-omnipotent powers in the colonies. Like Roman pro-consuls in ancient times, they took full advantage of their new powers; in so doing, they created administrative and native policy precedents that laid the foundations for authoritarianism under the *Estado Novo* after 1926.

The year 1913 was an important watershed. Norton de Matos, as new Governor-General, instituted two key measures: the 'Regulamento das circunscrições administratívas da província de Angola' which attempted to bring new control over the interior with more use made of civilian authority; and the establishment of a Department of Native Affairs, which he created without the prior permission of the Portuguese Overseas Ministry, thus illustrating his own boldness and high-handedness.[10] The department, instituted with the best intentions as an attempt to bring Angola into line with the colonial systems elsewhere in Africa, became no instrument for reform at all but was always a dead letter.

The new autonomy of Angola under the republic brought the dangers and turbulence of freedom with few of the benefits of co-operation and harmony. Changes both in Portugal and in Angola encouraged the instability. Portugal faltered under a wave of violence, strikes, assassinations, economic disasters and the costs of participation in the First World War. In the meantime, Angola was shaken by African revolts, occurring practically every year of the life of the republic. Military considerations over-rode the freedoms of the civilian both in Lisbon and in Luanda and tended to harden the attitude of the governors-general. For the first time in the history of Angola there were paralysing strikes of Africans and Europeans (in 1920 and 1926), race riots in São Tomé and the constant agitation of at least a dozen Angolan parties of *assimilados* and European settlers and businessmen. *Assimilado* hopes of advancement conflicted both with the hopes of fortunes and jobs of Portuguese immigrants encouraged to leave turbulent Portugal, and with the economic status quo desired by the European *patrão*.

The traditional dilemma for the governor—'order' or 'anarchy', 'progress' or 'chaos'—seemed to increase under the republic for, with new civil freedoms, the frustrated citizens tried to make up for lost time. It was very difficult to achieve a balance between stability and the necessity for economic development.[11] The problem was compounded by the characters of the governors and by the temptation to abuse their new powers to further their reputations and to speed economic development. Furthermore, the creation in 1921 of the post of high commissioner gave independence of action to the highest Portuguese official in the colony in order to sweep aside all obstacles to economic development. The result was colonial dictatorship and efficient authoritarianism, the republican prelude to the *Estado Novo* policy after 1930.

Four high commissioners served in Angola between 1921 and 1930: Norton de Matos (1921–23); Rego Chaves (1925–26); Vicente Ferreira (1926–28); and Filomeno da Câmara (1929–30). All of them had the powers, plans and personalities to act as modern Sousa Coutinhos, as Iron Surgeons, to propose and execute long overdue reforms and development. In a sense, each was a disciple of Governor-General Paiva Couceiro (1907–09) who had preferred original approaches to reform but insisted on making a reality of the traditional vague Portuguese policies of cultural assimilation and patriotism. But one high commissioner more than any other was responsible for destroying the budding Angolan nationalist movement and for crushing civil liberties in order to achieve absolute political 'unity' for economic progress: General José de Norton de Matos (1867–1953). It was he who set the legislative and executive precedents for efficient political repression of all political movements. His historical reputation is ambiguous. On the one hand, he is justly regarded as a great road-builder and as the protector of the African masses by means of enlightened labour and welfare policies executed during 1913–15 and 1921–24 (though he failed to solve the key labour problem and, after 1921, was more interested in road-building than in African rights).[12] On the other hand, the history of his high commissionership shows that he especially feared and distrusted the educated Angolan African and, in order to safeguard his economic programme, he thoroughly crushed the *assimilado* associations, newspapers and unions and deported many leading Angolan figures.[13] He befriended the African workers and peasant but slapped down the *assimilado*. His suspicion of 'conspiracy' among the Angolan associations as 'nativist' or 'separatist' movements places him in a category with most Iron Surgeons in Angolan history. His accomplishments as a builder of roads, schools and hospitals and the instigator of enlightened labour laws and efficient administration were remarkable, but they should not obscure his role as the Portuguese official who laid the foundations for the kingdom of silence under the *Estado Novo*. The end of the period of free Angolan press and associations began under Norton de Matos, not under Dr Salazar.

THE TURBULENCE OF FREEDOM, 1910–22

The Portuguese republican constitution of 1911 increased freedoms of the press, opinion and association for all citizens in Europe and in Africa. At first, the Angolan elite as well as Europeans benefited. Although sceptical governors might liken the creation of these new freedoms to the opening of Pandora's box, the new political parties and associations that the Angolans and educated Portuguese Africans organised were, for the most part, loyal to the republic. Indeed, Africans supported and counted on the republic for general reform more than Europeans because black Angola had more to lose if it failed. An explosion of organising in Angola followed the declaration of the republic. For several decades, beginning in the 1870s, there had been less spectacular organising of social clubs, secret republican clubs, masonic lodges, welfare societies and recreation groups, but the post-1910 groupings often had political goals and openly used political means to achieve them.

Earliest to organise openly were the European republican parties and trade unions in Luanda. Such groups as the Junta Revolucionária de Loanda (1910) led to the formation of the better-known Partido Reformista de Angola (November 1910), composed of anti-slavery elements, and the Partido Republicano Colonial (1910?). In the first two years, a number of Angolan *assimilados* joined these primarily European associations, but they soon drifted away to form parties of their own. Many parties had their own weekly newspapers: the most active in the early period was *A Reforma*,[14] the organ of the Partido Reformista, a

115

party which was less of an ideological group than a humanitarian coalition. The first goal in its programme was the abolition of 'slavery' in Angola. No common front of Europeans seemed possible in this political system. Personality clashes, ideological conflicts, factionalism and petty squabbling beset the groups and divided them into splinters. By 1916 many Europeans had become disillusioned with the republic, and new European associations were founded: the Partido Pro-Angola, the Liga Pro-Angola (1924) and the União dos Defensores de Angola (1924), groups of whites who united to seek government patronage for their interests after the controversial regime of Norton de Matos.

Like the European parties and politicians, the Angolan *assimilado* groups were neither united nor especially successful in achieving their goals. Despite attempts to form fronts or coalitions, they too remained divided on personalities, issues and ideology—and with an added problem: colour and race. They were composed for the most part of Luanda and Ambaca *assimilados*, almost to a man employed in the government service. The origins of the groups were more social than political; *mestiço* social clubs gave birth to the first Angolan party with African interests in mind, the Liga Angolana, probably formed in 1912 but officially established and approved by the government under Norton de Matos in 1913.[15] The beliefs of the members were influenced by the radical journalism of men like Fontes Pereira and the authors of *Voz D'Angola* but they saw in the early republic an opportunity to advance peacefully both their own circle of *assimilados* and the African masses in general. Norton de Matos did not at first oppose the formation of this party but rather courted it and attended its ceremonies. In the honeymoon era of republican politics and freedoms in Angola, there was just a slim possibility that Europeans and Africans might unite on reformist non-ideological grounds and bury their heated race antagonisms of previous decades. While the Liga Angolana complained of racial discrimination in Luanda, it supported the legal processes of political action and collaborated with the government. Its members were loyal republicans. The European moderates in the Partido Reformista de Angola, however, complained that the *assimilados* were too radical in their protests about the course of race relations, and in 1911 they asserted in their organ that there was no racial discrimination in Angola.[16] Their argument to support that interesting contention was typical of what became the official Portuguese viewpoint: Portuguese always lived with black women in 'perfect promiscuity'! With such a polarisation of arguments on both sides, few of the *assimilado* elite remained joined for long in parties with their European brothers. Shortly after the Liga was founded, several members, for reasons unknown, quit the party and formed their own party, originally called the Centro Africano but later named Grêmio Africano. Both groups represented the sum of accommodating *assimilados*; they later reformed in similar groups in 1930 as the government-sponsored associations, the Liga Nacional Africana and the Associação dos Naturaes de Angola.[17]

The stated goals of the Liga Angolana were moderate but firm: (i) to fight for the general interests of Angola; (ii) to further African education; (iii) to defend the interests of its members and protect their rights; and (iv) to establish physical education classes. Although Portuguese could join, members were usually Africans or 'natives of other Portuguese provinces', including the Cape Verde islands, São Tomé and Goa (in theory). It was not a true political party but an elite lobby of coloured Angolans with a programme of improving the lot of the mass of Africans as well as advancing *assimilados* within the European system. Its effective life was short—only nine years from 1913 to 1922. It was constantly being watched for good behaviour in terms of the Portuguese value system and apparently it accomplished little in the way of reform. Its effectiveness was hampered by consistent European enmity and suspicion as well as official oppression. From the beginning, it was suspected by colonists as being an anti-European organisation, linked with African traditional resistance in the interior. On at least two occasions, in 1914 and again in 1917, it was accused of conspiring with rebellious tribesmen. Out of these alleged connections, never proved and vehemently denied by its leadership, came the hate name applied to the organisation by hostile whites, Associação de Matabrancos (Kill-Whites Association).[18] The Liga was careful to state its loyalty to Portugal during crises, however, and few more loyal republican associations existed in Angola. Above all, it was composed of moderate and accommodating *assimilados* committed to the changes promised in the Portuguese system. It was no revolutionary group, except perhaps for a few radicals within it, and its strategy was to achieve African advancement within the traditional Portuguese politics of patronage. Like the Liga, the Grêmio Africano was intensely loyal to the republic; when European support for the republic flagged, the African associations continued their enthusiasm. Characteristically, on October 5, 1920, the Grêmio was reportedly the only Angolan association in a society oriented to public rituals to celebrate the tenth anniversary of the flagging republic, an event which aroused little enthusiasm among the other groups.[19]

From 1910 onwards, *assimilado* associations were formed in Lisbon also. The earliest organisations in the metropole were coalitions of *assimilados* from the various Portuguese African provinces, influenced

117

by current ideas of Pan-Africanism, Pan-Negroism, Garveyism and anti-slavery humanitarianism as well as accommodation to the republican structure of politics. Like the Angolan associations, they soon fragmented on a number of issues and they, too, were eventually reformed and absorbed as officially-sponsored associations by the *Estado Novo* after 1930. Perhaps the earliest coalition party was the Liga Ultramarina (1910), followed by the Liga Colonial (1911), then by the better-known Liga Africana (1919) and its rival organisation, the Partido Nacional Africano (1921). Most of these coalitions had branches in the Portuguese African provinces but conducted relations with international organisations, not just with the Portuguese authorities. In 1931 the Liga Africana and the Partido Nacional Africano, through the auspices of the Portuguese government, merged into one front or coalition, the Movimento Nacionalista Africano, a reformed and apparently purged group of *assimilados*.

These Lisbon associations claimed to be federations representing and promoting the progress, rights and interests of the masses of Africans in all five Portuguese provinces; they claimed also to be strictly constitutional and legal in all their activities. However, affiliated with the Liga Africana, founded in late 1919, were the Liga Angolana and the Liga Guineense of Portuguese Guinea, both of which were about to be banned in Africa by their respective governors-general.[20] It is interesting to note that the Liga Africana included in its published statutes a goal more radical than the programmes promised by the Liga Angolana—to revoke all discriminatory legislation in Portuguese Africa—and the Partido Nacional Africano included a similar goal in its programme.[21] No provincial *assimilado* party dared to publish such a political goal: an indication of the greater political freedom for Africans in Lisbon than in the colonies. While the Lisbon coalitions espoused ideas common to those of the provincial groups—educational reform, loyalty to the constitution of the republic, defence of African rights, land reforms in the Africans' interests—they differed in that they were able to espouse a more radical approach, organise on an international scale with the consequent freedom and publicity and seek aid from international organisations to apply pressure on the Portuguese government. Their final goal, African advancement, was not revolutionary, and they made it clear that they believed their ideas did not conflict with those of the republic. In their party organs,* published in Portugal and

* The Liga Africana for a period published its views in the *Correio d'Africa* (Lisbon), while the major organ of the Partido Nacional Africano was the *A Voz D'Africa*, which began in 1911 in Lisbon, but was published ephemerally from then until after 1930 from various presses in Lisbon, Oporto and Geneva.

sometimes in Geneva, the site of the League of Nations, these Pan-Portuguese African groups attempted to launch a negro movement that would transform the face of Portuguese Africa. They petitioned, pleaded, published and spoke in the interests of the African masses and elite. Their newspapers openly espoused Pan-Africanism and Pan-Negroism and urged African advancement in all levels of government, both provincial and national, in the face of the exclusivist policies of the European interests. They wrote of democracy, constitutionalism and freedom and urged economic advancement of Africans as a foundation for African political 'conquests' of the representative bodies of government. In order to strengthen themselves and to apply pressures on Portugal, they established contacts with the League of Nations and with W. E. B. DuBois's Pan-African Congresses.

The years 1921–26 marked the zenith of the Lisbon Pan-Portuguese African associations' freedom of movement. The Liga Africana supported the Pan-Africanism of W. E. B. DuBois, while the Partido Nacional Africano leaned towards the negro nationalism of Marcus Garvey during his heyday. The Liga acted as host for a brief portion of the Pan-African Congress in Lisbon in December 1923. This unusual session has remained an obscure episode in the history of Pan-Africanism. Apparently little about Portuguese Africa was discussed, for the two meetings concentrated on the Pan-African movement in the world and on the position of the negro in the United States. Interested Portuguese authorities and politicians participated and the Minister for the Colonies, Vicente Ferreira, made a speech sympathetic to the delegates' ideas in the second meeting.[22]

Little emerged from the Liga's brief relations with the Pan-African Congresses. The Partido Nacional Africano, however, vigorously protested against forced labour practices in Portuguese Africa by sending delegates on several occasions during 1923–25 to the International Labor Organization. Forced labour questions occupied the attention of the Partido throughout its brief life, and, like other African protest organisations, it felt obliged to defend the African character against European defamatory attacks and to assert that the African personality was one of 'invincible vitality'.[23] They proposed a new multiracialism for Portuguese Africa which would allow the free development of African culture. The Partido viewpoint on a sensitive racial issue was given in an article published in 1929: 'We are not simply Portuguese. Before being Portuguese, we are Africans. We are Portuguese of the negro [sic] race. We are proud of our double quality. But we possess, above all, the racial pride . . . of being negroes [sic] . . . we must co-operate with the whites.'[24]

Angola

Despite the well-meaning moderation of these Pan-Portuguese African associations, they soon fell foul of the authorities. Temporarily banned or persecuted from as early as 1922, they suffered from lack of funds, factionalism and official enmity. As late as 1929 the Partido petitioned the President of Portugal, protesting about government decrees that erected new educational barriers to African promotion in the colonial services in Africa: a 1929 decree barred African advancement in certain sections of the bureaucracy, such as the Treasury. However, the *assimilado* coalitions' appeals to the government's sense of republicanism and democracy were ignored. Their presses were shut down, their provincial branches banned and by 1928 the Partido's main offices were in Geneva, not in Portuguese territory. By 1931, their slight influence on Portuguese policy had gone and they were, in effect, purged and amalgamated into one government-sponsored federation, the Movimento Nacionalista Africano. Little more was heard from them. Although they gained temporarily more international attention than their provincial counterparts, these Lisbon *assimilado* organisations, made up of Africans and *mestiços*, were limited in their effectiveness by the Portuguese government of the day and by the situation in each African colony. Their much-publicised unity was hollow. They suffered from the republic's failure to execute a new deal in Portuguese Africa, and they, like the Liga Angolana and others, ended up as officially-sponsored and controlled associations under the dictatorship. The most they could hope for after the demise of the first republic was the gradual restoration through loyalty and 'order' of the modest fund of rights and jobs and the status they had enjoyed all too briefly during the turbulent days of republican freedom. As an early Angolan nationalist, Afonso Baptista Franque, said in a Lisbon interview in 1924: 'What we want is that our rights be respected.'[25]

ANGOLA BOUND

The policy of the republic towards Angola was bound to be affected by the fate of the republic itself. In assessing the effectiveness (or lack of it) of this policy, the condition of Angola is no more important a consideration than is the instability and ultimate failure of the republican government. In the short period of sixteen years, the republic was wracked by over two hundred incidents of violence and disorder; forty-four governments held office and only one president served his full term of office; on three occasions, dictatorial governments held power. During these years, the chaotic situation in Portugal encouraged dictatorial action by the governors of Angola.

The response of Portuguese authorities to alleged threats, in the form of rumours, misinformation and partial evidence, was customarily harsh if inefficient. There is a continuity of political repression which begins as early as 1912, under Norton de Matos. A protest march of Africans led by an *assimilado* civil servant, A. J. de Miranda, in 1911 was well-received by Governor-General Coelho, and the petition the marchers brought was taken and studied. But within three years a number of repressive measures were taken. In 1913 the entire provincial press was shut down temporarily. In 1914, Miranda, who had been actively promoting the idea of African education through his association, Educação do Povo—Socorros Mutuos,[26] and who had been transferred in 1912 from Luanda to Malanje, was fired from the civil service and exiled to Cabinda on charges that he allegedly had formed a secret political society which had tried to overthrow Portuguese rule. In 1913–14 Africans in the Congo district, reacting to increased forced recruiting for Cabinda, rebelled and attacked Portuguese installations at São Salvador. As has already been discussed (chapter 3, pages 80; 89), the Portuguese authorities in the district, acting on false reports, arrested the Baptist missionary, the Reverend J. Bowskill, and jailed him and several Protestant catechists for several months on charges that they had conspired with the rebels to end Portuguese rule.[27] The Miranda and Bowskill incidents both took place under the first regime of Norton de Matos.

In 1917 the government-general under Massano de Amorim reacted in much the same way to a rumoured 'nativist conspiracy' in the Kwanza valley. Simultaneous African tribal rebellions in the Amboim and Seles regions frightened the Luanda authorities. Reports from unreliable sources claimed that *assimilados* were conspiring with the tribes to massacre the Europeans and end Portuguese rule. Again, the evidence was based mainly on rumour, but certain concrete evidence of unrest seemed to be connected with the alleged 'plot' of 1917: the protest march of some forty repatriated African *serviçães*, armed with *catanas*, back from São Tomé, who threatened the life of the European farmer in the Cuanza-Norte district; the isolated murder of a European clerk; the discovery of hidden arms and dynamite, and the rumoured plotting of the Liga Angolana. In July and August 1917 many *assimilados* in northern Angola were arrested and several dozen were imprisoned in the Luanda fortresses for periods of up to five months. As rumour was king in the European communities, it ran riot in Malange, Benguela and Luanda during this incident and settlers responded by such acts as burning African villages.

António de Assis Júnior (1878–1960), an *Ambaquista assimilado* who became a lawyer in the civil service, was in the Dalatando area (now called Salazar) when the rumoured conspiracy unfolded. He was arrested and, while in prison, wrote a bitter protest that was published in two parts.[28] The material in this protest resembles that in previous *assimilado* defences of their loyalty and character before Portuguese authority but is also a shrewd analysis of the state of political Angola in 1917–18. Suggesting that the *assimilado* under those conditions was the most unfortunate of the varied groups in Angola, Assis Júnior hoped that the *civilizado* would be both 'Angolans and Portuguese'. His description of a rumour-ridden society complements the tone of the cynical Luso-African proverbs sprinkled throughout his memoir, such as 'The black can never be right'.[29]

The 1917 incident was not the end of Assis Júnior's involvement in political Angola. The regime of Norton de Matos enveloped him in a final and disastrous incident. On this occasion, rumour was a providential excuse which played into the hands of the High Commissioner. While he had appeared to be friendly towards African labourers' rights and *assimilado* organisations when he was Governor-General in 1912–15, during his second regime he put his new powers and his policy of 'unity' for Angola above all considerations of civil liberties and political rights. Behind his conviction that only through 'unity' would Angola achieve economic development was his patriotic belief that Angola could provide Portugal with the wealth and prestige it lacked in Europe.

His second period in office began, then, with measures to crush any threat to the efficiency of his economic development programme or the operation of his government. Such threats could come from any of several sources: foreign immigrants, such as the Boer trekkers or the new German immigrants from South West Africa and Germany; foreign Protestant missionaries; foreign concessions; European trade unions and associations; Angolan *assimilado* associations and their press, critical of his regime; or civil functionaries not carrying out his wishes. For every potentially threatening group, Norton de Matos had a decree or law to control their actions or eliminate them. He passed decrees limiting land-holding by foreigners, thus striking at the Boers in southern Angola at their most sensitive point; increased passport restrictions and foreign immigration controls were aimed at the Germans; Decree 77, passed in 1921, forbade the teaching of foreign languages in missions and the printing of literature in native languages, besides encouraging the teaching of Portuguese.[30] In 1921–22 Norton de Matos banned several European associations such as the Associação des Funcionários Públicos (founded in 1917) on the pretext that they opposed 'discipline' of the government service and injured the prestige of republican rule in Angola.[31]

In the meantime, he had built up the hopes of the Angolan *assimilados* by giving new powers of representative government to the Luanda Conselho Legislativo in 1921–22. The Liga Angolana and the Grêmio Africano were given the privilege of electing delegates to sit with European delegates on the Conselho; in 1921, each dutifully and expectantly chose its representatives, supposedly to speak for the African people of the colony, and urged greater political autonomy for Angola. Between January and April 1922, however, Norton de Matos turned around to crush the African associations and the free press of Luanda. The sudden change of policy took the Angolan community by surprise and produced a complicated controversy which before the year was out was debated in Lisbon.

The pretext for this particular burst of repression was the so-called 'Catete revolt' of 1921. António de Assis Júnior, now a *procurador judicial* in the Golungo Alto region, represented African groups there that were objecting to continued forced labour practices and confiscation of African farmlands. He petitioned the government through the proper local channels, and later took the issue to the higher echelons in Luanda. He was arrested with a number of other *assimilados* in Luanda and the Kwanza river valley, the beginning of a series of arrests, bannings and deportations. Norton de Matos took the opportunity of the rumours of a widespread 'nativist conspiracy' to crush all organised Angolan opposition. By February 1922, the Liga Angolana was banned, its newspaper, *O Angolense*, was closed down and the counterpart organisation, the Grêmio Africano was also banned.[32] The Luanda press was muzzled, including two other newspapers expressing an African *assimilado* viewpoint: *A Verdade* and *Independente*. Several dozen *assimilado* leaders, both functionaries and journalists, such as Assis Júnior, Narciso de Espirito Santo and Manoel dos Santos Van Dunem, were deported to isolated places such as Cabinda and Ganguela in eastern Angola. Others remained in Luanda jails. Several European journalists had already been deported by the High Commissioner in previous months for critical editorials. The suppression of the *assimilado* rights' movement completed the foundation for his 'unity' programme.

The allegation of the banning Decree 99, that the Liga Angolana was involved in a conspiracy to inspire the native populations to revolt against Portugal, was never proved. The 'Catete revolt' was largely a fabrication; none of the conspiracy evidence was conclusive and the promised investigative report of the affairs of 1921–22 was never published.[33] The bannings were based more on rumour than on fact, a situation that was common in the pre-1930 official repressions. Although many of the Angolan *assimilados* eventually returned from exile and jail terms, they and their intellectual descendants never forgave the 'Caligula in Angola' for his attacks on their advancement and organisations. Since 1930, the publications of the heir to the Liga Angolana, the Liga Nacional Africana, have criticised the effects of Norton de Matos's repressive regime and have perhaps oversimplified his role as the chief obstacle to pre-1930 *assimilado* advancement. They have pointed out the adverse effects—as he himself later admitted in a book—of a bureaucratic innovation in the structure of the Angolan civil service: the creation of a special African section for *assimilados*, the Quadro Geral Auxiliar in 1921.[34] In his account of his 1921–24 regime in Angola,[35] the High Commissioner explained that he instituted this, where there had hitherto been no distinction between Europeans and *assimilados* in the bureaucracy, in order to protect the *assimilados* from European competition and therefore to favour a gradual evolution of African advancement. Whatever his true intentions, the consequences of the Quadro were restrictive rather than protective. The change was attacked by Liga Nacional Africana literature into the 1960s as being responsible for setting back several decades the *assimilado* rise in society, through the pegging of salary scales, the limitation on entry by enforcing new educational requirements where few schools were available, and the imposition of a ceiling on positions to which Africans could rise. The Quadro was backed by a philosophy that resembled the motives behind the establishment of the Department of Native Affairs in 1913, another Norton de Matos creation.

Thus the controversial but active high commissionership of Norton de Matos in the period 1921–23 created a new political climate for Angola. It prepared the way for an official moratorium on European and African politics, a slowing down of *assimilado* and African advancement, the colonial mystique of the 1930 era and later, and the philosophy that brought the Estatuto dos Indígenas (native code) and its supporting laws later. Built upon tradition and precedent, of course, this new tradition stressed discipline and unity, terms heard again in 1926 with the emergence of a new authoritarian state in Lisbon. Even the liberal democrats who attacked the dictatorial repressions of Norton de Matos in Angola, however, based their attack on their belief that his actions would alienate the Angolan population and cause them to declare their independence from Portugal.[36] Thus, the final motive of the political debaters was patriotic and colonial at heart. Cunha Leal, European deputy representing Angola in the Portuguese Parliament while Norton de Matos was under fire, made a point of supporting democratic freedoms in Angola as long as the context was that of a Portuguese colony, not a free Angolan republic.

The period 1921–26 forms an important watershed in the history of Angola. A study of this era suggests not only the importance of Portuguese politics and nationalism in Angola but indicates also the intricacies of Angolan affairs and the conflicts of interest at work. Norton de Matos's brief regime prompted an angry reaction from several European groups, expressing their opinions in the Angolan press. The editorials concerned ignored the question of the suppression of the *assimilado* organisations and concentrated on the autocratic measures that affected them. Several papers outside Luanda, such as the *Jornal de Benguela* and *Mossamedense*,[37] had severely criticised his 'autocracy' and had suffered for their outspoken words. Certain European merchants and *patrões* in Luanda, however, favoured his reforms; they were willing to overlook his financial embarrassments with the deficit, currency and debts incurred, and agreed with his strong stand on African assertion. He found influential supporters in the *Província de Angola*, the Luanda weekly created on the occasion of, and because of, his resignation in late 1923. This well-financed paper, representing a coalition of settler interests, defended his regime and requested that he return to Angola to finish what he had begun.[38]

The paternalistic High Commissioner, perversely accused by his enemies of having 'an excess of personality', never returned to Angola, but his political handiwork survived. When, after May 28, 1926, the *Estado Novo* began to infringe traditional freedoms, many protests were made, albeit unsuccessful ones: even the European paper that had supported the High Commissioner, now a successful daily, openly protested against the first censorship laws of the new military regime as a violation of the 1911 republican constitution.[39] But the fact remained that the economic interest groups that had supported Norton de Matos's original measures of 'discipline' had no leg to stand on when Portugal began to enforce the policy of unity on the pretext of patriotic necessity. As Portugal's control over Angola tightened in new ways, the methods employed were those of Norton de Matos; those who now no longer applauded were silenced.

In a regime that stressed 'order' and 'discipline', in a way reminiscent of the Italian state of Benito Mussolini, a man Norton de Matos may well have admired,[40] the organised African elite could not but be suspected as elements of potential 'disorder'. To the Portuguese authorities the logical solution was to absorb such elements into the associations approved of and sponsored by the state. Thus the free *assimilado* civil servant of 1920 became the subservient puppet of 1926, enveloped in a patriotic ritual of political patronage. Those *assimilados* who did not co-operate were exiled to Lisbon or to more remote and less pleasant places, or they were jailed. *Assimilados* with ambitions beyond the status of sycophancy had once held a fleeting hope that they could act as cultural or racial middlemen between the African tribesmen and the Portuguese or perhaps between the European settler and Lisbon. Some had hoped Lisbon would protect them from the demands of the settlers. They had retained this feeling during the brief period under the republican new deal in 1910–11. Their dreams were shown to be largely hollow as repression became more continuous and efficient. The bitter comment of Assis Júnior on the European attitude towards the African in 1917 tells much about the mood of the frustrated Angolan elite: 'In his own land the native is no more than a Jew, and moreover a Jew as he was treated in the time of religious fanaticism.'[41]

The testing time for political principles in Portugal and Africa had come full circle by 1926. Principles of nineteenth century liberalism and humanitarianism seemed to be rejected in favour of a pragmatic policy of economic development, political stability and social status quo. In Angola much the same process occurred as economic development and a newly-established control were implemented largely for the sake of Portugal and the pockets of the European population. Much effort in those years was expended on debating questions of how to develop Angola economically; related issues like labour, finance, currency and economic autonomy were also discussed. Although economics appeared to dominate all, the question of Portuguese control over Angola and internal political liberty was perhaps more critical in the long run.

The quickening pace of the Portuguese efforts in Angola clashed with the political experimentation of the republic. In Angola this development was complicated by racial conflict and a conflict of interests. It was not unnatural that the uneducated Portuguese immigrant would fear and even hate the privileged *mestiço* bureaucrat of Luanda. Consider the strength of *assimilado* numbers and position in 1921: numbering over half the educated Westernised population and holding significant jobs, they seemed on the way to the enjoyment of African autonomy. The newly-regenerated European immigration and economic interests and, indeed, Portugal's control over Angola seemed threatened by the free African press and nascent political parties. Liberties in Angola were overwhelmed by developments in Portugal and Africa. The great reservoir of poverty, ignorance, disease and isolation afflicted the springs of progress as well as the soil of liberty.

The first republic died in 1926. Its demise marked the end of one important phase of Angolan nationalism and Angolan history. An entire generation of moderate *assimilado* nationalists was neutralised or purged in the 1922–30 period, and Angolan nationalism went into a phase of silence and inactivity. A new generation of protesters and activists would not go into action for another twenty years, while the aging *assimilados*, whose hopes had been raised by the republic, tried to save what they could of their jobs and positions. The hapless Assis Júnior, for example, twice-arrested in a five-year period, lost his militancy and reaffirmed his patriotic loyalty to Portugal in a ceremonial march to the governor's palace in early 1926.[42] Others refused to repudiate their past freedoms and preferred jail or exile. A general exodus of politically-minded *assimilados* came in 1928–30 in a wave of deportations by the government, thus completing the work begun in this department by Norton de Matos.[43]

From this survey of political activity over a century of Angolan history, a distinct continuity of action and grievance emerges. This continuity suggests a fundamental instability, never far below the surface of the ritual of the politics of patronage and patriotism.

Modest economic progress and administrative efficiency were the marks of the new look of Angola in the late 1920s. The bases were laid both for modern economic development (after centuries of frustration) and for a political moratorium on both African and settler politics. But more important than the new roads, schools, hospitals, laws and plans were the attitudes of the major interest groups, where there was very little change. The majority of Portuguese settlers treated most Africans in the old spirit of *com preto e mulato, nada de contrato*.[44] They scorned any governor or official who threatened settler access to African labour, and thought mainly of their pockets. To officials sent from Portugal (only one Angolan white settler briefly served as interim governor between the first and second high commissioners) Angola had a great economic future, but they were more aloof from local vested interests and were, more or less, reformist in attitude. Paternalism for all was their motto and policy. As in the past, the relative freedom of the settler to control the everyday life of the African in the interior undermined many Lisbon reforms.

With increasing economic progress, even better-informed Portuguese observers became more hopeful and complacent, seemingly assured that Portuguese justice and reform would easily undo centuries of injustice and stagnation and that all the *assimilados* were loyal to Portugal. Economic progress was both a blessing and a curse, for, while it brought some unity of purpose to the colony, it also brought a desire for more profits for the elite and did not encourage any attempt to understand the African. Portuguese leaders failed to perceive the continued survival among the Africans of the idea of freedom and independence in old Angola and the still fresh memory of the civil liberties enjoyed before the 1922–30 repressions.

As reform and improvement became more than dreams of nineteenth-century liberals, Portuguese leaders came to believe that reform would inevitably ensure peace and prosperity. Portugal could win African loyalty if only reforms were executed and unfair policies and suspicions and high-handed settler abuses brought to an end. This thought process was natural for the colonial setting, but failed to take account of African aspirations. The reformist solution was basically limited by Portuguese ethnocentrism and nationalism, factors that coloured most white attitudes. African 'nativism' (or 'separatism'), as African nationalism was termed in the 1920s, was considered an aberration, easily overcome by reforms. A Portuguese settler who knew Angola then thus concluded:

> Now, do those who rule, govern and administer in our country want the small separatist current in Angola to disappear?—Let them administer and govern without diverging from the path of justice, rectitude and the commonweal. If they do this, they will transform Angola into what it should be—a great, prosperous and rich country—then the separatists will disappear like magic.[45]

The protesting and warning voices of Angolan *assimilados* during 1870–1930 were accompanied in the succeeding decades by a few Portuguese voices, to be sure, but the basic failure of European leadership was to perceive the depth of African aspirations. As Angola entered a new era, the prevailing beliefs that reformism would produce automatic loyalty, and that loyalty was being Portuguese, became significant. Within twenty years, a regenerated Angolan nationalism rose to challenge these ideas.

6. Discovering Angola, 1926-61

Angola is quite far from being entirely changed from what it was forty years ago, because I am certain that we have travelled only a short way along the road opened up by the great Governor [Paiva Couceiro, 1907–09] . . . who knew certainly that unacknowledged vested interests swarm like highwaymen along the road great reformers try to follow.

> Norton de Matos, 1948,
> Opposition candidate for presidency of Portugal.

No useful proposal, no advantage, no wealth, no benefit of civilisation will be possible and lasting, if, at their very foundation, there is no free labour.   Augusto Casimiro, 1958,

> former Governor of Portuguese Congo.

THERE IS A distinct stage of development between the new colonial legislation of the *Estado Novo* (1926–33) and the outbreak of African insurgency in 1961. In effect, Angola was given one generation of classic colonial rule, relatively free of effective anti-colonial pressures. Despite an early stage of economic stagnation and continuing general poverty, conditions improved and standards of living rose. In the political sphere, nationalism revived during the last decade of the era, having been dormant during the 1930s and 1940s. For Portugal, it was a testing time for policy rather than a struggle to survive as a colonial power or coloniser, and Angola became a symbol of some pride. However, the lives of most Africans changed very little, apart from some economic improvements. They experienced at this time the most intensive European influences so far in the history of Angola and learned that the Portuguese not only had come to stay in the interior as well as on the coast but might stay forever. In 1961, Angola became the scene of the bloodiest anti-colonial insurgency in the history of Africa south of the Sahara. This chapter is an attempt to give the essential background and to explain the origins of the shattering days of 1961.[1]

NATIVE POLICY TO 1961

By 1930–32, the Portuguese administration had eliminated both European and African dissident political activity, had won the remaining tribal armageddons and had settled down to deal with two monumental problems, closely inter-connected: native policy and the economy. For the next generation, these problems dominated administrative activity.

Legislation passed between 1926 and 1933 formed the pillars of the new colonial policy towards the African. Except for initial legislation under the short-lived republic, Portugal had no 'positive' native policy until the *Estado Novo* regime.[2] The new native policy ended the nineteenth-century liberal approach to the treatment of the African. Gone was the assumption that the African would 'naturally' become assimilated into the European sector; the new philosophy learned from the generation of 1895 'realists' decreed that definite standards were to be set for the native to qualify for rights. Moreover, unless protected by legislation, the native could be abused. The new policy, known as the '*Indigenato*',* designated the native (*indígena*) as a legally separate element in the population. The means of bringing the native into a 'non-native' or '*não-indígena*' classification, that enjoyed by Europeans, was by a process of assimilation, *assimilação*. The old policy of *assimilação uniformizadora*, permitting the African to be subject to the laws and institutions of metropolitan Portugal, was replaced by selective assimilation, a policy philosophically aligned with the thoughts of the 'Heroes of Africa', the men who conquered the remaining independent tribes of Portuguese Africa. Those who felt that the old native policy was utopian and dangerous to Portugal's authority often felt the same way about civil liberties and party elections for Europeans.

This selective assimilation policy was in force from about 1926 until 1961. Historically, it represented one modern expression of executing what was called the 'civilising mission'. Unlike the old invertebrate policy, however, the new one was strictly regulated by a bureaucracy and dependent upon education for its ultimate success. The legislative origins are found in 1926 when the Colonial Minister João Belo drew up the Estatuto político, civil e criminal dos indígenas das colónias de Angola, Guiné e Moçambique ('Political, Civil and Criminal Statute for Natives in the Colonies of Angola, Guinea and Mozambique'), which was later replaced, but only partly modified, by a 1929 version. Two principles emerge from these two laws: firstly, the assurance of the natural rights of the African natives and their 'progressive fulfilment of their moral and legal duties of labour, education and self-improvement'; secondly, the duty of 'uplifting' the natives gradually and changing their ways to integrate them into the European sector of the colony.[3] Because *indígenas* did not have the rights or education of Portu-

* *Indigenato* means, literally, 'the quality of being a native'.

guese citizens, their lives were regulated largely according to native custom and law. They had separate courts, presided over by Portuguese officials. Two native *assessores*, or auxiliary judges, informed and advised officials. To guarantee the protection of native rights, the new regime established a Commissão de Defesa dos Indígenas ('Commission for the Defence of Natives'), whose members were often Portuguese missionaries.

In a sense, separate provisions for native institutions, customs, inheritance and family constituted a limited form of indirect rule. In some areas, the Portuguese retained the traditional chiefs and allowed them local powers, but under the supervision of European officials. As in the British system of indirect rule, native customs continued to be practised as long as (in the opinion of the Portuguese) they did not 'offend the rights of sovereignty [of Portugal] or repel the principles of humanity'.[4]

Later legislation more closely defined the legal meaning of 'native'. By a 1954 statute,[5] an *indígena* was an African, or descendant of an African, governed by native customs and not yet 'advanced' to the cultural level or degree of 'civilisation' that allowed him to come under the same laws as a Portuguese citizen. Three other documents formed the heart of the remainder of the *Estado Novo* legislation affecting Angola. These were the Colonial Act of 1930, the Imperial Organic Charter of 1933 and the Overseas Administrative Reform Act of 1933. The cornerstone principle, of course, was *political unity*, a euphemism for Portugal's colonial sovereignty in its African territories, which meant political centralisation as opposed to the greater autonomy allowed under the republic. Then and later, Portugal affirmed that its government would not accept the principle established in many British tropical colonies of 'the paramountcy of native interests'.[6]

From Portuguese articulation of their policies and from material published on such policies before Portugal joined the United Nations Organisation in 1955, several other key colonial principles emerge. A leading modern colonial theorist, Marcelo Caetano, asserted that Portugal had three other fundamental aims: spiritual assimilation, administrative differentiation and economic solidarity. Angola and the other Portuguese African colonies were to be integrated into metropolitan Portuguese territory. The term 'colony' was changed in 1951 to 'overseas province' (*província ultramarina*). The aim of native policy was to integrate the African into the Portuguese nation, while, in theory at least, respecting African culture and law. The state was to stand as a protector between the Africans and the settlers, and to some extent this was carried out. Early in the period 1930–61, however, agents other than the state had a much greater control over and contact with the African masses: the Catholic and Protestant missions with their schools and hospitals, the ubiquitous Portuguese trader, the European farmer, the labour recruiter and the tax collector. The demands of an efficient assimilation policy were great in a vast territory with a scattered population and during much of the era Portugal could not meet the challenge. More often than not, the dream of assimilation overwhelmed the reality.

There were many obstacles in the way of a successful policy of selective assimilation, many of them obstacles that had plagued previous regimes. Despite numerous laws and the newly-centralised control over the Angolan administration, Portugal failed to enforce an effective policy of assimilation—the theoretical guarantee of continued sovereignty—because little changed within Angola. To the traditional problems of Portuguese poverty, Angolan under-development, ethnic diversity of the African population, few health, welfare and education facilities and a lack of Portuguese supervisory personnel were added the consequences of continued forced labour—a daily fact of life—and the hostile attitude of certain European colonists towards assimilation (i.e. education) of Africans. The disintegration of African traditional authority and society also affected this policy, for many Africans were caught between allegiance to their village life and the attractions of the town, without the possibility of full satisfaction from either. The old power of the African chiefs and headmen was largely eroded, and although some European officials became, in effect, authority figures to the African, they could rarely take the part of the chief and often were obliged to enforce African respect and obedience towards superannuated chiefs who were no longer representative of the people. As the era progressed, intensified Portuguese influences further eroded the remaining African system without substituting a full-fledged educational system to ease the transition.

Until new legislation was passed in 1961, the state set the following standards for 'assimilation': the African had to be at least eighteen years of age, have proven ability to speak Portuguese, a good character and a clean police and military record (he could not be a deserter from the army). He had to submit his application to become an *assimilado* to local officials, and the state would then consider his case; if his petition was approved, the authorities issued him with an identity card, *o bilhete de identidade*. If the African could prove he held a job in the colonial bureaucracy, had a high school education or was a merchant or in industry or business, the application formalities were waived.

Although the legal machinery of the native courts was not clearly defined (Duffy has pointed out that there was no African penal code in Portuguese Africa),[7] the administrative system was thorough. There was a host of native labour laws, of course, and by law each African male had to carry a little book, the *caderneta*, whose origins were discussed in chapter 5. The carrying of the *caderneta*, both a native identity card and a pass-book, was enforced by a modestly-sized police force, staffed largely by Africans and officered by Portuguese—a similar racial composition to that of the Angolan army.

Paternalism characterised the native policy but the paternalism was not always a benevolent one. Much depended on the personalities of officials carrying out the policy. Corporal punishment was not uncommon: it was considered appropriate to the nature of the African. To the European official and settler, the whip (*chicote*) and the wooden paddle (*palmatória*) symbolised European supremacy over the African and the need for periodic punishment to instil fear and respect in the mind of the child-like African. To the African, such treatment meant that he was still a kind of slave. Moreover, paternalism meant that the measure of African rights was an exclusively Portuguese decision; hence, they were often vague and loosely interpreted. African land rights, for example, were protected in property legislation that supposedly prevented European land-grabbing but did little to stop such activities in northern Angola, especially after the new wave of farming settlers of the 1950s.

The two pillars of the assimilation policy were education and religion, and modest progress was made in both fields during this generation. Although what occurred in Angola was not spectacular or even respectable, compared with events in British and French Africa, to the Angolans some progress was evident. The great era of mission building had been from 1880 to 1930, and between 1930 and 1950 only eight new missions entered Angola.[8] By then, nearly half the African population was recorded as nominally Christian: the 1950 census showed 1,500,000 Africans listed as Catholics and 540,000 as Protestants. However, more than conversion, mission education constituted the foundation of Angolan education and assimilation. After Decree 77, in 1921, missions instructed most classes in the Portuguese language, and knowledge of the language spread more rapidly among the African masses. Until 1950, most schools in Angola were mission schools, but in the following decade the government increased its educational programme, built more schools and imported more teachers from Portugal. The expansion of government schools between 1955 and 1961 suggests the general wave of change in other fields in Angola:[9]

Angola

Education (all races)	1955–56 students	1960–61 students
Primary	68,759	105,781
Secondary academic	3,729	7,486
Secondary technical	2,164	4,501

While the growth rate in each category ranged between 54 and 108 per cent, a spectacular rise, not all the students recorded were African; in the upper levels, the majority were European, and the general illiteracy rate among black Africans was listed by UNESCO figures in 1958 as 97 per cent.

Despite the expansion of education, in the late 1950s no more than 1 to 2 per cent of Angola's population were in school, while at least 15 per cent were of school age. This situation worried several leaders on the Conselho Legislativo, the advisory council to the governor-general. In a debate on education in April 1958, the Bishop of Malanje, D. Manuel Nunes Gabriel, acknowledged the new educational expansion but strongly criticised the fact that Portugal was educating only a tiny portion of the African masses, despite the rule that 'all schools are open to people of all colours'.[10] He recommended rapid expansion to include the African masses. In reply, the Governor-General admitted the difficulty of getting qualified teachers to come from Portugal, but stated that there was no need for a basic reform of the educational commitment. The bishop's criticism was supported by Manuel Bento Ribeiro, a high official of the Liga Nacional Africana and a nominated member of the Conselho representing 'native interests', who gave educational statistics to show that Portugal's programme for native education was 'impoverished'. He argued that Portugal's 'obligations of sovereignty' required much more.[11]

Although politely worded and appropriately patriotic in form, these criticisms were significant. Certain Portuguese leaders realised that, in view of the rising pressures, the assimilation policy was in trouble and the educational system needed more rapid expansion. But to many, recalling the pitiful educational system of before, the statistics proved more than modest success. In a 1959 debate in the Conselho Legislativo,[12] members praised the assimilation policy and quoted figures to show an admirable increase in the rate of assimilation for the three years 1956–58, when some 2,000 Africans achieved citizenship—a number equivalent to about 25 per cent of the new Portuguese colonists who settled in Angola during the same period. The overall figures of the assimilated population, however, were not impressive. According to the 1950 census, out of an African population of over 4 million, only 30,089 had achieved *assimilado* status. Of this number it is unclear how many were Africans and how many were *mestiços*, for Africans and *mestiços* (and

134

even Europeans) were frequently confused in the official statistics. In any event, certain voices warned that few *black* Africans were benefiting under the *indigenato* policy, still complacently praised by many. These few critical voices made little headway but still spoke out. Augusto Casimiro pointed out the ludicrous deficiency in African education in agricultural schools: in a territory where most farmers were black, out of fifty students enrolled in the two agriculture schools in 1954, not one was a black African.[13]

There is some evidence that, by 1957, certain enlightened elements in Lisbon were not happy with the results of selective assimilation and may have been setting the stage for the abolition of the *indigenato* system before the events of 1961 speeded up the process of change.[14] New labour legislation, the raising of wages for some unskilled labourers and other measures by the Overseas Ministry, advised by men like Professor Adriano Moreira of the Portuguese Institute for Overseas Studies, presaged changes in the policy towards the African masses. Realism and new pressures from the outside as well as from within caused a quiet reassessment. Lisbon had adequate evidence that the policy, as administered, contained many barriers to African advancement. There was direct pressure on the governor-general from petitions submitted in 1953 and 1958 by the leadership of the Liga Nacional Africana. These petitions noted the great discontent among the African masses over the difficulty of obtaining the passport to *assimilado* status, *o bilhete de identidade*,[15] which, since 1942, had been issued to Europeans and *assimilados*. It was more than a document giving the bearer access to some civil rights: it was a sine qua non for economic advancement. Without it, the petitioners complained, the African could not obtain any decent job, a civil service position or even a driving licence. Without a job, and hence no money, self-improvement and 'civilisation' (in Portuguese terms) were impossible for all but the most fortunate. The 1958 petitioners recognised among the African masses of Angola 'an insatiable desire for improving themselves', for education, in order to aid their communities. They boldly asserted:

> The *bilhete de identidade* is for us natives a question of life or death. On it depend our future and the future of our children . . . you will pardon, Your Excellency, if we frankly state that . . . we cannot understand how, after four centuries of Portuguese rule, in order to obtain such an important document, we must report to the administrative authorities, not for them to tell us we are well-behaved or that we are not vagabonds, but to give us a document of social liberation. It is an abuse that only painfully will we tolerate.

These protests about the *indigenato* system from within indicate its failure. Even moderate, loyal Angolan leaders were convinced of its failure and the dangers inherent in it. The system was counter-productive, if, instead of smoothing African advancement, as it may have done in the days before the general awakening of African aspirations, now it impeded progress and thus alienated and frustrated many. But no real change was made at this time. The books, articles, speeches and petitions were considered and absorbed; but the system continued, relatively unaltered, into 1961.

AN ARCHAIC ECONOMY

As before, economic questions continued to dominate Angola's day-to-day affairs. The new development in this period was that the economy achieved a new prosperity; there was increased basic development and greater profits were rendered to the European business interests and settlers than ever before in history. The generation witnessed a slow but steady rise in wages, prices and standards of living. Closely connected with this new prosperity and development was cheap African labour, provided by the Angolan masses. The problems that arose from this crucial dependence of the economy on cheap labour had serious political consequences beginning as early as the 1940s.

The new regime in Lisbon eliminated Angola's serious deficits and debts, which had grown to scandalous proportions by 1926. Much of Angola's revenue depended upon customs and taxes since as yet agriculture produced little for export, diamond mining was only beginning and there was little or no industry. The Benguela railway was linked with the Belgian Congo system during 1929–31 and provided a new source of revenue.[16] Until at least 1932, Lisbon paid the deficits for Angola. However, beginning in 1930–31, officially at least, there was a perennially balanced Angolan budget. Portugal attempted to make Angola self-supporting, while at the same time using the country as a major market for Portuguese goods. Arrangements were made to eliminate the excess of imports over exports and to build up a basic communications network. Prosperity was the eternal eldorado. Angolan economic and financial autonomy were virtually ended during 1926–32 as Portugal drew a tight net over the system. Little economic prosperity came until after the Second World War, a period of stagnation and only slight progress. In this era Angola became, in effect, a coffee economy, and coffee enabled Angola's oligarchy to become prosperous, not merely self-supporting. Spectacular trade balances were produced in 1951 and

1953 and Portuguese colonists responded with a wave of new immigration.

The post-1945 coffee boom had profound consequences for the economy and society. The new prosperity, both real and imagined, to be found in coffee intensified an atmosphere of black-white conflict, as it encouraged white immigration, European land-buying, further forced labour abuses and economic and social competition between the races. Although coffee had been cultivated in Angola as early as 1830, its potential had little influence on settler immigration until the late 1920s, and only after 1940 did the higher coffee prices reveal the eldorado. During 1945–60, Angola became the first producer of coffee in Africa and the third or fourth in the world. The profits from the coffee crops represented the one bright spot in the period of economic stagnation between the collapse of the rubber boom and the end of the Second World War. The following figures reveal the increase in coffee production:[17]

Year	Tons of coffee produced in Angola
1893	8,000
1910	6,140
1926	9,343
1935	10,277
1942	18,966
1951	38,860
1956	66,543
1960	87,217
1961	168,000
1962	185,000

Just as revealing is the comparative value of the coffee export crops: in 1946, the exported crop was valued at 184,000 contos,* while by 1960 it had increased about seven times to 1,263,000 contos. Clearly, European companies and farmers gained considerable profits from the new export sales—but what of the African farmer and labourer? The labourer was paid very poor wages, while a surprisingly small number of African farmers contributed to the coffee exports. Between 78 and 80 per cent of the 1960 production came from European-owned farms. In 1961 coffee production, European-owned lands produced 74 per cent and Africans' land only 26 per cent.

In response to the coffee boom and to the colonising programmes of the *Estado Novo*, there was a new wave of Portuguese immigration.

* A conto in Portuguese currency is 1,000 escudos, roughly $(US)35.00 or £(UK)14 10s.

Angola

The post-1940 rapid increase of the white population had profound social, political and economic effects. The following figures illustrate this movement:

Year	Europeans in Angola
1900	9,177
1920	20,000
1940	44,083
1950	78,000
1955	110,000
1960	172,000

The Portuguese resident population increased nearly 400 per cent between 1940 and 1960, a startling development in view of the small immigration rate of previous years. By the mid-1950s, 10,000 Portuguese immigrants were arriving annually. More important than the overall increase was the precise location of the largest increases and how this affected Africans. The most intensified white settlement on farmlands, primarily coffee country, was located in precisely those areas with the highest incidence of forced labour practices and where African farmers were under pressures: the districts of Cuanza Norte, Luanda, Congo (redivided into two districts in 1961, Uíge and Zaire), Cabinda and Benguela.

The coffee boom brought racial and later political conflicts, especially in central and eastern sections of the Congo district.[18] Although there were few Portuguese settlers resident compared to numbers in other areas, the increase from 2,000 in 1940 to over 6,000 in 1957 were very important, in terms of the history and situation of the district. Between 1955 and 1957 the Portuguese population increased by one quarter; many acres of land formerly owned by African subsistence farmers were bought up, despite land laws which, in theory, protected African lands, and there was a burgeoning of hundreds of small Portuguese bush stores. Conflicts arose as a result of new and often unprepared immigration and settlement outside the government-sponsored plateau *colonatos* (colonies) and the vastly-increased demand for cheap African labour.

Angola's labour shortage was a chronic problem that no governor-general, high commissioner or minister had been able to solve, and there is no doubt that the post-war coffee boom encouraged forced labour and other abuses. The traditional lack of people in Angola was well-known; other reasons for the chronic labour shortage were more subtle.[19] They included: poor wages for both skilled and unskilled labour; primitive working conditions; corporal punishment;

138

malnutrition; poor health of the workers; the continued export of contract labour—save for intermittent years when determined governors ordered it stopped—to the islands of São Tomé and Príncipe during the era 1920–50;[20] the fear of forced labour itself; and the customs of African groups. Although poor wages and bad treatment may have been decisive historic reasons, always recognised but rarely ended, for the labour shortage, the dislike of agricultural or other wage labour by certain African ethnic groups did contribute to the problem.

From the 1940s onwards, the forced labour system came under new criticism from Portuguese critics. Petitions from the Liga Nacional Africana protested, but the first and most significant attack came from Captain Henrique Galvão (1895–1970), high inspector of the colonial administration. With over two decades of experience as an official in various parts of Angola, and as a student of African life, Galvão compiled in 1947 a detailed *Report on Native Problems in the Portuguese Colonies*, mainly on Angola and Mozambique.[21] He showed how the Angolan economy exploited cheap African labour and how the contract labour system was like slavery. This controversial report indicted the very foundations of the European sector of the economy, for without cheap, poorly-paid labour, even such modest profits as existed before 1950 would have been endangered. Galvão described 'demographic haemorrhage' and 'demographic anemia' that lead to heavy African emigration from Angola to other territories for better wages and treatment. The facts were appalling: infant mortality rates of 60 per cent, poor health of workers, bad treatment of workers on forced labour contracts and abuses connected with European store dealings with Africans. In 1947 Galvão warned the government in a secret session of the Portuguese National Assembly in Lisbon that there would be 'imminent catastrophe' if labour conditions were not rapidly improved. In essence, he revealed a sub-economic system of slavery in certain sectors. The administration banned Galvão's report and later arrested and imprisoned its author on charges of treason (in 1959, he managed to escape to Latin America). Some labour reforms were introduced between 1947 and 1959, but the system remained essentially intact in the Congo district, Cuanza Norte and Malanje, where labour shortages continued to plague officials and settlers committed to labour-intensive projects such as coffee and cotton. As late as 1961, recruiters were taking young and old Africans, some of them subsistence cultivators, to work in contract labour jobs in the coffee regions at starvation wages. Much the same occurred in the Malanje and Kasanje (Cassange) areas of cotton cultivation, where until 1961 rural labourers were often forced to pick quotas of cotton.

Certain voices in the 1950s echoed Galvão's criticisms. Foreign journalists such as Basil Davidson—in articles (1954) and a book, *The African Awakening* (1955)—carried on the English humanitarian tradition of attacking forced labour in Portuguese Africa; the South African journalist, Brian Parks, writing in the *Johannesburg Star* in 1958, also attacked forced labour in Angola.[22] However, the Portuguese government was more inclined to listen to, but not necessarily to act upon, Portuguese criticisms. In 1958 Augusto Casimiro, former Governor of the Congo district, provided a comprehensive critique, clothed in the language of patriotism.[23] He stated that forced labour remained a major Angolan problem. He feared the consequences of an African reaction to continued forced labour, European land-buying and general poor behaviour of the new immigrants. To Casimiro, poor wages explained the African reluctance to enter the wage economy, and he warned of the consequences of forced labour in passages reminiscent of warnings given by the Marquis Sá da Bandeira in his *Trabalho Rural Africano* (Lisbon 1873). In 1957, F. C. C. Egerton warned that Portugal should make reforms in its 'civilising mission' and that 'there was no time to lose'.[24] Casimiro's thesis was that, if forced labour continued, the current prosperity of Angola was built on sand. In effect, a continued forced labour policy would weaken and perhaps destroy Portugal's hold on Angola. Echoing earlier critiques by Galvão and Selvagem, that 'free' colonisation was a failure and that 'directed' migration was best for Angola, both for the settler and to strengthen Portuguese control,[25] he attacked the European colonisation programme as poorly-managed and badly-supervised, since many settlers were not fit to live with Africans in Angola. He echoed a hope of many Portuguese reformers for over a century when he wrote of the desirability that the European farmer 'should dispense entirely with native labour'. To Casimiro, the evils of European behaviour vis-à-vis the African were 'force' and 'egoism'. He held up the neighbouring Belgian Congo's free labour system of the 1950s as an example to the Portuguese in Angola.

Casimiro was not the only Portuguese critic to attack forced labour and the immigration policy. In the same year that Casimiro's important book appeared (subsidised, significantly, by the Gulbenkian Foundation in Lisbon), the Bishop of Malanje in a session of the Angola Conselho Legislativo attacked the colonisation programme for sending immigrants with no education or preparation for successful colonisation and harmonious race relations.[26] Indirectly, the Bishop was criticising the forced labour system, too, for the system was continued by new immigrants anxious to make profits on their new coffee lands by recruiting cheap labour from among African subsistence farmers and eager, in not a few instances, to set up small stores and to exploit the African customers by means of unfair prices and practices. Although Portugal passed a new rural labour code in 1957, an improvement over the old one, and signed the 1959 Convention of the International Labor Organization against forced labour, there was no great change in the labour field until 1962. The highest percentage of contract labour work continued to be carried on in the Congo district and in Cuanza Norte. So great was the Angolan Bakongo emigration to the Belgian Congo in the 1940s and 1950s that employers began to contract Ovimbundu from the densely-populated districts of Bié and Huambo to fill the labour shortage in northern Angola.

By the late 1950s, many Portuguese officials were satisfied that the few remaining abuses had been eliminated and that racial harmony prevailed everywhere in Angola. Particularly sanguine was the survey of Congo district by a former Governor, Hélio Felgas.[27] He recognised the African grievances of the mid-1950s, but believed they had been abolished by 1958. The Bakongo male, he asserted elsewhere,[28] generally considered farming degrading but was interested in the money to be had from coffee cultivation. His survey depicts the struggle between the new Portuguese immigrant farmer who bought up African lands, said to be uncultivated and therefore legally purchasable according to Portuguese law, and the peasant African farmer, angered at the loss of his land. In a message to Africans in the Congo district in early 1956, the failing King of Kongo, Dom António III (who died in July 1957), warned his subjects that they would lose their coffee lands to Europeans and *assimilados* if they did not occupy, clean and cultivate them by June 30, 1956.[29] He cited several serious incidents of conflict between whites and blacks over land in the district. Whatever the reception for the King's officially-sponsored warning, the land conflict continued unabated. Felgas interpreted the return, in 1955–58, of hundreds of Bakongo emigrants from the Belgian Congo as proof of new prosperity, successful reform and future harmony in race relations. Satisfied that the new intensification of European immigration and farming could be harmonised with the return of African migrants, with the administration protecting African land-ownership, he concluded his book with the statement that the area had 'no racial problems' and that there was 'no need to fear for the future'.[30] In short, Felgas, and undoubtedly other officials in the area at the time, were proud of their land reform programme and made only mild references to those they considered the culprits, 'some Europeans poorly endowed morally'.

Besides problems in the private sectors of the economy, there were problems in the larger sphere. The economy suffered from a lack of capital, a monopoly structure, heavy protectionism by Portugal and a highly conservative investment policy both in Lisbon and Luanda. The resentment of certain Portuguese Angolan business groups grew for what they considered Portugal's economic exploitation of Angola. Vested interest and monopoly, characteristic of the old economy, continued dominant in the coffee boom era. The government's first Six-Year Development Plan (1953–59) produced the first chinks in the wall of protectionism, lack of risk capital and tight monopoly. Portuguese private investment was encouraged, but little appeared. Some 95 per cent of the money for the first Six-Year Plan came from Angolan revenues. Large companies dominated most investment and credit schemes, and smaller groups, lacking the capital and unable to obtain it, due to the ultra-conservative credit policies of the few banks and loan companies, were shut out. The tight money policy, expressed in high interest rates, the dispensing of few loans without high collateral and a rudimentary credit system, combined with the natural deficiencies of the economy. Certainly, the lack of adequate utilities, transport and communications in Angola were serious problems and required a great deal of basic spending, first by the government and later by the more prosperous and progressive large companies, such as Diamang (Companhia de Diamantes de Angola) and the Benguela railway (Caminhos de Ferro de Benguela); but general neglect of health, education and welfare in the Six-Year Development Plans (a second one was inaugurated in 1959) was a marked characteristic of the distribution of development funds before 1961.

In short, the territory continued in the 1950s to be afflicted by the traditional 'economising' policy. The economic annals of Angola are filled with official and private complaints about the tight money policies of the banks and companies. Whether through private fears of competition or public and official fears of eventual foreign economic control, little foreign investment entered Angola during the early post-war era. There was Belgian, British, South African and some French capital in several of the major companies established before 1940, but the government carefully controlled such activity.

Revenues from minerals were impressively boosted in the mid-1950s with the significant discovery of petroleum reserves in northern Angola and iron ore deposits in the south. Although oil samples from Angola reached Lisbon as early as the 1790s, and perhaps earlier, little investigation of potential reserves came until the establishment in 1922 of Angoil (Companhia de Petróleo de Angola), an oil prospecting company based in Lisbon.[31] A Belgian company, Petrofina (Compagnie

Financière Belge des Pétroles),[32] began to exploit the oil in 1955. The discovery and exploitation of oil and iron gave the Angolan economy a new fillip. The oil especially promised to inject new life into the economy when and if the coffee revenues, so dependent upon world market prices and competition, decreased.

The new prosperity held lures for the poor white immigrant, the rural African subsistence farmer and the Portuguese *capitalista* or *Africanista*.* With the new opportunities for higher wages and profits came the danger of monopoly and unfair competition. Most of the Angolan population was not allowed to profit significantly from the economic movement; through either direct or indirect monopoly, most of the new gains went to the European sector. The great lack of skills and ignorance among the African masses had not been appreciably reduced, in spite of increased urbanisation, educational and religious expansion and the growing money economy. Over 80 per cent of the Africans remained in subsistence agriculture and in rural surroundings.[33] By 1961 only 11 to 12 per cent of the total territorial population was 'urban', and many of the 'towns' of over 2,000, which put them in the urban category, were mere villages. Only five cities—Luanda, Benguela, Lobito, Nova Lisboa and Sá da Bandeira—had populations of over 20,000. As usual, the capital, Luanda, dominated the urban pattern with some 40 per cent of the total urban population.

While African migration to Angolan cities increased during this era, so did the migration of labour to the neighbouring countries of South West Africa, Belgian Congo, Northern Rhodesia and South Africa. By 1961, over 30,000 Angolans annually migrated to these states for work. There was significant African and European unemployment in the Angolan towns, for not enough jobs had been created for the new arrivals, whether from Portugal or from the interior. In job competition, the newly-arrived white was better off than the resident African and sometimes the *mestiço*; thus Luanda became a very Portuguese city by 1950, and many services and trades, once Africanised, were now filled by new Portuguese arrivals. In 1952 some 35 per cent of the whites were native-born Angolans while 60 per cent were born in Portugal;[34] of the whites in Luanda in 1960, some 80 per cent were born outside Angola. While Luanda had the largest *mestiço* population (over 6 per cent) of any city and was more like a Rio de Janeiro than any other Portuguese African metropolis, the new immigration, partly directed to the plateau colonies but mainly sticking to the cities, made the capital more of a European city than ever. By 1961 Angolan Portuguese

---

* *Capitalista:* Portuguese with investments; *Africanista:* Portuguese with land and/or investments in Portuguese Africa, or a settler.

143

were claiming, with some justification, that Luanda was now in size and loyalty the 'third city' of Portugal, surpassing all others except Lisbon and Oporto.

To many African leaders, Angola remained the exploited Black Mother of the mid-twentieth century. The European settler with Angolan roots more and more resented the Portuguese metropolitan economic controls. That the monopoly economy and the oligarchic social structure were both wasteful and politically dangerous was realised by some insiders. Significantly, Augusto Casimiro concluded his 1958 critique with the warning that the greatest evils for Angola were 'exclusive economic or political interests', and that Angolans should be treated in the spirit of the majority.[35] Casimiro was convinced that little time remained, that reform was urgently required. Who took his conclusions to heart? Whatever the official reaction, the follow up had little impact.

OLD LOYALTIES AND REVIVED NATIONALISMS

If changes characterised the new era, these changes had differing effects. The European sector derived from them considerably more comfort and benefit than did the African. For many Africans, as well as those few thousands integrated into the system as *assimilados*, the promise of the pre-1930 days seemed betrayed. The changes of the 1940s and 1950s were often disruptive and destructive.

Neither the European settler minority nor the African majority was self-governing. The new prosperity encouraged thoughts of autonomy or even independence among certain European circles in the towns. Some thought of a separate Angolan path rather than a strictly national Portuguese future. Meanwhile, the government built, upon a foundation of new colonial publications, a mystique and rhetoric that began to talk of *Lusotropicalismo*, a concept that seemed to imply racial harmony but also an understood Portuguese national dominance. During 1945–61, Angolan nationalism was revived by several groups, rarely co-operating and sometimes conflicting with one another. Each had different ideas about Angola's future. It would be an oversimplification to state that there were only two nationalist groups, African and European,[36] for there were, broadly, four groupings comprising over sixty parties and associations: the old *assimilado* associations, now government-sponsored; the new militant clandestine African-*assimilado* parties; the African ethnic separatist groups; and the European settler parties. Having passed through its period of stirrings, from 1870 to 1930, Angolan nationalism now entered its era of struggle.

As both a reaction to political agitation and an assertion of control and development plans, the government placed a strict moratorium on settler and *assimilado* politics between 1930 and 1942. Following the emasculation of the original *assimilado* associations in 1922, the settlers were prohibited from organising and electioneering for local offices. Several incidents and influences combined to produce a conflict between forces for or against the new military dictatorship in Lisbon. Immediately after 1926, the government deported to Angola numbers of political exiles who agitated and combined with the disaffected in Luanda in an attempt to overthrow authority in Angola and to declare a free republic. The events of March 1930 brought to a climax the opposition movement. Dissident officer elements attempted an abortive coup in Luanda while the High Commissioner, Filomeno da Câmara, was in Benguela; for several weeks the government was in temporary exile in Benguela, publishing the *Boletim Oficial* away from Luanda. A Lieutenant Morais Sarmento, imbued apparently with more *loucura* (heroic madness) than *siso* (sound judgement), became the sole (and celebrated) casualty of the brief violence that followed in Luanda, when he was shot by a company of African troops. By April 1930 a new Governor-General was appointed by Lisbon and a political moratorium was declared, with deportations, jailings and investigations. Except for some bombings and bomb scares afterwards, the agitation died away by 1931, and the regime was surprised that the brief rebellion of Portuguese armed forces in the Azores islands in 1931 did not produce a similar uprising in Angola.[37]

In 1936 the government decreed an end to the prominent role played by the *degredados*, exiled convicts from Portugal, in Angola. Henceforth, all *degredados*, with the temporary exception of women, were to be imprisoned in remote parts of eastern and southern Angola or returned to Portugal rather than kept in the Angolan towns and the capital.[38] After this decree, the blue denim convict uniforms were less conspicuous in the European urban sectors. The act was one more measure to change the ways of old Angola, a harbinger of a more efficient political control from Lisbon.

Elective municipal and local politics were resumed, provisionally, by Governor-General Freitas Morna in December 1942.[39] His action gave him substantial popularity with the settler community, a feeling probably increased by his protection of the Angolan labour supply by banning the export of contract labour to São Tomé. With this partial restoration of civil liberties, the regime was testing the effects of concession to local aspirations and stated that absolute national loyalty was necessary. Thus, the politics of paternalism and patronage were

145

renewed around the banner of 'national unity'. Although the atmosphere remained fairly calm in the beginning, political activity and agitation increased with each new election, national or municipal. In the national presidential elections of 1948, 1951 and 1958, and as the home opposition to the Salazar regime gained some strength, Angolan leaders increased their political efforts. Each election became an opportunity to protest against unpopular laws and conditions in the European community. In the late 1940s, certain members of the Angolan African intelligentsia became involved in election activities. And it was during 1948–55 that the Communist Party of Angola (PCA) was secretly established in Luanda, probably a branch of the Lisbon party. Certain liberal European settlers were involved with some African groups at this stage, though the majority of Portuguese remained in associations involved in the politics of patronage and loyalty. During this post-war period, certain pro-autonomy parties, such as the Partido Pro-Angola, founded in 1924, were revived.

Angolan settler organisations achieved their greatest impact in the national presidential elections of 1958. Unlike previous elections, the growing opposition in Angola had some effect, even among black Africans, and attempted to raise support for the opposition candidacy of Air Force General Humberto Delgado (1900–1965), a moderate-liberal who encouraged ideas of political autonomy among Angolan Europeans. Rallies were organised and literature was distributed.[40] The regime sought absolute loyalty to the government party, the only legal political association, the União Nacional, and its candidate Admiral Américo Tómas. Although the election results were kept secret, information became available that Delgado received from 25 to 30 per cent of the total vote in all the Portuguese territories (including metropolitan Portugal), and perhaps a majority of the Portuguese vote in Angola and Mozambique. This clear proof of an upsurge of opposition prompted the regime to take new measures to assure its safety. In early 1959, there was a series of arrests and deportations of Europeans as well as Africans in Angola. Either shortly before this, in 1958, or early in 1959,[41] the first detachments of the national secret police, known as the Polícia Internacional e de Defesa do Estado (PIDE), were sent from Lisbon, and they came to play a prominent role in government surveillance and control from that time onward.

Like the other Angolan nationalist groups, the Angolan Portuguese groups were not united. They supported various ideas of separatism, absolute independence or a commonwealth association with Portugal. They formed lobbies rather than true political parties and rarely had any organisational strength beyond the traditional centres of separatism in Luanda and Benguela, with Lobito now developing in a similar manner. Not all these groups were members of the Portuguese opposition, which was itself fragmented and disunited. Some did adhere to the ideas of Captain Galvão and General Delgado (who also fled Portugal to exile in Latin America in 1959), but no coalition or united front of anti-Salazarists formed. In some respects, economic freedom was more an issue than the vote. As was customary, the governor-general appointed by the Lisbon government often played the role of high patron, a mediator between Lisbon and Luandan interests. His personality and programmes were important factors in Angolan Portuguese activities; the changes and reforms that took place were often attributed solely to his initiative rather than to that of Lisbon. The Lisbon government found that the lack of unity among the Angolan interest groups enabled the regime to maintain fairly close control.

THE POLITICS OF COLLABORATION: THE LIGA NACIONAL AFRICANA

The *assimilado* associations, now officially sponsored and even subsidised, were revived by government permission in 1930. The Liga Nacional Africana and the Associação dos Naturais de Angola relaunched themselves as primarily social and economic associations in Luanda. Most active was the Liga, whose activities still encompassed 'protecting the rights' of Africans and *assimilados*. If their post-1930 activities were more ritualised and controlled than before their eclipse in 1922, protest of a political nature did emerge from their relations with the government. By means of petitions to the government, reports, meetings and monthly literature,* the Liga played a key role as the dominant loyalist *assimilado* association. Led mainly by Luanda-born *mestiços*, most of whom were Roman Catholic, employed in the civil service and middle-class moderates, it had several thousand members. Although primarily urban-supported, it had contacts in the smaller towns and in the interior, and after 1935 became increasingly concerned and informed about the condition of the Angolan masses.

From 1930 to 1955, the older leaders dominated the Liga. These men, born between 1890 and 1910, soon met opposition and disagreement from the younger generation, born in the 1920s and 1930s. Young Africans and *mestiços*, who had had greater educational opportunities than their fathers and grandfathers, came to play a more important role

* The monthly bulletin of the Liga, still published, is *Angola: Revista Mensal De Doutrina E Propaganda Educativa*, a successor to the original publication, the *Boletim*.

in the organisation. Generation and ideological conflicts arose; and the establishment of the militant, clandestine African nationalist groups during 1953–60 was in part the result of the struggles within the Liga leadership, under increasing pressure to make a definite stand on the political future of Angola. Thus it was not an African nationalist group on the offensive, but an association allowed by the government as a lobby for African interests, expressed through 'acceptable' *assimilado* leaders. However, despite its weaknesses, it did have a significant function. Its effective expression of protest and interest has been obscured by the more militant African parties, but it did provide a consistent voice for Africans' grievances. In terms of African interests, its function was twofold: to protect and further *assimilado* advancement within the system, and to do the same for the less privileged African masses; and, because of the subordinate position of the Liga, the first function often took precedence over the second. But it was not merely a lobby for moderate *assimilado* advancement in the civil service of Angola. Its literature and petitions suggest it played a larger role during the 1950s. The Liga also supported welfare and educational benefits for its members. Subsidising schools, charity and medical benefits for its members and their families, it acted as a welfare association of some importance in Luanda. As government pressure on it increased in the late 1950s and early 1960s, the organisation took on the aspect of a social club and welfare society. But, earlier, the leadership had conceived of its role as that of a defender of African rights and the promoter of advancement in all spheres.

The preparation of petitions for government study represented a primary means of promoting advancement. In 1938, on the occasion of the presidential visit to Angola of Marshal Carmona, the Liga presented to the government a report entitled *The Needs and Aspirations of the Native Populations*. It included the major African grievances and requested that Africans be represented on the governor's advisory council, the Conselho do Governo (reconstituted as the Conselho Legislativo in 1955). In 1946, the Lisbon government, under the aegis of Marcelo Caetano, Minister for the Colonies, established 'native' representation on the Conselho with the nomination of two *assimilados* as members: the Reverend Manuel Joaquim Mendes das Neves, and a functionary, Euzébio Martins de Brito Teixeira, both from Luanda, the first Angolan African members to be represented on any official body higher than the Câmara municipal (city council or city hall) since 1922. Despite a one-year reversal of this innovation in 1954, African representation, nominated rather than elected, in what some moderates considered 'our little parliament' continued throughout this era. After

1955, with the nomination of other members from the Liga leadership and the *assimilado* community—Manuel Bento Ribeiro, Lourenço Mendes da Conceição, and a woman, Sinclética dos Santos Tavares—at least six Angolans served for a period on the Conselho.[42] Although it met infrequently and had, up to 1961, only rather limited advisory powers, it did serve as an outlet for expression and grievance. The governor-general, naturally, dominated its proceedings.

These developments suggested a slow movement towards self-government for a restricted group of European and *assimilado* interests. Nevertheless, there was little change in the government attitude towards Angola's political relationship with Portugal; 'political unity', the euphemism for Portuguese paramountcy, was the fundamental principle. This did not prevent the Liga from submitting other petitions to the government in 1953, 1955–56 and 1958. In either 1955 or 1956, it sent a manifesto to the United Nations, stating its dissatisfaction with Portuguese rule. Later, in 1957, when the government asked the leaders to send to New York a loyal delegation to speak for Portugal's official delegation at the United Nations, they either balked or refused. There followed a government-prompted purge and shake-up of the leaders responsible for the refusal.

Whatever its conflicts with the government and within itself, the Liga has prided itself on being a leader of African advancement in Angola. Its literature has claimed credit for the following advances and reforms: salary raises for Angolan civil servants; abolition of a separate administrative corps for Africans (Norton de Matos's 1921 creation); recognition of equality and rights of African nurses; improvements in the status of Africans in the Angolan army; African representation in the government Conselho, beginning in 1946; and, above all, 'a little more respect for the dignity of the human being'.[43] Although its methods were gradualistic and loyalist, there was always the hint in its petitions of disapproval and controlled impatience. In a sense, the limit of its effectiveness in achieving reform and redress of grievance was the extent to which it could work out a smooth relationship with the current governor-general.[44] Since most of the post-1938 governors tended to be paternalistic but benevolent, modest reforms were achieved. However, lasting satisfaction was missing, and the quiet that Portugal interpreted as proof of good relations was the calm before the storm.

Angola

DISCOVERING ANGOLA: AN ANGOLAN CULTURAL REVIVAL

The reawakening of Angolan political and social aspirations after 1940 was in part inspired by and accompanied by a cultural revival among the urban intelligentsia. It came mainly in the form of a literary revival that sought to express itself by developing African and Angolan forms and ideas. The medium of expression was, almost without exception, the Portuguese language, and it was employed by a younger generation of Angolans born after 1920. Unlike the Angolan 'Generation of 1890', the literary-journalistic writers of Luanda, this new group excelled in poetry and included Angolans with more formal education and greater experience abroad.

The literary harvest of the 1920s and 1930s was neither large nor inspiring. Literary activity was confined largely to newspapers, with a few obscure novels and several interesting but amateurish historical studies. Oscar Ríbas, born in Luanda in 1909, wrote several Portuguese short stories in the 1920s, but after 1940 began to study Angolan ethnography, chiefly the Kimbundu society of Luanda; in doing this, he became the intellectual heir to J. D. Cordeiro da Matta (1857–91), the brilliant poet, folklorist and linguist of Kimbundu. Ríbas's studies of Kimbundu custom and society in the 1950s and 1960s won him wide acclaim in the Portuguese-speaking world;[45] but, in terms of cultural leadership, he was of the older generation. In the 1940s new voices with original messages appeared.

In 1942, the scholar-poet from São Tomé, Francisco Tenreiro, published his volume of poetry, *Ilha de Nome Santo*, a pioneering Portuguese-*assimilado* expression of 'negritude'.[46] Other poets from the Cape Verde islands, São Tomé and Angola appeared in Portuguese publications and participated in a cultural revival. In Luanda, a movement grew up around a group of younger students, both *assimilados* and Europeans. Inspired in part by the Angolan poetry of the European Tómas Vieira da Cruz, this movement at one time named its efforts 'Discovering Angola'. In 1952, the group published a literary journal in Luanda, *Mensagem—A voz dos naturais de Angola*,[47] which published only a few numbers before it was banned by the authorities. Among the Angolan poets who edited and wrote for it were Viriato da Cruz and Mário de Andrade, later renowned as African nationalist leaders.

Vieira da Cruz was not the only European to leave a mark on Angolan letters and to discover the reality of Angola. Perhaps the most celebrated writer of Portuguese Africa (born in Mozambique but brought up in

Angola) was Fernando Monteiro de Castro Soromenho (1910–68). Spending most of his formative years in Angola as a student, labour recruiter, *chefe de posto* and journalist, he wrote about what he saw in remote eastern Angola, an area that provided the setting for much of his fictional creations. More than any other Portuguese storyteller of his generation, he was able to see Africans through realist and not ethnocentric eyes and to communicate his empathy to readers. In his writing career, he moved from a non-committal realism (*Homens sem Caminho*, 1946) to expressions of serious doubt concerning the consequences of European rule in Africa and to tragic themes of racial and cultural conflict in the Angolan context (*Terra Morta*, 1948, and *Viragem*, 1959).[48] Angolans of a younger generation who read the work of this sensitive and increasingly liberal writer were aided in their personal discoveries of the Angolan present and past.

The 'Discovering Angola' movement sought to redefine the Angolan past as well as the present. It rejected a total adherence to national Portuguese culture. Members began to research into old newspapers, pamphlets and books, and, in doing so, they rediscovered the stirrings of Angolan nationalism between 1870 and 1930 and also found a closer identification with African culture. With the new poets came a rediscovery of heritage. In the 1950s, several collections of their works were published in Lisbon,[49] as a number of the poets were attending universities in Portugal or were associated with Portuguese institutions. The Liga Nacional Africana encouraged some of the young poets and their early poems are found in its publications. The Angolan cultural revival was led by Angolan Africans and *mestiços*, although Portuguese did take part. Among the more notable poets not yet mentioned is Geraldo Bessa Vitor, with his *Ecos Dispersos* (1941), and his *Cubata Abandonada* which received the Camilo Pessanha Prize in 1957. The more militant poets, later to become nationalists, including Agostinho Neto, Viriato da Cruz and Mário de Andrade, had their influence on the movement with themes reminiscent of the 'negritude' and political protest of the French African school.

In some ways, the new cultural revival was faced with the dilemma of the *assimilado*—a spirit caught between two cultures, Portuguese and African. The offspring of such a process, however, need not be in conflict. The new poets could in some cases avoid following closely the path of either culture; they could choose a syncretic way. The cultural blendings of the new movement of the 1950s, for example, exhibited a universal spirit, a humanism that incorporated creativity and simplicity from both cultural sources.

The political aspect of the cultural revival illustrated the complexity

Angola

and difficulty of the political future of Angola within the Portuguese national orbit. Some of the most promising of the new poets went into exile in Europe or in other African territories; their militant nationalist activities came to dominate their creative efforts and few of them were producing poetry of the same quality after 1961. Within Angolan society, literary effort came under the surveillance of the government. In a brilliant effort, the Angolan novelist Luandino Vieira wrote *Luuanda*,* perhaps the first significant Angolan novel of social protest. The work received literary prizes in Angola in 1963 and a coveted award in 1965 from the Portuguese Society of Writers in Lisbon, an act that brought political repercussions and government disapproval.

In the mid-1960s a new Angolan poet of major stature emerged from the younger elements of the movement. Mário António, born in 1934 in Maquela do Zombo and educated in Dondo, Luanda and Lisbon, became a prolific poet, but also composed valuable works of research on Angolan social and intellectual history. As one of the intelligentsia who 'discovered' the cultural past of Angola, Mário António ranks today as a major literary figure. In such volumes as *Amor* (1960), *100 Poemas* (1963) and *Rosto de Europa* (1968), he shows a great range of interests and mastery of language and control. With such men of letters, the Angola of the new era could be proud of the past and confident of the future.

PEASANTS AND PROPHETS

One more background element to the 1960s remains to be discussed: African prophet and separatist religious beliefs and the peasant masses. While urbanisation, economic growth, increasing Portuguese control and influence, miscegenation, orthodox Christianisation and Western education made new inroads among some Angolans, many remained apart from this process. At least half of the Angolans were non-Christian and well over half of them remained in their rural, largely agrarian and traditional, tribal environments. In the context of all Angola, then, only a minority were Westernised to any great extent, while the majority were only partially Westernised and many of these were finding life in the towns strange and unsettling. Religious beliefs had played a vital role in traditional Angolan society and now, with the twentieth-century changes and new pressures, new hybrid religions were created by Africans to meet the challenges.

In 1958, the Portuguese authorities managed to obtain the following message, written by an Angolan prophet, Simão Toko, to his followers:

* Luuanda is the traditional Kimbundu spelling for Luanda.

152

There is no reason to fear the white man, because he has already lost the power previously given him by God. God is angry with him, because he has committed several great sins. A new Christ, a black Christ, shall come and Toko is his prophet. To him God has given the power which before he had given to the white man.

The land is ours and it was the white man who stole it. Now, we are very strong, and besides we have the help of the ancestors. Already we have occupied the north and the south; now we have only to build up churches in the east and west. Within a short time we shall command all Africa. The white shall submit to us and will become our servants. Within a short time, Simão Toko shall return as our liberator.[50]

Such a message expressed a strong belief in the future and in the power of an African prophet. Exactly what connection there was between the beliefs of the 1961 insurgents and the religious sects that espoused such messages is still unclear. That there was *some* connection cannot be doubted.

Recent prophet movements and separatist ('nativist') churches in Angola have their precursors in history. Perhaps the oldest recorded case occurred in 1704–06 in the Kongo kingdom. A Bakongo prophetess, Chimpa Vita, or Dona Beatriz, led the 'Antonian heresy',[51] preaching radical doctrines that featured black saviours and saints and urging the restoration of the Kongo kingdom to its former strength; she was captured and burned as a heretic. Another precursor movement came in 1891, in eastern Angola, when Mona N'Engana Nzambi ('Son of God'), a youth apparently afflicted with elephantiasis, was said to be divine.[52] Other African prophets, who preached more anti-Portuguese messages, arose in Bailundo (1902) and again in Kongo (1913–14), and in later cases.

One particular ethnic group and one area have traditionally spawned Angolan prophet movements and fed others: the Bakongo people and the lower Congo regions of the Belgian and French Congos. Since 1919, four African prophets, each named 'Simon', have appeared in or near Angola. All were Bakongo: one was born in northern Angola, and the other three grew up in the adjacent Congo states. Each experienced orthodox Christian mission teachings as well as the doctrines of more unorthodox sects such as Jehovah's Witnesses, the Salvation Army and Kitawala in the Belgian Congo. To some extent, each prophet's message found support in Angola. These prophets were: Simon Kimbangu (1889?–1950), born in the Belgian Congo and the most famous of the four prophets; Simon M'Padi, also born in the Belgian Congo, founder of the 'Khaki' uniform movement, and arrested in the Second World War as an agent for the Germans; Simon Zéphirin Lassy, born in 1908 in French Congo; and Simão Gonçalves Toko, who was born between 1900 and 1910 at Maquela do Zombo, northern Angola, spent at least seven years in the Belgian Congo, and in 1963 was exiled from Angola by order of the government. Emphasising Bible-reading and fetish destruction, each black prophet experienced similar calls and visions and often preached anti-European sermons. Significantly, they looked to the future for a time when there would be greater happiness for Africans.

How can the rise of these Angolan prophet movements be explained? Certainly, the Protestant missions played a role in the education of most of the African prophets, who later broke away and formed their own churches and sects. But during the period of greatest Protestant missionary expansion in Angola, 1890–1940, comparatively few prophet movements appeared. The new influences from Western civilisation in general provide a more complete explanation for this phenomenon, for the prophet movements found their greatest popular support in the areas where Portuguese and Roman Catholic influences were strongest: the towns and in the Bakongo area, where Africans early felt the weight of Christian influences. It was the Bakongo, not the more orthodox Christian Ovimbundu, who were especially receptive to the rebellious religious message and to the syncretist nature of African prophetic belief in the twentieth century. Sometimes linked to such prophet movements was the idea, reappearing like the forgotten phoenix, of the restoration of the old Kongo kingdom, now partitioned among three colonial powers. In many of the movements, leadership revolves about an extraordinary individual who claims special powers of healing and vision and who usually spent some years outside Angola. Kimbangu, M'Padi, Lassy and Toko promised an end to suffering for African masses and they offered new, messianic moorings for the drifting detribalised peoples.

The beliefs of the Angolan peasants featured the traditional past, ancestor worship and the old culture. While the new Christian missions undid some of these beliefs, much of the old culture remained in the anxieties, fears and aspirations of the Africans. This difficult transition process could produce a frustrated 'lonely African', to use Turnbull's now famous phrase.[53] As well as being a reaction to disintegrating traditions, the receptivity of the masses to the black prophet's messages was also an act of personal rebellion. The making of the prophet illustrated a similar process. Leaving behind a frustrating life in Angola in 1943, Simão Toko went to live in the Belgian Congo for seven years. In 1950 he returned to Angola, an energetic prophet now eager to spread his own personal message which clashed with his Baptist up-bringing. Of course, prophetic messages differed as did the audiences that listened to them. While Toko stressed an almost puritanical individual discipline as a means of achieving future changes, Lassy emphasised the power of holy water to destroy witchcraft.

By the 1960s the prophet movements in Angola, of which at least ten have been identified by Dos Santos,[54] had become increasingly popular. The most important, in terms of numbers and the area affected, appeared to be Tokoism. While Toko had preached anti-European ideas, he also urged personal reformism, and, after 1961, when the Portuguese authorities had him under close surveillance, he publicly asked his followers to remain loyal to Portugal. It is uncertain how much these public professions of loyalty may have meant during such a time of confusion and terror, but it is clear that the movement was then gaining rather than losing supporters. By the mid-1960s the movement had churches in many parts of Angola, chiefly in the urban areas. To the African townsman, in part uprooted from the old environment, such a futuristic message of hope had real appeal. Rather than a revival of tradition—although it contained traditional elements—the Tokoist movement spread a vision of a changed future, and it found fertile soil in Luanda and in other large urban concentrations of Africans.

It is a testimony to the strength of this particular prophet movement and its appeal to African masses that in 1963 the government felt obliged to exile its leader to the distant Azores islands. Furthermore, despite his exile, the movement has not died out but has prospered, in anticipation, perhaps, of the messiah's return. The ultimate appeal was to the masses, whose past tradition was eroding, whose present was unhappy and who resented the privileges of the new elites. To many who participated in these religious sects, the present was evil and only the millennial future and the power of the black prophet held promise.

Part Two

René Pélissier

Introduction

TRUTH is at a premium in contemporary as well as historical Portuguese Africa. One must tread warily between censorship by the antagonistic parties and a great deal of rumour.[1] There are such controversial questions as political support, prison camps within and outside Angola, military activities and casualties, to be dealt with.[2] Any study of Angolan problems must be an exercise in scepticism: one cannot rely entirely on any document, any allegedly dependable informant, any statement by the official information services of one side or the other. What is there left from which to assemble the facts? Little that is entirely indisputable; each time one seems to have unearthed an element of truth, some new information comes to light to invalidate it. The researcher's task is a thorny one.

In a Latin country such as Portugal and in a part of Africa like Angola, verbiage proliferates but is rarely applied to the letter. Hence weight will be given to a law, a party programme or a speech only if the author has personally been able to observe that it has had some effect on the ground. In any case, in a country where it is the exception for anyone, black or white, to speak freely to a foreigner without trying to preach the government or party line, one cannot hope to attain a level of authenticity comparable with that in a country where information is free. So, in good faith but with no illusions as to the paucity of the information available, the reader is offered a middle-of-the-road account of events which later historians with access to the archives will invalidate or confirm. This is but an introduction to a far wider task now in progress.

7. The Political Confrontation before 1961

The history of the modern revolutionary process in Angola will never be accurately written—most of it is hidden in administrative and police records and not everything is even written here.
António de Figueiredo,
Portugal and its Empire: The Truth, London 1961.

BEFORE THE outbreak of disturbances in 1961, several parties or political groups were clandestinely active. All movements whose overt or tacit aim was termination of Portuguese rule in Angola were, of course, banned and harried by the police. Only two paths were open to them: to stay in the country and create an underground network; or to carry on the political struggle abroad. The former were almost all penetrated by the Polícia Internacional e de Defesa do Estado (PIDE),* whose efficiency was and remains implacable. Meanwhile, those leaders who stayed in Europe, or Guinea, Ghana or the Belgian Congo, found their activity diminished or invalidated by their very remoteness from Angola. Their movements were characterised by weakness of organisation, resources, membership and leadership.

This weakness is easily accounted for. Whatever the attraction of nationalist ideals for the mass of the people, they were before 1961 ill-equipped for a political struggle and even more so for a military one. Ethnically they were divided, as everywhere else in Africa, but in Portuguese Africa there were certain special features. 1. The gulf between *assimilados* and *indígenas* introduced a new divisive factor, for their objectives were not always the same. 2. The role of the *mestiços* was often ambiguous, for their emotions pulled them towards now one civilisation, now the other, and even their ambitions, usually frustrated, could tug in divergent directions. 3. A small white minority with Marxist leanings or affiliations was active among some political groups, including *assimilados*. 4. A far larger section of the white community was autonomist in that its members wanted to break away from the control of Lisbon, but exclusively for the benefit of their own

* On November 18, 1969, by a decision of the Portuguese Council of Ministers, the PIDE became known as the General Directorate of Security within the Ministry of the Interior.

community. So there was a white anti-nationalist, anti-African movement seeking to perpetuate the colonial regime within the country but
with external autonomy. 5. Sociologically, African nationalism represented a servants' revolt against the white masters, but, although the
former had some white supporters, they had no Spartacus of their own
colour. And that was the rub: the lack of black African leaders was all
too obvious; it stemmed from the absence of a sufficiently large and
active new elite to run the movement. The traditional leaders were not
intellectually trained to direct other than a tribal revolt. 6. Potential
leaders existed before 1961: the African ministers and catechists of the
foreign Protestant mission churches. In their own churches, they were
accustomed to a more democratic administrative system than that of
the Catholic church, but they were to engage wholeheartedly in the
struggle only when they became the target of police repression; and by
then it was too late for them to take the lead of the dislocated nationalist
networks. Thus, at the start, the political struggle was heavily weighted
between the whites, masters of every method of repression, and the
mestiços and Africans contesting their rule. 7. In Angola, the rural
populace was passive unless some leader (*chefe do povo*), often a
Protestant, managed to carry with him a nucleus of the faithful. Given
these seven factors, for the nationalists who had stayed in Angola, the
outlook for armed rebellion before 1961 was bleak.

There were two main currents within Angolan nationalism before
1961: the modernists, subject to a definite Marxist influence; and the
ethno-nationalists, who were far more powerful since they had a
limited but secure tribal base in the ancient kingdom of the Kongo.

The Modernists

The modernists were formed in the towns, where the opportunities for
education enabled a tiny Angolan elite to come to the fore. Their cells
contained a strong proportion of *assimilados* and *mestiços* in contact with
Portuguese liberals or Marxists. The towns bred the germs of clandestine nationalism, especially Luanda and Malanje and the up-country
towns of the Cuanza corridor: Catete, Dondo, Salazar and Cacuso, for
example. This is Mbundu territory. Agents of the opposition were
thicker on the ground here than anywhere else: *Ambaquistas*, black
African Methodist ministers and catechists, *mestiços* and black African
Catholic priests and catechists. Moreover, there was every possible
form of urban friction, since competition between the poor whites and
the few qualified Angolans intensified ill-feeling. The presence of large
shanty towns in Luanda, the *muceques*, gave the leaders an opportunity

161

to work on a detribalised, alienated populace very receptive to words of protest. South of the Luanda-Malange line was another urban axis, similarly open for the growth of nationalism. It ran parallel to the first line, across Ovimbundu country, roughly from Lobito-Benguela to Silva Porto, via Nova Lisboa. A few outlying centres prolonged the line towards Mossamedes* and Sá da Bandeira but the backward state of the southern rural population precluded any hope of a development comparable with that in the central and northern districts.

In sketching the background one also defines the limits to which modern nationalism could aspire. This nationalism, with its pretentions to be pan-Angolan—that is, anti-tribalist—remained in most cases an elite and urban phenomenon,† lacking the support of the great rural masses without which any national uprising in Angola was doomed to failure. From the start, the obstacles were formidable. The movement inevitably arose in the towns, among the elite and the detribalised, under the eye of the police who could strike hard to prevent it building an organisation in the centres of white concentration and greatest strength.

The recent origins of this nationalism are obscure. It seems that the Portuguese Communist Party succeeded in infiltrating the authorised organisations open to Africans, notably the Liga Nacional Africana—LNA (African National League) and the Associação Regional dos Naturais de Angola—ANANGOLA (Regional Association of Angolan Nationals). There it recruited a few members or fellow-travellers, survivors of pre-war nationalist movements and young *assimilados* with literary interests of a nationalist bent. This is an important point: the Portuguese Communist Party did not create nationalism—this existed long before—but it provided leaders, methods and probably resources for the movement at a time when it was but a latent tendency, devoid of any means of expression due to suppression before and during the Second World War. From 1948 on, according to a Portuguese Salazarist writer,[1] there were three movements or clandestine groups: the Comité Federal Angolano do PCP (Angolan Federal Committee of the Portuguese Communist Party); Angola Negra (Black Angola); and the Comissão de Luta das Juventudes Contra o Imperialismo Colonial em Angola (Youth Struggle Committee against Colonial Imperialism in Angola). They concentrated on finding militants among the young *assimilados* and *mestiços* in Angola or studying in Portugal. They also widened the gap between

* Today, the town's name is spelt Moçâmedes, but the former spelling is retained in the text to avoid confusion.

† Except, that is, for a few places in the Mbundu area: around Catete and in part of the Dembos, for example.

members of the official associations dithering between a comfortable apolitical line and a dangerous participation involving loss of their economic positions. In 1952, these three clandestine organisations were reported to have combined to form the Conselho de Libertação de Angola (Angolan Council of Liberation). In 1954, the Associação Africana do Sul de Angola (South Angola African Association) was formed in Nova Lisboa by the Ovimbundu railwaymen of central Angola. Its formation was permitted by the authorities but it seems, nevertheless, to have had nationalist interests. Finally, in October 1955, the Partido Comunista de Angola—PCA (Angolan Communist Party) appeared in Luanda in the strictest clandestinity. It was probably a successor of the Conselho de Libertação. Despite affirmations to the contrary, it was not particularly active among the *muceques* of Luanda since police supervision in the capital was too efficient. Moreover, its best known leaders were in exile in Europe (for example, the *mestiço* poet Mário de Andrade) or in prison in Portugal (like the black African poet and doctor Agostinho Neto). The Angolan Communist Party was weak, and its Communist façade may have alienated African nationalists allergic to Moscow.

A new party appeared at the beginning of 1956 (or perhaps 1953),[2] the Partido da Luta Unida dos Africanos de Angola—PLUA (African United Struggle Party of Angola), which reassembled the young Marxists of the Angolan Communist Party, whose creature it seems to have been. The Partido da Luta Unida had only a brief existence as a distinct organisation for, in December 1956, it joined with other lesser-known clandestine organisations to form the Movimento Popular de Libertação de Angola—MPLA (Angolan Popular Liberation Movement). These young Marxist intellectuals pursued a policy of frontal attack; in December 1956 they published their first manifesto under cover of the MPLA. The PIDE tracked them down and Viriato Francisco Clemente da Cruz (secretary-general of the MPLA) fled to France to join Mário de Andrade. Out of reach of the Portuguese police, they were able to express their views freely and to create in exile an anti-colonialist movement (Movimento Anticolonialista—MAC), with representatives of some of the nationalist movements of Portuguese Guinea, Cape Verde, Mozambique and São Tomé. In Angola, the MPLA cells pursued their activities mainly among the *assimilados*, and penetrated certain Catholic *mestiço* circles, thanks to the work of Mário de Andrade's brother, the Reverend Joaquim da Rocha Pinto de Andrade.

The elections for the Portuguese presidency in May 1958 caused a considerable stir among the white electorate, and also among the *assimilados* and *mestiços* who had the right to vote. Towards the end of 1958, a handful of white intellectuals created a Movimento de

Libertação Nacional—MLN (National Liberation Movement) alongside the MPLA. These elections, which were open only to the *civilizados*,* seem to have provoked a political awakening among those Africans capable of expressing their dissatisfaction. An African organisation with no white members was formed: the Movimento de Libertação de Angola—MLA (Angolan Liberation Movement). These two groups were as impotent as the MPLA, and they decided to unite in a Movimento de Libertação Nacional de Angola—MLNA (National Angolan Liberation Movement), which may correspond to the Movimento de Independência Nacional de Angola—MINA (Angolan National Independence Movement). They were betrayed and their networks were swept by a wave of arrests in March 1959 and again in May 1959. These were followed by numerous arrests in July 1959, which also struck the leadership of the MPLA. By working up through the networks, the PIDE succeeded in shattering the organised progress of these rival cells, all of which were striving towards the same goal of independence. The situation must have seemed worrying to the Luanda authorities which, at an undetermined date, detected also a Movimento para a Independência de Angola—MPIA (Angolan Independence Movement), with cells in Luanda, Benguela, Malanje and elsewhere—not to mention the many supporters of Angolan nationalist movements in Portugal itself. Indeed, it seems that in the summer of 1959, notwithstanding multi-racialist and assimilation policies which should be the logical negation of Angolan nationalism, something came unstuck in the groundplan of Portuguese colonisation. Education and city life, far from producing Portuguese with black skins, were spawning malcontents who used their modern skills to deny allegiance to Portugal and proclaim it to Angola. All the same, one must not exaggerate the force of these micro-movements. Often they had only a few hundred, or even a few dozen, members, whose fear of the PIDE and its reputation relegated them to a more or less passive role. The masses were not roused, even in the *muceques*.

The great round-ups of 1959 were significant in that they deprived the modern nationalist movements of their main local leaders. The MPLA leaders in exile tried to compensate for their weakness in Angola by intensive political agitation. In January 1960, the Movimento Anti-colonialista became the Frente Revolucionária Africana para a Independência Nacional das Colónias Portuguesas—FRAIN (African Revolutionary Front for the National Independence of the Portuguese Colonies). At that time, one hears of a little-known *mestiço* leader who remained in the background until the late 1960s but is now perhaps the most active

* i.e., Portuguese residents, *assimilados* and *mestiços*.

and important MPLA leader: Lucio Lara. He opened an office in Conakry for the Frente Revolucionária (in fact, the MPLA), whence he tried to direct their few cells disabled by the PIDE.

These few leaders mastered the techniques of modern information methods and, taking advantage of the help of socialist countries and progressive supporters, they tried to mount a propaganda campaign in Western Europe against Portugal. Their most successful effort was on the occasion of the 'Trial of the Fifty Accused' (in fact, there were fifty-seven),[3] arrested in the 1959 round-ups or tried in absentia. But Salazar was not to be deflected from his policy by the pleas of the MPLA from Conakry. On June 20, 1960, he gave his reply: 'Portugal will never agree to discuss self-determination for its overseas territories.' In Angola, Agostinho Neto was arrested on June 8 and Father Pinto de Andrade on June 25. Local MPLA leaders roused the people in Neto's home village to demand his liberation. The troops opened fire on them at Catete and were reported to have killed thirty and injured about two hundred. This was the first known sign—although others may have occurred previously—that repression by the military was replacing that of the police before the outbreak of disturbances. They were not townsmen who fell forty miles from Luanda, but countryfolk from the cotton area.

The trials of members of the networks, arrested in 1959, began in Luanda in August 1960. A tremor ran through the *muceques* but, although there may now have been plenty of Africans determined to rise, they lacked weapons and, above all, leaders. The MPLA branch abroad continued in November 1960 its fruitless quest for unity with the ethno-nationalist parties of Léopoldville, but quarrelled with the outstanding leader—Holden Roberto—of another exile group, the Angolan Bakongo politically active in the independent Congo. Orders from Conakry were delivered in Angola with difficulty and there was almost no one left to carry them out. Most of the urban clandestine movements were decapitated by the arrests of 1959 and 1960. The towns were now capable only of convulsive tremors; they were no longer a promising terrain for a general uprising. Fear had become the common denominator of the party cells, around which the police net was closing, thanks to mounting denunciations.[4] From this time onwards, the Luanda cells, weakened and largely cut off from their leaders abroad, threw themselves into an improvised and suicidal operation doomed to failure, but the repercussions of which are still felt today: an urban insurrection at the heart of the strongest bastion* of the white

* *Baluarte* is the Portuguese expression, with very much the same connotations as the Afrikaans *laager*.

community. It sufficed to alert international opinion, but was inadequate to launch revolt throughout Angola, for lack of reliable rural bases.

THE ETHNO-NATIONALISTS

The ethno-nationalists themselves generally reject the description, which smacks too much of tribalism. All the same, their origins and relative strength lay in their powerful influence among the rural populations of the Bakongo region of Angola, a region that had many advantages for a nationalist struggle. Historically, it was the cradle of the ancient Kongo, with the psychological force deriving from memories of that kingdom and its southern marches (the Dembos). Geographically, it lay on the frontier of Congo-Kinshasa, which gained independence from Belgium on June 30, 1960. Ethnically, although divided into tribes, the Bakongo were a sufficiently large element in Angola (numbering 621,787 *indigenas* in 1960) to be able to raise troops. Economically, thanks to the cultivation of coffee, the Bakongo enjoyed a relatively high income by comparison with other Angolans outside the towns. In the field of religion, Baptist missions had created a slender elite of educated leaders, and welded significant sectors of the population behind the Bible. Topographically, the terrain is undulating, cut by rivers; in some places forests and jungles offer a refuge for partisans. Nowhere else was there such a mass of conditions favourable to warfare, except perhaps in the Dembos area, the people of which, partly Kimbundu-speaking, have always had a strong attachment to independence. So it was no coincidence that a flame of revolt broke out among the Bakongo and the Dembos which is still alight. But the fact that it did not ignite revolt anywhere else in Angola—before the guerrilla operations of the MPLA and the União Nacional para a Independência Total de Angola—UNITA (National Union for Total Independence of Angola) in the east in 1966—is clear indication of its tribal, and not national, character. It was indeed an expression of nationalism, but by a small fraction of the Angolan people (about 15 per cent in 1960, probably less than 8 per cent in 1970 after the exodus of refugees to Congo-Kinshasa and the losses of 1961).

Although active ethno-nationalism was essentially limited to frontier areas and only secondarily involved the major ethnic group of Angola, the Ovimbundu, or the major part of the Mbundu and southern and eastern tribes, before 1961 it was far more dangerous in the short term to the Portuguese than the pan-Angolan nationalist movements whose cells were fairly easily eradicated by the PIDE. In the bush, heads of posts and administrators were responsible for native politics and supervision of loyalty. Although the Portuguese had their informers, they were up against the physical impossibility of close control over their districts. Three or four *cipaios* (rural guards), not even always Bakongo or Dembos, were not enough to prevent political agitation in a post, especially where a largely 'open' frontier facilitated the despatch of emissaries from Léopoldville (Kinshasa).* So the Bakongo nationalists were able to prepare their assaults with virtually no loss of militant leaders and without ever being separated from their followers. In this, they had an obvious advantage over the MPLA. On the other hand, with the exception of the educated Baptists among them, they were short of top leaders capable of directing a well-planned campaign to be executed by the middle ranks.

Just as their intellectual urban rivals were rent by quarrels over ideology, personalities and tactics, so the ethno-nationalists fell prey to tribal and religious dissension. The peripheral irredentists, aiming not at an independent state of Angola but merely to end Portuguese rule over a part of their tribal territory cut off by colonial frontiers, will be dealt with first. Among the groups with some Angolan members were at least three Congolese organisations: the Abako group; the Parti de la Solidarité Africaine—PSA (African Solidarity Party); and the Association des Tchokwe du Congo, d'Angola et de Rhodésie—ATCAR. The Angolan Chokwe living in Northern Rhodesia founded a self-help association that was to pave the way for future ethnic claims encompassing all Chokweland. Similarly, in southern Angola the Ovamboland Peoples' Organisation (OPO), founded in 1959, which was to become the South West African Peoples' Organisation (SWAPO), demanded reunion of Angolan Ovambo with their brothers to the south. Their influence was not a serious threat to Portuguese control.

More important were the rather obscure movements that emerged within the most populous ethnic group in Angola, the Ovimbundu. With more than 1,750,000 out of an Angolan total of over 4,560,000 *indígenas* in 1960, they were (and are) the pivotal segment of the black inhabitants of Angola. Their ethnic area has the double advantage of containing great urban centres, such as Lobito-Benguela and Nova Lisboa, and Protestant and Catholic missions scattered over the plateau. They had some modern African elites but their efforts to rebel against Portuguese rule were largely unsuccessful before 1961. Ovimbundu

---

* For instance, the Congo district in 1960 was about 37,000 square miles in area and had fourteen *concelhos* or *circunscrições* and thirty-seven posts: an average of 725 square miles per administrative division. This inevitably meant that posts were dozens of miles apart, enabling anyone to cross the international frontier without formalities.

nationalism does not seem to have had the same impact on the rural masses as Bakongo movements or even the Mbundu-oriented MPLA. However, some secret societies did emerge around reduced nuclei of Catholic- and Protestant-educated young scholars. Most significant were the Juventude Cristã de Angola (Christian Youth of Angola) and various Protestant cells, such as the Grupo Avante, Grupo Ohio, the Organizacão Cultural dos Angolanos (Cultural Organisation of Angolans) and others. But, violently repressed by the police and far from welcoming foreign sanctuaries, the Ovimbundu nationalists as a whole could be considered no more than a minor nuisance by the Portuguese authorities. Their influence will be really felt years after the 1961 outbreak of violence. While some survivors from pre-1961 clandestine cells will move towards the modernist pan-Angolan MPLA, others will dig in among their fellow Ovimbundu to evolve an Ovimbundu branch of nationalism comparable to the Kongo one.

The really important segment of Angolan ethno-nationalism before 1960 was Kongo, with its Cabindan appendix. The Cabindans were not numerous (some 56,000 in 1960); they were separated from the rest of Angola, and both intellectually and materially they were better treated by the Portuguese than their brother Bakongo. Some of their leaders dreamt of independence for the ancient kingdom of Ngoio. Theirs was a micro-nationalism, encouraged from time to time by Congo-Brazzaville. They were not dangerous to the Portuguese since their protest was mainly verbal. Their principal organisation was the Movimento de Libertação do Enclave de Cabinda—MLEC (Cabinda Enclave Liberation Movement), headed by Luis Ranque Franque. Before 1961, there was also the União Social dos Maiombes de Luali (Mayombe Social Union of Luali), the Alliance du Mayombe— ALLIAMA (Mayombe Alliance) and the Comunidade Cabindense— COMCABI (Cabindan Community). All were in exile and lacked leaders, although a few traditional chiefs supported them.

The Bakongo nationalist movement south of the Congo river was much more important and the only group of its kind to receive aid and subsidies from countries outside Africa. Before 1961, it consisted of two elements: the 'hawks', the União das Populações de Angola—UPA (Union of Angolan Peoples), which had difficulty in breaking away from its initial tribalism; and a cluster of small groups suffering from the lack of even moderately competent leaders, and all inclined to seek illusory collaboration with the Portuguese. The most archaic in aspiration were the Catholic monarchists of the Ngwizani a Kongo, or Ngwizako group. Their only real interest was in restoring the kingdom of Kongo under a Catholic king. Their candidate for the throne, vacant since the death of Dom António III in 1957, was their president, José dos Santos Kasakanga, in exile in Léopoldville. The Portuguese were in no hurry to find a successor on account of the political repercussions that might have ensued, but, just before the outbreak of disturbances, they seem to have come to an agreement with the Ngwizako that the throne of São Salvador should be occupied by a Catholic. The coronation was planned for February 17, 1961.[5] The chief preoccupation of the Portuguese was to avoid the election of a Baptist king. This they achieved and thus thwarted the original plans of the only organisation genuinely determined to attack them militarily: the UPA.

The UPA was originally a modest tribal association of Angolan Bakongo, and more precisely Baxikongo (28·63 per cent of the Angolan Bakongo in 1959), whose leaders were both Baptists and royalists. While the Ngwizako had their Catholic pretender, their Protestant rivals were, from 1954 (or 1957),[6] grouped under the banner of the União das Populações do Norte de Angola—UPNA (North Angola Peoples' Union) whose president was Barros Nekaka, who had favoured the Protestant candidate, Manuel Kiditu, for the royal election of 1955 after the death of King Dom Pedro VII. It was the Catholic candidate, Dom António III, who was elected with the help of the Portuguese administration. He reigned from 1955 to 1957; during this time, he had to cope with an attempt at his deposition organised by royalist Bakongo from the Belgian Congo, known as the Kongo Palaver (1955–56). Barros Nekaka was the maternal uncle of a young clerk in the Belgian administration, born in Angola but brought up in the Belgian Congo: his name was Holden Roberto. The Portuguese authorities blocked the election of a new king of the Kongo from 1957 to 1962. They thereby obstructed the residual monarchist aspirations of the UPNA, which was unable to go any further in that direction under the combined eye of the Belgian administration and the Portuguese police. The UPNA turned to a more modern and more ambitious claim. In 1958, this organisation, whose relations with the American Committee on Africa gave it an international opening that strengthened its contacts with the Baptist Church, announced that it was no longer interested in winning the throne of São Salvador and restoring the Kongo monarchy. It now entered a pan-Angolan phase without losing its tribal ascendancy over the Baxikongo living in Léopoldville.

Consistently with this new orientation, the UPNA dropped the 'Norte' from its title and became the União das Populações de Angola—UPA. From 1958 onward, Holden Roberto took the ascendant over his uncle. The UPA sent the young man abroad to widen his education and to denounce Portugal before world opinion. Henceforward his personality

169

was indissolubly linked with UPA policy, which he guided and finally incarnated. He had several advantages over the other leaders of Angolan ethno-nationalist movements, who were eking out a living in the African quarters of Léopoldville. He was a Protestant, spoke English and was in contact with such distinguished anti-colonialist leaders of his day as Lumumba, Bourguiba, Nkrumah, George Padmore, Frantz Fanon and the Algerian FLN. He was based either in Accra or Léopoldville, out of reach of the Portuguese. Travelling widely, he was broadening his still modest education and learning the rudiments of organising a party with pretentions to modernity. He received subsidies and advice from a variety of sources with differing motivations.

There were, on the other hand, certain weaknesses in Holden Roberto's position as the new leader of the UPA. Since he had spent practically his whole life in exile in the Belgian Congo, the only Portuguese he had known were tradesmen: smart maybe, but peaceful. He therefore had no fear of them, but he also had little knowledge of them. His assumption that the psychology of the Portuguese settlers was the same as that of the Belgians was to lead to a serious tactical error. Furthermore, he made enemies among the itinerant emissaries of the MPLA who frequented international anti-colonialist conferences and regarded him as a dangerous rival. At Tunis in January 1960, he refused to join the Frente Revolucionária (FRAIN) which Viriato da Cruz and Lucio Lara had just formed to achieve independence for all the Portuguese colonies. They were divided on many points. The MPLA people were left-wing intellectuals, steeped to the marrow in Portuguese culture for all that they denied this; *mestiços* for the most part, their points of reference included Lisbon as well as Moscow and Paris. Holden Roberto, who alone constituted the UPA abroad, was Angolan by chance, and the poles of attraction for him were São Salvador, Léopoldville, Brussels and New York. There was manifestly a wide gulf separating the bright Marxist poets from the former clerk shaped in the Baptist tradition and the Belgian colonial mould.

Within Angola, UPA agents distributed leaflets and contacted the *sobas* (native chiefs). But the real propaganda effort among the masses began only after Holden's return to Léopoldville, following the independence of the Congo. He broadcast over Radio Léopoldville, edited a newspaper, threatened the Portuguese settlers and loyal *sobas* and made many promises for fulfilment after independence. And in Angola itself? He seems to have invoked all the grievances of the population of Congo district. The slogans were simple: the white man has stolen the black man's land; he grows rich by making the black man work in the coffee plantations; he beats him and treats him as a child; but the Golden Age will dawn after independence when everything belonging to the settlers will go to the native population. The Portuguese administration was alerted to this fermentation that was spreading particularly among the Baxikongo and in districts where the white coffee planters were particularly oppressive: the Dembos.

Holden Roberto felt confident. Before his eyes he was witnessing the sudden collapse of Belgian colonisation. He demanded negotiations with the Portuguese government on June 9, 1960, but, given Lisbon's traditional policy, his request was naturally refused. It was unthinkable for Salazar's government to deal with movements that it considered subversive, unrepresentative and foreign. This was one of the tenets of Portuguese policy. According to Lisbon, the exiles in Léopoldville were nothing more nor less than 'foreign opportunists'. Both sides refused to compromise and they moved towards armed combat. In Léopoldville, now capital of an independent country, Roberto became more exigent, bought a few arms and prepared for armed insurrection south of the frontier. Did he make this capital decision himself, or did his 'advisers' urge it on him? Whatever the case may be, the central committee of the UPA burst asunder in 1960. The moderates, under the leadership of J. P. Bala, withdrew, accusing Roberto of nepotism and extremism. They were mostly Bazombo opposed to the Baxikongo followers of Roberto and his uncle. J. P. Bala thereupon formed the Movimento de Defesa dos Interesses de Angola—MDIA (Movement for the Defence of Angolan Interests), which soon came within the Portuguese orbit. The UPA, purged of waverers, looked like the party best placed to act concretely, now that the MPLA had lost its local leaders. However, a glance at the map will show that its hold on the bush was still limited to northern Angola, with some infiltration along the Cuanza river, in Luanda and possibly east of Malanje. It was a rural party whose strength was mostly restricted to Kikongo-speaking districts (and not even all of them, for the eastern Portuguese Congo showed no inclination at the outset to rebel); it hardly touched the centre of the country and the south not at all. In short, it was to act as though the Bakongo area was the whole of Angola.

The other Kongolese associations and movements in Léopoldville were weak. Besides Ngwizako, there was the Aliança dos Naturais do Zombo—ALIAZO (Alliance of Zombo Natives), consisting of peaceful Bazombo tradesmen. Founded in 1956, it is typical of the tribal self-help organisations that proliferated in Léopoldville. At the end of 1960, the Nto-Bako movement, an alleged creation of the Congolese Abako, was founded, under the leadership of Angelino Alberto. It was to act as intermediary between the Portuguese and the distant refugees. There were a few other tribal organisations, such as the Associação dos Bassorongos (Bassorongo Association). But the main point is that all these groups were even weaker than the UPA and that all favoured negotiation since they had no power to put pressure on the Portuguese.

It seems that the UPA decided on armed combat before the departure of those who were to form the MDIA—that is, in December 1960.

8. The Armed Revolt of 1961

> While we were in this distress we received an account that the viceroy of the Indies had fitted out a powerful fleet against the King of Mombasa, who, having thrown off the authority of the Portuguese, had killed the governor of the fortress, and had since committed many acts of cruelty.
>
> Father Jerónimo Lobo (1596–1678),
> *A Voyage to Abyssinia*, translated by
> Samuel Johnson, London 1735.

THE YEAR 1961 was one of reckoning in Angola, the pivot of the country's recent history. It was to shake the Portuguese out of their lethargy and dreams, to awaken unfulfilled hopes in the Africans and to bring down on a whole racial group, the Bakongo, and on a good proportion of their neighbours, the Mbundu, as well as on other *assimilado* cadres, the horrors of war and repression. For the Portuguese, it marked the end of colonial tranquillity; for Africans, the beginning of an ordeal. For all it was the year of terror.

It is useful, first, to expose certain errors. The Portuguese were not taken totally unawares by the events themselves; what caught them off guard was the racial massacre that followed in the north. It was not the rebellion, but its intensity, its suddenness and its bestiality, which nearly brought about their loss of Angola. The settlers were expecting trouble,[1] as is shown by their arming: in 1959, Angola imported 156 tons of arms and ammunition; in 1960, 953 tons (six times as much); while, in 1961, this dropped to 424 tons and, in 1962, to 145 tons. It was certainly not to hunt elephants but to resist the Africans if they were to rebel that the Portuguese stocked their arsenals. But, in spite of the threat from within and without, Angola in 1960 was, militarily speaking, a no-man's-land. Even allowing for reinforcements (denied by Portuguese sources), it can be estimated that on the Portuguese side there were only 15,000 to 20,000 whites, *mestiços* and Africans in the army or para-military organisations: a derisory force to hold a country that might break into simultaneous, nation-wide revolt. It must not be forgotten that, if Angola failed to achieve independence by armed revolt in 1961, it was because only a small minority of its peoples and elite dared to demonstrate anti-Portuguese feelings. Whether through fear, lack of interest, ignorance, incompetence or loyalty, the peoples to the south of the Cuanza hardly budged; if only the nationalist chiefs had found there as favourable a terrain as they did in the north, it is virtually certain that the Portuguese would have been swept from Angola, or at the least confined to their strongholds along the coast.

THE BAIXA DE CASSANGE 'COTTON REVOLT'

The Baixa revolt is the least known yet most comprehensible of all the rebellions of 1960–61. It was an act of defiance against the system of obligatory cotton cultivation for which Cotonang, a monopolist company, had the concession in the region east of Malanje. Censorship was such that it is not known precisely when and where the revolt started. The causes were numerous: the local population was forced to cultivate cotton, to the exclusion of foodstuffs, in certain areas; the 31,652 producers of the Malange district were obliged to sell their whole crop at a price fixed by the government well below that of the world market; east of Malange there was a veritable 'cottonocracy' that relegated the rural African to the role of being merely a provider for the company. The annual income of an *indígena* family under this regime in 1959–60 was $20 to $30. This can justifiably be called exploitation; it was, indeed, denounced as such by some members of the Portuguese administration.

It is possible that leaflets from the MPLA cells in Malange reached the Baixa. There was also the messianic agitation by and the influence of the Congolese Parti de la Solidarité Africaine, and possibly UPA emissaries. In November-December 1960 the producers of this remote hinterland stopped work and refused to pay taxes. The Portuguese army carried out intimidatory manoeuvres around January 1961. The Africans attacked several shops, at least one administrative post and a Catholic mission. The rebels believed that they were invulnerable to bullets. A repression began, the degree of which is difficult to gauge, but there were certainly summary executions and bombardment with napalm. Estimates of deaths vary between several dozen (Portuguese sources) and 10,000 (nationalist sources.) It was a massacre of a population armed with *catanas* and *canhangulos** rather than a military operation. The government administrator of the Malange district, a Cape Verdian, reportedly recognised that the revolt was justified. It is not known for certain if it was aided by some leaders who escaped from Luanda after February 1961, but it seems probable that politics

---

* A *catana* is a kind of bushknife used for clearing dense vegetation. The *canhangulo* is a home-made gun: at times, a length of water-piping mounted on a rough stock and loaded with nails and bits of metal.

entered little into this affair. The disturbance was over by early March with the capture of a self-appointed prophet, António Mariano. This was a rebellion of poverty; it failed because the rebels lacked arms and leaders and support from neighbouring tribes. But it was a precursor of the events of March 1961.

An Attempt at Urban Revolt and its Consequences

The MPLA dates the start of what it calls 'the national revolution' as February 4, 1961. This is convenient, but it is not absolutely certain that the MPLA was the only organisation involved in these events. Indeed, police pressure on the *muceques* of Luanda intensified at the beginning of 1961. Many prisoners were forced to talk by the PIDE, the political cells saw their members at liberty melt away to swell the number in the prison of São Paulo, in the Casa de Reclusão Militar and in other hastily-equipped detention centres. The real motives and authors of the rebellion are still unknown. Was it an attempted coup d'état aiming at the centres of control (the governor's palace) and information (Radio Angola), or merely an attempt to release the leaders in prison? Or was there an agreement between the white opposition to Salazar and the modern nationalists? A combination of the three is probable. Whatever the case, it looks like a commando suicide action. Small groups of Africans (drugged, according to the Portuguese), about 80 to 180 in all, attacked on the night of February 3–4 a police patrol, the prison of São Paulo, the Casa de Reclusão Militar, a police barracks and the radio station. Everywhere they were repelled, leaving dead, wounded and prisoners behind them. On February 4, an armed white militia was formed in Luanda. The following day, Sunday, at the official funeral of seven police and soldiers in the presence of the Governor-General, Dr Silva Tavares, in the Luanda cemetery, there was a massacre of Africans (inoffensive onlookers according to the nationalists, armed terrorists according to the Portuguese); this reportedly degenerated into a bloody butchery of Africans in the *muceques* by the infuriated whites. No one has yet given a clear and impartial explanation of these events. One can only say that it was a racial massacre, the number of whose victims is not known.

The consequences were tragic. There is no doubt that, in the following days, round-ups by the police, army and militia, leading to summary executions, liquidated a fair number of the nationalists and probably many more innocent civilians. Unfortunately for Portuguese propaganda, numerous foreign journalists were in Luanda at the time, waiting for the *Santa Maria* which had been captured by Henrique Galvão.

This Portuguese luxury liner had been hijacked in the West Indies on January 22, 1961, to arouse world public opinion against Salazar's policies, and possibly also to land commandos in Angola. It never succeeded in coming within thousands of miles of Angola, but the disturbances in Luanda were deliberately sparked off at this moment to attract international publicity. It is not known whether local MPLA leaders, members of the European opposition or some other leaders gave the order. Tactically the operation was doomed in advance (unless they had expected support which did not materialise) but psychologically victory was complete. The populace was committed to react according to race: mutual fear and racial hatred took possession of both black and white communities, the position of the *mestiços* being the most vulnerable. The UPA seems to have played a minimal part (if any) in the attacks of February 3-4, and in those of February 10 in which some seventy men tried a second time to take the administrative post of São Paulo, an assault that became, according to some, a veritable slaughter. Luanda was a city of terror and sleepless nights. Africans no longer dared to enter the white areas for fear of being arrested or assaulted. The Governor-General was probably overwhelmed by the white extremists and some military chiefs who wanted to settle the nationalist question by a reign of terror. There are some parallels with the attitude of the French community in Algeria, faced with the rising tide of nationalism. In Luanda in February 1961, the Portuguese were faced with a population which not only lacked arms but was also little inclined to die. Many fled into the bush. Some escaped to the Dembos. Luanda did not rise en masse. A good number of Africans left, and also the rich whites, who began to retire to Portugal. As in Algeria, it was poor whites who stayed, and they were the most savage. Moreover, they were armed and determined to take the law into their own hands. The attacks were a provocation to them and also a warning for the future. Persecution of the African elite began on a larger scale.

At that time, however, the bush had not yet stirred, although some accounts suggest it was disturbed. The MPLA high command at Conakry virtually lost contact with its networks, or rather with the survivors. In Luanda, it had no more men willing to sacrifice themselves and only a few areas of influence where a 'native son' had a following (Neto in the Catete region), or where there lived an African minister who supported the MPLA (the Reverend Domingos da Silva in some parts of the Dembos). Apart from the Congo district and the Cuanza valley, there were no rural areas ready to follow party orders because, south of the Cuanza, there were no ethno-nationalist parties with mature plans for a rebellion co-ordinated with their northern competitors. This was the greatest handicap.

THE CONGO INSURRECTION OF MARCH 1961

At this distance of time, the Congo insurrection could be called a caricature of a successful nationalist revolt. There were nine cardinal errors in the assessment of the situation. 1. There is no indication that the tensions and conditions of the African rural populace were such that an explosion was inevitable, as in Baixa de Cassange. If the Kongo tribesman thought himself too ill-treated or exploited, he could always cross over into the Congo. 2. Tension was high only where there were European planters, and their presence weighed heavily on only a small fraction of the district. 3. It was not a spontaneous revolt against poverty as was claimed, but a series of operations organised by the UPA, inadequately agreed, but nevertheless prepared in advance. 4. It seems that the plan of attack was put into action too early. Possibly the UPA feared it would be outstripped by the MPLA; possibly it was advised to act quickly in order to take advantage of the fact that the Angolan question was before the United Nations Security Council. In any case, the date of the uprising seems to have been fixed several weeks in advance. 5. The tactics were at fault: if it were to succeed, the massacre and mutilation of Europeans should have been carried out in two or three days at the most, and on sufficiently wide a scale (4,000 to 5,000 at least)[2] to cause general panic among Europeans in Angola. 6. The UPA never grasped that it was fighting Portuguese and not Belgians. It was not up against Northern Europeans, prepared to pack their baggage, but against Latins who were poor, extremely tough and with no place to retire to back home. It had to contend with people who were of peasant origin, who had fled from poverty at home and now had their backs to the wall; they were armed and ready to defend themselves, careless of world opinion (of which in any case they had no knowledge, because of the censorship). When the UPA partisans left Congo-Léopoldville and entered Angola, they left twentieth-century white civilisation for a narrow world with a white community belonging to the nineteenth century and still reacting in many ways like the pioneers of the Far West, or of Rhodesia at the beginning of this century, or of South America in the seventeenth century. In 1961, northern Angola was still a frontier. To overcome force, one needs superior force and quickness of action. Both were lacking on the UPA side; failure to realise this was its capital mistake.

7. The UPA was an organisation directed by the Bakongo, exerting a

notable influence among them alone. It still smacked of the tribal origins of the former União das Populações do Norte de Angola. Hence the UPA had worked out in 1961 not a national strategy but a purely tribal one for the Bakongo and the Dembos people. They sent emissaries to the south but neither the Mbundu nor the Ovimbundu nor the eastern races were really prepared to rise. So, from the beginning, the UPA could call on only limited potential support. Further, it was to alienate the real or enforced sympathy of three major elements in Angolan society. From the beginning of the revolt, there were massacres not only of whites but of *mestiços*, *assimilados* and some of the Ovimbundu contract workers on the coffee plantations. Portuguese propaganda immediately seized on this error, which can only be accounted for by basic tribalism, group resentment against the African elite and hatred of colonial institutions. The rebellion not only rejected the white overlord but also the heritage of colonisation: the *mestiço* and the 'assimilated' (and hence educated) African.

While the influence of messianic sects in the development of the revolt is in doubt, one can take it that the Portuguese were equated with evil. From many points of view, the rebellion of March 1961 was much closer to the Mau Mau revolt and the Congolese rebellions of 1964 than to the far more 'scientific' revolts of Guinea-Bissau or even of Mozambique. It rejected the Portuguese, and also considered the Ovimbundu a friend of the white man, and therefore the UPA's enemy. Of course, not all contract workers, *assimilados* and *mestiços* caught in the north were killed, but the number of those assassinated was sufficient to show Angola, and especially the townsfolk, that although the Bakongo had risen for independence—a goal approved by many Africans—it entailed the possibility of the elimination of other Angolans by the UPA. And that might include some 80 per cent of the population.

8. The UPA used terrorist tactics within the Bakongo and Mbundu groups against those who did not want to take part in armed revolt. Villages that were loath to rebel were burned and sometimes a massacre of part of their inhabitants followed. But this policy pays only in the short term, if victory is rapid. After the first euphoric moments, such refugees and press-ganged combatants disband, flee or surrender. This was the case particularly among the Bazombo tribesmen and generally east of the line Maquela do Zombo-Carmona-Camabatela. In some places, the insurrection became a pretext for Protestants and Catholics to settle old scores—the Catholics being considered more pro-Portuguese. 9. It is clear that the UPA was counting on a rapid victory that would not require complicated logistic organisation or the despatch of leaders, which they did not have. After the first reverses in summer

6. An Ovimbundu recruit

7. Portuguese soldiers in Lucunga

8. *Canhangulos:* museum pieces captured from the guerrillas

1961, the rebels were left without instructions, leaders or aid. As the urban networks did not provide leaders, the revolt slipped rapidly into anarchy until some trained cadres could be sent.

The Portuguese, for their part, also made some tragic mistakes. This is no place to elaborate on the sickening massacres perpetrated on them on March 15 and the following days. They are well known: rape, dismemberment, disembowelment of nearly all Europeans caught by the rebels. These atrocities have been explained by the extensive use of drugs, by the type of weapons (*catanas, canhangulos* and the like), by the belief that the enemy must be mutilated to prevent his resurrection on the day of independence, and so on. But the truth remains that, by their attack on civilians (since there were few troops), sparing neither women nor children, the rebels assailed the Portuguese at his most sensitive point: his pride as a male and father of a family. The number of Portuguese settlers killed in March and April 1961 has been greatly exaggerated. Despite the lack of reliable figures, the number of Europeans can be estimated as being between 200 and 300, in addition to the *mestiços* and innumerable Bakongo, Mbundu and loyal Ovimbundu.

The reaction of the Portuguese could have been predicted, given a knowledge of their psychology. The law of retaliation was resorted to, with fire-arms and the modern techniques at their disposal. Their reactions were those of Latin peasant-settlers, living psychologically in frontier territory, fifty or sixty years behind industrialised Europe, in a society where relationships were based on force. Inflated by rumour, the horror stories launched a train of revenge by the survivors in the north who had resisted or fled to Luanda and then by the Portuguese army. It was here that the Portuguese mistake was to rebound against them. There is no doubt at all that in some places, during these early months, the white and *mestiço* militia, reinforced by Ovimbundu, regarded every African who had not taken refuge with them as a terrorist. They fired on sight, burned down villages and spared prisoners only until they had talked. The massacre of Africans was as brutal and indiscriminate as that of the whites had been. This was a frankly racial war, without pardon and without foreign witnesses, apart from a few Baptist and Methodist missionaries who were gradually eliminated. Its victims were villagers who had had nothing to do with the commandos and the more or less organised guerrilla bands. By this indiscriminate killing, the militia, and then the army, caused the Africans to unite on the side of the UPA. The racial gulf opened by the UPA was widened by the Portuguese. It led to massacres, instigated by the Portuguese, of Mbundu in the Cuanza valley as far as beyond Malanje, and in some parts of central and southern Angola, and to the

179

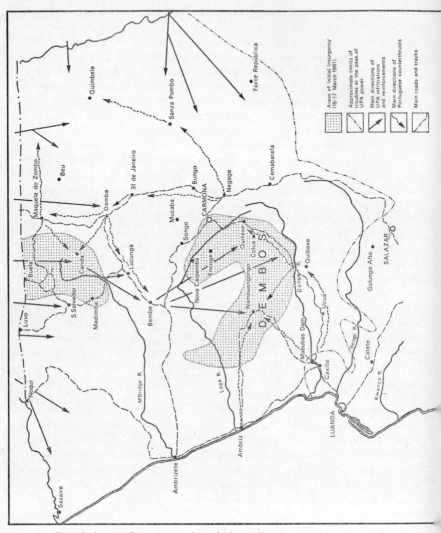

4. Revolt in north-western Angola in 1961

persecution, imprisonment and sometimes disappearance of the African elite in the towns. Now there were only enemies and suspects. Everyone was afraid. The only people not affected were the rural populace far from towns and Protestant missions. Although these represented a majority, the mistrust and hatred accumulated in 1961 still weigh heavy on Angola's future. At least a generation must pass before the dead of 1961 are forgotten in the areas affected by terrorism and counter-terrorism.

The First Phase: Terrorism and Counter-Terrorism

Anyone wishing to give an exact account of the first days of the rebellion and the period immediately preceding it, would be hard put to it to sift out reliable evidence from the fragmentary and contradictory information available. It is still too soon to know who ordered and planned the attacks, chose the operatives and commanded complicity. The UPA, through its spokesman Holden Roberto, then in New York, first denied and then claimed the initiative. One must also take the Dembos into account. It does seem, however, that some Portuguese knew that serious trouble was in the offing. They may even have been the first to move, here and there, by imprisoning potential leaders or even trying to cause their disappearance. Reliable sources are lacking. It is not impossible that some of the Protestant missionaries had been warned of what was coming. Holden Roberto maintained that the revolt broke out in the Primavera plantation, then spread throughout the north.

There were several leading events on March 15. There were attacks on the Congolese frontier to give free passage to UPA commandos who included not only Angolans but a sizable number of troublemakers from the Léopoldville population. Best known of these attacks were those at Buela, Madimba, Luvaca, Cuimba and Canda close to the frontier. There were activities against isolated plantations in the Dembos, then on the Mbridge and in the Nambuangongo region. And there were attacks on the Quitexe and Dembos posts on and south of the Mbundu-Bakongo ethnic boundary, then on the capital of the district, Carmona. No general uprising of the Bakongo occurred, but there were local actions that may have involved several hundred assailants (at Carmona) or youth commandos (at Quitexe). There was no question of a mass uprising against the whites: central and southern Angola were apparently calm. It was during the following days that the scale of the massacres of whites and of villagers who remained loyal to them became known to the Portuguese. Refugees poured into Luanda, where the memory of the events of February 1961 was still fresh. The Portuguese authorities were silent. In the plantations, deprived of information by censorship of the radio, planters continued to fall victim to the rebel bands. Ovimbundu resisted them with their employers. No great number of troops arrived in the north.

Violence now begot more violence. The northern whites had two choices: either to flee with their families, or to withdraw, arms in hand, to the posts. Reprisals started. Without reliable sources, one can only reconstruct a situation which in Portuguese received the apt title *confusão*. There was panic in Luanda, and generally throughout the country where rumour carried more weight than information. Each tale of tragedy sowed mistrust between black and white communities. There were arrests and executions in the *muceques* of Luanda, and, because uprising in the African shanty towns was feared, the troops could not leave the big towns. A few reinforcements were sent out from Portugal on March 21. A witch-hunt started: many African ministers were arrested, some never to return; every African *assimilado* regarded as a potential leader was suspect, and many were arrested and some were executed.

It is not clear just what did happen in the north where the UPA was free to disseminate its commandos in a land of rough tracks and less than a dozen military aircraft, but massacres of Africans by the militia, troops and police took place all along the Luanda-Malanje railway line. One must be cautious here. Local Portuguese questioned in 1966 maintained that plots had been discovered to massacre all the whites and divide their women and belongings among the blacks. What is one to believe? There is, however, no doubt that killing occurred in Massangano, in Dondo, in Cacuso, in Malange and elsewhere. Massangano, abandoned by its inhabitants, became a semi-desert. All this is well known to the Angolan whites who, if not proud of it, blame the catechists and minor Protestant religious and scholastic leaders—in fact, any Africans likely to contest the whites' status.

The southern Dembos was the site of a minor popular uprising. Militarily, the situation is not clear. The Portuguese had very few troops in action (certainly less than a thousand men). There were no major encounters; it was more a question of ambushes, such as that of Colua mentioned for the first time in a Portuguese despatch of April 2. There were few skirmishes since the Portuguese were not numerous and the Africans were disorganised, armed only with traditional weapons, badly led and without guerrilla experience. It is not known what the UPA was doing in this vast no-man's land of the Portuguese Congo. The Africans fled from their villages; the Portuguese, in their posts, carried out a few patrols and waited for help. The fact that they resisted as the north slid slowly into chaos illustrates the difference between this situation and that in the Congo after the mutiny of the Force Publique. In any case, the Portuguese had no choice but to stay put, for the roads were not safe and the coffee crop was not ripe. This is an important point. Many northern settlers were in debt because they had settled there too recently to have recovered their initial investment. These were not old settlers, as in the Huíla or central Angola, but newcomers out for gain and determined to hang on to their only wealth, their land and their shop in the bush (*a loja do mato*). This withdrawal of the Portuguese to some of their *postos*, to wait until the situation calms down, is characteristic of Portuguese history in Angola. In a colony settled by northern Europeans, massive support would have arrived and the trouble would have been handed over to the army, but there was no hope of that in Angola. Each armed civilian (and all now were armed) who stayed on in the north prayed to Providence for help. But this was slow to materialise. On April 10, Ucua, eighty miles from Luanda on the direct coffee route, was attacked (twelve Portuguese civilians were killed and about a hundred Africans). The position of the northern settlers was now frankly perilous. But although alleged 'plots' were uncovered in the centre and south, the rural populace there did not budge. The disappearance of potential chiefs deprived the masses of leaders other than the traditional *sobas*, the overwhelming majority of whom stayed on the Portuguese side. In the towns, the *assimilados* strove to survive by giving proof of their loyalty to the Portuguese.

On April 12, Lucunga was attacked; its eighteen civilian defenders disappeared. The Cabinda Enclave was attacked by UPA troops but no great damage was done. It is not known what the Portuguese soldiers were doing, apart from holding the towns and the more important northern posts. Then Providence at last smiled on the Portuguese, in the shape of a speech (on April 13) by the Portuguese Prime Minister, Salazar, who took over the Ministry of Defence. Whatever the settlers' attitude to the regime, they must have welcomed with relief this firmness and determination not to give in to international or domestic pressure.

From this date there was renewed activity in the north. A minimum of organisation appeared among the insurgents—and here and there a few automatic weapons. The eastern corner of the Congo district was now Portuguese in only nine fortified posts; the rest was abandoned to the rebels. The UPA brought forward its commandos unopposed in the north-south central corridor, from the frontier down to the Dembos. It registered its greatest psychological success in forcing the Portuguese into the error of abandoning the powerful fortress of Bembe—powerful, that is, in the face of adversaries armed with stones and *canhangulos*—attacked on April 17 and abandoned the next day. But the Portuguese at home sent out reinforcements, in numbers at least sufficient to restore white morale, if not to regain full control of the rebellious areas. At this stage, UPA tactics were to assault the posts; their inferior weapons and methods (mass attack by men and children badly armed and often drugged) led to appalling slaughter before the sub-machine guns of a couple of dozen embattled civilians. Their supporters were sacrificed as cannon fodder and kept going only by promises of resurrection after independence and by witchcraft. (For example, the *indigenas* were made to believe that white man's bullets changed to water, *maza*, which became the warcry of the assailants, along with 'UPA' and 'Lumumba'.) Such archaic means were effective in the short term but prejudicial to the struggle, for the blind support they engendered quickly turned to disillusion in the face of the slaughter. Better tactics were to ambush convoys or civilian vehicles, since troops were spread thinly over the vast theatre of operations. In this field guerrilla operations fulfilled their potential, whereas they failed before the walls of the posts.

There is no point in naming all the places attacked, with more or less enthusiasm, by the Africans. The story of Mucaba has taken its place in Portuguese historical mythology alongside the glorious deeds of innumerable sieges withstood by them in the East and in East Africa in the sixteenth, seventeenth and eighteenth centuries. Less than thirty civilians, a few soldiers and a *mestiço* Cape Verdian head of post took refuge in a church and resisted some thousands (?) of rebels throughout the night of April 29–30. Their ammunition exhausted, they were saved by air-strikes. African losses before this insignificant little refuge were over 300 dead. Such figures must have given cause for thought to the most convinced nationalists and the most ardent partisans. The Portuguese adopted the only possible policy in the absence of massive reinforcements: they evacuated weak and isolated posts and concentrated the few available civilians in the strongest centres and these held fairly well (apart from the loss of Lucunga and the evacuation of Bembe), for they were supplied by an air force which, although insufficient, was unopposed.

In the rest of Angola, the PIDE and frightened civilians uncovered plenty of alleged 'plots', but repression was so radical and the masses so little involved outside the towns that precautionary measures were enough to keep the peace in the bush. It was in the towns that conditions were bad for everyone. Economic deterioration and lack of confidence in the future paralysed investment, closed down some

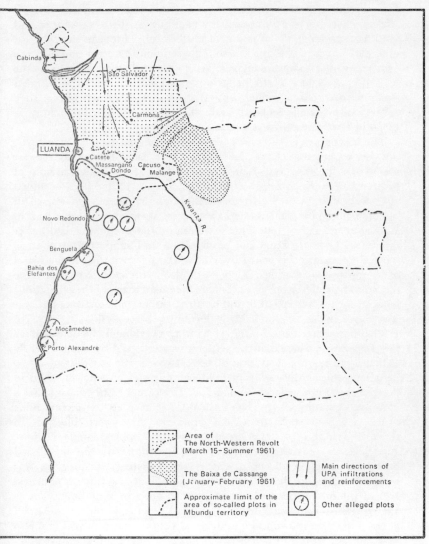

Area of
The North-Western Revolt
(March 15 – Summer 1961)

The Baixa de Cassange
(January – February 1961)

Approximate limit of the
area of so-called plots in
Mbundu territory

Main directions of
UPA infiltrations
and reinforcements

Other alleged plots

5. Troubles in Angola in 1961

sectors (building, for instance) and restricted commerce. Urban Africans tried to pass unnoticed by avoiding in their appearance and attitudes anything (the wearing of clothes too European in style, for example) which might give rise to the suspicion that they would like to oust the whites. The Portuguese accept the tribalised African of the bush if he remains a 'child' or 'primitive'. Their enemy is the *calcinhas* (wearers of trousers), the semi-Westernised Africans whom they suspect of economic jealousy and political ambition. And politics is taboo in Portuguese Africa just as it is in Portugal.

The Portuguese in the north remained strong in their defence posts, but the UPA began to change its tactics. The season of the coffee harvest was to give the rebellion a new direction. Apart from Lucunga, no post had been taken by force; those which the UPA held had been occupied after evacuation by the Portuguese. Although the guerrilla bands had an increasing number of automatic weapons, their only success was in ambushes and skirmishes. This was because the Portuguese had better discipline, far more arms and ammunition and support from the air. Their courage was sharpened by fear for the safety of their families and of losing their belongings. They were also apprehensive of losing the forthcoming coffee crop, since the UPA men held many of the plantations in the Congo, Cuanza-Norte and north of the Luanda district. The war was to become an economic struggle.

The first phase, from March 15 to May 15, though characterised by the desperate resistance of the settlers, was followed by a more clearly military phase. The fact that it took two months to despatch two battalions will hardly figure in military annals as a model of speed in the command of a colonial expedition. It was not until May 13 that a motorised column set out from Luanda; it avoided the direct coffee route (Luanda–Caxito–Quitexe–Carmona) which was blocked in the Dembos, and took the longer but safer route (Luanda–Dondo–Vila Salazar–Camabatela–Carmona). It reoccupied all the abandoned posts and supplied all those which were resisting. Its progress was incredibly slow, due to endless obstacles (felled trees, traps, ambushes) and to the authorities' visible concern to keep to a minimum losses among the troops from Portugal who had practically no experience of guerrilla warfare in tropical countries. On this journey the column also took the opportunity of destroying villages which the administration had classed as rebel.

At Negage, an important air base, the column divided. One battalion reoccupied the posts in the east of Congo district, the other turned north towards Maquela do Zombo, then west to Bembe. This influx of troops, however limited, together with those who had been in the north from the beginning, relieved pressure on the posts and restored the settlers' confidence. There was, however, some disagreement between the settlers who wanted unconditional extermination of all Africans in the bush and the troops anxious not to lose too many men; also the settlers wanted all plantations to be reoccupied but the officers had to keep enough men to face the guerrillas.

The African population at that time was caught between two lines of fire: blind repression by the settlers, and threats and killings by some guerrilla leaders who claimed to be UPA adherents but in some cases became veritable warlords left to their own devices for long periods without arms or orders from the party leaders in Léopoldville. The Africans had in general abandoned their villages en masse and set up refugee villages in the forests and the *serras** (the Dembos were ideal for this, and also some of the isolated ridges in the north). The men of these villages engaged in some local operations, reinforcing the more mobile commandos who were moving in a country where they always had the initiative in attack. The UPA, or its local leaders, in an effort to rally the numerous waverers, massacred the lukewarm and the loyal *sobas*.

What were the main features of this racial war? It began with massacre, and continued with a more skilful form of guerrilla warfare. The UPA enjoyed the support of the Bakongo masses but it had forced them to abandon their means of livelihood and, instead of making hundreds of thousands of combatants of them, it only created refugees. More serious, the flight of the Bakongo into the bush, though giving it short-term support, deprived it of the indispensable complicity of a settled population, essential to a long struggle. The combined action of the Portuguese and the UPA emptied in part the rich country of its inhabitants, before emptying it completely at a later stage and in certain areas. The MPLA, despite its claims, seems to have had no influence on strictly military operations, since its supporters in the Dembos and the Cuanza valley appear at that time to have been carrying out UPA orders, under pain of death. The other ethno-nationalist parties at Léopoldville seem merely to have had a moderating influence. They dared not openly oppose the warfare, but contributed a link among refugees who wanted to return or to give themselves up to the Portuguese: notably the Nto-Bako, the Movimento de Defesa (MDIA) and the Ngwizako. The International Red Cross gives an estimate of 103,000 Angolan refugees in Congo-Léopoldville by the end of June 1961.

* In the Angolan context, a *serra* is not always a full orographic complex or mountain range; the word is also used in connection with a single feature, such as a hill or ridge. The *serras* in north-western Angola are heavily forested.

The Economic Guerrilla Campaign, and Portuguese Recapture of the Posts

It is here that the UPA nearly overwhelmed the Portuguese. If it had adopted a scorched-earth policy from the start, it might well have succeeded in making the northern settlers lose heart. The UPA plan now was to destroy plantations and ravage coffee plants before the harvest in order to ruin the settlers and break their ties with the country. The reason the UPA did not use these methods sooner was probably because it was counting on an early victory and hoping to sell the harvest after independence. June, July and August were the hardest months for the Portuguese. They took inadequate counter-measures to the destruction of the plantations by occupying the accessible ones with armed civilians formed into para-military militia; by recruiting more or less voluntary workers from the Ovimbundu to replace the Bakongo and the contract workers from the south who had fled or been killed; by tentative moves to attract the refugees from the *serras*. They had to find labour and stamp out fear of the white man. On some days in July as many as sixteen plantations were destroyed. The poorest settlers lost their footing, left the north or enrolled in the Corpo de Voluntários (Volunteer Corps).

Simultaneous with this race for the coffee (which, though not yet ripe everywhere, burned well because the high grass had not been cleared from March to May), Portuguese troops were easily recapturing the posts abandoned in the east. It was the dry season, the most favourable to military convoys and aerial expeditions. The Governor-General, Silva Tavares, was replaced by the air force general, Venâncio Deslandes. The initiative passed to the military who, although at first bewildered by this guerrilla warfare, now had at least 20,000 land forces. They now had to prove to the white settlers, who had accused them of lack of ardour, that they could fight the enemy wherever they chose. They mounted an operation aimed at reoccupying Nambuangongo, deserted in March and never finally retaken. It was one of the main centres of the rebellion and its proximity to Luanda was a constant threat and humiliation to the Portuguese. This first major offensive ran up against fairly stiff resistance, to start with, from Africans blocking the advance of the three columns from Ambriz, Caxito and the eastern Dembos. The slow progress of the columns gave the partisans plenty of time to evacuate Nambuangongo before they entered it on August 9 after taking twenty-six days to cover 100 to 150 miles. This was above all a psychological victory; it showed that the army could go where it liked, that it was active and held the initiative. Strategically, it was clearly only a relative victory, since the jungle around Nambuangongo is still held by guerrillas, whose presence is felt despite their lethargy. It would not be wrong, however, to take the Portuguese reoccupation of Nambuangongo as the turning point in their recovery of the initiative.

This blow to the Nambuangongo bands led some of the guerrillas to filter south and try to infiltrate the Catete region towards the Cuanza valley, possibly in the hope of cutting the only road still open to Carmona. This was a region of longstanding nationalist sympathy (with the MPLA) but which had been so heavily scoured from the start by Portuguese troops that its inhabitants were only too well aware of their vulnerability.

In the Congo and the Dembos, the coffee war continued but the guerrilla groups' ardour diminished for they were short of food and often of ammunition. Rivalry arose among their leaders. The number of partisans is not known for certain (it may have been between 8,000 and 10,000 men in July), but what is certain is that they fought little, they were dispersed, uncoördinated and showed little vigour. One may even suspect that they fought more among themselves than against the Portuguese. Their lack of military leaders, not to mention policies, was manifest. Their organisation was below the minimum for Africa. It is not surprising that the Portuguese forces announced only ninety-seven dead of the army, three of the navy and ten of the air force from February 4 to the end of August 1961—110 dead all told, including accidental deaths, in five and a half months of combat over an area of 60,000 square miles if one includes the rebel fringes of the Malanje district. Even if these figures were an understatement—which has never been proved—they are certainly closer to the truth than the thousands of dead claimed by the rebel leadership in Léopoldville.

While burning and pillaging of plantations continued around Carmona, in the Vale do Loge and elsewhere, the planters were making every effort to reoccupy their farms before they were destroyed. At the same time, they harvested the 'terrorists' ' coffee. The authorities urged the settlers who had withdrawn to Luanda to return to their plantations, for, although a plantation reoccupied by its owner was often attacked, it was rarely destroyed since the assailants gave up in the face of resistance. The UPA partisan bands were tired and discouraged and began to dig in among the *serras* rather than take the offensive. Life in the forest gave security against napalm bombardments and parachute drops but tended to sap the spirit of combat. They tried to live by their own resources, but the cold, the September rains and lack of food decimated the weakest—the women and children. There can be no comparison between these refugee villages in the forest, struggling to survive, and the Algerian maquis, or even less the Viet Cong.

The Portuguese gave no detailed military information to the press after October 7, 1961. Did this silence denote reversals? Hardly, for, with the collapse of the rebellion, they succeeded in occupying the last abandoned post, Caiongo (October 3), in the extreme east of the Congo district. They had gone a long way in a few months. Apart from the Cabinda Enclave, where an outpost of the Miconge post had been abandoned, from the beginning of the rebellion the Portuguese had given up two *concelhos* headquarters and thirty-three posts in the north of Angola, leaving an administrative vacuum that gave the UPA a free hand for six months. The restoration of this administrative infrastructure—usually without a shot being fired—enabled the Governor-General to declare optimistically on October 7 that the military operation was complete.

But the Portuguese came back to devastation and a human desert. Probably some 300,000 had left their villages to escape the war, and had fled to Congo-Léopoldville or hidden in the forests and *serras*. This voluntary or forced withdrawal from the whites was the most serious defeat for the Portuguese. There was a veritable exodus of Bakongo to the north. To stem it, the troops started a psychological and social campaign of recuperation. They succeeded where the frontier was too far away, where UPA influence did not go deep (as in the eastern district of Congo), and where the settlers had not carried out too many reprisals. This velvet-glove technique was backed by bombardment of refugee columns making for Congo-Léopoldville. Elsewhere, the lack of material resources on the Portuguese side rather than guerrilla effectiveness prevented the troops from controlling completely the natural strongholds: for instance, the partisan refuges in the Dembos and the Mucaba, Pingano and Canda *serras*. The settlers, apart from the tradesmen, many of whom were ruined in the north by lack of business, were delighted by the departure of the Bakongo and Mbundu of the Dembos. The more extremist of them would have liked to see all the northern Angolans disappear and their replacement by Ovimbundu contract labour. This extremist view was opposed by (among others) Major Rebocho Vaz, the new Governor of the Uíge district (the Congo district was split in two—Zaire in the west, Uíge in the east), who tried to restore peace by offering a pardon to the refugees in the bush.

From October 1961 until the end of 1962, a considerable number of *indígenas* (more than 236,000 in the Uíge district alone) surrendered to the Portuguese, who screened them but helped them rebuild their ruined villages. The official line was to punish the 'terrorists' but to welcome peaceful villagers, 'children led astray by witchcraft and the UPA'. Portuguese policy now held that, to restore confidence, kindness needed to be substituted for extermination. This policy is still followed and has brought undoubted local successes; but it has failed in the empty bush and among the well-led maquis. Whatever the true feelings of those who surrender to the Portuguese, exhaustion has made them 'docile children'. In the north, the war is not ended but stifled.

South of the Luanda-Malange line, the country did not experience economic and material losses. In the east, the diamond mine of the Lunda achieved a record output of 662,133,000 escudos, exported by Diamang (Companhia de Diamantes de Angola) in 1961. Better still, in spite of the destruction of plantations, in this year coffee exports amounted to 118,122 tons at a value of 1,398,449,000 escudos. The UPA certainly ruined dozens of planters in the north by destroying part of the crop; but, paradoxically, this gave Angola the chance to clear unsold stock, to stabilise overproduction and, by reducing imports from 3,669,610,000 escudos in 1960 to 3,267,692,000 in 1961, to make up a deficit in the Angolan balance of trade. This was certainly not the result anticipated or intended in Léopoldville.

The 1961 Balance Sheet

In human terms, the reckoning is tragic. The precise number of African dead is not known. Various sources have put it at 8,000, 25,000 and 50,000. The present writer inclines to the view that it was nearer 50,000 than 8,000. Most died not as a direct result of warfare but as victims of disease and famine among the partisans. Compared with the slaughter in Algeria, the Congo and Biafra, this is a relatively modest figure. But it holds a bitter lesson for the Angolans; if they wish to break free from Portuguese colonisation, they must be prepared to pay a heavy price in men. A reliable estimate of the Portuguese victims would be about 400 civilians by the end of 1961, which illustrates the partisans' lack of success.

Economically, in spite of appearances, the rebellion was a spur and an indirect advantage to the Portuguese, as has been shown. Socially, however, the revolt succeeded beyond all expectations. Everyone went in fear. Africans in the north had but one solution: refuge far from the Portuguese, and scorched earth. Those of the rest of Angola were obliged to return to the submissive attitude of the past, and keep their thoughts to themselves, away from informants of the PIDE and the administration. This applied especially to the educated Angolans. For the mass of the *indigenas*, the repeal of the Native Code in September 1961 did not bring much change in their lives. They had to wait until 1962 for the situation to improve. The Portuguese solution was to increase the armed forces and the number of white settlers, and to stay on guard. Bloodshed lay between white and black communities in the north and along the Cuanza, in Luanda, some port cities and in some parts of the Ovimbundu area where so-called plots had been discovered and harshly repressed. Elsewhere mistrust was rife. Clearly, the Portuguese will never again be as unprepared to crush a revolt as they were in 1961. Contrary to the opinion of many foreign observers some evidence suggests that, at least in the short run, and with the aid of Southern African white neighbours, Portugal will control Angola.

9. Political Aftermath of the Revolt, 1961-70

How is it that we can cross the entire length of Angola or Mozambique with no other aid than the goodwill of the people and their brotherly help?
Vasco V. Garin, the Portuguese representative,
in a speech to the 946th meeting of the
United Nations Security Council, March 15, 1961.

In 1961, a storm of international indignation broke over Portugal. The Portuguese government refused to give way before the widespread condemnation of its response to the rebellion. Instead, it began to play its cards with all the skill at its command. It did not lack trumps: a sound financial and monetary position; a monopoly of internal information and the ability to suppress effective action by the political opposition in Portugal; support from foreign interests with extensive capital investments in Angola and Mozambique; and deployment of the threat not to renew to the United States the usage rights of its air bases in the Azores.

The Portuguese point of view was clear. Portugal was at home in Angola; it faced a foreign invasion and threatened nobody; Angola was not a colony and Portugal was not going to leave. The determination of Salazar coincided for historical, economic and personal reasons with the interests of some sections of the business community and with those of the army, the Church (after some hesitation) and the police. So the regime was able to impose on Portugal a silent acceptance of the financial and human sacrifices that a simultaneous triple war in Africa would entail. No modern democratic European country, however rich, has been able to undertake such a task for so long. Faced with the inflexible attitude of a man holding complete power and backed by the only vocal elements in the country, external pressure appeared powerless and derisory. Most of the speakers at the United Nations and elsewhere do not seem to have grasped this fact. They are dealing not with a simple colonial power but with the very incarnation of European ultra-nationalism. And its essence is to admit no rivals in Angola, which it affirms to be part of the national homeland.

As seen from Angola, the affair of Baixa de Cassange may have been a

193

revolt of despair, the Luanda attacks a suicidal reaction by some hundreds of nationalists, and the revolt of the Bakongo and a fraction of the Mbundu a frankly racial rebellion with nationalist undercurrents. But, as seen from Lisbon by the power establishment, these were serious threats that could endanger the stability of Portugal and hence of the regime and the hegemony of its supporters over Portuguese society and economy. They must be suppressed, with concessions in secondary matters but intransigence in the essentials: that is, the preservation of Angola, the overseas provinces and their wealth. So reforms would be practically nil in the concrete political field, but much more important in terms of everyday life for the average African.

EXTERNAL PRESSURE AND THE REFORMS OF 1961

The ritual of the annual debates of the United Nations on Portugal's African policies has done nothing to affect the aims and actions of the government in Lisbon. The United Nations' most positive effect has been to provide help for the Angolan refugees driven by the war to Congo-Kinshasa, Zambia and even Congo-Brazzaville. Their numbers have continued to grow from 1961 to the present, in spite of the returns to Angola which began in late 1961. In fact, all the areas held firmly by the UPA have lost nearly all their inhabitants (e.g., the population of the Zaire district fell from 102,777 inhabitants in 1960 to some 30,000 in 1968) while the non-Baxikongo areas (that is, east of the line Maquela do Zombo–Carmona–Negage) have seen the gradual return of their people, as has Cabinda.[1] The High Commissioner for Refugees has quietly helped tens of thousands of Angolans to remake a more normal existence outside their country.[2] Another field in which the United Nations has achieved a direct, positive result is in the publications by its Secretariat, which carried out some fundamental and unparalleled studies on Portuguese Africa.

Nevertheless, the international storm over the Portuguese territories, helped by direct pressure from a few major Western powers, did produce indirect results. On August 28, 1961, the then Minister of Overseas Affairs, Adriano Moreira, announced a series of reforms that were to precede the fundamental new Labour Code in 1962. The most important reform was the repeal of the Native Code of 1954 (Decree 43893). The distinction between *indígenas* and Portuguese citizens was removed, and equal rights were given to 'civilised' and 'non-civilised' citizens. In theory, everyone suddenly became 'civilised' by the law's magic. Moreira, who elsewhere would be considered an intelligent conservative, was regarded in Portugal as a 'Young Turk' of advanced views within the regime; for some time he had been worried by the contradiction which made Angolan Catholics and Protestants (48·50 per cent and 17 per cent respectively in 1960) adults in religion but legally minors in administrative and political matters. There was a great uproar in Portugal over this repeal of the Native Code, but the main handicap was that it came fifteen years too late and appeared merely as concession to foreign pressure. So, in principle, 'non-civilised' black Africans and *mestiços* joined their 'civilised' brothers and the whites who were 'civilised' ipso facto, even if illiterate (and in 1950 there were 18,153 illiterate whites).

Initially, this change had little practical effect, for the former *indigena* still had his *caderneta* and was still under the moral obligation to work; hence, he was likely to be subjected to a period of contract work (*contrato*) against his will. Politically, the Portuguese electoral law remained unchanged; adult members of the former *indigena* community (4,562,606 in 1960) were thus excluded from the ballot on account of illiteracy. Rarely are reforms introduced in time in a colonial society. This was the case here, for this measure could satisfy only some of the Africans' social aspirations. For Angolan nationalists in exile, it was useless. It lacked even the psychological power of the French integration offer to Algerians, since (with very few exceptions) the illiterate were still barred from political life. According to the nationalists, the Portuguese were offering their civilisation to a people demanding independence. This basic misunderstanding between nationalists and Portuguese was bound to continue. For the masses, such considerations were irrelevant; they could understand only that they were still liable to the obligation of working under the *contrato*, and that they could not travel without a permit (*guia*).

Moreira's other reforms of September 1961 concerned matters of secondary importance in everyday life: co-ordination of the application of traditional and codified law; reorganisation of the *regedorias* (*indigena* administrative units in the bush); and occupation of land and concessions. Decree 43894 sought to avoid clashes between the indigenous population and settlers wanting to expand. Each *regedoria* obtained a reserve of land equal to five times the amount exploited by Africans. There was certainly no need for agrarian reform in Angola, but some writers have mentioned disputes over land ownership as one of the causes of the Congo district revolt.[3] A Junta Provincial de Povoamento (Provincial Settlement Board) was created to speed up settlement in Angola by Portuguese peasants. This policy was violently denounced by Angolan nationalists but was a logical move for Lisbon, since it aimed at a 'whitening' of Angola by installing colonists in the

Roman sense of the term, that is to 'civilise' Angola, with Lisbon claiming the role of a latter-day Rome among the barbarians.[4] Given administrative slowness in general and that of the Portuguese in particular, one must not imagine that these measures notably modified in 1961 the situation of a country in the throes of a latent civil and racial war in the north.

In the field of economic planning another decree (dated November 8, 1961) envisaged the creation of a common market between Portugal and its overseas territories, aiming to abolish within ten years (between January 1962 and January 1972) discriminatory tariff restrictions on national products within the escudo zone.

THE NEW RURAL LABOUR CODE, 1962

It was not until 1962 that a really fundamental reform was introduced to modify social relationships between Africans and the white community. Whatever may have been said to the contrary, there is no doubt that international pressure, and especially Ghana's complaint to the International Labor Organization, led to a recasting of the Rural Labour Code (Decrees 44309 and 44310 of April 27, 1962). This repealed the former code of 1928, the source of so many recriminations and accusations of forced labour and coercion. Moreira had for long been thinking of abolishing this labour system which, in practice, gave European employers the opportunity to recruit—sometimes by fraudulent or coercive means—a cheap labour force (the average monthly wage for a rural labourer in 1960 was 442·5 escudos). It is probable that the report of the Commission of Inquiry sent by the International Labor Organization to Angola and Mozambique[5] gave Moreira the necessary strength to impose this regulation on the ultra-conservatives and Portuguese economic lobbies in Angola. He was as a result accused of 'communism' by some members of the administration.

What were the actual consequences of the 1928 Labour Code? In 1960, out of a male population of 1,351,623 economically active, there were 367,851 wage-earners (27·2 per cent), and the rural labour force* amounted to only 299,861 workers, of whom 115,904 had a written contract (that is, were genuine *contratados*). On October 1, 1962, to the chagrin of the settlers (planters, fisheries and mines) who employed this labour —and one can say without hesitation that it was far from always voluntarily employed—every Angolan became free. Free to work for himself, to choose an employer, or to do nothing at all if he had the

---

* That is, the non-specialist *indígena* labour force, working for someone else, with or without a contract.

means to pay the capitation tax (which, incidentally, was increased at about the same time as the abolition of the Native Code). The African's moral obligation to work was abolished; the Portuguese had to attract his labour by other means than pressure: a rise in monthly wages was one, from 487·50 escudos to 540 escudos in 1962, settling at around 562 in 1964–65. Early in 1962, a body was set up to ensure compliance with the new law: the Instituto do Trabalho, Previdência e Acção Social (Institute of Labour, Welfare and Social Action). Particularly relevant to its task are the following provisions: no form of forced labour is permitted; no penal sanction is envisaged for failure to fulfil a labour contract; there is no paternalistic guardianship of labourers; recruiting of labourers through the authorities or by use of their facilities is not permitted. Before the establishment of this body, there were only eighteen officials in the whole of Angola concerned with labour problems, all of them in Luanda. In practice, therefore, supervision was left to the heads of posts, that is to say, to the people who had acted as intermediaries between employers and employees during the more or less forced recruitment of the latter. The Institute began its inspection of business firms in 1963. At the same time, from 1962 on, the government took stricter measures against heads of posts who continued to oblige *sobas* (chieftains) and *regedores* (African village administrators) to provide unwilling labourers. Obviously the administration ought to have started here if it was genuinely interested in suppressing the abuses of its subordinates. The problem stems from the conception of public office in Portugal and Angola. If the state paid its officials properly, they would be protected from the temptations and financial pressures of the settlers; and it would at the same time be able to demand complete integrity from them. In paying them a starvation wage it had to tolerate extortion or else to clamp down by sacking its personnel (and dismissals did indeed increase in 1962, when some areas were cleared of staff that were too openly corrupt). This second method was unfortunate since, as wages remained low, public service still attracted too many mediocre candidates or opportunists hoping to supplement their pay by illicit financial transactions.

Nevertheless, Moreira's Labour Code of 1962 must be reckoned a fundamental reform, since it abolished almost completely one of the sources of humiliation for Africans. Legally and in practice, every worker was henceforward free, although some observers living in the country estimated that, in 1966, the law was still infringed in some 5–10 per cent of cases. But the fact that 90–95 per cent of *contratados* were genuinely voluntary labourers reduced the doubtful cases in the whole of Angola to less than 10,000. This is an improvement which would have been unimaginable in 1960, and every Angolan knows it. One can assume that, in areas affected by the fighting and massacres of 1961, there was in 1966 no forced employment of those whom the Portuguese call *recuperados* or *apresentados* (i.e. people who have left the nationalist maquis and live under military protection). It is also likely that virtually all Ovimbundu contract workers on the northern plantations are genuinely voluntary labourers. As one administrator said: 'It is simply a question of common sense: there is no point offering the pre-1961 system to former "terrorists". Bees are drawn by the honeypot, not the vinegar bottle.'

The introduction of authentic voluntary labour, a new pillar in the Angolan economy, was completed by additional measures. One no longer sees groups of women and children working on the roads to fulfil the obligations that their men, away on *contrato* duties, could not accomplish. Upkeep of roads classified as of provincial importance is the responsibility of the Junta Autónoma de Estradas de Angola—JAEA (Autonomous Angolan Highways Authority), which does not employ labour provided by administrators* of posts.[6] The abolition of compulsory labour thus removed another source of friction.

Even more important, perhaps, was the creation in 1963 of the *mercados rurais* (official rural markets), particularly in the agricultural coffee zones in the north. These markets have tended to eliminate the abuses practised on the small African producer by the Portuguese tradesmen (no weighing, overvaluation of goods given, undervaluing of those accepted in exchange, pressure, and so on). Development of these markets has been of special benefit to the coffee growers of Uíge and Cuanza-Norte (168 million and 171 million escudos turnover, respectively, in 1966). The markets are held under proper administrative supervision, on a fixed date; transactions are carried out according to price and quality restrictions laid down by the government. Having visited one of these markets, the present writer believes that they have done more to improve the standard of living of north Angolans than all the other forms of state assistance and supervision. By enforcing cash payments, thus ending barter, and imposing forced saving (a proportion of all payments to Africans was temporarily withheld), they have rectified dealings between customers and sellers, removed causes of misunderstanding and rancour, and introduced the rural African to the market economy. This is one of the most beneficent consequences of the 1961 upheavals.

These are the chief measures that have notably improved the lot of

* The new official title of a head of post (*chefe de posto*) is *administrador de posto*.

Angolans who stayed on the Portuguese side. To outsiders they may seem belated, timid and rudimentary. But in Angola they appeared to revolutionise social routines and relationships inherited from the nineteenth century. Portuguese paternalism did not disappear after 1961; on the contrary it was strengthened by becoming somewhat more humane. Of course, abolition of the Native Code and the African's obligation to work (for the European's benefit), was resented by most of the white community; now that the immediate danger of general uprising was past, thanks to the inertia of the northern guerrillas, they were once again demanding revenge for the fear they had suffered in 1961. The administration, with considerably stronger military and police forces, had taken over control of public order from the white civilians. In some places the administration and police reclaimed the arms they had distributed earlier, although private arsenals were maintained more or less clandestinely and fire-arms permits for Portuguese are still prevalent.

THE SITUATION SINCE 1961

The revolt is not over in the interior. Although the Portuguese authorities tend officially to regard it as simple banditry—and locally in some cases they are right—this is not supportable as a general diagnosis of the situation. However, because the Angolan population as a whole has not joined in the revolt, for the reasons already given, it is limited to particular regions, despite the nationalists' efforts to give it a nationwide basis. It has become the longest war recorded in black Africa and, although losses are comparatively small on both sides, since there is little fighting, there is no visible prospect of a military solution.

It affects in two ways the Portuguese and Angolan economies. Along with the war in Guinea and Mozambique, it involves Portugal in very heavy expenditure for a country itself underdeveloped. Portugal's military expenditure may represent between 7 and 7·5 per cent of the gross national product—a figure that is probably exceeded only by Israel and super-powers such as the United States. In Angola, on the other hand, the presence of some 50,000 European soldiers with a relatively high purchasing power (in 1966 both black and white ordinary soldiers at Luanda earned 1,500 escudos without board, and at Cabinda 700 escudos with food) has at least three consequences: it stimulates trade in all garrison towns and villages; it increases by a fifth the white community; and it adds to the young generation of *mestiços*. So a war which slowly exhausts Portugal develops Angola, thanks to expenditure on sovereignty and the very considerable investment undertaken to catch up on the backlog. At the same time, it increases the white and *mestiço* proportion of the country's total population which, moreover, lost about 7 per cent of its 1960 African population by the death or exodus of Bakongo tribesmen.[7]

A major effect of the war has been to awaken the Portuguese from somnolent routine, forcing them to maintain their vigilance and not to allow the spread of abuses that could upset the rural masses. In effect, the Portuguese are now compelled to initiate a measure of economic, social and cultural progress.

The Nationalist Movements and their Activities in Angola

Without the nationalist movements, Angola would certainly have had a more peaceful and less bloodstained history, but probably the 1961–62 reforms would not have materialised so soon. Their strength and weakness before and during 1961 have been reviewed. Their evolution since 1961, a long period for exiles, is extremely complex, but one can pick out certain outlines without getting bogged down in details. They were weak in 1961; they were still weak in 1970. They were not remarkable for their achievements, for their unity in the struggle, for their leadership, or for the quality of their guerrillas. The quarrels between the African nationalist parties escalated in some cases to a point where the two principal movements seemed to spend more time opposing each other than fighting the Portuguese on the battlefield. If one is to assess the real influence of the nationalist groups in Angola after these years of struggle, what does one find? Their military presence in Angola faded away steadily until 1966, when the MPLA and then UNITA guerrilla operation opened in the east. At the time of writing, they are still a threat to the Portuguese, but their chances of defeating the Portuguese army and settlers by force of arms seem remote. The converse is equally true. More important, in spite of their claims, none of the Angolan nationalist movements has succeeded in paralysing the economic development of the country, and it is by this criterion that one must judge the success of the rebellion.

Situation of the north Angolan maquis after 1961. There is no doubt that, from 1961 to 1965, the UPA was the most active movement, relatively speaking, in Angola, and the most dangerous to the Portuguese. At the end of 1961, they had lost the first round of the rebellion; the racial explosion had subsided, its Bakongo supporters were dead or in exile in the Congo, or had gone over to the Portuguese side, or taken refuge in the jungles and mountains. There alone UPA strength was alive. Geographically, it did not amount to much; in human terms it

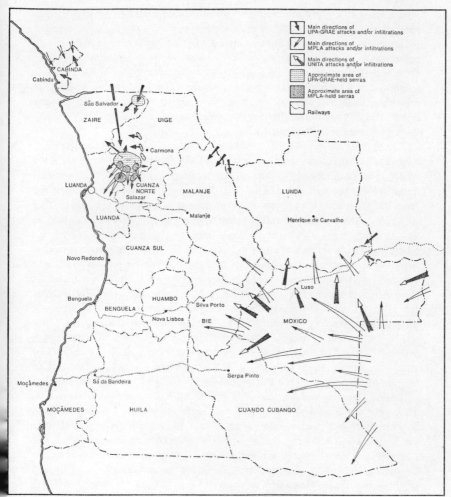

6. Troubles in Angola in 1970

was a tragedy. The tactics of the UPA and the Portuguese had a dual result: the scorched-earth policy drove the villagers out to refuges inaccessible to the Portuguese army; by emptying the land of its inhabitants, it deprived the UPA of the support it would have received from a stable population. Whole stretches of country in the Zaire and Uíge districts became literally deserts where the Portuguese knew that anything that moved was an enemy. Outside these natural strongholds, the UPA is not the 'fish in the water' of Mao Tse-tung's theories, for there is no water left in the pond.

The Portuguese army, physically incapable of sealing off the frontier, adopts simple tactics. Bombardments of the forests have little military effect, but psychologically they inspire fear. Meanwhile, patrols and machine-gunning in the plains and open country near the Congolese frontier prevent the kind of mass exodus that occurred in 1961. The military count on hunger and disease to drive the refugees to surrender, as did most of the Bakongo not belonging to the Baxikongo subgroup. Such a policy relies on there being no help from the north, but this is impossible to eliminate. Hence, new village cells have been gradually reconstituted by the insurgents in the forest, often with the name of their original home, and supporting as best they can a few combatants for whom they are principally a refuge. These guerrilla groups are almost economically self-sufficient: that is their only strength. Only small commando groups, more or less well-armed and aggressive, venture beyond the *serras*, for they know they get no help until they reach the next maquis village. It is a free field for extermination. The targets of these bands are Portuguese convoys and patrols, plantations (*fazendas*) reoccupied by the Portuguese and their armed *contratados*, and, very occasionally, a garrison site such as Bembe. In fact, there is little contact between opposing sides and each seems happy with this passivity. The only new development in guerrilla combat technique is the appearance of mines which, as in Mozambique and Guinea, are becoming the major obstacle to Portuguese movements.[8] The position of the guerrilla bands varies. If they do not launch attacks, and if the smoke of their camp fires is not noticed, there is every chance that a village cell will not be discovered. Difficulty of access prevents the Portuguese from penetrating these terrible *serras*, some of which extend to several hundred square miles of jungle.[9] Gradually, the Portuguese army also began to mine the jungle paths and the tracks leading to the frontier in order to hem in the rebel zones and prevent any large-scale exodus.

The UPA leadership in Léopoldville faced many problems. They had to arm the guerrilla bands, provide them with cadres, prevent desertions to the Portuguese from spreading and reanimate the combatants' courage. At the same time, they had to defend their pre-eminence in the nationalist struggle by preventing soldiers sent by their rivals, the MPLA, from reaching the Dembos where it seems that, from late 1961 if not earlier, rivalry between partisan leaders led to inter-guerrilla massacres when some leader or other questioned the UPA's political monopoly. Ethnic differences between the Bakongo and the Mbundu also played a part in this settling of scores. It seems certain that rivalry between African Methodist and Baptist ministers and catechists, who had become guerrilla leaders and the more or less accepted rulers of the lives of their flock, resulted in clashes on the political level. The Brazzaville and Léopoldville headquarters passed these off as 'doctrinal differences' between MPLA and UPA partisans.

In fact, the few MPLA guerrilla groups were concentrated around Nambuangongo and in the eastern Dembos. They consisted entirely of Mbundu refugees, either from the towns and villages of the Luanda-Vila Salazar corridor, or from the Dembos (as far north as Quitexe) or from the region touching the outskirts of Caxito. The UPA guerrilla groups were all Bakongo, except for a few Mbundu from the ethno-linguistic frontier (Quitexe and also Nambuangongo). In general, the UPA partisans were far better off because of their more northerly position, with shorter lines of communication to the Congo, and because of the UPA's policy—mistaken from the point of view of the pan-Angolan nationalist struggle, but understandable in a party claiming a 'combat monopoly' in the war—of intercepting and destroying reinforcements sent by the MPLA to the Mbundu who were asking for help from Nambuangongo and the Dembos. Whoever was responsible for this fratricidal warfare among the Angolans, there is no doubt that it suited the Portuguese very well. Since 1961 the rivalry between guerrilla factions has enabled them to eliminate many of those hornets' nests from which, from time to time, a few partisans emerge to kill one, two or three Portuguese before returning to their jungle retreats to send a communiqué to Kinshasa or Brazzaville announcing massive Portuguese losses.

In fact, it is only in its own tribal territory (near the Congolese frontier and particularly in the Serra da Canda) that the UPA administration succeeded in building up a rudimentary organisation within Angola. At Fuesse, in 1962–63, they could show foreigners a decided and effective front. But, with grim irony, the villages in this area were destroyed one by one as the Portuguese followed up reports of them in the international press. There are several places like Fuesse in the forest. Militarily this does not signify much; but, from the propaganda point of view, these trips into the Angolan interior have given the UPA the chance to appear as the only organisation fighting on the ground, whereas the MPLA, before 1964, could only go the rounds of capital cities without ever showing any concrete results—and for good reason.

The UPA *and its satellites.* It would be a grave mistake to conclude that the UPA was militarily inactive after its rough treatment by the Portuguese in 1961. Indeed, its military potential was reinforced after that date, but this was largely outside Angola. By comparison with 1960, the party was definitely progressing in 1962. It had retained its initial support from the exterior; to this there was added the weight of the Baptist church (which cared for its refugees), the help of the Algerian FLN (which trained a few dozen future officers in its Tunisian bases), the funds from various sources (especially the United States), the American technical advisers and the international stature of Holden Roberto, who had by now eclipsed his rivals. However, closer inspection shows that, even though the party claimed 40,000 members in 1962 (not much out of an Angolan refugee population of several hundred thousand men), the circumstances of war had driven its major strength outside the country. The only region in Angola where it could hope for ethnic support had lost between a third and a half of its population, many of whom were now in refugee villages north of the frontier. Despite its guerrilla bands, the UPA was more than ever a party of exiles. While a small portion of the Bakongo exiles kept fighting, most of the Angolan Bakongo in Congo-Kinshasa did not participate in the war. The UPA was not able to arouse the enthusiasm of the refugee population. And (as we have seen) in Angola itself, the tribal aspects of its struggle had alienated most of the other ethnic groups.

Within the party there was rivalry on two counts: Holden Roberto favoured too openly the Protestant Baxikongo, to the detriment of other Bakongo and other Angolan ethnic groups; and he exercised too great a monopoly of power, refusing to ally with the MPLA intellectuals, who, in any case, regarded him as a 'foreigner'. In this way, the UPA was deprived of leaders. The Angolan nationalist leaders were in some cases aware of their weaknesses, but few wished to change their positions.

In February 1962, João Baptista Traves Pereira, a Cuanhama commander of the UPA forces in Angola, was killed near Bembe (by the Portuguese, the UPA claims). At the beginning of March 1962, the UPA chief of staff, Commander Marcos Kassanga, left the party, accusing Holden Roberto of tribalism (Kassanga was a Ganguela) and of responsibility both for the death of Baptista and also for the deaths in October 1961 of twenty-one or twenty-three members of an MPLA armed band.[10] Even more serious, he blamed Roberto for the deaths of 8,000 Angolans (non-Bakongo, *assimilados* and *mestiços*). Whatever the truth of these accusations, they illustrate the troubles arising from Roberto's personality and 1961 tactics. Possibly to stem this incipient disintegration, the UPA on March 27, 1962, formed the Frente Nacional de Libertação de Angola—FNLA (National Liberation Front of Angola), in association with Emmanuel Kunzika's diminutive Partido Democrático de Angola—PDA (Angolan Democratic Party), formerly the Aliança dos Naturais do Zombo—ALIAZO. The Frente Nacional was destined to pre-empt the Frente Angolana de Libertação Nacional—FALN (Angolan National Liberation Front): a more or less still-born organisation formed by Marcos Kassanga with part, it seems, of the Liga Geral dos Trabalhadores de Angola—LGTA (General League of Angolan Workers). The LGTA was a trade-union group in exile, one of whose leaders at that time was André Martins Kassinda (an Ovimbundu). The Frente Nacional, dominated by the UPA, was the kind of front that all Angolans in exile would have liked to have had created. But, since it did not include the MPLA or the non-violent groups (Movimento de Defesa, Ngwizako, Nto-Bako, etc.), it was based on two Bakongo parties: the one responsible for the rebellion, the other which had now renounced non-violence, ever since the Bazombo had found themselves caught between the two fires of the UPA and the Portuguese.

On April 5, 1962, the Frente Nacional created a 'Government of the Angolan Republic in Exile', later renamed the 'Revolutionary Government of Angola in Exile' (GRAE in its Portuguese abbreviation, by which it is more familiarly known). The major office-holders were: president, Holden Roberto; vice-president, Emmanuel Kunzika; foreign affairs, Jonas Malheiro Savimbi (Ovimbundu); armaments, Alexandre Taty (Cabinda). The main function of the GRAE was as a diplomatic weapon to crush the MPLA and provide a valid spokesman in dealings with the Congolese authorities. In this respect, the UPA's position was not always easy. Before June 30, 1960, its activities were officially banned in the former Belgian Congo, but the support of Joseph Kasavubu, the most eminent Bakongo politician, saved them from interference. But once he became President of the new Congolese Republic, Kasavubu's Abako movement advocated reuniting the Kongo peoples, and, by late 1960 and early 1961, he was against the UPA. However, Cyrille Adoula's promotion to Prime Minister of Congo-Léopoldville in August 1961 compensated the UPA, for he was a long-standing friend of Holden Roberto.

The GRAE strengthened its position in 1962 by creating allied organisations, closely attached to the UPA. There was a Serviço de Assistência aos Refugiados de Angola—SARA (Refugee Aid Service); an Associação das Mulheres de Angola (Angolan Women's Association); a União Nacional dos Estudantes Angolanos—UNEA (National Students' Union of Angola); a youth association; a trade union (the Liga dos Trabalhadores de Angola, retaken in hand); and so on. The whole set-up corresponded closely with rival organisations set up by the MPLA.

In May–June 1962, there were serious but sporadic clashes in Angola, in the Serra do Uíge (near Carmona), the Vale do Loge and the Bessa Monteiro region. The UPA-GRAE organisation received its first twenty-four Angolan trainees from the Algerian FLN camps in Tunisia in June 1962. Contrary to the claims of the Governor, Venâncio Deslandes, the war was not over, but it claimed so few Portuguese victims (289 Portuguese and Angolan soldiers killed between February 4, 1961, and June 8, 1962) that Portugal could stand it. The Congolese government appeared to back Roberto's revolutionary government in exile entirely when it put the Kinkuzu training camp at the disposal of the UPA-GRAE on August 21, 1962. Roberto's movement should now logically have progressed towards a more skilled and intensive form of guerrilla activity. But there was no massive invasion of Angola by the more or less real forces of its Exército de Libertação Nacional de Angola—ELNA (National Liberation Army). To put it bluntly, the Kinkuzu soldiers and their officers felt more at home in the independence parade in Kinshasa than among the guerrilla units to which the UPA-GRAE claimed to have sent 3,000 trained men. However, the UPA did open an office in Lubumbashi (Elizabethville). In the absence of military victories over the Portuguese, it was to register a brilliant success over its main political opponent, the MPLA.

Following the conference of African heads of state in Addis Ababa in May 1963, the committee entrusted with reconciling the Angolan national movements was short-circuited by the decision of Congo-Kinshasa, announced on June 29, 1963, to recognise de jure the GRAE. During the ensuing period of extreme confusion in July, the MPLA sustained a political collapse and the ascendancy of the UPA-GRAE seemed assured. However, a new party was formed at Lubumbashi in that same month: the União Nacional Angolana—UNA (Angolan National Union), consisting of former UPA partisans (particularly Ovimbundu, several thousand of whom, it would seem, were living in the Katangese capital). This new formation, which denounced the tribalism of the UPA-GRAE, was in fact an Ovimbundu splinter-group of the UPA. Including Marcos Kassanga and André Kassinda, the UNA tended to draw closer to the UPA's great rival, the MPLA; but the difficulties of communications, the lack of means and the narrow horizons of its leaders were to render it practically paralysed.

The 'conciliation committee' of the Organisation of African Unity in Kinshasa gave Holden Roberto his biggest political victory by recommending the recognition of the GRAE to the exclusion of all other Angolan movements. Its supremacy was sealed by its official recognition by some twenty African governments, including those as diverse as Algeria (pro-MPLA in tendency), Senegal and the United Arab Republic. But these diplomatic successes did not solve the deep problems troubling the GRAE, even though they brought subsidies (especially from Algeria and Tunisia) and almost complete hegemony over the refugees in the Congo. The GRAE lacked trained leaders and, for all its efforts to place students in Western universities, the Marxist intellectuals of the MPLA, although temporarily powerless, were able to lay a base of future influence by offering far more scholarships in Communist countries than its rival was able to obtain in the West. From the summer of 1963 until 1964–65, the GRAE tried to mitigate its predominantly Bakongo character by working on the refugees and Angolan workers in Katanga. But it had little success here, for these people were either apolitical or attracted by the UNA and other incipient groups stemming from pre-1961 central Angola ethnic groups, as they were of Ovimbundu, Quioco (Chokwe), Lunda or Luena stock. In practice, the GRAE headquarters remained in Kinshasa, the bulk of its army in Kinkuzu, and its guerrilla bands in the *serras*. There was no progress, except for an occasional ambush in the west (such as occurred near Tomboco). No new theatres of war were opened beyond the region that had rebelled in 1961.

Even so, albeit at a snail's pace, the war continued. From February 4, 1961, to July 10, 1963, the Portuguese lost 511 men,[11] 200 of them being killed in a period of eight months. For an army estimated at 40,000 men on October 6, 1963, these were minimal losses, though they do not include those of the Volunteer Corps. At the same time, the Portuguese command estimated that only some 6 per cent of Angola was still troubled by some 4,000–5,000 guerrilla fighters. The Bessa Monteiro region was especially affected in July 1963, but the UPA incursions in Cabinda in August were without future since they received no support from the population.

Hopes raised in some quarters in August 1963 by the Portuguese announcement of limited elections in Angola did not affect the GRAE, which reiterated the conditions it regarded as indispensable for a return to peace: the acceptance by Portugal of the principle of self-determination; the liberation of political prisoners; the withdrawal of Portuguese forces; the commencement of negotiations leading to the transfer of power to the Angolans. This was asking a lot of the Portuguese government which sent the President of the republic on a month's visit to Angola in September-October. After the Congolese authorities had officially evicted the MPLA from Kinshasa in November 1963, the GRAE had a free hand and strategically stifled any stray MPLA impulse to battle by preventing its adherents from crossing the frontier to supply the Dembos and Nambuangongo.[12]

There was nothing of great import in GRAE affairs in late 1963, except that Holden Roberto came up against a less encouraging American attitude and threatened to turn to the Chinese for aid. During this period, the *serras* in the north of Angola, increasingly harried by the Portuguese, lost yet more of their refugees who made for the Congo (some 12,000 in March 1964). Recognition of the GRAE by African states was maintained, but it suffered a further crisis in July 1964. Its Minister of Foreign Affairs, Jonas Malheiro Savimbi, resigned his post in the middle of an OAU conference in Cairo, on July 16, 1964, and on July 24 José João Liahuca, director of SARA, the refugee aid service, also resigned. Both denounced GRAE inefficiency, the lack of unity in the nationalist movement and, more serious, the lack of support for the forces inside Angola. They were probably motivated by acceptance into the GRAE of Viriato da Cruz and his followers (a minority faction of the MPLA), which brought a pro-Chinese *mestiço*, highly skilled in Marxist dialectic, into the bosom of an organisation where the intellectuals could be counted on the fingers of both hands. The departure of the two leaders, followed by that of the Cabindan Alexandre Taty, robbed the GRAE of some of its leading non-Baxikongo members. Three years after the outbreak of rebellion, Holden Roberto was once again at the head of a tribal movement, as unrepresentative as the MPLA.

Militarily, the UPA and MPLA made no progress, but their presence was enough to tie down in Angola a substantial Portuguese army which, although it fought little (seventy-five killed between March 17 and September 17, 1964),[13] cost a lot. It was a war of attrition. Tshombe's presence at the head of the Congo-Kinshasa government did not favour reactivation of the fight, since passage of arms was forbidden by him. What was chiefly lacking was the will to win and enthusiasm for the fight. The leadership did not set an example, for in this fourth year of war some of its members appeared to have settled down as professional bureaucratic nationalists, leaving the guerrilla forces short of arms. Moreover, OAU aid to the GRAE was not materialising (only 500,000 French francs in two years, according to the GRAE). Some of its combatants lost heart and surrendered to the Portuguese. The struggle against the MPLA sharpened (twenty-five MPLA men were reportedly killed in an ambush on September 28, 1964). Enmeshed in Congolese politics, the GRAE undertook some activity in Katanga and a little along the Cuango frontier.

A serious weakness of the GRAE arose from the alienation of the sympathies of an important section of the Ovimbundu trained at Kinkuzu, including the chief of staff, José Kalundungo. This withering of the struggle was exemplified by the attempt on June 21, 1965, of Alexandre Taty (former Minister for Armaments) to carry out a putsch against UPA headquarters and to dismiss Holden Roberto. On June 23, a commando unit lead by Taty, Kassinda and two Europeans sacked the GRAE offices in Kinshasa and, more important, carried off their archives. It is not impossible that the PIDE and the Portuguese embassy in Kinshasa may have had a hand in this obscure affair. Violent attacks were directed at Roberto but he retained the support of the troops in Kinkuzu, which was vital for his position.

Tshombe's replacement by General Joseph Mobutu in November 1965 improved Roberto's prospects somewhat, at least in the struggle against the galaxy of mini-groups competing for the loyalty of the Angolan refugees. In June 1966, the GRAE security chief arrested several of its dissident leaders and rivals and despatched them to the Kinkuzu camp.[14] Despite a stillborn reconciliation in Cairo on October 17, 1966, between the GRAE and the MPLA, any unity between the two movements was impossible on personal, ethnic and political grounds.

Although Portuguese losses increased in 1966–67 (from July 3, 1966, to July 4, 1967, the Portuguese lost 220 regular soldiers and at least 100 Volunteers) due to the entry into the field of the MPLA and the União Nacional para a Independência Total de Angola—UNITA (National Union for Total Independence), the renewal of the struggle cannot be attributed to any intensification of GRAE activity. On the contrary, although it was the only movement with reasonably well-armed forces, apart from the MPLA, it seemed to prefer to keep them close to Kinshasa, probably to counter any new putsch by its rivals or even an improbable frontier-crossing by the Portuguese army. For all Roberto's asserting before the United Nations in May 1967 that he had an army of 30,000 men controlling a territory inhabited by 400,000 people, one might well ask whether, six years after the start of hostilities, even these inflated figures indicated progress in a movement that had been claiming similar or higher figures in 1961. Indeed, apart from the support of General Mobutu's government and of the moderate African states, the UPA-GRAE at the present have only three real trump cards. In the first place, there is the presence of hundreds of thousands of Bakongo refugees—who, although they may now have few illusions about the likelihood of a speedy return to Angola, suffice to keep alive the structures created in 1962 with their UPA membership fees—and of several thousand volunteers. Then there is the political acumen of Roberto himself who, despite all setbacks, has managed to keep one step ahead of his rivals within the GRAE. His knowledge of the Congolese environment, with which he has been intimately associated since childhood, is probably the movement's surest guarantee of survival. The third strong card is his organisation's control of the Congolese frontier, which crosses the ethnic territories where the revolt began. The UPA-GRAE retains local supremacy over the rival MPLA by preventing it from supplying its northern guerrilla bands with men and arms.

Roberto's movement, all the same, has been put in a bad light by repeated MPLA denunciations of it (including accusations of genocide), by the inertia of its combatants and by its inability to bring unity to the Angolan nationalist cause. In theory, the GRAE includes three parties within the FNLA (National Liberation Front): the UPA, the Partido Democrático de Angola, and some secessionist members of the MPLA lead by Viriato da Cruz. But, in fact, it is the creature of Holden Roberto. The decision of the OAU heads of state, meeting in Algiers in September 1968, to reconsider their recognition of the GRAE as a 'government' is a distinct victory for MPLA progressives, even though it meant little in the context of a guerrilla war.

In the period 1968–70, a certain reanimation of GRAE partisan activities was visible in northern and eastern districts, including Cabinda, Zaire, Uíge, Cuanza-Norte, Luanda and Malanje, with sporadic forays into parts of Lunda and Moxico where they have to contend with MPLA and UNITA guerrillas operating there. The Benguela railway close to the Congolese border has been a favourite, albeit dangerous, target for GRAE commandos. But except in the Dembos and other *serras* of north-western Angola where they still have partisans providing shelter, the GRAE forces spasmodically operating in Cabinda, Malanje, Lunda and Moxico have apparently no inland bases, so they have to resort to hit-and-run raids from the Congolese border, their best sanctuary.

The MPLA and its satellites. The MPLA has experienced an unexpected revival after its near-extinction in 1963. There are three main reasons for its survival and later revival. In the first place, it is headed by a small group (probably fewer than ten people) of long-standing militant Marxists, used to clandestine struggle and with an apparently sincere faith in the socialist future of Angola, in spite of all the obstacles. The

9. São José de Encoge, a northern fort, two hundred years after its foundation

10. Political prisoners and former *terroristas* in a camp near Serpa Pinto

key man seems to be Lucio Lara, a cold, methodical organiser, a convinced Marxist of European ways, a *mestiço* apparatchik from Nova Lisboa. He saved the life of the MPLA in 1963. In his function as officer in charge of cadres, he exercises in the background an overwhelming influence on the life of this party, which has mastered the language and methods of European left-wing parties (at least in appearance). Secondly, it enjoys the effective support of the Soviet Union, the East European people's democracies and Cuba and, at one time, China. It never seems to be in any financial difficulty over equipping its still modest but increasingly numerous troops, especially since 1964–65. Thirdly, after a lethargic existence in Kinshasa, the removal of its headquarters to Brazzaville in 1963 was a distinct advantage, for thereby it could escape the direct attacks of the GRAE, the discouraging atmosphere of Kinshasa and PIDE intriguing.

However, it still suffers from some weaknesses which it has not been able to eliminate. There is a wide gulf between the Marxism of its brilliant, intellectual leaders (of whom its new president, the poet Agostinho Neto, is a good example) and the Angolan people whom they aspire to liberate. Overwhelmingly illiterate, the people prefer to follow leaders of their own ethnic group rather than exiled intellectuals. Hence the MPLA has succeeded in retaining a few strongholds in Angola where Mbundu tribesmen have taken refuge under leaders whom they knew, such as a few African Methodist ministers or Tókoist leaders from the Dembos or the Luanda-Malange corridor, who happened also to be MPLA supporters. Herein the MPLA resembles the UPA as being an ethnonationalist party. And, as with the UPA, this carries a penalty. Its almost total failure in Cabinda stems from the fact that the Cabindans see it as a movement of 'foreigners' come to disturb them and compromise them in the eyes of the Portuguese. By contrast, its relative success in eastern Angola is due to its initial care to establish local leaders before launching a guerrilla war.

Claiming to be pan-Angolan and having from the start a nation-wide support, but limited to the *assimilados* and detribalised urban Africans (except for the rural Mbundu bases), the party had its original leaders disappear in the PIDE arrests of 1959 and 1960, and in the storm that burst on the *assimilados* in 1961. Working throughout Angola, it suffered the repeated attacks of the PIDE. Where it lacks Mbundu rural leaders, or newly-enrolled local leaders (as in the east and also in the Malanje, Bié and probably Huambo districts), it can prosper only in the towns where clandestine activities are recrudescing, since 1969 if not earlier.

Moreover, the *mestiço* and Mbundu preponderance among its leaders

8—A

cuts it off from the mass of Bakongo refugees in Congo-Kinshasa; it is thus deprived of the potential support to which the UPA-GRAE can lay claim. Crossing the Congo river in 1963, to establish its headquarters in Brazzaville, accentuated this alienation from the Angolan Bakongo masses. To contact its rural Mbundu bases, its partisans have to cross a great river, pass Congolese control posts, and avoid the GRAE troops of the Exército de Libertação Nacional (ELNA), the Portuguese soldiery and the UPA guerrilla bands. It is hardly surprising if its partisans have hesitated before such obstacles. It was very difficult for the MPLA to establish easy communications; but they tried to compensate for this military weakness by obtaining aid from some socialist countries. The difficulty of the MPLA's access to Angolan centres was somewhat alleviated in 1966 when it began to work on the 'soft belly' of eastern Angola. Here its chances of beating its rival and the Portuguese were better, for it was dealing with a new population, not tired of the war, and with an easy refuge in Zambian Barotseland, where the MPLA was able to build up a similar position to that which was so favourable to the UPA in Congo-Kinshasa.

It would be true to say that the MPLA was a mere spectator of the Bakongo revolts in 1961. Its claims to have had its own guerrilla bands at that date do not hold water, since the UPA by terror or promises won over all alleged MPLA supporters in the Dembos and Nambuangongo. It was only when the UPA's hold weakened, and when a local leader such as the Reverend Domingos da Silva managed to get out of Angola and establish contact with the MPLA abroad, that groups in the existing guerrilla movement declared for the MPLA. In fact, the MPLA office in Léopoldville in 1961 remained passive, for its best leaders were either in prison (Agostinho Neto), or travelling (Mário de Andrade), or else in Conakry (Lucio Lara). Moreover, in 1961 the MPLA was clinging to the well-known tactics of a 'front' to cover its own weakness by setting up a larger organisation which it could manipulate. Very obviously, its first preoccupation was left-wing opinion in Western Europe and among the rulers of progressive African states. Action within Angola was relegated to second place. It tried to drag the UPA into an avatar of the Frente Revolucionária Africana (FRAIN): an organisation called the Conferência das Organisações Nacionalistas das Colónias Portuguesas— CONCP (Conference of Nationalist Organisations of the Portuguese Colonies), which was founded in Rabat (April 18–20, 1961) one month after the revolt of March 1961 and comprised ten nationalist organisations from Africa and Goa. The UPA refused to join, giving the struggle in the interior precedence over the exterior. Since the MPLA was more or less devoid of troops, its tactics in 1961–62 were to seek an alliance with the UPA and, once inside the works, to deploy its intellectuals and seize the control levers. Holden Roberto saw through the manoeuvre and rejected the proposed alliance, which prompted the MPLA to accuse him of tribalism and sectarianism.

The MPLA refused to accept as full members Portuguese progressives born in Angola,[15] but maintained a somewhat eventful relationship—dictated by schisms within the Portuguese opposition—with Salazar's 'domestic' opponents from Henrique Galvão to the Frente Patriótica de Libertação Nacional—FPLN (Patriotic Liberation Front) based in Algiers and including, notably, the Portuguese Communist Party. It was probably thanks to the help of this opposition that they succeeded in enabling Agostinho Neto to escape from Portugal and rejoin the MPLA headquarters in Kinshasa in July 1962. The situation he found on his arrival was not particularly hopeful for the MPLA. It was vain to denounce the UPA as non-representative; the MPLA's only concrete activities at this period seem to have been assistance to the refugees through the intermediary role of the Corpo Voluntário Angolano de Assistência aos Refugiados—CVAAR (Angolan Refugee Aid Volunteers), founded in August 1961. Thanks to MPLA recruitment of *assimilados* in exile, the CVAAR was able to open a medical centre with eight Angolan doctors in Kinshasa.

To re-establish itself, the MPLA called its first national conference in December 1962, and there elaborated a battle programme. Its leaders wanted to approach the Angolan masses but, since Roberto and the GRAE kept the frontier closed to them, this remained a theoretical hope. Agostinho Neto was elected president of the steering committee and Mário de Andrade moved from president to foreign affairs; Manual Lima took the department for war, and the key post of organiser of cadres went to Lucio Lara. Viriato da Cruz was removed from the leadership. On paper, the organisation seemed well balanced. However, apart from the CVAAR, none of the MPLA's satellite bodies—neither the Exército Popular de Libertação de Angola—EPLA (Popular Liberation Army of Angola), equivalent of the GRAE's Exército de Libertação Nacional (ELNA), nor the Organisação das Mulheres de Angola—OMA (Angolan Women's Organisation), nor the Juventude do MPLA (Youth Movement), nor the União Nacional dos Trabalhadores de Angola—UNTA (National Union of Angolan Workers)—was other than a subsidiary movement in search of serious militants. And these were in short supply in all of the MPLA's satellites. The same thing applied to a union of students in exile in Europe and North Africa, based in Rabat: the União Geral dos Estudantes da Africa Negra sob Dominação Colonial Portuguesa—UGEAN (General Union of Black African Students under

213

Portuguese Rule) which was attached to the Conferência das Organis-ações Nacionalistas (CONCP) in Morocco after September 1961.

The main features of the first MPLA conference were: redirection of activities, with the accent changing from external propaganda to armed struggle; theoretical non-alignment; precedence of politics over military matters; training of leaders. The MPLA was still trying to establish a political front with the GRAE but the latter replied with bullets. The sole solution for the MPLA was to try to open a military front where they would not be hampered. The only accessible one then was the Cabinda Enclave, to which it sent a few guerrilla fighters in January 1963. Cabinda had been quiet throughout 1962, after minor UPA attacks in 1961, directed by Alexandre Taty. If the MPLA had had really competent keen soldiers and the support of the Cabindan population, there is no doubt that its operations in the virgin forest of Mayombe could have driven the Portuguese from an untenable position, since neither artillery nor aviation had any effect in this mountainous jungle. But such was not the case; it seems that Fulbert Youlou, President of Congo-Brazzaville, was reluctant to encourage a Marxist movement that could have involved him in frontier problems; and, in any case, he supported the separatists of the Movimento de Libertação do Enclave de Cabinda—MLEC (Cabinda Liberation Movement).

Crisis struck the MPLA in the summer of 1963. Still in pursuit of their dreams of the political front, the MPLA leaders tried to weaken Roberto's stand against them by aggregating the Movimento Nacional Angolano—MNA (Angolan National Movement), a Bakongo ethno-nationalist micro-party, to their organisation and its trade-union satellite, the UNTA. But a sharp check to this manoeuvre was given by Cyrille Adoula's recognition of the GRAE on June 29. A further blow came from Viriato da Cruz, who had left the MPLA in December 1962; on July 5, he announced that *he* represented the MPLA, not the Neto-Lara or any other group.

By this point in time, Agostinho Neto had formed, with the UNTA and the MNA, a new alliance of parties: the Frente Democrática para a Libertação de Angola—FDLA (Angolan Democratic Liberation Front). To begin with, this included the MPLA, the UNTA and the MNA; but it was gradually joined, in toto or in part, by the moderate Bakongo parties that were vegetating and proliferating in Kinshasa: the Movimento de Defesa (MDIA), the Ngwizako and, finally, a section of the Nto-Bako. For an allegedly Marxist party, such an alliance with tiny groups, deeply compromised with the Portuguese who financed them, meant grasping at political survival at the expense of an entire past policy of intransi-gence.

Mistakes of this kind by the MPLA, and the attacks on it by Viriato da Cruz and the UPA, finally convinced the Organisation of African Unity that the MPLA was a movement in dissolution, seeking to prolong its existence by allying with 'doubtful' politicians. It became known that dissensions among the MPLA's combatants (all 250 of them, in 1963) were such as to render them completely innocuous to the Portuguese. The OAU's 'conciliation committee' in July asked its member-states to recognise the GRAE. Mário de Andrade resigned from the MPLA on July 22; the Neto-Lara section was on the rocks; the Viriato da Cruz wing tried to join the GRAE, but was not accepted. Algeria's recognition of the GRAE in August might have proved the last straw for the MPLA if Lucio Lara had not succeeded in rallying its remnant of supporters (five doctors of the CVAAR had left in August) by allowing the still-born and compromising Frente Democrática to fade out, and by moving to Brazzaville after the closure of the MPLA and CVAAR headquarters in Kinshasa by Cyrille Adoula in November 1963. It was the end of a chapter for the MPLA: one in which doctrinaire preaching and propaganda abroad had completely disguised its intrinsic weakness and its lack of partisans willing to take up arms.

Henceforward, if the MPLA was to operate south of the Congo river, it would need to employ secrecy and guile to survive the attacks of GRAE partisans seeking to eliminate its militants. A conference of some fifty MPLA leaders at Brazzaville from January 3 to 10, 1964, took stock of the situation. They had only two or three hundred soldiers left. However, Youlou's overthrow at Brazzaville, the associated drift to the left in that country, and, above all, the arrival of substantial Russian and even Chinese aid stiffened the movement, while Viriato da Cruz, who had stayed at Kinshasa, now entered the GRAE (and incidentally precipitated the departure of Jonas M. Savimbi). The MPLA came to rely more and more on Communist assistance, which it strove to obtain and justify by accentuating its 'revolutionary' character and to this end launched a leaders' training campaign (350 students were sent to Europe between 1961 and 1964). It published three magazines: *Vitória ou Morte*, *Unidade Angolana* and *Boletim do Militante*, all employing Marxist terminology and themes. Under the 'post-revolutionary' reign of Massemba-Débat at Brazzaville, the MPLA no longer needed to hide its convictions and methods. In July 1964, the Congo-Brazzaville government allowed it to receive an important arms cargo.

Since the MPLA could no longer openly influence the refugees in Congo-Kinshasa, it began to concentrate on those in far-away Angola, around Nambuangongo and in the eastern Dembos, who had neither surrendered to the Portuguese nor gone over to the UPA. These were

Mbundu survivors—Protestants who had rebelled in 1961 and whom the MPLA had more or less abandoned perforce. Their endurance was to enable the party to forget its setback among the Cabindans, many of whom refused to co-operate with the MPLA guerrillas. The elderly Domingos F. da Silva, vice-president of the party, was the indispensable ethnic and religious link, keeping alive the Mbundu's flame of rebellion. He and Agostinho Neto (also a Mbundu) were the only MPLA top leaders whom the rural combatants still in the field knew and followed. The present fate of the MPLA rested with men like him; the future belonged to the young, enrolled in the Pioneers, then in the Juventude and finally in the military training camp organised at Brazzaville by the Cubans or the revolutionary instruction centre at Dolisie (near Cabinda). The most active and best-educated of these young militants were given scholarships to study military techniques or in universities in East European countries (80 per cent of the total).

The MPLA's problems in 1965 were complex. It was a party of intellectuals cut off from the towns of Angola where it recruited its members before 1961, and it held sway over only a small minority of the Mbundu (perhaps 15,000) who had stayed in the resistance movement less because of Communist beliefs than through their religious (Methodist) ties with the Reverend Domingos da Silva[16] and other African pastors living with their flocks. In Cabinda, its partisans suffered from the passive hostility of the Frente de Libertação do Enclave de Cabinda—FLEC (Cabinda Liberation Front) and the active opposition of a dissident UPA group that might have joined the MPLA but went over to the Portuguese to continue, on their behalf, the UPA versus MPLA struggle. This group was led by Alexandre Taty, who chose to command former UPA troops bought up by the Portuguese in 1965 in order to combat the MPLA in Cabinda. (In this context, one can affirm that the PIDE networks and Portuguese informants in Congo-Kinshasa are equal in effect to a division of parachutists on the ground.) The Sino-Soviet dispute complicated the international work of the MPLA which, on the whole, followed the Soviet line, especially as Viriato da Cruz tended to be pro-Chinese. Desertions to the Portuguese among the higher military ranks (including Commander José Ferreira, in March 1965) led the MPLA to apply a policy similar to that of the GRAE. Two former MPLA men, followers of Viriato da Cruz, were reported to have been arrested in November 1965; they have not been heard of since.

Thanks to its *mestiço* leaders, with their pan-Angolan vision of nationalism, the MPLA grasped that it must breach the Congo blockade and direct its effort to opening a guerrilla front in new terrain and among new ethnic groups. This indicated eastern Angola as the new theatre of operations from which it might hope to win the key racial group which so far no one had been able to bring into the fight against the Portuguese: the Ovimbundu. This simple geo-political calculation prompted the MPLA to send clandestine leaders from 1964 onward into the eastern Angola bush to cultivate carefully the pre-insurrectional ground. In these vast open spaces, impossible for a scattered Portuguese administration to control (the average area, in 1966, of the twenty-eight administrative divisions of the Moxico district was 2,800 square miles each, and that of the twenty-one divisions in the Cuando-Cubango district 3,600 square miles each), underpopulated and partially unexplored, the MPLA militants went undetected until May 1966. At that date they laid an ambush near Luso; by this stroke the nationalist war, which had vegetated for five years in the north, gained truly pan-Angolan dimensions. Although the MPLA battle communiqués were even more exaggeratedly optimistic than those of the UPA,[17] there is no doubt that their partisans, moving in small, well-armed and mobile bands, achieved considerable successes, not so much against Portuguese soldiers as by converting whole villages, whose inhabitants fled towards Zambia thanks to brutal Portuguese repression (razing of 'infected' villages) and MPLA tactics.

In June and July 1966, the MPLA succeeded for the first time in sending a column (of 150 to 200 men) to the Nambuangongo region; they crossed the frontier at several points where the vigilance of the GRAE and the Congolese authorities had been lulled by the MPLA's unofficial representative in Kinshasa, Luis de Azevedo. In September 1966, they created a União de Estudantes Angolanos—UEA (Angolan Students' Union) equivalent to the União Nacional dos Estudantes Angolanos—UNEA of the GRAE. The GRAE resented the reinforcement of MPLA potential in the Dembos and Nambuangongo; it stepped up its ambushes of MPLA guerrilla bands and, in 1966–67, intensified arrests and partial liquidation of the opposing militants, both in Angola and Congo-Kinshasa.

In 1967–69, the MPLA engaged in a 'scientific' struggle for the first time in eastern Angola; they had moved part of their military and political staff from Brazzaville to Lusaka, Zambia. The MPLA's success was largely due to the virtual absence of UPA interference, and also to the support of some of the Luchaze, Bunda, Luena, Chokwe and other branches of the Ganguela and Mbundu (southern Malange district) who were less under the control of the Portuguese administration because of their remoteness from centres of white economy. In this period, it was the only movement pursuing the war in five regions, in three of which the campaign was not based on ethnic influence. Encouraged by the success of its commandos in blowing up some of the few bridges of eastern Angola and attacking areas as far from the frontier as, for example, Cazombo, Lucusse, Cangamba and Cangombe, in 1968 the MPLA moved part of its organisation into Angolan territory and abandoned Brazzaville for Lusaka as its main external centre. It was the first time the leadership of any nationalist party in Angola had felt strong enough to abandon its refuge abroad.

In 1970, the MPLA had recovered enough confidence to implant various formation centres for political cadres, women leaders, young 'Pioneers' and above all guerrilla training in Cuando-Cubango and Moxico districts, some located 200 miles from the Zambian border. At the present time, the MPLA is reported to be moderately active in five so-called military regions. The first of these is the Dembos area, which serves as a base for attacks against such distant targets as the oilwells about twenty-five miles from Luanda. The Dembos area figures prominently in MPLA history as the cradle of the 1961 resistance to the Portuguese and for refusing to surrender to the UPA in subsequent years. In spite of the GRAE blockade, it hopes to instil new life into the largely lethargic Dembos maquis; there has been renewed agitation in as safe a region for the Portuguese as Massangano in the Cuanza valley. The second region, the Cabinda Enclave, is the weakest of the so-called fronts, activities being pinioned to border posts along the frontier with Congo-Brazzaville. The third region, Moxico district and a large part of the Cuando-Cubango district, is the most promising ground for the MPLA because of its vast size and its proximity to Zambia. In this sparsely-populated area, MPLA groups were reported to have shot down three Portuguese planes in July, September and October 1969 and to have scored some success in ambushes and skirmishes with Portuguese ground forces. The fourth region, the districts of Lunda and Malanje, is a recent creation in the military set-up of the MPLA. The Portuguese hit the guerrillas there hard in June 1969, killing two of their local commanders. Apparently, by expanding westward the MPLA hopes to reach the Cuanza valley from the south-east and link with the beleaguered Dembos. The fifth region, the Bié district, is the more dangerous for the Portuguese, because activities there affect the populous central Angolan plateau. Hopes to win over the Ovimbundu to the MPLA side are still premature. Moreover, while it tries to consolidate or expand its control in the bush the MPLA leadership is secretly hoping to undermine Portuguese confidence in the towns by resurrecting or creating underground cells. Some of their Luandan activists managed to hijack a regular civilian plane on the Cabinda run and take it to Pointe Noire in Congo-Brazzaville in June 1969. Numerous obstacles still face the MPLA, however. It must prevent UPA competition in the east; completely eliminate UNITA partisans from the region, retain the support of the Zambian government which tolerates its convoys to the frontier and its bases; overcome tribalism; outmanoeuvre the PIDE and the administration, both of which are now powerful and skilled, even in rural areas; resist the Portuguese air force and defeat the enemy shock troops—*caçadores especiais* (special light infantry) and paratroops—in guerrilla warfare; overcome the backward state of the population it seeks to 'liberate'; and, above all, win from the people the massive support that it does not yet have. If it can achieve all this it may hope to reach the stage attained by the Partido Africano da Independência da Guiné e Cabo Verde (PAIGC) in Guinea—that is, the installation of a rudimentary administration beyond the reach of the Portuguese cooped up in their garrisons.

If the MPLA overcomes all these obstacles in the east, it can hope to live off the land indefinitely, unless a military counter-offensive mounted jointly by Portugal and South Africa were to reduce Moxico and Cuando-Cubango to the state of Zaire, now a semi-desert whose former inhabitants have fled over the frontiers. Its major trump-card is perhaps the absence of settlers in the east (in contrast to northern Angola).[18] If the MPLA were to succeed in winning the support of the Ovimbundu and Chokwe, it would become a dangerous threat to the plateaux of Bié and Huambo and to the Diamang mines, two major props of Angola. If not, it would either be relegated for good to this Angolan backyard or expelled from it. Its attacks on the Benguela railway are, in this respect, a double-edged weapon, for they alienate Congo-Kinshasa, where the MPLA has nothing to lose, but also Zambia on which it depends for logistic reasons.

Although about a hundred of its militants are reported to be incarcerated by the UPA-GRAE in Kinkuzu and Kamuna in Congo-Kinshasa, the MPLA, after focusing its efforts on eastern Angola and trying to infiltrate the central plateaux, may be considered in the short term as having an edge on the GRAE. In the long term, it may be the most dangerous adversary, since it is preparing an Angolan and not a merely Bakongo take-over. It remains to be seen whether its leaders will be more skilled than the Portuguese in gaining the allegiance of the most apolitical ethnic groups: those with the fewest complaints against the Portuguese who more or less ignored them until 1966. One should not forget that, for Luanda, the east—and particularly Cuando-Cubango and Moxico— are *as terras do fim do mundo*, 'the end of the world'. Starting from the

Angola

world's end, will the MPLA find the strength to win the economic heart of Angola, when it failed in Cabinda, the Dembos and Nambuangongo? Moreover, it is not only Portugal that the MPLA is facing, since in the third region some evidence shows that South African forces operating from their Caprivi Strip airbase help patrol the Angolan bush of the Cuando-Cubango and Moxico districts against MPLA commandos. Whatever the result of its action, it will be a long trek for the MPLA to reach the sea-coast of central Angola. So it is in the political sphere that its struggle against the UPA seems most successful, as its bitter rival loses ground.

The nationalist 'spectators'. Even experts in the political fragmentation of Congo-Kinshasa may well be appalled by the veritable labyrinth of Angolan ethno-nationalist parties which, not entirely by chance, grow up, flourish and die in that same Congo-Kinshasa. There is little point in listing all of them and following their meanderings, which have all the characteristics of micro-tribalism: opportunism of leaders, and a lack of seriousness and maturity among heads of mini-groups who are first and foremost refugees and only secondly politicians. They are frustrated by the easy atmosphere of Kinshasa, where they see former Congolese companions rising to the top while they vegetate in the shanty towns because their nationality deprives them of a slice of the Congolese political cake. A careful observer is reported to have collected the names of fifty-eight Angolan nationalist organisations from the beginning to 1967, together with twenty-six associations or groups of a social or trade-union nature.[19] This proliferation of parties is the best possible present the Angolans could offer the Portuguese, who have skilfully grasped the advantage to be gained from this fragmentation, and have added to it by the offer of pensions and subsidies to some leaders who have become professional exiled nationalists: an honourable sinecure in Kinshasa as long as one can find a dozen or so compatriots to form a new party.[20] All are weak; most are aware of this, but extremely rare is the leader prepared to renounce the first place in his own tiny group, to become number two or three in a more serious organisation. In fact, after the negative results of the MPLA's desperate efforts in 1963 to win over these micro-parties, neither its revolutionary Marxists nor Holden Roberto and the Baxikongo intransigents of the UPA seem to have made further efforts at recruitment among these groups whose nuisance value politically is minimal but who are ethnically strong enough to prevent either of the main rivals from succeeding completely within their tribal fiefs.

The irredentists are little heard of and seem to have abandoned their claims or gravitated towards the stronger UPA, as did some Chokwe militants. The Ovimbundu nationalists of the former Grupo Avante or the Comité Secreto Revolucionário do Sul de Angola (Secret Revolutionary Committee of South Angola) have either tended to look to the UPA (but following their disillusion with the policies of the GRAE they have showed less interest in their formal affiliation) or have slowly taken stock of the potential value of their ethnic base and will wait for a leader with a modicum of charisma. They believe that Jonas Savimbi, the GRAE dissident, will be the man in a position to raise the Ovimbundu masses and a good number of the pre-1961 activists will turn to the UNITA. The South West African People's Organisation enjoyed UPA-GRAE support for a brief moment.

The Cabindan separatists pose a more important and persistent problem, which has increased with the economic development of the Enclave, due to the discovery of offshore oil in September 1966. Politically they are pacifists, perhaps because of their knowledge of their compatriots' pacific nature, and the futility of MPLA efforts in the Mayombe jungle. The principal party, the Movimento de Libertação do Enclave de Cabinda (MLEC) spawned a splinter group, the Comité de Acção da União Nacional de Cabinda—CAUNC (Cabinda Action Committee), which broke away in December 1961 only to return to form, at the Pointe Noire conference on August 4, 1963, the Frente de Libertação do Enclave de Cabinda—FLEC (Cabinda Liberation Front) in association with the MLEC and the Alliance du Mayombe (ALLIAMA). President of this front was Luis Ranque Franque. Verbal opponents of the UPA-GRAE and also of the MPLA when its forces attacked the Enclave, the groups in the front sought a constitutional conference with Portugal, an amnesty and independence for Cabinda alone. Based at Pointe Noire, they probably had some influence over Cabindan refugees in Congo-Brazzaville, for whom they competed with the MPLA. Some Cabindan refugees in Congo-Kinshasa returned home in 1966 and 1967. The high standard of living in Cabinda, which is experiencing an unprecedented oil boom, is the surest ally of the Portuguese; they now have to face only small frontier skirmishes with the MPLA, and the Congo-Kinshasa frontier is rather peaceful, except for an occasional GRAE incursion. Despite its propaganda, the MPLA does not control a third of the Enclave; not even a twentieth. The most exposed posts are Miconge and Massabi, open to attack from Congo-Brazzaville, since northern Mayombe can be crossed clandestinely by small groups, at times pursued by Alexandre Taty's troops now with the Portuguese.

The refusal of the Frente de Libertação and of some exiled Cabindans to join the nationalist movements in the rest of Angola probably received secret encouragement from the Portuguese; and the Luanda authorities had the bright idea of appointing a pro-Portuguese Cabindan *mestiço* as Under-Secretary for Education for Angola. Far from diminishing, Cabindan separatism is actually on the increase and it is kept in check only by the iron grip of the Portuguese, who have no intention of losing the revenues from the American-controlled Cabinda Gulf Oil Company.[21] Ignoring the 'revolution', they have laid a tarmac surface on the vital highway linking Cabinda with Guilherme Capelo (formerly Landana), Dinge, Buco-Zau and farther north.

Among the Bakongo ethno-nationalists, the Catholic Ngwizako still survives, oscillating between liaison with the Portuguese and with the MPLA (as in 1963). As Catholics, they had suffered UPA-GRAE threats, but it was a Catholic king, Dom Pedro VIII, who was elected on September 9, 1962, at São Salvador, with Portuguese approval. After a brief reign of several weeks, Dom Pedro VIII died, leaving a Queen Regent and their former president, José Kasakanga, in a Luanda prison. More or less penetrated by the Portuguese, they suffered a split in October 1961, then a reconciliation in July 1963. They allied with various organisations, all virtually without members and composed of non-violent Bakongo exiles demanding independence for the Kongo.

Among this hotch-potch was the Nto-Bako, the leader of which, Angelino Alberto, visited Lisbon in 1961 and arranged the return of some refugees. Even for Kinshasa, it was far too openly a party of collaborators. It split apart in July 1963, when three rival groups claimed to be the Nto-Bako. Some of its militants were reportedly arrested in Angola, despite a Portuguese safe conduct.* One part of the Nto-Bako joined the Ngwizako in 1965 to set up, in association with some even weaker organisations, typical of the proliferation of Lilliputian Kongolese groupings, the Frente Patriótica para a Independência do Kongo Português—FPIKP (Kongo Patriotic Front). Some of these movements are known only by their French names, which they have not even bothered to translate into Portuguese: for example, the Union Progressiste de Nso (Nso Progressive Union), the Rassemblement des Chefs Coutumiers du Kongo Portugais—RCCKP (Association of Portuguese Kongo Traditional Chiefs), the Parti Progressiste Africain—PPA (African Progressive Party), formerly a youth organisation of Bazombo, Alliance des Jeunes Angolais pour la Liberté (AJEUNAL). The most obvious activity of all the groups combined in the Frente Patriótica is the collection of subscriptions wherever possible, and the directing of two or three petitions a year to the United Nations.

* Some of those living in Kinshasa were reportedly arrested in September 1969 by the Congolese authorities.

Traditionalist and non-violent, these nostalgic supporters of the kingdom of the Kongo are completely innocuous to the Portuguese who may even be financing them on the side.

The Frente Patriótica does not exhaust the list of Kongo mini-groups. For example, the Movimento de Defesa (MDIA) still survives from 1961; it is openly financed by Lisbon to which it has rendered signal service by sending refugees home, and competing with the UPA for the loyalty of those who have remained in Congo-Kinshasa. In 1963, it expelled its secretary-general, Jean-Pierre Bala, and made common cause with the MPLA for a brief moment in the Frente Democrática, before rejoining the Bazombo in the Partido Demo-crático Angolano, an ally of the UPA within the Frente Nacional (FNLA), and subsequently meeting with even more Byzantine adventures in which some of its leaders were arrested by the UPA-GRAE.

There is little to be said of the Partido Democrático Angolano—PDA (Angolan Democratic Party) except that, on March 27, 1962, it became a satellite of the UPA which used it as a screen to justify the claim that the GRAE was not exclusively *Upista*. Its president, Emmanuel Kunzika, was especially interested in the education of Angolan refugee children. His influence among the Bazombo was useful to Holden Roberto since it brought the more or less nominal support of the small traders of that tribe.

Finally, among the leading Bakongo mini-groups there were: the Comité da Unidade Nacional Angolana—CUNA (Angolan National Unity Committee) composed of people from the Bembe region, includ-ing elderly UPA dissidents of a 1963 schism; and the Movimento Nacional Angolano (MNA), formerly the Frente Nacional Angolana, started in 1962 and comprising Bakongo from the coast (Bassorongo).

These micro-parties have one thing in common; with the exception of the PDA, they are all opposed to the UPA and envious of the aid it has received from America. Hence, UPA dissidents have tried to recruit from among them, especially during the UPA-GRAE lethargy in Tshombe's heyday. In April 1965, in addition to the exclusively traditionalist Bakongo regrouping within the Frente Patriótica do Kongo, another organisation was formed under André Kassinda, ex-leader of the Liga Geral dos Trabalhadores, the UPA trade-union satellite; this was the Concelho do Povo Angolano—CPA (Angolan People's Council), which was to encompass two Bakongo parties: the CUNA and the MNA. To broaden its base, it was joined by a Quioco (Chokwe) party, the Partido Nacional Africano—PNA (African National Party), led by José Paulo Chiringueno, based at Tshikapa (Kasai), and by an Ovimbundu party led by UPA dissidents, the União Nacional Angolana (UNA), which had close relations with President Kaunda of Zambia. The Concelho was also joined by the União Geral dos Trabalhadores de Angola—UGTA (General Union of Angolan Workers), a breakaway from the Liga Geral dos Trabalhadores (LGTA). It was in the name of the CPA that André Kassinda attacked the GRAE offices in June 1965 in company with Alexandre Taty (see page 209). Although failing in his attempted putsch, Kassinda was still powerful enough to transform, on paper, his CPA in May 1966 into a National Executive Committee (CNE in its Portuguese abbreviation), which he tried to make militant. His arrest in July 1966 by the UPA-GRAE police put an end to his activities, and probably also to those of the CPA-CNE as such.[22]

A Comité des Bons Offices Angolais (CBOA), led by an Angolan Kongo who naively hoped to achieve the Sisyphean task of unifying the Angolan nationalist parties, was still active in Brazzaville in May 1969. Further, the União Progressista Nacional de Angola—UPRONA (National Progressive Union of Angola) was still petitioning the United Nations in May 1969, as was the Cartel dos Nacionalistas Angolanos—CNA (Cartel of Angolan Nationalists) which regrouped such familiar figures as Angelino Alberto of Nto-Bako. The list is still open for more names.

The UNITA. Although this political chaos leaves the head reeling, there is one more party which requires examination and which has at least a leader of above-average calibre: Jonas M. Savimbi, former Minister of Foreign Affairs in the GRAE. An Ovimbundu from the Nova Lisboa area, a Protestant and a graduate of the University of Lausanne, Savimbi seems to have had connections with the MPLA before joining the UPA; he left this latter in 1964 and tried to rejoin the MPLA in 1964–65. He was not accepted, and so he decided to set up on his own account with a nucleus of Ovimbundu ex-GRAE militants from Kinshasa and Lubumbashi, and to recruit support from Angolan workers in Katanga and Zambia. Away from the poisoned atmosphere of Kinshasa and his enemy, Holden Roberto, he hoped to open a new front from which to win his Ovimbundu fief. He had little to fear from the UPA, but he was to follow in the footsteps of the MPLA which became active in the east in 1966. Savimbi appears to have formed his party in March 1966, in the Moxico district inside Angola. It bore the resounding title of the União Nacional para a Independência Total de Angola—UNITA (National Union for Total Independence of Angola).

Some of UNITA's guerrillas may have trained in China—which could explain recent MPLA coolness towards Peking—and Savimbi began to mount hit-and-run operations; but his troops made some of the same mistakes the UPA committed in 1961.[23] The reception he got from the populace, already solicited by the MPLA, does not seem to have been any more enthusiastic than that accorded to the men from Brazzaville. Indeed, although the UNITA had some guerrillas in 1966, commanded by a former UPA Ovimbundu commander, José Kalundungo, they fell back on methods which one had thought completely out-of-date, such as mass attacks by hundreds of bare-chested Africans, drugged and led by a woman witchdoctor, with a few partisans armed with automatic weapons concealed among them. On the night of Christmas Eve, 1966, about 500 men attacked the frontier town and station of Teixeira de Sousa (containing perhaps some hundreds of Portuguese, including troops). How could they hope to take such a white fortress, supported by rail and air communications, when in 1961 thousands of Bakongo failed before insignificant little Mucaba? The only Portuguese losses were the deaths of the local PIDE chief and four civilians, but the Chokwe, naively engaged in this hopeless adventure, left 243 or 295 dead (accounts vary) in front of the machine-guns. Despite this setback, at the beginning of 1967 the UNITA was still blowing up the railway line which fed Zambia. The Portuguese, in a strong position, closed the line for a time. But at this point the Zambian government, apprehensive over its life-line towards Lobito and probably suspicious of the UNITA's occult role in its internal politics, expelled Savimbi, who left his organisation in a crippled state.

In 1970, the UNITA claimed to be active in the Moxico, Cuando-Cubango, Lunda, Bié, Malange and even Huambo districts, where half the population was reported by the UNITA as having stopped paying taxes. Whatever the grain of truth in these communiqués, the UNITA faces formidable handicaps since it must vie with the MPLA, the GRAE (near the Katanga border) and the Portuguese. Moreover, its terrorist UPA-like actions against the African civilian population is a double-edged weapon if they are not channelled by a core of educated cadres. The main trump-card of the UNITA is its ethnic appeal to the Ovimbundu.

Only the UPA-GRAE, the MPLA and, more remotely, the UNITA have any potential for effective action. When one knows how easily PIDE agents enter Congo-Kinshasa (and probably Congo-Brazzaville and Zambia), where they have no hesitation in setting off alone over hundreds of miles of track to collect information or pay some informant (perhaps a local or Angolan politician), one can have no doubt of the Luanda authorities' determination to ensnare in their meshes all these diminutive groups who are fighting a system which disarms or buys them. This is a far cry from the triumphant communiqués but probably much nearer to the harsh and naked truth.

10. The Social and Economic Situation in Angola

> A man forewarned is worth two, and it needs four men to evict
> him from his house.
>
> Governor-General Horácio de Sá Viana Rebelo,
> *Angola na África deste Tempo*, Lisbon 1961.

DÉTENTE IN THE BUSH

The reader should not be confused by the labyrinth of the post-1961 explosion, but should view African nationalist affairs in true perspective. Some two hundred politically-active men command probably 5,000–6,000 guerrillas fighting more or less actively in Angola, and are supported by perhaps 50,000–70,000 peasants hiding in the bush of northern and eastern Angola. On the periphery are some 350,000–400,000 old refugees (of the 1961–64 exodus) or new ones (since 1966). Because of the impossibility of open political activity in Angola, they stay outside the country, either resignedly or under duress, but vocal.

In 1965 there were 5,153,672 people in Angola, according to an official estimate; this means that, allowing for the whites, at least twelve times as many Angolans have stayed under Portuguese rule as have gone into exile. It would obviously be wrong to count all of them as partisans of Lisbon, but equally inexact to attribute to them feelings of which one knows little. The fact is that, today, there must be at least 5·2 million people in Angola with no hope of political self-expression, due to their fear of the police, when they have an opinion to express, or to their ignorance. This simple fact should not be lost to mind when one considers Angola ten years after the outbreak of the rebellion. The overwhelming majority of Angolans (black Africans and *mestiços*) who remain in the country obey the Portuguese; having abolished most of the pre-1961 conditions, the Portuguese are now more popular with the Angolan population. The most serious complaint that an Angolan labourer in the bush can level at the Portuguese is that the minimum wage for manual labourers is notoriously insufficient (in 1966, some types of work in the interior of Angola earned no more than 10 escudos a day; in 1968, this was raised to 25 escudos in Luanda). But since he may now stay at home if he wants to, the only contribution which he must make to the state is a fairly low tax (250 to 450 escudos a year in 1966), which he can pay by selling his own produce. Today, a rural Angolan usually gets a job with a white employer only when he needs a large sum of money, for the construction of a house, for a dowry, a bicycle, cattle and so on. It is the slow but inexorable spread of material civilisation, as represented by European society in its Portuguese variant, which stimulates need in the rural African.

In 1960, contract labour affected less than one-eleventh of the economically active African male population. In 1964, out of 241,351 rural wage earners, 102,851 were under written contract; this is a reduction of only one tenth over the 1960 figures (115,904). Although these are only estimated figures, one can affirm that only a small proportion of Africans are working for a Portuguese employer (the percentage of wage-earners to the active male population in 1960 was 27·2 per cent in Angola as compared with 32·3 per cent in Ghana) and this is steadily decreasing (there were 241,351 non-specialist Angolan wage-earners in 1964, as against 299,861 in 1960). The significance of these figures is their revelation that, since 1960, the number of Angolans working for a Portuguese employer has diminished notably, despite a developing economy. Hence sources of friction between the rural African and the white economy have been reduced. Except in the guerrilla-affected areas, the majority of rural Angolans find their traditional habits little disturbed by white colonisation and administration, which now only asks of them that they eschew politics and pay their taxes. In exchange, they are offered new opportunities to educate their children, at least at a rudimentary level, and to obtain medical treatment if they live near a post or mission. Some foreign observers believe that rural Africans are still subjected daily to physical brutality. This is a misconception for a number of reasons: conditions have improved, many Angolans do not openly resist the Portuguese, and those individuals who do are rapidly apprehended by the authorities. There is much less friction than before 1961–62 for the simple reason that the Portuguese are concentrated in the towns, while the network of informants to the police, administration and army is sufficiently effective to uncover, sooner or later, anyone with views too openly 'political' (which implies, in the Angolan vocabulary, 'subversive'). It is here that repression comes into play and it is radical in eliminating 'contagious elements'. In the whole of Angola, such politically fever-stricken regions are not yet numerous: the Bakongo heartland (though only in part), some Mbundu areas and some areas in eastern and central Angola. The

Angolan bush is still an unknown quantity, passive on the whole but beginning to stir where UPA-GRAE, MPLA and UNITA agents are active.

THE LONG WAIT IN THE TOWNS

In the towns, things are more complicated but, as the Portuguese are numerous there, the PIDE even more vigilant and the troops in garrison, neither Portuguese nor Angolans express their strong feelings openly. The real thoughts of both races are heavily dissimulated. The undisclosed mind is a façade that is turned to the outside world. The Africans have learnt that this Portuguese racial characteristic can serve as a protection to them also. In the towns ravaged by serious disturbances in 1961 (Luanda and the Luanda-Malange corridor) or by fairly undisguised repression, foreign observers who do not speak Portuguese or have no other than official contacts, are profoundly surprised by the calm and serenity of relations between the different segments of the population. On the surface, all seems forgotten (including massacres and imprisonment); and the numerous mixed police patrols (black, white and *mestiço*), since they rarely have to intervene, seem 'decent types'. This is one of the façades of Angola. Anyone living for some time in the country sees that reality is less simple, and that urban tensions exist, as is to be expected in a multi-racial society which suffered such a severe shake-up as that of 1961.

It is clear that the police and military authorities have no intention of allowing the bloody confrontations of 1961 to be repeated, and take every precaution to keep the situation well in hand and avoid provocation by agitators. They succeed easily, with a minimum of effort, but there is no doubt that they would use far sterner methods in a case of serious trouble. In Luanda, a sizable proportion of the African and European population is at the call of the police; some Africans live entirely from their subsidies (500 escudos was the going rate for an important piece of information in 1966). A military barbed-wire enclosure surrounds the town and suburban districts, and everyone who enters or leaves the capital is screened. Under these circumstances it is very difficult for the nationalists from abroad to infiltrate and work in the Luandan *muceques*. An urban maquis would be suicidal. Propaganda does filter through but, having visited several Angolan prisons, the present writer can assert that, by 1966 at least, the period of the great *confusão* begun in 1961 was over. The prisons were huge but few (if any) were packed; other measures have been employed since 1961–62 to 'evacuate' excess inmates, 'definitively' for some, provisionally for others.

The Social and Economic Situation in Angola

Undoubtedly MPLA networks have reappeared here and there in Luanda, in Lobito and its industrial zone, but towns as important as Nova Lisboa and Malanje apparently have, for various reasons, only insignificant clandestine activity. It is always easier to insure liaison with a port, even though PIDE vigilance may be stricter there, as at Mossamedes; but even in these towns where *assimilados* and *mestiços* are numerous, there is a gulf between the political aspirations of the Angolan lower middle classes (mostly civil servants) and their willingness to face the hazards of clandestine political life of which they all know the cost. Fear of the PIDE is the surest means of shutting mouths, if not ears. The recollections of former prisoners who were released from the gaols of 1960–61 are sufficiently fresh to silence the impulse to protest. Moreover, the lack of Angolan cadres is so great, and the Portuguese policy of 'vigilant pardon' so clever, that there are many former 'pseudo-terrorists' and minor nationalists of 1961 who, on leaving prison, found their place in the administration still waiting for them. So long as they remain politically quiescent, they can earn their living as before. The *cabecilhas* (ringleaders) disappeared for good or were sent to the Chão Bom camp in Cape Verde, or to the *campos de trabalho* (labour camps) and other places in the interior from which it is probably impossible to escape or communicate with the outside world.[1]

UNIVERSAL VIGILANCE

Angola is not given over to fire and bloodshed. In point of fact, one can cover 10,000 miles in Angola without hearing a single shot fired, although there may be plenty of soldiers. It is virtually impossible to get exact and reliable information on this subject. Portuguese military strength was generally reckoned at 60,000 men in 1966 (army 55,000, navy 1,000 to 2,000, air force 3,000 to 4,000). These combatants seem to have risen by 1970 to 70,000, 50,000 of whom are white and 20,000 *mestiço* or black. To these must be added 1,116 PIDE officers (1969 figures), more than 11,000 members of the Polícia de Segurança Pública, 10,000–20,000 agents of the Organização Provincial de Voluntários e Defesa Civil—OPVDC (Provincial Volunteers and Civil Defence Organisation): a paramilitary body very active in defending plantations and protecting convoys in the north.[2]

These are the official forces. Brigades of railwaymen and air volunteers add to this total. Less well-known is the role of Angolans on the Portuguese side against the guerrillas. From April–May 1961, the Portuguese were arming partisans: tribal chiefs in the Dembos and Ovimbundu volunteers seeking revenge for the UPA massacres of their brothers in the north. They went further and, as they recovered Bakongo and Mbundu villages which were not involved in the massacres or now wanted to make peace with the Portuguese, they provided these 'sheep led astray by sorcerers' with firearms also. Without needing to create veritable strategic hamlets, by 1970 they could count in the north on the mistakes of the MPLA and UPA (whose partisans at times indulged in looting and killing their tribal brothers who had gone over to the Portuguese) to provide a buffer between the guerrilla bands and their own troops. There is no doubt that ten years of guerrilla warfare strains the nerves of those who wage it and suffer from it. Whatever their real political aspirations may be, some Angolans give or sell food and clothing to the partisans, while others open fire on them with ancient Portuguese weapons.

This is perhaps the major success of the psycho-social campaign of the Portuguese army. And they have been able to employ another counter-insurgent technique, thanks to the ethnic divisions in Angola: one which was largely ineffective in Algeria. Ovimbundu animosity towards the Bakongo and Mbundu who martyred them in 1961 is real and persistent, at least where they are in contact in the north-west coffee region. Since they work in the coffee plantations and are most exposed to attack from the *serras*, the Portuguese have armed them in some particularly strategic plantations, and their employers pay an insurance on their lives. So the racial war in northern Angola still burns today. In addition to about 100,000 Portuguese civilians fit to bear arms, there are today in Angola—taking into account the *cipaios* and other forms of defence and including police and soldiers—probably 100,000 armed men on the Portuguese side.

If the Portuguese with such forces have not been able to check the latent guerrilla warfare, there are numerous reasons for this: the frontiers can be crossed; the nationalist political organisations, albeit weak or little obeyed, still have their top leaderships intact, and the MPLA and UNITA have a recruitment campaign afoot; the terrain is unfavourable to a regular army; there is an irreducible nucleus of reconstituted insurgent villages; part of the African population gives the partisans tacit or active support; there is a lack of enthusiasm among some Portuguese officers who, not convinced of a victory which they judge problematical, do not go to the limit of their human and material resources. In this respect, although the nationalists themselves recognise that the rough and hardy Portuguese peasant is a good soldier, often an excellent soldier for counter-guerrilla warfare, the morale of the junior officer corps is another matter. Many of them are young graduate conscripts, recently out of university and no great supporters of the regime; their main concern is that they and their men should emerge unscathed from a military service that may last four years. The war is allowed to drag on because to end it would demand considerable efforts in human terms. It is not an impasse but just a typical Portuguese reaction: let time do the work for us!

Yet, although the MPLA eastern offensive should not give cause for any great optimism among the general staff in Lisbon (which is faced with the possibility of another Guinea-Bissau experience), the calm in the rest of Angola and the remarkable economic development of the country lead Portugal's military leaders to exhibit official confidence. They know that, in case of a major confrontation, they can count on the support of South African forces and on their own rearmed civilian compatriots—not to mention the possibility of unleashing a tribal war by setting the Ovimbundu against the northern and eastern peoples. The greatest asset of the Portuguese troops is not the superiority of their armaments and training but the manifest inferiority of the nationalist command. In ten years of war, and with an armament now hardly inferior to that of the Portuguese (except in aviation and artillery),[3] the partisans (according to Portuguese official sources) have not been able to inflict more than about 1,000 deaths in combat: which, with deaths from accident and disease, may bring Portuguese losses to between 2,000 and 2,500 only.[4] This, for an army of 20,000 to 70,000 men over a period of ten years, constitutes a statistically negligible rate, given the terrain and climate.

THE DEVELOPMENT OF ANGOLA

A factor of capital importance to the anti-guerrilla struggle, and of even greater importance to the country's economy, has been the undreamed-of development in communications.

Admittedly, there has been little change in the railway network, apart from the new line to Serpa Pinto, completed in 1961. But most important is the road network. Here the Portuguese have made an amazing effort to overcome the backward state of the country and the great distances. Their strategic interest is clear. They aim to link all district capitals (fourteen, excluding Cabinda) with Luanda by metalled roads open in all weathers. Anyone familiar with the dreadful tracks, rutted now that the Africans are no longer obliged to maintain them, will appreciate the efforts of the Angolan highways authority, which spent 637 million escudos in 1965–67 and has been one of the successes of the post-1961 period. A measure of the importance of this work can be judged from the example of the Cela *colonato*: this used to be a week's journey by lorry from Luanda in the wet season (hence its produce was not collected); now it is only about ten hours' drive from the capital.

By 1971, one could go from Carmona, Luanda, Malanje, Lobito, Nova Lisboa, Sá da Bandeira or Mossamedes to the South West African frontier by metalled road, with roads off to the east, and in particular to Henrique de Carvalho and the Diamang mines in the north. The significance of this can scarcely be overstated: there is now safe, cheap and rapid contact between the main centres of white population. For the first time in their history in Angola, the Portuguese can now, within twenty-four to forty-eight hours, bring up massive reinforcements to any point where an urban white population is in danger, whereas in 1961 each white settlement was an island in an African sea, reached easily only by air. The highways council's 15,000 miles of roads, and the 13,000 miles of rutted tracks, may seem modest, but the Portuguese are planning for the future by concentrating on the main strategic axes (and particularly liaison with South Africa); at the same time, they have given the country an infrastructure which it lacked. In peacetime, buses, lorries and *carrinhas* (light 'pick-up' vehicles) keep the country's commercial life flowing; but these 70,000 to 80,000 four-wheeled vehicles could possibly be equipped with light armour as they were in 1961 in the north.

To this as yet slight but, for black Africa, astonishing development of the road system, the Portuguese have added a network of aerodromes of which some are well-known (Luanda, Nova Lisboa, Lobito, Sá da Bandeira, Silva Porto, Mossamedes, Malange, Luso and Cabinda) because often frequented by civilian traffic. There are others far less known: for example, the military bases of Negage and Toto, and especially the little-visited base of Henrique de Carvalho with a landing strip some two miles long (built since 1962) and a garrison of over 1,000 airmen keeping an eye on the diamond territory of Lunda and the trouble spot of Moxico. Other aerodromes, such as Neriquinha on the Zambian frontier, are almost secret, and there are even more quite unknown in the bush. The Portuguese have not forgotten that, if they held the north in the violent days of 1961, it was due to civilian resistance and enemy incompetence, but also to air support. The civil airlines carry a modest load (130,797 passengers and some 3,600,000 miles covered in 1969), but the air taxis and aeroclubs which are particularly active in the north could well be enlisted to reinforce the air force in case of serious trouble. It is no mere chance that the Plano intercalar de Fomento (Intermediate Development Plan) of 1965–67, forecasting expenditure of 3,039,500,000 escudos, could only be 78 per cent fulfilled, whereas 98.1 per cent of the 1,076,100,000 escudos allocated to transport and communications was utilised. In the words of a former governor of Angola, who became Minister of Defence in 1968: 'A man forewarned is worth two, and it needs four men to evict him from his house.'[5]

Paradoxically, then, it is clear that, since the rebellion broke out, Angola has been kept in hand more firmly than ever before by the Portuguese—and this in contrast to the case of Guinea-Bissau. Tightening of police and military control has gone hand-in-hand with an unprecedented economic boom that could be even greater if the capitalists in Portugal showed an eagerness to invest in tune with the optimism of the Lisbon authorities and their compatriots' determination to stay put in Angola.

A few figures will indicate the true influence of the nationalist guerrilla campaign on the country's development, and show that it has provided an unprecedented stimulus. The contest has been engaged between Portuguese and nationalists, the former to develop to the maximum, the latter trying to prevent them, but failing utterly so far since the only guerrillas who could bleed the country of its wealth are those in the coffee zone. The results of their efforts are doubtful.

There was a deficit in Angola's balance of trade in 1960; it was still there in 1968 but this was due to increased imports (produced in part by the purchase of capital goods to equip the Cassinga iron mines and the export railway to Mossamedes, and also for exploitation of the Cabinda oil) and not to a decrease in exports. On the other hand, the 1969 balance of trade showed a deficit of over $4,000,000.

Angola is a typical underdeveloped African country, prevented from exploiting its potentialities to the full by the weak economy of the Portuguese homeland. The Portuguese lack capital, technicians and economic imagination and impetus. This would be a sign of bankruptcy in any other colonising system. There is no doubt that under the control of more modern colonisers, Angola would experience a lightning development, for the mineral wealth now exploited there is, in the opinion of some geologists, but a minute proportion of the Angolan potential. Traditionally, the Portuguese have been very wary of foreign investors, and it is only their own investment incapacity that has led them to accept in Angola Belgian, British, American, German, French, Japanese, Scandinavian and South African capital participation in mining development which will play an essential part in the coming years. One must stress the fact that Angola is probably the African country south of the Sahara with the brightest prospect of economic development (apart from South Africa). This is known in Luanda, in Lisbon, in New York, in Moscow and, possibly, in Peking.

Principal Exports

	1960		1969	
	Quantity	Value (escudos)	Quantity	Value (escudos)
Coffee	87,217 tons	1,263,964,000	182,798 tons	3,234,435,000
Diamonds	933,646 carats	496,168,000	1,980,394 carats	1,843,173,000
Sisal	57,941 tons	375,479,000	59,035 tons	197,123,000
Maize	31,964 tons	164,952,000	177,393 tons	305,129,000
Iron ore	545,800 tons	151,553,000	5,102,179 tons	1,098,718,000
Fish meal	45,085 tons	108,341,000	92,391 tons	347,210,000
Timber	90,674 tons	96,749,000	152,071 tons	224,104,000
Fuel oil	nil	nil	250,800 tons	99,083,000
Raw cotton	8,894 tons	146,376,000	18,807 tons	329,751,000
Oil	nil	nil	1,502,391 tons	485,110,000

	Total exports		Total imports	
	Quantity	Value (escudos)	Quantity	Value (escudos)
1960	1,806,109 tons	3,565,492,000	520,505 tons	3,669,610,000
1969	7,997,883 tons	9,390,424,000	860,896 tons	9,261,182,000

Portugal, for its part, has decided at all costs to hold on to a territory which involves heavy military 'expenses of sovereignty' (paid in escudos) but which enables it to correct in part its balance of payments (Angolan exports are transacted in dollars) and gives it an outlet for its exports of wine (539,011,000 escudos' worth taken by Angola in 1969) and textiles (465,754,000 escudos' worth in 1969) which sell poorly abroad at the same quality. In other words, the Angolan balance of trade, traditionally in deficit to Portugal (negative balance of 518,138,000 escudos in 1967, positive balance of 73,907,000 escudos in 1969), but generally positive towards other countries (with the recent exceptions of 1967, 1968 and 1969: minus 200,873,000 escudos in 1969; but plus 636,597,000 escudos in 1966) enables Portugal to repatriate foreign currency earned with Angolan coffee, diamonds, oil and iron ore. Although subordinate to the political considerations of the Portuguese regime, this double advantage of an assured and more or less obligatory market for its agricultural and manufacturing products,[6] and a source of hard currencies, must weigh in favour of retaining under the 'colonial pact' a country whose situation is so beneficial to Portugal.

From this dry arithmetic, which all the same is a key factor for Angola's future within Lisbon's sphere of influence, one fact which is not open to discussion should be isolated. Slowly but inexorably, Angola is outgrowing its reputation as an economic Cinderella and is moving into a rate of growth which is remarkable, given Portugal's lack of means. This is happening despite the lack of enthusiasm on the part of private Portuguese capital. The main stimulus, of course, comes from public investment. Between 1965 and 1967, 2,372,201,000 escudos were spent by the state in the civil sector. For the Third Development Plan (1968–73), the expenditure of 25,384,000,000 escudos is forecast: 11,600,000,000 for mining industries (semi-privately financed); 3,779,000,000 for transport; 3,361,000,000 for the manufacturing industry; 2,041,000,000 for agriculture, forestry and livestock; 1,358,000,000 for education and research; and 1,238,000,000 for energy. If the country's position in 1971 is compared with that of 1960, Angola might join with the melancholy humorists of Luanda in saying: 'Thank you, Mr Roberto, you have wakened Lisbon. Now they know that we (the Angolan whites, that is) exist!'

RACE RELATIONS

There is a decided improvement in Angolan race relations. In places not daily affected by the war the social climate is amazingly relaxed for a country with such a sombre past. In Carmona, for example, in 1966

235

one could observe on the main street a black woman and white woman arm in arm.

With the Portuguese one cannot generalise, but one thing is sure: their behaviour is illogical and even if one takes dissimulation into account, they still retain a great measure of confidence in the African which is difficult to sap—even if they are rather wary since 1961. Perhaps an ethno-psychological study might explain this phenomenon, but in Angola it stems from well-rooted conviction in the settler mentality that the rural African (*preto do mato*) is basically inoffensive, 'harmless and irresponsible like a child'. The poorer settler, who himself has come from an archaic rural society, semi-feudal in some provinces, often tries to cheat the African because he is weaker, and because he himself is used to being humiliated in his poverty back home and has come here to get rich. But he does not hate him. As long as the bush African is docile or indifferent, the Portuguese will not take exception to eating at the same table, and even less to sleeping discreetly with his daughter. It is only when the 'child' rebels that incomprehension starts. As a male member of a patriarchal society where the father's authority is often absolute in the countryside, the poor settler will punish the 'ungrateful child' with all the vigour of an outraged 'father' whose will is opposed. So the rapings and macabre cruelties perpetrated on the northern settlers in 1961 were probably the UPA's greatest psychological mistake, for the Portuguese subconsciously equated them not only with rebellion against the father's authority but also with 'incest within the colonial family'. That was something he could not tolerate. The fury with which he reacted to a revolt which, psychologically, he could not understand and even less acknowledge, is well-known. It is not just by chance that the only Portuguese to side with the Angolan nationalists before 1961 were recruited among the bourgeoisie and intelligentsia of the towns, and never from the poor settlers:[7] the first to be threatened by the 'child's' growing up to replace the 'father'.

The whites who experienced the drama of 1961 now show an understandable suspicion of the Bakongo and Mbundu; but this suspicion is far less noticeable among recent arrivals.[8] In order to see the 1961 Bakongo-Mbundu revolt in its true psychological light, one should consider it not as a purely modern nationalist rebellion, but rather as of a kind with the Herero revolt of South West Africa some fifty years earlier. The settlers' reactions in the two cases were identical to begin with: extermination for extermination. But the Portuguese soon came to prefer the subtler method of reclaiming the 'rebellious child'. Perhaps that is the secret of their continued settlement in Angola.

Manifestly, this simplistic plan is upset by the irruption of modern

life and twentieth-century pressures—diminished though they be by
Angola's isolation. It is also threatened by a new phenomenon of broad
scope. White feelings towards the educated African and the *mestiço* are
far from idyllic. For the poor white, the 'child' has grown as big as his
'father' and is sometimes better qualified than he. Under pressure from
Lisbon, which aims to transform the Angolan into a black Portuguese,
there has been a scholastic explosion of which many observers,
hypnotised by the pre-1961 situation, may not be aware. In 1960–61, in
the whole of Angola there were 105,781 pupils in pre-primary and
primary schools, 7,486 in academic secondary schools and 4,501 in
technical secondary schools. Five years later, 1965–66, the figures were
225,145, 14,577 and 13,220 respectively: increases over the 1960 figures
of 113 per cent, 95 per cent and 194 per cent respectively.[9] In 1966–67,
the respective totals were 267,768, 16,700 and 15,371; and 712 were
following theological studies and 607 attending the University, which as
yet does not provide arts and law courses. About 1,000 were taking
primary school teachers' courses.

This remarkable development in the provision of education exhibits
interesting features. There has been an important extension of rural
schooling, whereby the Angolan child learns the rudiments of Portuguese language, civilisation, history and geography.[10] As a result, there
is a substantial increase in the number of Portuguese speakers. The
widespread use of Portuguese, even in the bush (except in the south and
east) is striking; indeed, its extension is probably far more rapid than
the increase of English-speakers in Nigeria and of French-speakers in
Congo-Kinshasa. Against this, however, there is a rapid regression in
the number of Africans in secondary schools,[11] which they leave as
soon as they have the qualifications needed to enter the administration:
that paradise for *mestiços* and black Africans who find there a wage equal
to that of the whites and an escape from manual labour (despised in
Africa as in Portugal). There is a resulting increase in competition
between Angolans and Portuguese from the 'mother country' for semi-
qualified jobs. There are few Angolans taking higher education, either
at the university level or in parallel institutions (perhaps less than 10 per
cent of the 800 students in Angolan scientific and technical colleges and
the 1,000 students who go from Angola to Portugal). Briefly, the
official doctrine is to 'lusitanify' with the greatest rapidity as many
young Angolans as possible to put them out of reach of the sirens of
nationalism.

In the lower echelons, the Portuguese have been succeeding for
some years in catching up on arrears. But once the black or *mestiço*
student reaches a certain level, he becomes a competitor of the white

settler economically and probably also politically. So the Portuguese have taken a chance on the future. By educating the young they hope to make Portuguese of them, but at the same time they give them, on a vast scale, the intellectual tools to become aware of their Angolan character. In other words, if, like the rest of black Africa, Angola is really a white political creation, the theory of total (as opposed to selective) assimilation, if it is to work, must bridge in a few years the material, intellectual and social gap between the coloured neo-Portuguese and his white cousin. Is this possible? The poorer whites doubt it. They see the school simply as a nursery for future competitors, if not future subversives, who will one day want to eliminate them. Working with their backs to the wall in the bush, or in the white metropolis that Luanda has become (at least 25,000 newly-arrived whites since 1961), they scent danger and, *lusotropicalismo* apart, they are probably right. No elites, no trouble, at least in the short term! So it is Lisbon and the central authorities which push on along the path leading to liberalisation of education. This model is not original; similar ones have been implemented in recent years in all European colonies.

The future of Angola will depend on the silent role of these thousands of Angolans who are now receiving secondary or higher education. Having learned to keep quiet if they value their peace, their apparent passivity is officially accepted as acquiescence in present policies. In fact, in all black Africa (except for the old communities under French statute of the former colonial Senegal in and around Dakar and Saint Louis) there is no comparable case of such avid acceptance of the colonizer's civilisation and ways as that of the Angolan *mestiços* and a section of the African *assimilados*,* some of whom no longer speak a black-African tongue. But there is a gap between the acceptance of the elements of Westernisation which they judge positive, and the approval of particular policies. At the moment, a large part of the *mestiço* community and virtually all black-African heads of family with secondary education depend on the Portuguese for a living, either in public administration or private enterprise. Subjected to information depicting the chaos in independent Africa, knowing the weakness of the nationalist movements (and, for the *mestiços*, aware of the black African masses' hatred of them, since historically they have been among the first to exploit them), this intermediary class plays the official Portuguese

* Strictly speaking, one should speak of 'former *assimilados*', for assimilation as an administrative distinction ceased to operate with the repeal of the Native Code in 1961. But the term is retained here and elsewhere in the text to avoid confusion.

game, whether sincerely or no, in its efforts to preserve its privileges. *Primum vivere, deinde philosophari*. They would be the first to benefit from the overthrow of the political status of Angola, since they are the elite, but they know by experience that, cornered in the country as they are, they would also be the first to pay the cost of another upheaval like that of 1961. So they wait.

But while they are waiting, paralysed, between two fires, the Portuguese and their allies abroad, and especially in the white bastion of Southern Africa, are growing steadily stronger. So there is no significant exodus abroad nor large-scale desertion by the *mestiço* and black African elites. In the first place, controls make such a move almost impossible; and secondly, the saddening spectacle of the nationalist parties devouring each other abroad is hardly encouraging. Many are waiting for an independence which they know will probably not take the form which they would like, but they hope all the same that it will be favourable to their interests. But will their interests necessarily correspond with those of the millions in the bush? Those who want freedom know that many must die if it is achieved by warfare. So they prefer to wait until economic and political factors in Portugal and Southern Africa change and the erosion of time—a secondary factor in the Portuguese world—accomplishes a development whose final direction is difficult to predict, but which must be of long duration while the views of the Portuguese army and settlers continue to correspond with those of Premier Marcelo Caetano who, for various reasons, is bound to follow, for an indefinite period, Salazar's policies.

Part Three

Douglas L. Wheeler

11. Angola Infelix

In the realm of international politics, the events in Northern Angola showed the world that Portugal does not defend merely a territory under its administration. It defends, indeed, a piece of itself.

Hélio Felgas,
Guerra em Angola, Lisbon 1961, p. 227.

Tomorrow, or after tomorrow, Angola is going to change.

Américo Boavida,
Angola: Cinco séculos de exploração portuguesa,
Rio de Janeiro 1967, p. 125.

ANGOLA AND SOUTHERN AFRICA

Southern Africa is more than a geographic region; it is also the only remaining area of Africa where European-ruled states predominate: the Republic of South Africa, South West Africa, Rhodesia, Angola and Mozambique. (In West Africa, Portuguese Guinea is the last colonial enclave.) These states of Southern Africa vary in importance, but the bulwark and in some ways the lodestone of this 'subordinate state system',[1] is the imposing Republic of South Africa, with Angola, officially an overseas province of the Republic of Portugal, ranking a close second in geo-political significance in the area.

Southern Africa is more than a political bastion for white rule, a *laager* to the Afrikaner. Anachronistic though it appears in a rapidly decolonising world, there remains in southern Africa a pervasive white attitude of superiority over the black African. Observers of that part of the world cannot doubt that the majority of white inhabitants sincerely assent to the credo that 'the blacks cannot rule themselves or the country without us'. There may be friendly race relations in some parts of the area—even beyond traditional paternalism—but everywhere within it there is European dominance. This fact may be obscured by the propaganda and high-sounding statements coming from Lisbon, Salisbury and Pretoria, but the white man-in-the-street in Southern Africa is not reticent in decrying any 'favouritism' shown the black man. This attitude derives from present fears and a past of racial and economic conflicts; it unites the rulers of Southern

9—A * *

Africa, even though their racial policies differ, and it would unite them even if their mutual economic interests did not draw them into what some have called 'the unholy alliance'. During the past decade, the ties among these European-ruled states with African majorities have grown and have supported opposition to the anti-colonial attitudes dominant north of the 'African battleline'.[2] There are historic roots to this growing nexus of alliances, communications, investment and protection: roots which first grew in the nineteenth century when the Portuguese and the Afrikaner seemed destined to suffer subjugation under Bantu and Briton. The fear that unites Southern Africa's whites is not new. Before the partition of Africa, the Afrikaner and Portuguese in Africa had two mutual enemies: the British (or so they were stereotyped) and the black Africans. The first treaties between Portugal and the South African Republic (Transvaal), dating from the mid-nineteenth century, were in part based on interests and hatreds that prevail in a more modern form today.

What role will Angola and Angolans play in Southern Africa? And how will their neighbours, both white and black, influence their destiny?

By the late 1960s, Angola's geographic, political and economic resources were formidable, but they were at least in part neutralised by new factors in the struggle between the continent's independent black states and the Southern African white states. These latter enjoyed economic superiority over their black neighbours. The sanctions imposed by the United Nations against the Ian Smith regime in Rhodesia were ineffective. The independent black states of Tanzania, Zambia and Congo-Kinshasa struggled to counter-balance the economic strength of their southern neighbours by ending their dependence on the Southern African economy and transport system, and attempted to reorient their trade and communications to avoid using the Portuguese-controlled railroad outlets to the Atlantic and Indian Oceans. With aid from the Communist powers, from Britain and the United States and others, Zambia and Tanzania began building a railroad linking the port of Dar es Salaam to the copper mines of Zambia, thus ending the existing heavy dependence on the Benguela railway. Congo-Kinshasa also planned to build a line that would preclude the necessity of using the same Portuguese-controlled railroads.

By 1970, a much smaller percentage of copper from Zambia and Congo was being exported via the Portuguese routes. More than before, these independent states became oriented towards East Africa and, to an extent as yet undetermined, the economic significance of the Benguela railway was diminished. Nevertheless, the Portuguese in Angola retained a transport asset which, at least for the immediate future, was highly significant. They had strategic access to Central Africa and the reduction of Central African traffic allowed them greater use of the railroad for their own purposes, to compensate for the loss of revenue.

With the exception, already mentioned, of industrialised South Africa, Angola in the Southern African context is the most economically independent. Unlike Mozambique, it has a rich and varied assortment of minerals, and its budget does not depend on transit revenues from a neighbouring state. Then, too, Angola is a larger and far more compact territory, with more internal development and larger healthy plateaux, than is Mozambique. Recently discovered reserves of iron and oil in Angola promise great economic potential. Not land-locked like Zambia, the former High Commission Territories or Malawi, and with less desert and arid lands than South West and South Africa, Angola has most promising economic prospects.

While South Africa, in terms of development and of power to resist African nationalism, appears to be the major factor in the maintenance of white dominance in the southern region of the continent, Angola retains an independent position by virtue of geography and resources. If Angola must look to South Africa, it must also pay heed to the independent black states to the north and east: the two Congo Republics and Zambia. What occurs there has influenced events in Angola, and will continue to do so. Kinshasa is closer to São Salvador, capital of the old Kongo kingdom, than is Luanda; and Lusaka, Zambia's capital, is nearer to the heart of eastern Angola than is Luanda. Long frontiers and sparsely-settled areas characterise the extremities of Angola and combine to make the borders as much filters and transmitters of peoples and ideas as barriers. Indeed, the history of Angolan labour migration to these outlying states is a long one. An equally significant, if more recent, trend (and one which played a role in the 1961 insurgency) has been the return to Angola over these boundaries of African political exiles Since 1963, however, a certain number of Africans have returned from the Congo area professing loyalty to the Portuguese government: an act which in some cases may be merely ceremonial.

Since the first Force Publique mutinies of the 1890s and during the civil war of 1960–64, troubles in the Congo basin have spilled over into Angola. The precipitous decolonisation of the Belgian Congo in 1960, more than any other recent external event, has affected the destiny of Angola. And while South African troops may continue to aid Portugal in Angola, as they have reportedly been doing since 1967, such an intervention cannot alter the fundamental West-Central African orientation of the heart of Angola on the capital, Luanda.

245

Both an asset and a liability, Angola's massive size complicates the struggle between Portugal and African nationalists. On the one hand, the large amount of sparsely-settled territory gives Portugal scope for its landless peasant farmers and potential for mineral discoveries. On the other hand, much of the eastern half of the country is rather empty, a vast preserve of nature where even an army of 50,000 European troops from Portugal cannot effectively patrol, much less prevent, infiltration from across lonely frontiers. As the pattern of Portuguese expansion remained largely coastal until recently, the occupation by a large white army is a stopgap measure of limited effectiveness. Even in the late 1960s, Portuguese occupation in eastern Angola, the scene of increasingly effective African nationalist incursions, did not seem to be tenable. In the last few years, certain voices in the Angolan Portuguese community have expressed anxiety over Portuguese vulnerability in the large open spaces of the country. In a popular weekly magazine published in Luanda, a writer recently likened Angola to the giant baobab tree, a common sight in the western sections: 'The baobab is a tree which confounds . . . it is vast; the baobab, however, has a fragile root. If one could surround [its mighty base], a half-a-dozen men, perhaps, could fell the giant tree. . . . Its defect was to be born so large . . . like Angola.'[3]

However much they may be presently limited in power by the trials of new nationhood, Angola's independent black neighbours to the north and east constitute an increasingly important factor in its future. Proximity and naturally beneficial trade relations between Angola and the two Congos and Zambia in the long run may outweigh whatever temporary effort may be forthcoming from South Africa to draw Angola into its orbit to the south. In order to make its commitment effective over the long run, South Africa would in effect be forced to take over Angola, in a latter-day version of counter-revolutionary imperialism. Such a development would have uncertain support from Portugal and the South African white electorate. In terms of South African interests and resources, such an intervention in Portuguese territory is more feasible, if not more probable, in the case of Mozambique than of Angola.

Despite certain weaknesses in its position in Angola, Portugal is capable of bringing effective counter-pressure to bear on the outlying independent black states which aid exiled Angolan nationalists. As early as the secession of the Katanga regime of Moise Tshombe in 1960, the Portuguese demonstrated they would use counter-pressure to alleviate the hostile nationalist pressure. This counter-pressure has taken several forms: the harbouring (and perhaps supplying in some cases) of white mercenaries from Katanga between 1961 and 1964, the aiding of white mercenaries who had broken with the Congo government between 1964 and 1966, the temporary closing of the Benguela railway to copper shipments from Congo and Zambia in 1967, the selective bombing of the eastern border of Zambia in 1968,[4] Portuguese secret police activity in the two Congos and Zambia during the post-1961 era, and the policy Portugal adopted during 1967–69 of allowing the breakaway regime of Biafra in Nigeria to use airfields in Lisbon and on São Tomé island for transport and supply.

Portuguese counter-pressure against African nationalists in outlying states has produced concessions by the Mobutu and Kaunda regimes in Congo-Kinshasa and Zambia. The official support of those regimes for the Angolan nationalist parties in exile (some of which maintain military camps on their borders) has in some cases wavered. Perhaps the most notable concessions won by Portugal's counter-pressure occurred in 1967–68 in Zambia, where Kaunda was obliged to deny officially that Angolan nationalists enjoyed his support and his government to cancel the visa of a leading Angolan nationalist chief, Jonas Savimbi (which, in effect, meant his deportation).[5]

For the moment, at least, Lisbon holds the decisive balance of power in Angola, enabling the Portuguese to do their part in continuing white rule in Southern Africa. There is a certain fragility, however, in the Lisbon-controlled situation. The exercise of the necessary power in Angola is dependent on the political decisions of a government thousands of miles from Luanda. Although the new government under Marcelo Caetano, who was sworn in as Prime Minister on September 27, 1968, is not likely to make a decision of withdrawal from Portuguese Africa, there was sufficient uncertainty and doubt during the transition period in late 1968 for the leaders of the Portuguese army to feel obliged to promise support for Caetano only on the basis of maintaining the Salazarist colonial policy despite Salazar's departure from leadership.[6] The most decisive potential factor of change for Angola's future seems to lie in Lisbon rather than in Luanda. If, by any chance, Portugal were to withdraw from Angola, the balance of power in Southern Africa would alter significantly, and the European local leaders in Angola would be open to aid from their white Southern African neighbours.

REFORM VERSUS REVOLUTION

The 1961 crisis encouraged economic and social reforms in Angola. There was also an increase of local political autonomy in the form of

247

greater decision-making power on the part of more elected representatives in the provincial organs of the Legislative Council and the Social and Economic Council. However, the major decisions were still made in Lisbon or by the governor-general, the chief Portuguese representative in Angola. More important than political change, then, was the general economic expansion during 1961–70.

The 1961 insurgency encouraged a certain change of perspective on the part of the Lisbon government. Before 1961, Portugal felt obliged to defend its administration in Portuguese Africa almost exclusively through diplomatic relations with its major allies, Britain and the United States, and through the United Nations. Reforms and changes were for foreigners' consumption: a new form of the old Portuguese saying, 'for the Englishman to see' (*para o inglês ver*). The traumatic events of 1961, however, convinced many Portuguese leaders that Portugal could remain in Africa only if it could eradicate some of the African grievances which had caused the 1961 risings in northern Angola. In effect, reforms would now have to be designed to win loyalty from the black African masses. Now, *para o preto ver* ('for the black man to see') would be a more truthful saying. To this extent, Portuguese colonialism after 1961 had a more realistic programme.

The reforms in Angola, none the less, occasioned considerable criticisms and doubts from both local and outside observers. To what extent were these reforms real? To what extent were they like many of the paper changes of past centuries? Many observers noted that, while the Lisbon government sought reform and the local Angolan white community applauded it only to the extent that it furthered their economic opportunity, such changes did not solve the ultimate political question of who would control Angola. Furthermore, the effect of the new reforms on the black masses was an unknown quantity.

Angolan nationalists in exile have severely criticised these reforms in revolutionary terms. Dr Américo Boavida, a leader of the MPLA, in his book, *Cinco séculos de exploração portuguesa*,[7] has constructed a pseudo-Marxist theory on the nature of Portuguese activity in Angola. Boavida asserts that the true dangers of continued Angolan dependence and colonisation come not from Portugal, an underdeveloped colonial power deeply indebted (he claims) to international capital interests, but from Western international capital: companies like Diamang and the Anglo-American Corporation. Portugal, he says, is in effect a colonial dependency of these monopoly companies. Its recent reform programme ('pseudo-reformism') has been prompted by the 1961 insurgency and is largely mythical. To Boavida, the Angolan urban workers represent the most revolutionary force in the country in the future.

While exiled nationalist leaders tend to dismiss the post-1961 reforms as façade, these changes are significant since, at least in economic and social terms, they are at last bringing Angola into the twentieth century.[8] Relaxed controls are attracting foreign investment on a large scale. Increased government spending has expanded educational facilities for Africans, especially at the primary levels. In general, Angola has developed at a more rapid rate in the 1961–70 period than in the previous two decades.

The crucial question is not whether the reforms are hollow, but whether the reforms will win for Portugal sufficient mass African loyalty to keep the nationalists at bay. Optimistic Portuguese leaders believe that they can do so if given sufficient time, and the Lisbon government has favoured the appointment of officials with reformist ideas. In late 1966, it appointed as governor-general (replacing Silvino Silvério Marques) a popular district governor, Rebocho Vaz, whose activities in Uíge had attracted favourable attention. A Portuguese journalist in 1963 interviewed Rebocho Vaz, then a major, and his statement quoted and published in Lisbon is an important one:

> It is difficult at present to make prognostications on future events in the district. But there is one certainty: that we will be able to win this war—and we are in a war—only with a radical transformation of the social environment that still exists today.[9]

Not military power, but ultimately change and reform, then, would bring Portuguese success. This inherent belief at the top levels of the administration, at least, was exhibited in several ways in the late 1960s. The governor-general of Angola became more than a high patron to the settler community and to *assimilados* (a designation no longer official after the legislation of 1961); in a sense, his function now included that of being a director of a kind of colonial peace-corps dedicated to African welfare as well as to the preservation of Portuguese sovereignty. The idea expressed in the 1920s, that reform of conditions would prevent revolution in Angola, was revived in practice in the 1960s. This was also illustrated in a speech in Lisbon on May 20, 1968, by the Minister of Overseas Affairs, Dr Silva Cunha, at the swearing-in ceremony for a new governor-general of Portuguese Guinea. Silva Cunha made clear that the 'loyalty and dedication' of the Africans were crucial to the success of military defence and that the 'well-being and prosperity' of the masses had a high priority in administrative goals.[10] Such policy statements by key officials in the late 1960s appeared to be much more free of patriotic rhetoric than before the *confusão* of 1961.

Portugal's reforms in Angola will have ambivalent effects on the cause of black Angolan nationalism. To the extent that Angolan youth become less amenable to political dependence after further educational opportunities, to the extent that Angolans as a whole desire more change after initial gestures in that direction, and to the extent that the changes train a new national leadership prepared to disavow Portuguese suzerainty, the new reforms will be to Portugal's disadvantage. To the extent, however, that the post-1961 improvements draw back to Angola increasing numbers of Angolan refugees, pacify the masses and create a loyal pro-Portuguese black and brown elite who shun nationalist connections, the exiled parties will have trouble and their hopes of a rapid victory will be deferred.

The ideology of the exiled Angolan nationalists has responded to continued Portuguese viability and to the new reforms by becoming more radical and anti-Western.[11] Internecine struggles within and between the exiled parties have had their effect too, and made Portuguese survival a bitter pill to swallow. Communist interests have taken advantage of this situation and have increased their aid to certain parties, notably the MPLA based in Brazzaville. The radicalisation of the nationalists' theory and policy has also been a consequence of a situation which takes on the character of a competition over the destiny of the Angolan peoples between the Portuguese regime and the exiled nationalists and their friends among the independent African states. Radicalisation seems likely to continue for as long as the exiled nationalists and the new states of Congo-Kinshasa and Zambia do not enjoy strong economies and steady development.

Has a stalemate been reached? Or is the fact that Portugal still holds the upper hand in the struggle of fleeting importance only? Certainly, neither Portuguese colonialism nor Angolan nationalism seems foreordained to win a rapid or complete victory in the near future. The stakes of victory in Angola have been raised further by the discovery in 1966–67 of massive oil reserves. Similar complications, and the fact that the Angolan nationalist parties are bitterly divided, make the possibility of Angolan independence rather remote in the next decade.

If this is true, and if Portugal is to remain in control of Angola for the immediate future, what can be said about a transition era that would lead peacefully to independence? Such a transition might help prevent thousands of African deaths in post-independence turmoil. Only Portugal would appear to have the unity and resources necessary to effect such a transition, if ever a decision favourable to independence were to be made. Although the United Nations, the United States and certain Western European powers have urged Portugal to accelerate the process of decolonisation in Angola, there has been offered so far no viable alternative to the established Portuguese administration other than that of handing Angola over to a hastily formed coalition of feuding African nationalists.

THE VOICE OF ANGOLA

The history of Angola is replete with the failures of its rulers; at the same time, the problems that Portugal has faced in Angola have been to some extent more difficult than those confronting colonial powers elsewhere. Despite the weaknesses of Portuguese colonialism, despite the awful cost in human life of the tragic days of 1961, Portuguese rule has tended to improve the condition of the peoples of Angola. When all the criticisms are said, the fact remains that, of all the European groups in Africa, the Portuguese have maintained the friendliest and least race-conscious relations with black Africans. Not that there have been no racial conflicts or bad feelings. Nor is it true that today Africans bear no hatred towards the Portuguese. Nevertheless, in the context of modern Southern Africa, Portugal has racial policies that are more natural and more humane than those of South Africa and Rhodesia. This being said, improved race relations in Angola are no guarantee of future tranquillity, or of continued Portuguese sovereignty, of Angolan happiness, or of an African nationalist unity after independence. Mistrust exists between *branco*, *preto* and *mestiço* and it will continue at least as long as the chief political questions of Angola's future remain undecided, and perhaps longer. To this extent, the Portuguese moratorium on Angolan politics has been a disservice to the country and has postponed the solution of crucial problems.

Historians can rarely provide answers and few can safely make judgements on the affairs of men. But they can pose questions. How long will Portugal continue to rule Angola? For the sake of the welfare and daily needs of the peoples of Angola, would ten more years under Portugal be a better prelude to independence than a rapid freedom tomorrow? If African nationalists gain control, which parties will dominate? If Portugal wavers or withdraws for reasons of internal politics, will the Portuguese settler community take over? Would Portugal consider a partition of Angola into a white-dominated western section, controlling the mineral-rich enclaves, and a poor, landlocked African nationalist-led section to the east? Would Portugal under certain conditions set up a pro-Portuguese puppet government of settlers and *assimilados*?

There are no ready answers to these questions, but an appraisal of the possibilities is best made through paying attention to facts rather than

251

propaganda. Much misinformation and propaganda on Angola have been fed to the world community. Doctrinaire Marxist-Leninist propaganda ('all Portuguese reforms are myths'; 'exploitation is the sole purpose of the Lisbon regime'), or reactionary European attitudes ('Africans are childlike savages'; 'Angolans cannot rule themselves'), shed little light on the issues. If Angola were given independence tomorrow, the resulting loss of life might well make the Congo crises of 1960–64 pale in comparison. In the opinion of some observers, an acceptable alternative to this holocaust is an orderly transition period supervised by the Portuguese government.

As yet, the Caetano regime shows no sign of planning such a transition. Some pressure has already been brought to bear on Portugal by the United Nations and by its Western allies in NATO. While greater pressure could bring results, internal pressure within Angola or an explosion of strife in Portugal itself would be ultimately more decisive in bringing changes in Angola. Neither the government in Lisbon nor any settler-controlled regime will be brought to the bargaining table by the current lingering guerrilla war on the frontiers. Certainly, a popular mass struggle such as occurred in Algeria during 1954–62 would be a different matter; but as yet no significant terrorism or urban guerrilla sabotage has struck Angola. Until they do, the African nationalists will have failed to apply a crucial revolutionary principle. Terrorism in Angolan cities or widespread conflict in Lisbon would do more to end Portuguese control than all the outside aid to the exiled nationalists of the past decade.

Still, the decision to leave Angola would have to come from a government in Lisbon, and such a decision is now no more likely than the reappearance of a Sebastian or a Vasco da Gama. If a government were to emerge in Lisbon with the strength to decolonise Portuguese Africa, its political survival in the context of army paramountcy would be little short of miraculous. Portugal, then, faces in Angola and Mozambique an Algerian-like situation but with a greater relative economic stake and without a De Gaulle to lead it out of the wilderness. Under certain conditions, Angola could well present the world with another Vietnam situation. A partition by Portugal could be a prelude to such a dilemma, where one part of Angola, supported by Communist powers, would attempt to conquer the Western-supported section; in which case Portugal might call for outside troop reinforcements. Meanwhile, time is running short in Angola and, as jostling interests battle for control—apparently with no long-range plan in mind—the acceptable and peaceful alternatives are fast disappearing.

Portugal is not alone in its unhappy situation. The destinies of

Angola and Portugal for long have been linked, and Angola also faces an uncertain future. Although it is no longer the orphan of the Portuguese empire, or the 'coming colony' of Africa, its destiny has been influenced by the tragic impacts of slavery, slave trade, forced labour and a narrow political environment. Too often extreme solutions have been applied where statesmanship and generosity of spirit were required. Too often both the Portuguese and their African friends and enemies have mis-understood each other's aspirations and capacities, and have failed to benefit from a realisation of their common humanity. And too often the man-in-the-street in Luanda has not appreciated the ideals of Lisbon. Ultimately, Portugal's dilemma in Angola is linked with tradition and aspiration at home. Although some critics in Portugal have proposed a Commonwealth-like solution to the problem of Portuguese Africa, the government in power has actually increased Lisbon's political controls in Africa. Apparently a certain group in Portugal still nourishes the traditional fear that the demise of the Portuguese African empire would result in a Spanish takeover in Portugal. Whatever the extent of such a belief, the question of Portugal in Africa is not being actively debated in Lisbon, and the futures of at least Angola and Mozambique are not considered negotiable by the Caetano regime.

The independence of Angola is inevitable. Much less certain is the form it will take. A just response to the aspirations of Angolans of all races will require statesmanship of the highest order. This task will indeed be more demanding than the abolition of the old evils of Angola, the black mother of the New World. Perhaps its future may be more vital to world peace than the fate of South Vietnam. The things at stake exceed the importance of Angolan minerals or of a possible economic loss by Portugal.[12] At stake may be the future political course of Portugal, of Southern Africa, of situations in Africa that could develop into Vietnam- or Korean-like crises. At stake is the manner in which Angolans become masters in their own house, their long-dreamed-of destiny.

253

APPENDIX I

Governors-General of Angola since 1854*

José Rodrigues Coelho Do Amaral	1854–60
Carlos Augusto Franco	1860–61
Sebastião Lopes De Calheiros e Meneses	1861–62
José Baptista De Andrade	1862–65
Francisco António Gonçalves Cardoso	1866–69
José Rodrigues Coelho Do Amaral	1869–70
José Maria Da Ponte E Horta	1870–73
José Baptista De Andrade	1873–76
Caetano Alexandre De Almeida E Albuquerque	1876–78
Vasco Guedes De Carvalho E Meneses	1878–80
António Eleutério Dantas	1880–82
Francisco Joaquim Ferreira Do Amaral	1882–86
Guilherme Augusto De Brito Capelo	1886–92
Jaime Lobo De Brito Godins	1892–93
Álvaro António Da Costa Ferreira	1893–94
Francisco Eugénio Pereira De Miranda	1894–95
Álvaro António Da Costa Ferreira	1895–96
Guilherme Augusto De Brito Capelo	1896–97
António Duarte Ramada Curto	1897–1900
Francisco Xavier Cabral De Oliveira Moncada	1900–03
Eduardo Augusto Ferreira Da Costa	1903–04
António Duarte Ramada Curto	1904–06
Eduardo Augusto Ferreira Da Costa	1906–07
Henrique Mitchell De Paiva Couceiro	1907–09
José Augusto Alves Roçadas	1909–10
Manuel Maria Coelho	1911–12
José Mendes Ribeiro Norton De Matos	1912–15
Fernando Pais Teles De Utra Machado	1915–16
Pedro Francisco Massano De Amorim	1916–17
Filomeno Da Câmara Melo Cabral	1918–19

* Not included in this list are 'interim' governors or officials charged temporarily with governing duties in place of a governor. From Paulo Dias De Novais (1575–89), 'Governor and Captain-Major', until 1854 there were ninety-four governors and governing councils.

Francisco Coelho Do Amaral Reis	1919–20
José Mendes Ribeiro Norton De Matos	1921–23 (H.C.)*
Francisco Da Cunha Rego Chaves	1925–26 (H.C.)
António Vicente Ferreira	1926–28 (H.C.)
Filomeno Da Câmara Melo Cabral	1929–30 (H.C.)
José Dionísio Carneiro De Sousa E Faro	1930–31
Eduardo Ferreira Viana	1931–34
António Lopes Mateus	1935–39
Manuel Da Cunha E Costa Marques Mano	1939–41
Álvaro De Freitas Morna	1942–43
Vasco Lopes Alves	1943–47
José Agapito Da Silva Carvalho	1947–55
Horácio José De Sá Viana Rebelo	1956–59
Álvaro Rodrigues Da Silva Tavares	1960–61
Venâncio Augusto Deslandes	1961–62
Silvino Silvério Marques	1962–66
Camilo Rebocho Vaz	1966–

* H.C. = High Commissioner and Governor-General.

APPENDIX II

The Angolan Population in 1960

Whites	Mestiços	Blacks	Others	Total
172,529	53,392	4,604,362	166	4,830,449

Number of non-*Indígena* Blacks:* 41,756
Number of Angolan-born *Assimilados*: 37,873
Number of *Indígenas*: 4,562,606
Main ethnic divisions of *Indígenas*:
  Bakongo: 621,787
  Ganguela: 329,259
  Lunda-Quioco: 396,264
  Lunkhumbi (Humbe): 114,832
  Mbundu: 1,053,999
  Nhaneca: 138,191
  Ovambo: 115,442
  Ovimbundu: 1,746,109

* Including Black *Cape Verdians*, *São Tomenses*, etc., living in Angola.

Notes and References

Part One

1. LAND, PEOPLES AND KINGDOMS

1. J. J. Monteiro, *Angola and the River Congo*, London 1875; reprinted London 1968, Vol. II, p. 314.
2. José Ribeiro da Cruz, *Geografia de Angola*, Lisbon 1940, p. 49.
3. D. S. Whittlesey, "Geographic Provinces of Angola", *The Geographical Review*, Vol. XIV, No. 1, January 1924, pp. 113–26.
4. I. S. Van Dongen, "Angola", *Focus* (American Geographical Society), Vol. VII, No. 2, October 1956.
5. Lavrador Ribeiro, "Os Serviços de Saúde e Higiene", *Revista Médica de Angola* (Luanda), Vol. III (2a Series), No. 9, 1961, p. 12.
6. See James Stevens Simmons, ed., *Global Epidemiology*, Philadelphia 1944, Vol. II: "Angola", pp. 324–34; and Douglas L. Wheeler, "A Note on Smallpox in Angola, 1670–1875", *Studia* (Lisbon), Nos. 13–14, January–July 1964, pp. 351–62.
7. *Revista Médica de Angola*, Vol. III, No. 8, 1960, p. 27.
8. Harold Livermore, *A New History of Portugal*, Cambridge 1966; Charles Nowell, *A History of Portugal*, New York 1952; J. B. Trend, *Portugal*, New York 1957, especially pp. 175–95.
9. Trend, op. cit., p. 179.
10. Livermore, op. cit., p. 330.
11. Salvador de Madariaga, *Spain: A Modern History*, New York 1958, p. 253.
12. V. Bragança-Cunha, *Eight Centuries of Portuguese Monarchy*, New York 1911, pp. 13–14.
13. Ronald H. Chilcote, *Portuguese Africa*, Englewood Cliffs 1967.
14. António de Figueiredo, *Portugal and Its Empire. The Truth*, London 1961, pp. 19–25.
15. Aubrey Bell, *Portugal of the Portuguese*, London 1915, p. 162.
16. Ralph Delgado, *História de Angola*, 4 Vols., Lobito 1948–55, Vol. IV, p. 419.
17. See journals of António F. F. da Silva Porto, *Viagens e apontamentos de um portuense em Africa. Diario*, 13 Vols., copies in Society of Geography, Lisbon, and in Municipal Public Library, Oporto.
18. Raymond Cantel, *Prophétisme et messianisme dans l'oeuvre d'António Vieira*, Paris 1960, p. 167.
19. António de Saldanha Gama, *Memória Sobre as Colónias de Portugal, Situadas na Costa Ocidental da Africa*, Paris 1839, pp. 1–5.
20. Quoted in Richard J. Hammond, *Portugal in Africa 1815–1910*, Stanford 1966, p. 27.
21. Ibid., p. 35.
22. Miguel de Unamuno, *Por Tierras de Espana y Portugal*, Madrid 1914, pp. 122–3.
23. Miguel Torga, *Portugal*, Coimbra 1957, 2nd edn., pp. 57, 111–17.
24. F. C. C. Egerton, *Angola In Perspective*, London 1957, pp. 27–8.

25. Figueiredo, op. cit., p. 19.
26. C. R. Boxer, *Portuguese Society in the Tropics*, Madison 1965, pp. 86–7, 146.
27. 'Sebastianism' was the common belief of the masses that the dead King Sebastian would return to save the country. Imposters posing as the King appeared as late as 1813. Cf. Trend, op. cit., pp. 155–7.
28. Serpa Pinto to Luciano Cordeiro, May 16, 1878, *Cartas de Serpa Pinto ao Secretario perpétuo da Sociedade de Geographia Luciano Cordeiro*, Manuscript No. 35, Society of Geography, Lisbon.
29. See Douglas L. Wheeler, "Anti-Imperial Traditions in Portugal: Yesterday and Today", *Boston University Graduate Journal*, Vol. XII, No. 2, Spring 1964, quoted on p. 132.
30. 'Iron Surgeon' is a term used by Raymond Carr, *Spain 1808–1939*, Oxford 1966, pp. 171, 531.
31. Charles Vogel, *Le Portugal et ses Colonies*, Paris 1860, p. 122.
32. Gladwyn M. Childs, *Umbundu Kinship and Character*, London 1949, p. 191.
33. Henrique Galvão, *Santa Maria: My Crusade for Portugal*, New York 1962, pp. 14–23, 71; Figueiredo, op. cit., pp. 30–77.
34. See *The New York Times*, September 27 and 28, 1968; *Keesing's Contemporary Archives*, October 5–12, 1968, "Portugal", p. 22960; Hermínio Martins, "Opposition in Portugal", *Government and Opposition*, Vol. IV, No. 2, Spring 1969, pp. 250–63.
35. J. Desmond Clark, *Prehistoric Cultures of Northeast Angola and Their Significance in Tropical Africa*, 2 Vols., Lisbon 1963, Vol. I, p. 295.
36. Paul Bohannan, *Africa and Africans*, Garden City 1964, pp. 190–8.
37. G. P. Murdock, *Africa: Its Peoples and their Culture History*, New York 1959, p. 271.
38. David Birmingham, *Trade and Conflict in Angola*, Oxford 1966, pp. 1–9.
39. Jan Vansina, "Notes sur l'origine du royaume de Kongo", *Journal of African History*, Vol. IV, 1963, p. 1.
40. Birmingham, op. cit., pp. 19–20.
41. David Livingstone, *Missionary Travels and Researches in South Africa*, New York 1858 edn., p. 434; Robert Verly, "Le 'Roi divin' chez les Ovimbundu et Kimbundu de l'Angola", *Zaire* (Brussels), June 1956, pp. 675–703.
42. Birmingham, op. cit., pp. 64–77. Birmingham's reconstruction of the Imbangala invasion of Angola is more plausible than that of Vansina. See also, David Birmingham, "The Date and Significance of the Imbangala Invasion of Angola", *Journal of African History*, Vol. VI, 1965, pp. 143–52.
43. Childs, op. cit., pp. 181–9.
44. José Redinha, *Etnossociologia do Nordeste de Angola*, Lisbon 1956; rev. edn., Braga 1966, pp. 2–3; see also, José Redinha, *Distribuição Etnica de Angola*, Luanda 1962.
45. Childs, op. cit., p. 20.
46. António de Almeida and J. Camarote França, "Reçintos Muralhados de Angola", *I Encontro de Escritores de Angola*, Sá da Bandeira 1963, pp. 109–24; Lenk-Chevitch, "Vestiges d'anciennes constructions en Angola", *Zaire*, No. 11/6, 1948, pp. 675–7.
47. Gladwyn M. Childs, "The Kingdom of Wambu (Huambo): A Tentative Chronology", *Journal of African History*, Vol. V, No. 3, 1964, pp. 376–7.
48. Inácia Teixeira Gomes de Oliveira, *A Evolução Historica dos Cuanhamas*, Lisbon 1962; unpublished dissertation for the bachelor's degree, Faculty of Letters, Lisbon University, p. 1.

49. Ibid., pp. 41–3.
50. Padre Carlos Estermann, *Etnografia do Sudoeste de Angola*, 3 Vols., Lisbon 1958–62, Vol. I, p. 189. Estermann suggests that Kwanhama oral literature contains a folk story of the "Lion and the Jackal", which he considers comparable to the Antigone of Sophocles, 'one of the most sublime works of world literature'.

2. BLACK MOTHER AND WHITE FATHER

1 Basil Davidson, in *Black Mother*, London 1961, discusses King Afonso I and the effects of the slave trade on his kingdom.
2. C. R. Boxer, *Race Relations in the Portuguese Colonial Empire, 1415–1825*, Oxford 1963, pp. 21–2.
3. Jan M. Vansina, *Kingdoms of the Savanna*, Madison 1965, p. 192.
4. David Birmingham, *The Portuguese Conquest of Angola*, Oxford 1965, p. 2.
5. David Birmingham, *Trade and Conflict in Angola*, Oxford 1966, pp. 42–50.
6. Quoted in ibid., p. 27.
7. J. D. Cordeiro da Matta, *Ensaio de Diccionario Kimbundu-Portuguez*, Lisbon 1893, pp. 109–10.
8. Ibid., p. 87.
9. For a thorough discussion of early Portuguese contacts with Angola, see Birmingham, *Trade and Conflict*, op. cit., pp. 30–41.
10. Ibid., p. 47.
11. A. da Silva Rego, *O Ultramar Português no Século XIX*, Lisbon 1966, pp. 247–50.
12. António de Oliveira Cadornega, *História Geral das Guerras Angolanas*, 3 Vols., Lisbon 1940–42, edited by José Matías Delgado and Manuel Alves da Cunha, Vol. I, pp. 33–8.
13. Ibid., Vol. II, p. 589.
14. Figures from Birmingham, *Trade and Conflict*, op. cit., pp. 40–155, and unpublished documents.
15. Ibid., p. 115.
16. Cadornega, op. cit., Vol. II, pp. 298–358.
17. Ibid., Vol. III, pp. 382–6; translation from the Portuguese by Douglas Wheeler.
18. Birmingham, *Trade and Conflict*, op. cit., p. 27.
19. Boxer, op. cit., pp. 30, 40.
20. *Almanak Statístico da Província d'Angola . . .* , Luanda 1851, pp. 51–5.
21. E. A. da Silva Correia, *História de Angola*, Lisbon 1937, Vol. I, p. 13.
22. António F. F. da Silva Porto, *Viagens e apontamentos*, 13 Vols. in MSS., Municipal Public Library, Oporto, see Vol. III.
23. C. R. Boxer, *Portuguese Society in the Tropics*, Madison 1965, pp. 197–208.
24. C. W. Newbury, *The Western Slave Coast and its Rulers*, Oxford 1961, pp. 16–17.
25. H. Galvão and C. Selvagem, *O Império Ultramarino Português*, 4 Vols., Lisbon 1952, Vol. III, pp. 84–8.
26. Silva Correia, op. cit., Vol. I, p. 26.
27. C. R. Boxer, *Four Centuries of Portuguese Expansion*, Johannesburg 1959, pp. 86–92.
28. Silva Correia, op. cit., Vol. II, pp. 61–5.

3. A BARREN SOVEREIGNTY EXPANDED

1. A good deal of the material on expansion and policy in this chapter derives from my unpublished Ph.D. dissertation, Douglas L. Wheeler, *The Portuguese in Angola, 1836–1891: A Study in Expansion and Administration*, History Department, Boston University 1963.
2. The quotation beginning this chapter and referred to here is from Lord Russell to Count Lavradio, October 13, 1860, British Parliamentary *Accounts and Papers*, C 3531 (1883), XLVIII, p. 63.
3. Roger T. Anstey, *Britain and the Congo in the 19th Century*, Oxford 1962, pp. 50–3; 84–112. Britain's policy towards Portuguese expansion in north Angola was, according to Anstey, 'of arguable legality' (p. 229).
4. Amaral to Lisbon, August 16, 1869, Angola file, Pasta 40, *Arquivo Histórico Ultramarino*, Lisbon.
5. Ruben A. Leitão, *Cartas de D. Pedro V Aos Seus Contemporáneos*, Lisbon 1961, p. 307.
6. S. Lopes de Calheiros e Menezes, *Relatório do Governador Geral da Província de Angola*, Lisbon 1867, pp. 66–7; 70 ff.
7. David Livingstone, *Missionary Travels and Researches in South Africa*, New York 1858 edn., p. 466. Livingstone recuperated in Luanda after his journey and spent about sixteen months in Angola, 1854–55.
8. Letter signed by five Portuguese merchants, December 30, 1865, Angola file, Pasta 34, *Arquivo Histórico Ultramarino*, Lisbon.
9. See J. J. Monteiro in *Angola and the River Congo*, London 1875 and 1876 edns.
10. Quoted in Wheeler thesis, op. cit., p. 10; cited in Manuel Ferreira Ribeiro, *As Conferencias e o Itinerário do Viajante Serpa Pinto*, Lisbon 1879, p. 754.
11. Albuquerque to Lisbon, October 19, 1877, Angola File, Pasta 47, No. 267, *Arquivo Histórico Ultramarino*, Lisbon.
12. Ferreira do Amaral to Lisbon, April 9, 1884, Angola File, Pasta 4, *Arquivo Histórico Ultramarino*, Lisbon.
13. Recent studies discussing the 1890 ultimatum: P. R. Warhurst, *Anglo-Portuguese Relations in South-Central Africa, 1890–1900*, London 1962; Richard J. Hammond, *Portugal and Africa, 1815–1910*, Stanford 1966; and Eric Axelson, *Portugal and the Scramble for Africa, 1875–1891*, Johannesburg 1967.
14. Edward Hertslet, *The Map of Africa by Treaty*, London 1909 edn., Vol. III, "Great Britain and Portugal, Treaties, 1807–1906".
15. R. Oliver and J. Fage, *A Short History of Africa*, London 1962 edn., p. 198.
16. Lopes de Calheiros e Menezes, op. cit., pp. 66–7.
17. Discussions of slavery and forced labour in Portuguese Africa, with reference to Angola, are in Hammond, op. cit., pp. 311–42; James Duffy, *Portuguese Africa*, Cambridge, Mass., 1959, chap VI, pp. 130–73; James Duffy, *A Question of Slavery*, Oxford 1967.
18. Sá da Bandeira, *Trabalho Rural Africano e a Administração Colonial*, Lisbon 1873, p. 102.
19. *Dizimo* abolition is discussed in *Boletim Oficial* (Luanda), January 4 and 11, 1873.
20. Silva Porto, *Viagens e apontamentos*, Oporto MSS, Vol. IX, August 4, 1882, p. 389.
21. Ibid., Vol. XI, entries for 1885, pp. 19–87.

22. Ibid., Vol. xi, April 5, 1885, p. 53.
23. Jan Vansina, *The Kingdoms of the Savanna*, Madison 1965, p. 201.
24. Henrique Dias de Carvalho, *Ethnographia e História Tradicional dos Povos da Lunda*, Lisbon 1890, pp. 709–22.
25. Gladwyn M. Childs, *Umbundu Kinship and Character*, London 1949, pp. 202–4.
26. From Mary Kingsley, *West African Studies*, London 1900, p. 290.
27. 'Creole' is the term used by Mário António in "Música e danças tradicionais de Luanda", *Boletim Cultural da Câmara Municipal de Luanda*, April–June 1966, pp. 61–3.
28. Manuel Da Costa Lobo, *Subsídios Para A História De Luanda*, Lisbon 1967, pp. 197–8; 107–9.
29. Ibid., pp. 29–36.
30. Amândio César, *Angola 1961*, Lisbon 1961, p. 50.
31. See the analysis of *carnaval* songs and dances by Óscar Ribas in his *Izomba*, Luanda 1965.
32. A trek Boer view of the half century stay in Angola may be found in P. J. Van der Merwe, *Ons Halfeeu in Angola, 1880–1928*, Johannesburg 1951.
33. A. de A. Felner, *Angola. Apontamentos sobre a Colonização dos Planaltos e Litoral do Sul de Angola. Documentos*, 3 Vols., Lisbon 1940, Vol. i, p. 95.
34. Manuel V. Guerreiro, " 'Boers' de Angola", *Garcia de Orta*, Vol. vi, 1958, pp. 11–31.
35. The fascinating story of the last major Boer trek out of Angola may be read in *The Cape Times* (Cape Town), March 5 to October 9, 1928.
36. Hammond, op. cit., pp. 253–6.
37. Alberto de Almeida Teixeira, *Naulila*, Lisbon 1935, pp. 8–9. A study of German documentation has yet to confirm this conspiracy.
38. Horst Drechsler, "Germany and South Angola, 1898–1903", *Présence Africaine*, Nos. 42–43, 1962, pp. 51–69.
39. See attacks by Gastão Sousa Dias in *África Portentosa*, Lisbon 1926; and Augusto Casimiro, *Naulila*, Lisbon 1922.
40. António Barroso, *O Congo, Seu Passado, Presente e Futuro*, Lisbon 1889.
41. James Johnston, *Reality vs. Romance in South Central Africa*, New York 1893, p. 33.
42. *The Times* (London), March, April 1914; R. H. Carson Graham, *Under Seven Congo Kings*, London 1930, pp. 128–43.
43. Duffy, *Portuguese Africa*, op. cit., p. 127.
44. Term employed by A. da Silva Rego in *O Ultramar Português No Século XIX*, Lisbon 1966, p. 401.
45. Bento Carqueja, *O Futuro De Portugal*, Oporto 1920, p. 289.
46. *Cape Times* (Cape Town), March 19, 1928, editorial "Portugal in Africa".
47. Israel Zangwill, ed., *Report on the Work of the Commission Sent out by the Jewish Territorial Organization under the Auspices of the Portuguese Government to Examine the Territory Proposed for the Purpose of a Jewish Settlement in Angola*, London 1913.
48. *Província de Angola* (Luanda), September 17, 1923.
49. Quoted by Quirino de Jesus, "A Delimitação Effectiva de Angola", *Portugal em Africa*, Vol. i, 1894, pp. 43–6.

4. ANGOLA IS WHOSE HOUSE?

1. *O Futuro d'Angola* (Luanda), April 8, 1882.
2. See the definition of K. R. Minogue, *Nationalism*, New York 1967, pp. 29, 153.
3. See Douglas L. Wheeler, "Nineteenth Century African Protest in Angola: Prince Nicolas of Kongo (1830?–1860)", *African Historical Studies*, Vol. I, No. I, 1968, pp. 40–59.
4. Georg Tams, *Visita as Possessões Portuguezas Na Costa Occidental D'Africa*, 4 Vols., Oporto 1850, Vol. II, pp. 17–19.
5. R. H. Carson Graham, *Under Seven Congo Kings*, London 1930, pp. 2–3.
6. *Jornal do Commercio* (Lisbon), December 1, 1859.
7. Alfredo de Sarmento, *Os Sertões D'Africa*, Lisbon 1880, pp. 66–8.
8. See Carson Graham, op. cit., pp. 132–63 for the history of this uprising.
9. Carlos Selvagem and Henrique Galvão, *O Império Ultramarino Português*, 4 Vols., Lisbon 1953, Vol. III, pp. 95–6.
10. Documents in the *Arquivo Histórico Ultramarino*, Lisbon, Caixas 70, 73, letters of February 23, 1825; August 26, 1829; Governor-General.
11. Amaral to Sá da Bandeira, April 1860, *Papéis de Sá da Bandeira*, Maço 1, *Arquivo Histórico Ultramarino*, Lisbon.
12. Cited in Mário António, "Aspectos Sociais de Luanda inferidos dos Anúncios publicados na sua imprensa-Análise Preliminar Ao Ano De 1851", *Boletim Do Instituto De Angola*, No. 17, January–December 1963, p. 101.
13. Sarmento, op. cit., p. 67.
14. Sousa e Oliveira published with M. A. Francina, *Elementos Gramaticaes da Lingua NBundu*, Luanda 1864, one of the earliest books printed in Angola.
15. For a history of Angolan journalism, see Júlio de Castro Lopo, *Jornalismo de Angola. Subsídios Para A Sua História*, Luanda 1964.
16. For a complete example of an *Ambaquista*-composed letter in Portuguese written in 1910, see João Evangelista de Lima Vidal, *Por Terras D'Angola*, Coimbra 1916, pp. 20–1.
17. *O Arauto Africano* (Luanda), March 17, 1889.
18. *Voz D'Angola Clamando No Deserto*, Lisbon 1901, p. 69.
19. Ibid., pp. 128–144.
20. Ibid., pp. 144–51.
21. António de Assis Júnior, *Relato dos Acontecimentos de Dala Tando e Lucala*, 2 Vols., Luanda 1917–1918, Vol. II, pp. 55–6.
22. See Douglas L. Wheeler, "An Early Angolan Protest: the radical journalism of José de Fontes Pereira (1823–1891)", in Robert I. Rotberg and Ali Mazrui, eds., *The Tradition of Protest in Black Africa*, Oxford, 1970.
23. *O Cruzeiro do Sul*, No. 12, September 1, 1873.
24. *O Futuro d'Angola* (Luanda), April 29, 1882.
25. *O Arauto Africano* (Luanda), January 20, 1890, one of a series of articles by Fontes Pereira that month.
26. The title was changed from *O Arauto Africano* to *O Polícia Africano*, in the issue of February 4, 1890. The January 27 number was the last of *O Arauto Africano*, a title suggestive of later African newspapers in Mozambique, such as *O Brado Africano*.
27. *O Mercantil* (Luanda), January 30, 1890.
28. Mário António, *A Sociedade Angolana Do Fim Do Século XIX E Um Seu Escritor. Ensaio*, Luanda 1961, pp. 15–18, 56, 69.

29. Governor-General to Lisbon, October 14, 1885, Angola, Pasta 4, *Arquivo Histórico Ultramarino*, Lisbon.
30. José Tengarrinha, *História Da Imprensa Periódica Portuguesa*, Lisbon 1965, pp. 225–30.
31. Heli Chatelain to US State Department, 1891–92, in *Despatches from United States Consuls in St Paul de Loanda*, 1-430, roll 5, National Archives, Washington DC.
32. *O Commercio de Loanda*, September 18, 1867.
33. José de Macedo, *Autonomia de Angola*, Lisbon 1910, pp. 162–3; 207–8.
34. "Associações", Caixa 11-3/20-4, *Arquivo Histórico de Angola*, Luanda.
35. An economic recession, 1906–1910, stranded Portuguese immigrants in Angola and discouraged emigration from Portugal. In 1909 only nine Portuguese emigrated to Portuguese Africa. F. E. da Silva, *Emigração Portuguesa*, Lisbon 1917, p. 192.
36. *Voz D'Angola*, op. cit., p. 88.
37. Ibid., p. 35.
38. Ibid., p. 29.
39. Ibid., pp. 97–8.
40 Ibid., p. 20.
41. Ibid., p. 68.

5. ANGOLA AND THE REPUBLIC, 1910–26

1. Norton de Matos, *Memórias e Trabalhos Da Minha Vida*, 4 Vols., Lisbon 1944–5, Vol. III, pp. 26–8.
2. James Duffy, *Portuguese Africa*, Cambridge, Mass., 1959, pp. 153–73; James Duffy, *A Question of Slavery*, Oxford 1967, 3cc csp. 60–229.
3. Duffy, *Portuguese Africa*, op. cit., p. 155.
4. *A Reforma* (Luanda), March 25, 1911. The article noted that in 1907 the new colonial laws alone filled 2,113 pages.
5. Ibid. December 10, 1910.
6. Norton de Matos, *Memórias*, op. cit., Vol. III, p. 24.
7. Richard J. Hammond, "Race Attitudes And Policies In Portuguese Africa In the Nineteenth and Twentieth Centuries", *Race*, October 1967.
8. Norton de Matos, *Memórias*, op. cit., Vol. III, pp. 148–9.
9. Ralph Delgado, *Ao Sul do Cuanza*, 2 Vols., Lisbon 1944, Vol. I, p. 488.
10. See *Revista Colonial* (Lisbon), No. 11, November 1913.
11. Duffy, *Portuguese Africa*, op. cit., p. 251.
12. Ibid., pp. 253–6.
13. Francisco Cunha Leal, *Calígula em Angola*, Lisbon 1924; Júlio Ferreira Pinto, *Angola. Notas E Comentários De Um Colono*, Lisbon 1926; J. Norton de Matos, *A Província de Angola*, Oporto 1926.
14. *A Reforma* (Luanda), No. 1, December 1, 1910.
15. *Boletim Oficial* (Luanda), March 8, 1913. In this number the Liga's statutes were published in full.
16. *A Reforma* (Luanda), October 28, 1911.
17. *Boletim Oficial* (Luanda), II series, No. 29, July 19, 1930.
18. António de Assis Júnior, *Relato dos Acontecimentos de Dala Tando e Lucala*, 2 Vols., Luanda 1917–18, Vol. II, p. 29n.
19. *Independente* (Luanda), October 7, 1920.
20. Eduardo Dos Santos, *Ideológias Políticas Africanas*, Lisbon 1968, pp. 64–5.

Angola

21. *A Voz D'África* (Oporto), October 18, 1928.
22. Dos Santos, *Ideológias Políticas*, op. cit., pp. 66–9. Du Bois's account of his visit to Lisbon and the Liga Africana is found in his *The World and Africa*, New York 1947, p. 241.
23. *A Voz D'África* (Lisbon), July 8, 1929.
24. Ibid.
25. *Província de Angola* (Luanda), October 25, 1924, published the candid plea of an African *assimilado*, Afonso Baptista Franque.
26. *O Eco d'África* (Luanda), April 20, 1914, and November 1, 1914.
27. *The Times* (London), March 2, 3, 11 and 24, 1914.
28. Assis Júnior, op. cit.
29. Ibid., Vol. I, p. 36.
30. *Boletim Oficial* (Luanda), II series, December 9, 1921.
31. Ibid., I series, April 30, 1921.
32. Ibid., I series, No. 7, February 25, 1922, for text of Decree 99, dated February 21, 1922, signed by Norton de Matos.
33. Francisco de Cunha Leal, *Calígula em Angola*, Lisbon 1924, viciously attacks Norton de Matos for his 1921–23 regime; many of Cunha Leal's facts are accurate, if exaggerated, and can be checked in newspapers and local sources.
34. *Angola* (Luanda), January–June 1960, "Figuras Angolanas", pp. 15–17.
35. Norton de Matos, *A Província de Angola*, Oporto 1926, p. 234.
36. Cunha Leal, op. cit., pp. 138–40.
37. *Mossamedense* (Mossamedes), September 27, 1924.
38. *Província de Angola* (Luanda), August 16, 1923 to January 10, 1924.
39. Ibid., September 11, 1926.
40. For Norton de Matos's colonial philosophy see his *Província de Angola*, op. cit., pp. 7, 15, 232–5; *Memórias*, op. cit., Vol. II, pp. 223–33; Vol. III, pp. 49–65.
41. Assis Júnior, *Relato*, op. cit., Vol. II, p. 55.
42. *Província de Angola* (Luanda), January 20, 1926.
43. Ralph Davezies, *Les Angolais*, Paris 1965, p. 237.
44. From the editorial of José de Fontes Pereira in *O Futuro d'Angola*, April 29, 1882.
45. Júlio Ferreira Pinto, *Angola*, Lisbon 1926, pp. 291–2.

6. Discovering Angola, 1926–61

1. James Duffy, *Portugal in Africa*, Cambridge, Mass., 1962, chapter 7, "The Death of the Dream".
2. James Duffy, *Portuguese Africa*, Cambridge, Mass., 1959, p. 291.
3. *Grande Enciclopedia Portuguesa e Brasileira*, 40 Vols., Lisbon and Rio de Janeiro, Vol. 13, p. 705, "Indigenato".
4. Ibid.
5. Duffy, *Portuguese Africa*, op. cit., p. 291.
6. Marcelo Caetano, *Colonizing Traditions, Principles, and Methods of the Portuguese*, Lisbon 1951, pp. 31–42, 43.
7. Duffy, *Portuguese Africa*, op. cit., p. 302.
8. Ibid.
9. Figures from Michael Samuels, "The New Look in Angolan Education", *Africa Report*, Vol. 12, November 1967, p. 64.

10. *Boletim Oficial de Angola* (Luanda), Acta No. 50, April 22, 1958, session, pp. 991–2.
11. Ibid., Acta No. 60, October 20, 1958, session, p. 1178.
12. Ibid., Acta No. 62, April 1, 1959, session, p. 1225.
13. Augusto Casimiro, *Angola E O Futuro (Alguns Problemas Fundamentais)*, Lisbon 1958, p. 268.
14. Marvin Harris, "Race, Conflict and Reform in Mozambique", in Stanley Diamond and Fred G. Burke, eds., *The Transformation of East Africa*, New York 1966, pp. 162–3.
15. "A Questão do Bilhete de Identidade", *Angola, Revista de Doutrina e Estudo* (Luanda), Vol. XXIX, No. 162, January–June 1961, pp. 11–15.
16. H. L. Bishop, "Angola", *Encyclopedia Britannica*, 12th edn., New York 1944, Vol. I, p. 951.
17. Walter Marques, *Problemas do Desenvolvimento Económico de Angola*, 2 Vols., Luanda, 1964–65, Vol. I, pp. 173–80.
18. Hélio Felgas, *História do Congo Português*, Carmona 1958, pp. 193–8.
19. Afonso Mendes, *Trabalho Assalariado em Angola*, Luanda 1966, cited in *Area Handbook for Angola*, Washington 1967, pp. 345–7.
20. Álvaro de Freitas Morna, *Angola. Um Ano No Governo Geral (1942–1943)*, Lisbon 1944, p. 246.
21. Duffy, *Portuguese Africa*, op. cit., p. 327; Henrique Galvão, *Santa Maria: My Crusade for Portugal*, New York 1962, pp. 57–71, for a synopsis of the 1947 report, later published by the Portuguese opposition to Salazar.
22. Duffy, *Portuguese Africa*, op. cit., pp. 323–7.
23. Casimiro, op. cit., pp. 289–321.
24. F. C. C. Egerton, *Angola in Perspective*, London 1957, p. 28.
25. H. Galvão and C. Selvagem, *O Império Ultramarino Português*, 4 Vols., Lisbon 1953, Vol. III, pp. 233–4.
26. *Boletim Oficial* (Luanda), Acta No. 60, October 20, 1958, session, p. 1178.
27. Felgas, op. cit.
28. Hélio Felgas, *As Populações Nativas Do Norte De Angola*, Lisbon 1965, pp. 72–4.
29. Ibid., pp. 106–8.
30. Felgas, *História*, op. cit., p. 198.
31. *Angola: Exposition Internationale Coloniale de Paris: Monographie d'Angola*, Luanda 1931, p. 95.
32. Duffy, *Portuguese Africa*, op. cit., p. 345.
33. Allison B. Herrick, et al., *Area Handbook for Angola*, Washington DC 1967, pp. 55–66.
34. Galvão and Selvagem, op. cit., Vol. III, p. 233.
35. Casimiro, op. cit., pp. 345–6.
36. Thomas Okuma, *Angola In Ferment*, Boston 1962, p. 58.
37. Francisco Cunha Leal, *Oliveira Salazar, Filomeno da Câmara e o Império Colonial Português*, Lisbon 1930, pp. 1–110; José de Sousa e Faro, *Angola: Como eu a vi em 1930–31*, Lisbon 1932, pp. 14–21.
38. *Boletim Oficial* (Luanda), 1 series, No. 44, October 31, 1936.
39. Álvaro de Freitas Morna, *Angola: Um Ano No Governo Geral (1942–1943)*, Lisbon 1944, pp. 325–7.
40. Okuma, op. cit., pp. 60–1.
41. Mário de Andrade, "Angolese Nationalism", *Présence Africaine*, Vols.

14–15, Nos. 42 and 43, 1962, p. 13. Andrade claims the PIDE came to Angola in early 1957.

42. Duffy, *Portuguese Africa*, op. cit., p. 286. Duffy stated that not one member directly represented African interests up to 1959.
43. *Angola* (Luanda), January–June 1962, Vol. xxx, No. 164, pp. 11–12.
44. "Figuras Angolanas", *Angola*, January–June 1960, Vol. xxviii, pp. 15–17.
45. Oscar Ribás, *Ilundo*, Luanda 1958; *Missosso*, Luanda 1964; *Izomba*, Luanda 1965; a trilogy study of Kimbundu traditional literature, religion and associations.
46. José Montenegro, *A Negritude: Dos Mitos Ás Realidades*, Braga 1967, pp. 157–61.
47. Mário António, "Literatura Angolana. Contributo para uma definição", *Ultramar* (Lisbon), Vol. v, No. 15, 1964, pp. 81–92.
48. Gerald M. Moser, "Castro Soromenho, an Angolan Realist", *Africa Today*, December–January 1969, pp. 20–4.
49. Francisco Tenreiro and Mário de Andrade, eds., *Primeiro Caderno de Poesia Negra de Expressão Portuguesa*, Lisbon 1953; Mário de Andrade, *Antologia da Poesia Negra de Expressão Portuguesa*, Paris 1958.
50. Quoted in Padre A. da Silva Rego, "Conflicting Religious Orientations in Angola", in Ronald H. Chilcote, ed., *Brazil and Portuguese Africa*, forthcoming.
51. Jan Vansina *Kingdoms of the Savanna*, Madison 1965, p. 154; Eduardo dos Santos, *Maza. Elementos de etno-história para a interpretação do terrorismo no noroeste de Angola*, Lisbon 1965, pp. 310–11.
52. Dos Santos, *Maza*, op. cit., pp. 312–13.
53. Colin Turnbull, *The Lonely African*, New York 1962.
54. Dos Santos, *Maza*, op. cit., pp. 259–315. Dos Santos includes other religious movements, such as the traditional religious beliefs of Angolan peoples and eight secret societies. See also the research of Silva Cunha, *Aspectos dos Movimentos Associativos na África Negra*, 2 Vols., Lisbon 1958–59.

Part Two

INTRODUCTION

1. The following example of rumour (*boato*) is typical. On September 19, 1966, this writer was told a story with an unusual wealth of detail at Dundo in the Diamang concession. It was related that Angolan 'terrorists' had, some time before, killed by machine-gun fire a lieutenant-colonel in his jeep near Luso. The case was so important (probably the first death in combat of so senior an officer) that I was astonished the Portuguese press had not mentioned it. On September 21, a senior official of the Diamang company's private police denied that a lieutenant-colonel had been killed near Luso, but admitted that at the beginning of the month there had been an ambush in an African village ten miles from Luso, and that a Portuguese had been wounded. Determined to get at the root of the matter, I followed the trail of the story for hundreds of miles. On September 25, I hear at Luanda, from apparently reliable sources, that a Portuguese lieutenant-colonel was indeed dead, but that he had committed suicide (though at Cabinda, not Luso) because of his wife's infidelities. The next day, having arrived at Luso, I was informed that neither of the lieutenant-colonels in the garrison could see me, but that both were

well. A small ambush was admitted, but there was no news of a dead lieutenant-colonel, either at Luso or at Cabinda.

The fact is, fabrication and silence are so widespread in Angola that the truth itself is suspect. The pursuit of truth becomes an exercise in the art of the relative; one advances only to become more enbogged. The foregoing anecdote illustrates the care needed in dealing with information in Portuguese Africa. It would be naive to accept one version alone. The present-day problems of Angola are epitomised in this report of the death of a lieutenant-colonel who may never have existed.

2. One rarely has the chance to check personally on military information. Daniel Chipenda, MPLA representative, stated before the United Nations that his party's troops had killed 2,165 Portuguese soldiers in the Cabinda Enclave in 1965. (Cf. UN Document A/6300/Add. 3, First Part, p. 93 in the French text.) Personal investigation on August 3, 1966, in the cemetery of Cabinda town revealed twenty-four military graves from 1964 to 1965. Now, all soldiers killed in the Enclave whose bodies are recovered—and they almost always are—are buried there. Only the bodies of officers are returned to Portugal at the army's expense; the families of other ranks have to pay for repatriation of the corpses. Allowing for the poverty of these families, probably not more than half as many again of the bodies buried in the cemetery were repatriated. This would give a figure of around thirty-six dead in 1965. It would be a mistake to assume automatically that all of these had been killed in fighting. About a third of this figure could well be accounted for by deaths in road accidents (the tracks are terrible and these young country boys are inexperienced drivers). Hence, Chipenda, relying on the accounts of his partisans, multiplied the Portuguese losses at least eighty times. Such figures no longer deceive anyone, not even journalists favourable to the nationalist cause. (Cf. John Marcum, "Three Revolutions", *Africa Report*, Vol. XII, No. 8, November 1967, p. 9.) It is significant that, at Cabinda, the number of military graves was thirty-six from 1963 to 1965, with a further thirty-two up to August 1966: sixty-eight graves in all; yet the cemetery is vast.

7. THE POLITICAL CONFRONTATION BEFORE 1961

1. Amândio César, *Angola 1961*, Lisbon 1962, pp. 93–109.
2. Contradicting himself, Mário de Andrade subsequently changed the date to 1953, perhaps to ante-date the creation of the rival UPA. Cf. Mário de Andrade, "Et les colonies de Salazar", *Démocratie nouvelle*, Vol. 14, No. 9, September 1960, which gives the 1956 date; Mário de Andrade, "Le nationalisme angolais", *Présence africaine*, No. 42, 1962, which gives the 1953 date.
3. These were people actually brought to trial, but by no means all who were detained had a trial. Many were sentenced without trial; others 'disappeared'.
4. In some of the Luanda party cells, MPLA members were so afraid of PIDE informers that they attended clandestine meetings in masks so as not to be recognised at possible future interrogations.
5. *Courrier d'Afrique*, January 10, 1961.
6. For a discussion on the controversy surrounding the date of the UPNA's foundation, see John Marcum, *The Angolan Revolution*, Vol. 1: *The Anatomy of an Explosion*, Cambridge, Mass., and London 1969, p. 63.

8. THE ARMED REVOLT OF 1961

1. In some places, the heavy buying of salt by Africans a few days before March 15 gave tradesmen a warning.
2. This figure was given by a Portuguese writer in an article in *Economía e Finanças*, quoted in *Le Monde*, April 24, 1961.

9. POLITICAL AFTERMATH OF THE REVOLT, 1961–70

1. There is no exact figure for the number of Angolans in exile. Estimates vary between 200,000 and 500,000 in Congo-Kinshasa; cf. Sven Hamrell, ed., *Refugee Problems in Africa*, Upsala 1967, p. 36. An estimate of 350,000 has been made for the whole of Africa; cf. *Le Monde*, January 30, 1968.
2. The High Commissioner for Refugees has been helped in this by Catholic and, above all, Protestant relief organisations, as well as by other charitable bodies.
3. Obviously this problem arises where land is coveted by Europeans. The example this author is best acquainted with is that of the white *colonato* of Cela, where land was expropriated from Ovimbundu cultivators (who are the best in Angola) in order to provide the whites with homogeneous plots. In 1966, the state took some land from Africans but reclaimed for them, a short distance away, an area that was five times the extent originally cultivated by them. The Africans were also given some technical assistance within the *colonato*.
4. The setting up of this Junta Provincial de Povoamento, in fact, merely institutionalised the existing policy of emigration for poor peasants, subsidised by the government. In 1959, 3,141 *colonos* (settlers) had their fares paid to Angola. The figure fell to 2,900 in 1960 and to 1,379 in 1961 (the drop was due to fear of war among potential emigrants); it rose to 2,578 in 1962, 2,956 in 1963, 4,033 in 1964, 2,810 in 1965 and 2,574 in 1966—that is, about a quarter of the total of Portuguese arriving in Angola each year with the intention of staying.
5. International Labor Organization, *Official Bulletin*, Vol. XLV, No. 2, Supplement II, April 1962.
6. The writer does not know who is responsible for the upkeep of local tracks, but their dreadful state leads one to suppose that no African is any longer obliged to keep them in good condition.
7. In the north, the presence of soldiers sometimes went to filling up some of the gap left by Africans who had fled to the Congo. For instance, the Bembe post in 1960 consisted of 31,409 black Africans; in 1966, there was one family of traders, a dozen civilian and military families, only thirty *recuperados* (former 'terrorists') and more than 300 black and white soldiers. Otherwise Bembe was a human desert. Lucunga is an extreme case: in 1960, it had 111 whites and 12,850 blacks; in 1966, the population consisted of one white civilian, 165 soldiers and about fifty 'redeemed' Africans.
8. The UPA's first mine in the Uíge district exploded on June 14, 1962.
9. In 1966, and probably later, it sometimes happened that Portuguese patrols came across camps in the jungle and took prisoner a few women and children. Some of the latter, born in the jungle, had never seen white men. This writer met a 'terrorist' who had attacked the post of Bessa Monteiro in

1961; he had just been made prisoner by the Portuguese, who had come to his part of the jungle for the first time in 1966.

10. This was probably the only MPLA armed band to leave Congo-Léopoldville for the Dembos in 1961. It was commanded by Tomas Ferreira. The killings took place near an armed base of the UPA.

11. These 511 fatalities from February 4, 1961, to July 10, 1963, were made up as follows: 287 in battle, 100 by road accidents (mines and overturning of vehicles), 42 by accidents with fire-arms, 23 by accidents in aircraft accidents, 28 by other accidents and 31 by sickness. It is interesting to note that, between February 1961 and September 1962, there were only 320 deaths (16 career officers, 8 reserve officers, 16 career NCOs, 16 reserve NCOs, 238 white other ranks and 26 black other ranks). Cf. Artur Maciel, *Angola Heróica*, Lisbon 1963, p. 217.

12. In April 1963, a detachment of the MPLA still at Kinshasa appears to have been annihilated on the Loge river by UPA-GRAE forces; the dead are estimated as being thirteen or twenty-eight.

13. In 1964, the Portuguese army lost only 241 soldiers in its three wars (Angola, Mozambique and Guinea); cf. *Le Monde*, August 4, 1965.

14. If MPLA statements are correct, the GRAE was more concerned with liquidating its rivals (cf. the alleged massacre on May 19, 1966, of thirty-one MPLA partisans at Kamuna in Congo-Kinshasa) than in carrying on the fight in Angola.

15. Some of these Angola-born Portuguese progressives spoke Angolan African dialects. In contrast, some of the MPLA *mestiços* did not know a single one.

16. The MPLA, with the Reverend Domingos da Silva as its mouthpiece, invoked 'God, Our Father, and Jesus Christ, Our Saviour and Redeemer'. It distributed Bibles, matches, membership cards, radio sets and so on; but at this time it was unable to run arms and ammunition, so its leaders contented themselves with urging the exhausted guerrilla combatants not to abandon the revolutionary struggle (communiqué of November 6, 1965).

17. An MPLA communiqué of June 18, 1966, announced that one of its units had destroyed two jeeps and five *carrinhas* (light 'pick-up' vehicles), killed seventy-five Portuguese soldiers and captured important supplies, with no loss to itself. This is the kind of exaggerated claim that amuses the experts.

18. In 1960, the white populations in the eastern districts of Lunda, Moxico and Cuando-Cubango amounted, respectively, to 1,807, 3,432 and 314. They included almost no planters, but Diamang employees, tradesmen and foresters.

19. Name withheld, by request.

20. A metropolitan Portuguese senior official, with the duty of being well-informed of the activities of his enemies, said of the nationalists: 'Seven dogs to one bone, and each of a different breed.'

21. The 1968 estimate of the investments of the Cabinda Gulf Oil Company was 2,000 million escudos.

22. Kassinda is said to have disappeared from the Kinkuzu camp, which was in many respects an ideal internment centre for dangerous opponents of the UPA, ranging from MPLA supporters to those of its own ranks who opposed Holden Roberto's methods.

23. As, for example, the massacre of the family of a Portuguese tradesman isolated on the Zambian frontier at Chicote and the looting of the shop.

10. THE SOCIAL AND ECONOMIC SITUATION IN ANGOLA

1. The Portuguese, anxious to restore their image abroad in this respect, organise excursions to the São Nicolau camp for 'terrorists' near Mossamedes for the few journalists allowed into Angola. This publicity stunt is easily successful, for the Africans are indeed well-treated and earn even more than if they were working for Diamang or the Benguela railway. But at São Nicolau they are only confederates or heretics (like the *tocoistas*: the followers of the messianic sect founded by Simão Toko) who are living with their families. A camp for real political prisoners and partisans—'terrorists' in the Portuguese state vocabulary—is at a remote spot in Serpa Pinto, at Missombo to be precise. Here the conditions of life are harsher, though far from inhumane; and here also a velvet-glove policy is applied. The prisoners, some of whom are MPLA Methodist ministers or catechists, sometimes earn more than in civilian life. But the Portuguese have cleverly mixed UPA and MPLA partisans, which has several advantages: they can find out what is going on among camp inmates; they can afford a smaller guard; and they can manipulate the strife between the rival factions. These camps are not mentioned in official statistics. The PIDE can thus avoid public trials by removing 80 per cent of political prisoners alongside 20 per cent of common-law prisoners. In September 1966, there were 460 prisoners at Missombo and another 132 working in supervised freedom at Serpa Pinto: an interesting example for the political geographer of a pioneer and penitentiary site some 500 miles from the sea.

2. The Volunteers (OPVDC) are the successors of the spontaneous militia of 1961. They consist of unemployed whites and *mestiços* with a taste for danger, and of reliable Africans who are attracted by the pay (3,600 escudos a month was the rate in 1966 for an ordinary Volunteer). The Africans in the OPVDC are mainly Ovimbundu. This force wears uniforms and has light modern weapons, including machine-guns. It is paid for by a percentage tax on the price of coffee. Highly mobile and hardy, the Volunteers live in strategically-sited camps, whence they are despatched to threatened plantations with which they are in contact by continuous radio link. Militarily, it is an elite force which plays a very important role and suffers heavy losses in fighting with the guerrillas.

3. Not that Portuguese superiority in these two respects is of great avail. Artillery is of no use in the jungle against mobile guerrilla bands; and aircraft are only useful in the savanna and against village bases in the *serras*.

4. If the Portuguese had realised that their secrecy would rebound against them, since it gives their adversaries the chance to put forward fantastic figures, they would not have obliged the researcher to make such hazardous calculations. The truth is mostly favourable to them. According to a letter from the Information Services of the Portuguese Armed Forces, the deaths in combat of Portuguese troops between 1961 and 1968 are as follows: *1961* 134; *1962*, 115; *1963*, 83; *1964*, 101; *1965*, 87; *1966*, 90; *1967*, 88; *1968* (to December 1), 102.

5. Horácio de Sá Viana Rebelo, *Angola na África deste tempo*, Lisbon 1961, p. 224.

6. Industrial development in Angola is not always encouraged by Portugal since it may lead to competition with its own industries (cloth-making, chemical products etc.). This is a considerable disadvantage to Portuguese

settlers in Angola, who feel that they are being sacrificed to the metropolitan economic juggernaut. Hence the latent separatism of a section of the white community, which would welcome independence on Rhodesian lines but tends to forget that its security depends on the protection of an army that is composed largely of metropolitan Portuguese.

7. The Frente de Unidade Angolana (FUA), which recruited mainly among certain white residents of Benguela, Lobito and Nova-Lisboa and among the Ovimbundu of central Angola, was an offshoot of the pre-war separatist tendencies of some white settlers who included a few Africans and *mestiços* in their ranks. With survivors of the pre-1961 clandestine networks, they created in January 1961 a movement that was briefly active until May 1961, when the leaders were arrested by the PIDE. Whatever the aspirations of its adherents for an independent, truly multi-racial Angola of leftist leanings, the fact is that, though this group revived on the liberation of its white leaders, it never succeeded in capturing the allegiance of a significant section of the white population; nor could it compete with the UPA and the MPLA among the Africans. It seems by now to have died.

8. There were 2,207 whites in Carmona in 1960; in 1966, the number was estimated at between 4,000 and 5,000, including soldiers. (Incidentally, the price of a square metre of land in the centre of Carmona, a pioneer coffee town, was at least 80 escudos in 1966.)

9. Figures from Michael Samuels, "The New Look in Angolan Education", *Africa Report*, Vol. 12, November 1967.

10. Questions in an entrance examination for a Luanda high school on July 29, 1966, were as much on Portuguese as on Angolan matters. For example, this test for an African child of 10–12 years: *Q*. What is your nationality? *A*. Portuguese. *Q*. Where did Magellan die? *A*. No answer. *Q*. What are the products of Macau? *A*. No answer.

11. It was estimated that, in 1966, in the modern Liceu Salvador Correia de Sá in Luanda, the Angolans formed 20 per cent of the 1,700 pupils; but in the final year they represented only 10 per cent. Among these urban black Africans and *mestiços* formal assimilation had gone so far that there was almost no African family name.

Part Three

11. ANGOLA INFELIX

1. See Larry W. Bowman, "The Subordinate State System of Southern Africa", *International Studies Quarterly*, Vol. XII, No. 3, September 1968, pp. 231–61.

2. Waldemar Nielsen, in *African Battleline*, New York 1965, advances the notion of an imaginary line formed by the frontiers between independent black Africa and white-ruled Southern Africa.

3. "O Imbondeiro Ex-Libris Angola", *Notícia* (Luanda), January 21, 1967. For modern Portuguese expansion, see Douglas L. Wheeler, "Portuguese Expansion in Angola since 1836: A Re-examination", a *Local Series Pamphlet* of the Central Africa Historical Association, Salisbury, Rhodesia, August 1967, pp. 1–16.

4. "Portuguese Africa", special issue of *Africa Report* (Washington), Vol. XII, No. 8, November 1967; see articles therein by John Marcum, William

Hance, Alberto Franco Nogueira (Foreign Minister of Portugal), Douglas L. Wheeler and Michael Samuels. For earlier reports on the Angolan nationalists and on internal conditions in Angola, see John Marcum, "The Angola Rebellion: Status Report", *Africa Report*, Vol. ix, No. 2, February 1964, pp. 3–7; and Giovanni Giovannini, "Can Colonialism Make It?", *Atlas* (New York), Vol. ix, No. 6, June 1965, pp. 353–9. On activity involving Zambia and Portugal, see *Africa Report*, issues of April, May and June 1968.

5. See infra, Part Two, chapter 9, p. 224.
6. *Keesing's Contemporary Archives* (London), "Portugal", October 5–12, 1968, p. 22960.
7. Américo Boavida, *Cinco Séculos de exploração portuguesa*, Rio de Janeiro 1967.
8. Another result of the 1961 crisis has been the gradual exclusion of Protestant missionaries from Angola. By mid-1968, these missionaries had been reduced from an estimated number of '261 to under 50': see Theodore Tucker, "Protestant Missionaries in Angola", *Africa Today*, Vol. xv, No. 3, June–July 1968.
9. Quoted in Artur Maciel, *Angola Heróica: 120 Dias com os nossos soldados*, Lisbon 1963, p. 280. For a survey of the activity of the Portuguese army in Angola, see Douglas L. Wheeler, "The Portuguese Army in Angola: Its Changing Character and Role", *Journal of Modern African Studies*, Vol. vii, No. 3, October 1969.
10. Cited in *Boletim Geral do Ultramar* (Lisbon), Vol. xliv, No. 515, May 1968, pp. 57–60.
11. Exiled Mozambican nationalists, even those regarded as pro-Western, have tended to view developments in more doctrinaire terms than they did before the initial wave of insurgency. Dr Eduardo Mondlane, head of FRELIMO, wrote that the disease which Portuguese reforms would not cure was 'a class system which clearly runs along racial/cultural lines': see his article, "Race Relations and Portuguese Colonial Policy—With Special Reference to Mozambique", *Africa Today*, Vol. xv, No. 1, February-March 1968, p. 18. (Dr Mondlane was assassinated by an unknown party in Dar es Salaam in February 1969.)
12. For Portuguese affairs, 1968–70, see Douglas L. Wheeler, "Thaw in Portugal", *Foreign Affairs* (New York), July 1970, pp. 769–81.

Select Bibliography

Part One

I. Bibliographical Sources

Blake, John W., *European Beginnings in West Africa*, London 1941–42
Borchardt, Paul, *La Bibliographie de l'Angola, 1500–1910*, Brussels 1912
Chilcote, Ronald H., *Portuguese Africa*, Englewood Cliffs 1967
Gibson, Mary Jane, *Portuguese Africa: A Guide to Official Publications*, Washington 1967
Gulbenkian, Fundação Calouste, *Boletim Internacional de Bibliografia Luso-Brasileira*, Vol. I, No. 1, 1960 to present
Werner, Manfred W., *Angola: A Selected Bibliography 1960–1965*, Washington 1965

II. Archives and Libraries

Arquivo Histórico de Angola, Museu de Angola, Luanda
Arquivo Histórico Ultramarino, Depository of Overseas Ministry, Lisbon
Biblioteca da Câmara Municipal de Luanda, Luanda
Biblioteca da Sociedade de Geografia de Lisboa (Library of Society of Geography of Lisbon), Lisbon
Biblioteca Municipal Pública de Porto, Oporto
Biblioteca Nacional de Lisboa, Lisbon
Houghton Library, Harvard University, Cambridge, Mass.
National Archives, Washington
Public Record Office, London

III. Dissertations

Miller, Joseph C., *Chokwe Expansion, 1850–1900*, unpublished M.A. thesis, History Department, University of Wisconsin
Oliveira, Inácia Teixeira Gomes de, *A Evolução Histórica dos Cuanhamas*, unpublished dissertation, University of Lisbon 1962
Samuels, Michael A., *Educação or Instrução? A History of Education in Angola, 1878–1914*, unpublished PH.D. dissertation, Columbia University's Teacher's College 1969
Wheeler, Douglas L., *The Portuguese in Angola, 1836–1891: A Study in Expansion and Administration*, unpublished PH.D. dissertation, Boston University 1963

IV. General and Reference Works

Almada, José de, *Tratados aplicaveis ao Ultramar*, Lisbon 1961
Archivos das Colónias, Lisbon 1917–31
Arquivos de Angola, Luanda 1933–59

273

Angola

Boxer, C. R., *The Portuguese Seaborne Empire 1415–1825*, Hutchinson, London
1969
Brásio, António, ed., *Monumenta missionária africana, Africa Ocidental*, Lisbon
1952 to present
Delgado, Ralph, *História de Angola, 1482–1836*, Benguela and Lobito, 1948 to
present
Duffy, James, *Portuguese Africa*, Cambridge, Mass., 1959; *Portugal in Africa*,
Cambridge, Mass., 1962; "The Portuguese Territories", in Colin Legum,
ed., *Africa: A Handbook to the Continent*, 2nd edn., London, New York 1967
Grande Enciclopédia Portuguesa e Brasileira, Lisbon and Rio de Janeiro 1924–60
Herrick, Allison Butler, et al., *Area Handbook for Angola*, Washington 1967
Livermore, Harold, *A New History of Portugal*, London 1966; ed., *Portugal and
Brazil*, London 1953
Pattee, Richard, *Portugal and the Portuguese World*, Milwaukee 1957
Peres, Damião de and Eleutério, Cerdeira, eds., *História de Portugal*, Barcelos
1928

V. Periodical Literature

African Historical Studies (African Studies Center, Boston University, since 1968)
Africa Report (Washington, DC); see November 1967 issue devoted to Portuguese
Africa
Angola. Revista Mensal de Doutrina E Propaganda Educativa (Luanda; since
1933, organ of Liga Nacional Africana)
Annaes do Conselho Ultramarino (Lisbon, 1854–64; 4 Vols.)
Boletim Cultural Da Câmara Municipal De Luanda (Luanda)
Boletim da Sociedade de Geografia de Lisboa (Lisbon, since 1877)
Boletim do Instituto de Angola (Luanda, since 1953)
Boletim Oficial de Angola (Luanda, since 1845; now in three series)
O Cruzeiro do Sul (Luanda, 1873–79)
O Futuro D'Angola (Luanda, 1880s)
Garcia de Orta (Lisbon), technical publication of the Junta das Missões Geo-
graficas e de Investigações do Ultramar, Lisbon
Hispanic American Historical Review
Journal of African History (Cambridge University Press, since 1960)
O Mercantil (Luanda, 1870–97)
New York Times
Portugal em Africa: Revista de Cultura Missionária (Lisbon)
Présence Africaine: Cultural Review of the Negro World (Paris, since 1947)
Província de Angola (Luanda newspaper, since 1924)
Race (Institute of Race Relations, London)
Revista Médica de Angola (Luanda; in two series)
Revue française d'études politiques Africaines (Paris, monthly since 1966)
The Times (London)
Ultramar (Lisbon: "Revista da comunidade portuguesa e da actualidade ultra-
marina internacional")

VI. Land, Peoples and Culture

Bettencourt, José de Sousa, "Subsídio para o Estudo Sociológico da População
de Luanda", *Boletim do Instituto de Investigação Científica de Angola*, Vol. II,
No. 1, 1965, pp. 83–125

Carson Graham, R. H., *Under Seven Congo Kings*, London 1930

Chatelain, Heli, *Folk-tales of Angola*, Boston 1894

Childs, Gladwyn Murray, *Umbundu Kinship and Character*, London 1949

Clark, J. Desmond, *Prehistoric Cultures of Northwest Angola and their Signifi-cance in Tropical Africa*, Lisbon 1963

Cruz, José Ribeiro da, *Geografia de Angola*, Lisbon 1940; *Notas de Etnografia Angolana*, Lisbon 1940

Dos Santos, Eduardo, *Maza. Elementos de etno-história para a interpretação do terrorismo do noroeste de Angola*, Lisbon 1965

Edwards, A. C., *Ovimbundu Under Two Sovereignties*, Oxford 1962

Estermann, Carlos, *Etnografia de Angola*, Lisbon 1956–57; *Características da Literatura Oral dos Bantos do Sudoeste de Angola*, Sa da Bandeira 1963; "O Tocoismo Como Fenomeno Religioso", *Garcia de Orta*, Vol. XIII, No. 3, 1965, pp. 325–42

Felgas, Hélio, *Populações Nativas do Congo Português*, Carmona 1960; *As Populações Nativas do Norte de Angola*, Lisbon 1965

Franque, Domingos José, *Nós, os Cabindas*, Lisbon 1940

Hambly, Wilfrid D., *The Ovimbundu of Angola*, Chicago 1934

Redinha, José, *Distribuição Etnica de Angola—Introdução, Registo Etnico e Mapa*, Luanda 1952; *Etnossociologia do Noroeste de Angola*, Braga 1966

Ribas, Óscar, *Ilunda. Ritos e divinidades angolanas*, Luanda 1958; *Missosso. Literature tradicional angolana*, Luanda 1961–64; *Izomba. Corporativismo e recreio*, Luanda 1965

Silva Cunha, J. da, *Aspectos dos Movimentos Associativos na Africa Negra*, Lisbon 1959

Urquhart, Alvin W., *Patterns of Settlement and Subsistence in South-western Angola*, Washington 1963

Van Wing, J., *Etudes Bakongo: Sociologie, Religion et Magie*, Léopoldville 1959

VII. ANGOLA AND KONGO TO 1836

Almanak Statístico da Província d'Angola e suas dependencias, Luanda 1851

Balandier, Georges, *The Kingdom of the Kongo: From the 16th to the 18th Century*, London 1968

Battell, Andrew, *The Strange Adventures of Andrew Battell of Leigh in Angola and the Adjoining Regions*, London 1901

Birmingham, David, *The Portuguese Conquest of Angola*, Oxford 1965; *Trade and Conflict in Angola: The Mbundu and their Neighbours under the Influence of the Portuguese, 1483–1790*, Oxford 1966

Boxer, C. R., *Salvador de Sá and the Struggle for Brazil and Angola, 1602–1686*, London 1952; "The Old Kingdom of Congo", in Roland Oliver, ed., *The Dawn of African History*, London 1959; "Background to Angola: Cadornega's Chronicle", *History Today*, Vol. XI, October 1961, pp. 665–72; *Four Centuries of Portuguese Expansion, 1415–1825: A Succinct Survey*, Johannesburg 1961; *Race Relations in the Portuguese Colonial Empire, 1415–1825*, London 1963; *Portuguese Society in the Tropics: The Municipal Councils of Goa, Macao, Bahia and Luanda, 1510–1800*, Madison 1965

Cadornega, António de Oliveira de, *História Geral das Guerras Angolanas, 1680–1681*, Lisbon 1940–42

Cunnison, Ian, "Kazembe and the Portuguese, 1798–1832", *The Journal of African History*, Vol. II, No. 1, 1961, pp. 61–76

Cuvelier, J., *L'Ancien Royaume de Congo*, Brussels 1946; and Jadin, L., *L'Ancien Congo d'après les archives romaines*, Brussels 1954
Davidson, Basil, *Black Mother*, London 1961
Delgado, Ralph, "O Governo de Sousa Coutinho", *Studia*, Vol. III, Nos. 6–10, Lisbon 1960–62
Paiva Manso, Visconde de, *História do Congo (Documentos)*, Lisbon 1877
Silva Correia, E. A. da, *História de Angola*, Lisbon 1937
Silva Rego, A. da, *A Dupla restauração de Angola (1641–1648)*, Lisbon 1948
Sousa Dias, Gastão, *Os Portugueses em Angola*, Lisbon 1959
Vansina, Jan, "Long Distance Trade-Routes in Central Africa", *Journal of African History*, Vol. III, 1962, pp. 375–90; "Notes sur l'Origine du Royaume de Kongo", *Journal of African History*, Vol. IV, No. 1, 1963; "The Foundation of the Kingdom of Kasanje", *Journal of African History*, Vol. IV, No. 3, 1963; *The Kingdoms of the Savanna*, Madison 1965

VIII. ANGOLA AND PORTUGUESE EXPANSION, 1836–1921

Anstey, Roger, *Britain and the Congo in the Nineteenth Century*, Oxford 1962
Axelson, Eric, *Portugal and the Scramble for Africa, 1875–1891*, Johannesburg 1967
Calheiros e Menezes, Sebastião Lopes de, *Relatório do Governador Geral da Província de Angola, 1861*, Lisbon 1867
Castelbranco, Francisco, *História de Angola*, Luanda 1932
Chagas, Pinheiro, *As Colónias Portuguezas no Século XIX, 1811–1890*, Lisbon 1890
Crowe, S. E., *The Berlin West African Conference, 1884–1885*, London 1942
Delgado, Ralph, *Ao Sul do Cuanza*, 2 Vols., Lisbon 1949
Dos Santos, Eduardo, *A Questão Da Lunda (1885–1894)*, Lisbon 1966
Egerton, F. C. C., *Angola in Perspective*, London 1957
Felgas, Hélio, *História do Congo Português*, Carmona 1958
Felner, A. A., *Angola: Apontamentos Sobre a Colonização dos Planaltos e Litoral do Sul de Angola: Documentos*, 2 Vols., Lisbon 1940
Hammond, Richard J., *Portugal and Africa, 1815–1910; A Study in Uneconomic Imperialism*, Stanford 1966
Hertslet, Sir Edward, *The Map of Africa by Treaty*, London 1909
Kingsley, Mary H., *West African Studies*, London 1899
Monteiro, J. J., *Angola and the River Congo*, London 1875; reprinted (2 Vols.) London 1968
Pélissier, René, "Campagnes Militaires au Sud-Angola, 1885–1915", *Cahiers d'Etudes Africaines*, Vol. IX, No. 1, 1969, pp. 4–73.
Serpa Pinto, Alexandre, *How I Crossed Africa*, Hartford 1881
Silva Porto, António Francisco Ferreira da, *Viagens e apontamentos de um portuense em Africa*, 13 Volume diary at Biblioteca Municipal Pública de Porto, Oporto
Silva Rego, A. da, *O Ultramar Português No Século XIX (1834–1910)*, Agencia geral do Ultramar, Lisbon 1966
Wheeler, Douglas L., "Livingstone and Angola: Some New Letters 1854–56", *Rhodes-Livingstone Journal*, Vol. XXXII, December 1962, pp. 23–45; "Portuguese Expansion in Angola since 1836: A Re-Examination", Local Series Pamphlet, No. 20, in *The Central Africa Historical Association*, Salisbury, Rhodesia, 1967

IX. ANGOLAN POLITICS, NINETEENTH AND TWENTIETH CENTURIES

Assis Júnior, António de, *Relato dos Acontecimentos de Dala Tando e Lucala*, 2 Vols., Luanda 1917–18

Castro Lopo, Júlio de, *Subsídios Para A História do Jornalismo De Angola*, Luanda 1952; *Jornalismo De Angola. Subsídios Para A Sua História*, Luanda 1964

Dos Santos, Eduardo, *Ideologias Políticas Africanas*, Lisbon 1968

Hauser, George M., "Nationalist Organizations in Angola: Status of the Revolt", in Davis, John A. and Baker, James K., eds., *Southern Africa in Transition*, New York and London 1966.

Macedo, José de, *Autonomia De Angola. Estudo de administração colonial*, Lisbon 1910

Marcum, John, *The Angolan Revolution*, Vol. 1: *The Anatomy of an Explosion (1950–1962)*, Cambridge, Mass., and London 1969

Neto, J. Pereira, "Movimentos Subversivos de Angola", *Angola. Curso de Extensão Universitaria no ano lec. 1963–64*, Lisbon 1964; *Angola (Meio Século de integração)*, Lisbon 1964

Norton de Matos, José M. R. de, *A Província de Angola*, Lisbon 1926

Sarmento, Alfredo de, *Os Sertões D'Africa*, Lisbon 1880

Voz D'Angola Clamando No Deserto, Lisbon 1901 (collection of newspaper articles, 1889–1901)

Wheeler, Douglas L., "Nineteenth Century African Protest in Angola: Prince Nicolas of Kongo (1830?–1860)", *African Historical Studies*, Vol. 1, No. 1, 1968, pp. 40–59; "Origins of African Nationalism in Angola: Assimilado Protest Writings, 1859–1929", in Ronald H. Chilcote, ed., *Brazil and Portuguese Africa*, Berkeley 1971; "An Early Angolan Protest: the Radical Journalism of José de Fontes Pereira (1823–1891)", in R. Rotberg and Ali Mazrui, eds., *The Traditions of Protest in Black Africa*, Oxford. 1970

X. ANGOLA, 1921–1961

Caetano, Marcelo, *Colonizing Traditions, Principles, and Methods of the Portuguese*, Lisbon 1951

Casimiro, Augusto, *Angola E O Futuro (Alguns Problemas Fundamentais)*, Lisbon 1957

Coles, Samuel B., *Preacher With a Plow*, Boston 1957

Cunha Leal, Francisco de, *Calígula em Angola*, Lisbon 1924; *Oliveira Salazar, Filomeno da Câmara e o Império Colonial Português*, Lisbon 1930

Cushman, Mary, *Missionary Doctor*, New York 1944

Ferreira Pinto, Júlio, *Angola. Notas E Comentários De Um Colono*, Lisbon 1926

Freitas Morna, Álvaro de, *Angola. Um Ano No Governo Geral 1942–1943*, Lisbon 1944

International Labor Organization, *Report of the Commission to Examine the Complaint Filed by the Government of Ghana Concerning the Observance by the Government of Portugal of the Abolition of Forced Labor Convention, 1957*, Geneva 1962

Lemos, Alberto de, *História de Angola*, Luanda 1929

Lima Vidal, João Evangelista de, *Por Terras d'Angola*, Coimbra 1916

Moreira, Adriano, *Política Ultramarina*, Lisbon 1956; "Les Elites Dans Les

Angola

territoires portugais sous régime de l'indigénat", *International Bulletin of Social Sciences*, Vol. VIII, No. 3, 1956

Norton de Matos, José, *Memórias E Trabalhos Da Minha Vida*, Lisbon 1944–56

Okuma, Thomas, *Angola in Ferment: The Background and Prospects of Angolan Nationalism*, Boston 1962

Silva Cunha, J. M. da, *O Trabalho indígena*, Lisbon 1955

Sousa e Faro, José de, *Angolo. Como eu a vi em 1930–1931*, Lisbon 1932

Van Der Merwe, P. J., *Ons halfeeu in Angola*, Johannesburg 1951

Wilson, T. Ernest, *Angola Beloved*, New Jersey 1967

XI. ANGOLAN LITERATURE

Andrade, Mário de, *Antologia da Poesia Negra de Expressão Portuguesa*, Paris 1958

António, Mário, "A Poesia Angolana", *I Encontro dos Escritores de Angola*, Sá da Bandeira 1963

Casa dos Estudantes do Império, *Poetas Angolanos*, Lisbon 1962

Montenegro, José, *A Négritude. Dos Mitos Às Realidades*, Braga 1967

Moser, Gerald M., "African Literature in the Portuguese Language", *The Journal of General Education*, Vol. XIII, No. 4, January 1962; "African Literature in Portuguese: The First Written, The Last Discovered", *African Forum*, Vol. II, No. 4, Spring 1967, pp. 78–96

Nobre, Maria Da Conceição, *Antologia De Poesias Angolanas*, Nova Lisboa 1958

Tenreiro, Francisco, *Ilha de Nome Santo*, Lisbon 1942; and Andrade, Mário de, eds., *Primeiro Caderno de Poesia Negra de Expressão Portuguesa*, Lisbon 1953

Vieira, Luandino, *Luuanda*, Luanda 1961

Part Two

Addicott, Len, *Cry Angola*, S.C.M. Press, London 1962

Amaral, Ilídio do, *Aspectos do povoamento branco de Angola*, J.I.U., Lisbon 1960; *Luanda*, J.I.U., Lisbon 1968

Anderson, Perry, *Le Portugal et la fin de l'ultra-colonialisme*, Maspero, Paris 1963

Anuário estatístico, Repartição de Estatística Geral, Luanda, yearly

Banco de Angola, *Relatório e contas*, Lisbon, yearly

Borchert, Günter, *Die Wirtschaftsräume Angolas*, Deutsches Institut für Afrika-Forschung, Hamburg 1967

Caetano, Marcelo, *Portugal e a internacionalização dos problemas africanos*, Ática, Lisbon 1963

Caio, Horácio, *Angola: os dias do desespero*, 18th edn., author's edn., Lisbon 1966

Centro de Estudos Angolanos, *Angola—Cultura e revolução*, Algiers, since 1964

César, Amândio, *Angola 1961*, 8th edn., Verbo, Lisbon 1962

Chaliand, Gérard, "Problèmes du nationalisme angolais", *Les temps modernes*, Paris, No. 231, 1965, pp. 269–88

Chilcote, Ronald H., *Emerging Nationalism in Portuguese Africa*, Hoover Institution, Stanford 1969; et al., "Documenting Portuguese Africa", *Africana Newsletter*, Hoover Institution, Stanford, Vol. I, Summer 1963, pp. 16–36

Comte, Philippe, "Les provinces portugaises d'outre-mer ou la force des choses", *Revue juridique et politique. Indépendence et coopération*, Paris, No. 2, April–June 1964; No. 4, October–December 1964

Coret, Alain, "Les provinces portugaises d'outre-mer et l'ONU", *Revue juridique et politique d'Outre-Mer*, Paris, Vol. xvi, No. 2, pp. 173–221

Costa, Pereira da, *Um mês de terrorismo*, Editorial Polis, Lisbon 1969

Davezies, Robert, *Les angolais*, Editions de Minuit, Paris 1965; *La guerre d'Angola*, Ducros, Bordeaux 1968

Ehnmark, Anders and Wastberg, Per, *Angola and Mozambique*, Pall Mall, London 1963

Felgas, Hélio, *Guerra em Angola*, 5th edn., author's edn., Lisbon 1968

Figueiredo, António de, *Portugal and its Empire: The Truth*, Gollancz, London 1961

Fryer, Peter and McGowan, Pinheiro, *Le Portugal de Salazar*, Ruedo Ibérico, Paris 1963

Gersdorff, Ralph von, *Wirtschaftsprobleme Portugiesisch-Afrikas*, Verlag Gieseking, Bielefeld 1962

Gonçalves, José Júlio, *Protestantismo em Africa*, J.I.U., 2 Vols., Lisbon 1960

Hammond, Richard J., *Portugal's African Problem: Some Economic Facets*, Carnegie Endowment for International Peace, New York 1962

Houk, Richard J., "Recent Developments in the Portuguese Congo", *Geographical Review*, Vol. xlviii, April 1958, pp. 201–21

Institute for Race Relations, *Angola: A Symposium: Views of a Revolt*, Oxford University Press, London 1962

Maciel, Artur, *Angola heróica*, 2nd edn., Livraria Bertrand, Lisbon 1963

Marcum, John A., "The Angola Rebellion: Status Report", *Africa Report*, Vol. ix, February 1964, pp. 3–7; *The Angolan Revolution*, Vol. 1: *The Anatomy of an Explosion (1950–1962)*, M.I.T. Press, Cambridge, Mass., and London 1969

Margarido, Alfredo, "Les partis politiques en Guinée portugaise, en Angola et aux iles du Cap-Vert", *Le Mois en Afrique*, Paris, No. 7, July 1966, pp. 43–71; "As Ideologias do Colonialismo", *Cadernos de circunstancia*, Paris, Nos. 4–5, 1968, pp. 26–55

Marques, Walter, *Problemas do desenvolvimento económico de Angola*, Junta de Desenvolvimento Industrial, Luanda 1964

Massart, Jean-Jacques and Suetens, Nicole, *L'espace commun portugais*, Editions de l'Institut de Sociologie Solvay, Brussels 1969

Mendes, Afonso, *O trabalho assalariado em Angola*, Instituto Superior de Ciências Sociais e Política Ultramarina, Lisbon 1966

Ministerio do Ultramar, *Nova legislação ultramarina*, A.G.U., Lisbon, since 1953; *Organic Law of the Portuguese Overseas Provinces*, A.G.U., Lisbon 1963; *Political and Administrative Statute of the Province of Angola*, A.G.U., Lisbon 1963

Moreira, Adriano, *Política ultramarina*, J.I.U., Lisbon 1961; *Batalha da esperança*, Edições Panorama, Lisbon 1962

Moser, Pierre A., *La révolution angolaise*, Société l'Action d'Edition et de Presse, Tunis 1966

M.P.L.A., *Angola: exploitation esclavagiste, résistance nationale*, n.p., n.d.

Moutinho de Pádua, Mário, *Guerra em Angola*, Brasiliense de Bolso, São Paulo 1963

279

Angola

Nogueira, Franco, *Les Nations Unies et le Portugal*, Fayard, Paris 1963; *The Third World*, Johnson, London 1967

Pélissier, René, "Nationalismes en Angola", *Revue française de science politique*, Paris, Vol. XIX, No. 6, December 1969

Présence Africaine, Paris, special issue on Angola, No. 42–3, 1962; "Angola Casebook", No. 45, 1963

Rossi, Pierre Pascal, *Pour une guerre oubliée*, Julliard, Paris 1969

Salazar, António de Oliveira, *Discursos e notas políticas*, Vols. I–VI, Coimbra Editora, Coimbra, since 1935

Silva Cunha, Joãquim Moreira da, *O Trabalho Indígena*, 2nd edn., A.G.U., Lisbon 1960; *O sistema português de política indígena*, Coimbra Editora, Coimbra 1963

Silva Rego, A. da and Santos, Eduardo dos, *Atlas missionário português*, J.I.U., Lisbon 1964

Tam-Tam (Revue des étudiants catholiques africains), Paris, Nos 3–4, 1961

Teixeira, Bernardo, *The Fabric of Terror*, Devin-Adair, New York 1965

United Nations, *Special Reports on Territories under Portuguese Administration*, Documents A/4978; A/5160; A/5280; A/5286; A/5446/Add. 1; A/5800/Add. 3; A/6000/Add. 3; A/6300/Add. 3; A/6700/Add. 3; A/6868/Add. 1; A/7200 (Part II); A/7200/Add. 3 ; A/AC/109/L.625/Add. 1;*Background Papers*, Documents A/AC/108/L.5 and Add. 1; A/AC/108/L.7.

Viana, Horacio de Sá Rebelo, *Angola na África deste Tempo*, author's edn., Lisbon 1961

Index of Names

Adoula, Cyrille, 205, 214–15
Afonso I, King of Kongo, 29–30, 32
Aimbiri, King, 26–7
Albuquerque, Mousinho de, 113
Alexus, Prince, 87, 90–1
Almeida, João de, 75
Almeida, Salles, 95
Almeida e Albuquerque, Alexandre de, 59–60
Amaral, Francisco Ferreira do, 60
Amaral, José Rodriques Coelho do, 54–6, 59
Amprim, Massano de, 121
Andrada, Paiva de, 60
Andrade, Rev. J. da Rocha Pinto de, 163, 165
Andrade, Mário de, 150–1, 163, 212–13, 215
Andrade Corvo, João de, 59
Angelino, Alberto, 171, 222, 224
António, Mário, (Fernandes de Oliviera) 152
António III, King of Kongo, 141, 169
Antunes, Fr J. M., 78
Assis Júnior, António de, 113, 121–3, 126–7
Azevedo, Luis de, 217

Bala, Jean-Pierre, 171, 223
Baracho, Dantas, 98
Barroso, Fr António, 78
Beatriz, Dona, 153
Belo, João, 130
Birmingham, David, 22, 33, 35
Boavida, Américo, 243, 248
Bohannan, Paul, 20
Bosman (Dutch trader), 46
Botha, Jacobus Frederick, 71
Bourguiba, Habib, 170
Bowskill, Rev. J. M., 80, 121
Boxer, C. R., 15
Braga, Arantes, 95
Bragança-Cunha, V., 12

Brito Teixeira, Euzébio Martins de, 148
Buta, Tulante Álvaro, 89–90

Cadornega, António de Oliveira, 33, 37, 42–3, 112
Caetano, Marcelo, 12, 17–19, 131, 148, 239, 247, 252–3
Cakahanga, Domingos, 26
Calheiros e Menezes, Sebastião Lopes de, 56–7, 62–3
Camara, Filomeno da, 114, 145
Camara, Mattoso da, 95
Cameron, Verney Lovett, 61
Camões, Luis de, 11, 12, 15
Cão, Diogo, 28
Capelo H.C.B. (explorer), 34, 57, 59–60, 68
Cardoso, Augusto (explorer), 60
Carmona, Antonio de Fragoso, 148
Carpo, Ancenio de, 95
Carqueja, Prof. Bento, 82
Carvalho, Henrique Dias de, 60
Casimiro, Augusto, 128, 135, 140, 144
Castro Soromenho, Fernando Monteiro de, 151
Catendi, Marquis of, later Pedro V, King of Kongo, q.v.
Chatelain, Heli, 92, 104
Chaves, F. Rego, 114
Chilcote, Ronald H., 12
Childs, G. M., 25–6
Chiringueno, José Paulo, 223
Clark, J., Desmond, 19
Coelho, Manuel Maria, 109–10, 121
Coelho do Amaral, see Amaral
Conceiçao, Lourenço, Mendes da, 149
Cordeiro, Luciano, 59
Cordeiro da Matta, J. D., 70, 150
Cordón, F.M.V. (explorer), 60
Cortez, Hernando, 37
Costa, Eduardo, 113
Couceiro, Paiva Henrique de, 73, 114, 129

Angola

Coutinho, *see* Sousa Countinho
Cruz, Tómas Vieira da, 150
Cruz, Viriato da, *see* Viriato
Cunha, Dr Silva, 249
Cunha Leal, Francisco de, 124

Davidson, Basil, 140
Delgado, Gen. Humberto, 146–7
Deslandes, Venâncio, 188, 206
Dias, Bartholemeu, 35
Dias de Novais, Paulo, 33, 35–7, 41, 58
Dos Santos, Eduardo, 155
Dos Santos Tavares, *see* Tavares
Dubois, W. E. B., 107, 119
Duffy, James, 110, 133

Egerton, F. C. C., 15, 140
Enes, António, 112–13
Espirito Santo, Narciso de, 123

Faidherbe, Louis, 55
Fanon, Franz, 170
Felgas, Hélio, 141, 243
Ferreira, Africano, 95
Ferreira, Commander José, 216
Ferreira, Vicente, 114, 119
Ferreira Gomes brothers, 91
Figueiredo, António de, 12, 15, 160
Flores, Francisco, 56, 92
Fontes Pereira, José de, 84, 86, 95, 99–102, 106, 113, 116
Francina, M. A., 70
Franco, João, 17
Franque, Afonso Baptista, 86, 109, 120
Franque, Luis Ranque, 168, 221
Furtado, Pinheiro, 47

Gabriel, Manuel Nunes, 134
Galvão, Capt. Henrique, 139–40, 147, 175, 213
Gama, Vasco da, 15, 252
Garin, Vasco V., 193
Garvey, Marcus, 119
Gouveia, Father, 33
Gungunyane, Chief, 82

Harris, John, 110
Henrique, Bishop of Kongo, 29–30
Henriques, Carvalhal, 110
Henry of Aviz, Prince, 28
Henry II, King of Kongo, 87

Herculano, Alexandre, 14, 16

Ivens, R. (explorer), 34, 57, 59–60, 68

João, King of Ndongo, *see* Ngola Ari II
João I, King of Kongo, 28–9
Johnston, James, 80
Junqueira, Guerra, 12

Kalundungo, José, 209, 225
Kandonga, Kabuku, 39
Kasakanga, Jose dos Santos, 169, 222
Kasavubu, Joseph, 205
Kassanga, Marcos, 204–6
Kassinda, André Martins, 205–6, 209, 223–4
Kaunda, Kenneth, 224, 247
Kiambu Ndongo, Álvaro, 88
Kiditu, Manuel, 89, 169
Kimbangu, Simon, 153–4
Kingsley, Mary, 68
Kunziku, Emmanuel, 205,223

Lang, Dr, 54
Lara, Lucio, 165, 170, 211–15
Lassy, Simon Zepherin, 154–5
Léopold II, King of the Belgians, 61
Liahuca, José João, 208
Lima, Manuel, 213
Livermore, Harold, 12
Livingstone, David, 34, 57, 61, 68
Lobo, Fr Jerónimo, 173
Lopes de Sequeira, Luis, 31
Lumumba, Patrice, 170, 184
Lux (explorer), 74

Macedo, José de, 105
Madariaga, Salvador de, 12
Mandume, King, 27
Maniquitango, Marquis of Mossul, 47–8
Manuel I, King of Portugal, 11
Mao Tse-tung, 202
Maria II, Queen of Portugal, 87
Mariano, António, 175
Marigny, Admiral, 47
Marques, *see* Silverio Marques
Martins, J. P. Oliviera, 14, 16, 83, 112
Massemba-Débat, 215
Melo, Fontes Pereira de, 17
Mendes das Neves, Rev. M. J., 148
Miranda, A. J. de, 121

Index of Subjects

Angola

Markets, official rural, 198
Marxists, 160–1, 163, 170, 207, 210–11, 214
Massabi, 221
Massangano, 95, 113, 218
Matamba kingdom, 38–9
Mau Mau revolt, 178
Mayombe jungle, 214, 221
Mbaka tribe, 8, 40
Mbangala tribe, 56
Mbanza, 4, 20, 22 (*See also* São Salvador)
Mbridge river, 180–1
Mbundu kingdom, 22–3, 32
Mbundu peoples, 6–8, 39, 43, 56, 161, 211–12, 217; in armed revolt, (1961), and after, 173, 178–9, 190, 194, 203, 216, 230, 236; slave traders, 34
Mbwila, battle of, 31
Mensagem . . . , 150
Mestiços (mulattos), 36, 40, 43–5, 112, 143, 200; acceptance of colonialism, 238–9; massacre of (1961), 178
Mexico, 37
Miconge, 221
Missionaries: Catholic, 76–81, 132; Protestant, 71, 76–81, 100, 106, 111, 122, 132, 153–4, 161, 167, 181, 204; reduction in numbers, 179, 272 n.8.
Missombo prison camp, 270 n.1
Moçâmedes, *see* Mossamedes
Modernist movement, 161–6
Modern Slavery, A, 110
Molembo, 46
Mongoloid racial group, 9
Morocco, 214
Mossamedes (region), 2–4, 20, 74–5, 110
Mossamedes (town), 47–8, 54, 57–8, 64, 88, 162, 229; transport to, 68, 232–3
Mossamedense, 125
Mossul war, 47
Movimento Anticolonialista (MAC), 163–4
Movimento de Defesa dos Interesses de Angola (MDIA), 171–2, 187, 205, 214, 223
Movimento de Independência Nacional de Angola (MINA), 164

Movimento de Libertação de Angola (MLA), 164
Movimento de Libertação do Enclave de Cabinda (MLEC), 168, 214, 221
Movimento de Libertação Nacional (MLN), 163–4
Movimento de Libertação Nacional de Angola (MLNA), 164
Movimento Nacional Angolano (MNA), 214, 223
Movimento Nacionalista Africano, 118, 120
Movimento para a Independência de Angola (MPIA), 164
Movimento Popular de Libertação de Angola (MPLA), 163–8, 170–1, 174–7, 187, 189, 200, 203–25, 228–31; communist help for, 215, 250; evicted from Kinshasa, 208, 215; first conference (1962), 213–14; future of, 219–20; magazines, 215; military regions, 218; revival of, 210–14, 217–18; satellites of, 210–20; training campaign, 215
Moxico, 113, 210, 217–20, 224–5, 232
Mozambique, 26, 34, 46–7, 59–61, 82, 130, 146, 150, 163, 193, 243, 245–6; Commission of Inquiry on labour, 196; future problems, 252–3; Report on native problems, 139; war in, 178, 199, 202
Mpinda, port of, 30
MPLA, *see* Movimento Popular de Libertação de Angola
Mucaba, 184, 190, 225
Muceques (shanty towns), 161, 163–5, 175, 182
Mueneputo, 28, 32n.
Muxicongo, 8

Nambuangongo, 181, 188–9, 203, 208, 212, 215, 217, 220
Napoleonic invasions, 49, 90
Nationalism, Nationalists, 85–6, 90, 92–3, 99–100, 108, 126–8, 151; areas of, 161–2; armed revolt (1961), *q.v.*; Bakongo, 86–90; clandestine African groups, 148, 162–3; European resistance to, 90–3; evolution of movements since 1961, 200*ff.*, exiled nationalists criticise reforms,

292

Angola

Police Force, 69, 70, 94, 98, 133, 162, 193, 199
Polícia Internacional e de Defesa do Estado (PIDE, secret police), 146, 160, 163–6, 175, 184, 191, 209, 211, 216; in Congo-Kinshasa, 225; in the towns, 228–9
Political unity, principle of, 114, 131, 149
Pombeiros, 49–50, 54, 65–6, 80
Pombo tribe, 8
Population, 3, 4, 6, 8, 134, 256; Luanda, 68, 94; rural and urban, 143; white, increase in, 138, 200
Porto Alexandre, 75
Portugal, Portuguese: *assimilado* protest to, 106–8; church, 17; colonial principles of, 59, 131, 164; conquest of Angola, 32–40, 81–3, 96–7; early contacts with Angola, 2–5; early history and culture, 10–16, 28; European resistance to, in Angola, 90–3, 104–5; immigration increased in Angola, 97, 137–8; military expenditure, 199, 235; native policy (1926–61), 129–36; overseas expansion, 10–11, 13, 15, 18, 22–3, 25–30, 51–71; policies for national revival, 16–19; policy in the towns, 228–9; psychological problems of élite, 13–15; relations with Angolans improved, 226; relations with Boers, 71–3; relations with Germans, 73–6; relations with Kongo kingdom, 28–32; relations with missionaries, 76–81; '*século maravilhoso*', 11, 15, 18; trade in Angola, 26, 44–50, 64–7; treatment of 'rebels', 39; wars in Angola, 40–5 (*See also* Angola, Race relations, *and* Slave trade)
Portuguese Communist Party, 162, 213
Portuguese Republic, first (1910–26), 11–12, 80–1, 99, 103, 108–28; effect on Angola, 113, 120, 126
Portuguese slavery: Britain's Dilemma, 110
Portuguese Society of Writers, 152
Presídios, (forts), 36–7, 39–40
Press, 84, 92–3, 96, 99–106, 118–19, 125, 190; freedom of, 84, 115, 123

Príncipe Is., coffee crop, 64; export of labour to, 30, 38, 99, 109, 139
Prophet movements, 152–5
Protestants: churches, 77; numbers of, 133, 195 (*See also* Missionaries)
Provincia de Angola, 125
Pungo Andongo fortress, 39, 49
Punta da Lenha, 54–5

Quadro Geral Auxiliar, 124
Quiballa, 55–6
Quilengues, 40
Quioco, *see* Chokwe
Quitexe, 181, 186, 203
Quitungo, *see* Ambriz

Rabat, 212, 213
Race relations, 41–5, 97–8, 116, 126, 138, 141; deterioration under republic, 111–15; improvement in, 227, 235–9, 251; massacres, 175, 179, 187; PNA protests, 119; racial war today, 230; in Southern Africa, 243–4
Railways, 68, 75, 231, 233, 244
Rassemblement des Chefs Coutumiers du Kongo Portugais (RCCKP), 222
Reforma, 115
Reformism, 99–108, 128
Reforms, (1961) 194–9, 247–50
Refugees, 189–90, 202, 204, 206–9, 215; in the bush, 187, 226; MPLA help, 213, 215; political groups in Kinshasa, 212, 220–5; UN help, 194
Regedorias, regedores, 195, 197
Religions, new African, 152–4
Report on Employment of Native Labour, 110
Republicanism, 99–106
Revolutionary Government of Angola in Exile, *see* GRAE
Rhodesia, 23, 60–1, 177, 243–4; Northern, 66, 143, 167,
Roads, 71–2, 114–15, 127, 198, 222, 231–2
Roman Catholic Church, 29, 31, 33, 43, 70, 76–81, 96, 133, 154, 161, 163, 178; monarchists, 168–9; percentage of, 195; supports Salazar's policy, 193